MONOPOLY TELEVISION

CRITICAL STUDIES IN COMMUNICATION AND IN THE CULTURAL INDUSTRIES

Herbert I. Schiller, Series Editor

Monopoly Television: MTV's Quest to Control the Music, Jack Banks

The FAIR Reader: An Extra! *Review of Press and Politics in the '90s,* edited by Jim Naureckas and Janine Jackson

Communication and the Transformation of Economics: Essays in Information, Public Policy, and Political Economy, Robert E. Babe

A Different Road Taken: Profiles in Critical Communication, edited by John A. Lent

Consumer Culture and TV Programming, Robin Andersen

Marketing Madness: A Survival Guide for a Consumer Society, Michael F. Jacobson and Laurie Ann Mazur

Public Television for Sale: Media, the Market, and the Public Sphere, William Hoynes

Counterclockwise: Perspectives on Communication, Dallas Smythe (edited by Thomas Guback)

The Panoptic Sort: A Political Economy of Personal Information, Oscar H. Gandy, Jr.

Triumph of the Image: The Media's War in the Persian Gulf—A Global Perspective, edited by Hamid Mowlana, George Gerbner, and Herbert I. Schiller

The Persian Gulf TV War, Douglas Kellner

Mass Communications and American Empire, Second Edition, Updated, Herbert I. Schiller

FORTHCOMING

The Social Uses of Photography: Images in the Age of Reproducibility, Hanno Hardt

Introduction to Media Studies, edited by Stuart Ewen, Elizabeth Ewen, Serafina Bathrick, and Andrew Mattson

Invisible Crises, edited by George Gerbner, Hamid Mowlana, and Herbert I. Schiller

The Communications Industry in the American Economy, Thomas Guback

Hot Shots: An Alternative Video Production Handbook, Tami Gold and Kelly Anderson

Ideology, Government Broadcasting, and Global Change, Laurien Alexandre

MONOPOLY TELEVISION

MTV's Quest to Control the Music

JACK BANKS

WestviewPress
A Division of HarperCollins*Publishers*

Critical Studies in Communication and in the Cultural Industries

Copyright © 1996 by Westview Press, Inc., A Division of HarperCollins Publishers, Inc.

Published in 1996 in the United States of America by Westview Press, Inc., 5500 Central Avenue, Boulder, Colorado 80301-2877, and in the United Kingdom by Westview Press, 12 Hid's Copse Road, Cumnor Hill, Oxford OX2 9JJ

Library of Congress Cataloging-in-Publication Data
Banks, Jack.
    Monopoly television : MTV's quest to control the music / Jack Banks.
        p.   cm. — (Critical studies in communication and in the cultural industries)
    Includes bibliographical references and index.
    ISBN 0-8133-1820-3 (hc.) — ISBN 0-8133-1821-1 (pbk.)
    1. Rock videos—United States.   2. MTV Networks.   I. Title.
II. Series.
PN1992.8.M87B36   1996
384.55'51—dc20   96-2163
                                                                           CIP

The paper used in this publication meets the requirements of the American National Standard for Permanence of Paper for Printed Library Materials Z39.48-1984.

10   9   8   7   6   5   4   3   2   1

Contents

Acknowledgments   xi

1 Constructing Video Dreams: Music Video in a
       Commercial Culture   1
       Quantitative Empirical Studies, 2
       Cultural Studies, 4
       Limitations of Textual Analysis, 7
       The Political Economy of Communications, 8
       The Study of Corporate Activity, 10
       Relationship Between Economic Function and Ideological
          Content of Commoditized Culture, 12
       Trends in Ownership and Control of the Mass Media, 14
       A Political Economic Study of Music Video, 18

PART ONE
THE HISTORICAL DEVELOPMENT
OF THE MUSIC VIDEO BUSINESS

2 The Early Years of Music Video   23
       Early Combinations of Recorded Music and Visual Media, 23
       MTV: The Novel Early Years, 29
       Expanded Record Industry Involvement in Video Music, 41

3 The Growth of Other Video Music Program Services   47
       Cable Music Channel, 48
       Discovery Music Network, 50
       Hit Video USA, 51
       MTV's Sister Service VH-1: Video Hits One, 52
       The Box, 55
       Black Entertainment Television, 57
       The Nashville Network and Country Music Television, 59
       WTBS's *Night Tracks,* 60
       Video Music Shows on Commercial Broadcast Television, 61

4   Monopoly TV: A History of MTV's Anticompetitive Practices   63
        MTV Exclusivity Agreements with Record Companies, 63
        Label Payola Agreements with Other Music Programs, 78
        Major Labels Create Own Music Video Channel, 79
        MTV Attempts to Coerce Artists, 83
        MTV Attempts to Control Access to Cable Systems, 84

5   MTV and the Globalization of Popular Culture   89
        Corporate Incentives to Develop International Markets, 89
        MTV Europe, 91
        MTV Australia and MTV Japan, 97
        MTV Asia, 98
        MTV in Latin America, 102
        MTV's International Youth Culture, 104
        MTV's Global Advertisers, 105
        Major Record Labels' Global Marketing Campaigns, 106
        A One-Way Flow of Music and Culture, 109
        Alternatives to MTV, 110

6   MTV's Corporate Intrigue and Sagging Ratings   117
        Corporate Acquisitions of MTV Networks, 117
        The Decline of Video Music in the Mid-1980s, 122
        Resurgence of MTV, 127
        MTV Networks' Future: Multiplexing, Home Shopping, and
           Videos for Tots, 130

PART TWO
THE STRUCTURE OF THE
MUSIC VIDEO BUSINESS:
FORCES THAT SHAPE MUSIC CLIPS

7   The Record Companies' Role in Video Music Production
           and Distribution   137
        Video Music Incorporated into Record Companies, 137
        Record Label Video Production Dependent Upon Exposure
           Media, 138
        Video Clip Promotion, 139
        Record Companies and Artists, 143
        Music Video at Independent and Major Record Labels, 147

8   Video Clip Producers and Directors   155
        Music Video Clip Producers, 155
        Music Video Clip Directors, 158

Music Video Production as a Transitional Occupation, 160
The Music Video Producers Association, 161
Record Label Contracts with Video Clip Producers and
    Directors, 162
Record Label Constraints on Video Clip Content, 166
Emerging Patterns in the Record Companies' Use of Video
    Clip Producers and Directors, 167

9   MTV as Gatekeeper and Censor   175
MTV's Acquisition Committee, 176
MTV's Standards: Stated and Unstated, 176
The "Committee," 178
A Survey of Music Clips Rejected by MTV, 180
Record Company and Artist Reaction to MTV, 182
Music Clip Rotation Categories, 184
External Social Forces Influencing MTV's Standards, 185
Political Attacks on Popular Music, 190
Content Regulation of Music Television Programs, 191

10 MTV, Music Video, and Creative Expression   195
The Power of Record Labels and MTV in the Video
    Music Business, 195
Established Trends in Ownership and Control of the Music
    Video Business, 197
Relationship Between Economic Structure and Ideology
    Within the Video Music Business, 201

Notes   207
References   237
About the Book and Author   271
Index   273

Acknowledgments

Even though I sometimes think of myself as the Lone Wolf toiling away in isolation, many people, whom I want to acknowledge, have helped me with this book along the way.

Diane Prusank, the graduate director of the School of Communication at the University of Hartford, regularly provided me with research assistants who were helpful in the preparation of this manuscript. Mary Lawrence and Melissa Gettins were graduate research assistants who did much library research for me with speed and accuracy, checking facts and hunting down needed information about references, names, and figures.

John Dlugosz, T. J. Feldman, and Mary Lawrence, graduate students at the University of Hartford, all provided useful and thoughtful critiques of the book. Margaret Bennett, a lifelong friend, contributed valuable comments with a critical edge. I also had enlightening conversations with Nancy Breaux, a scholar and musician, about the role of popular music in society.

The members of my dissertation committee at the University of Oregon, Deanna Robinson, Janet Wasko, Carl Bybee, and Val Burris, offered thoughtful insights and criticisms on an earlier version of this manuscript, helping me to further clarify arguments. I was enriched by knowing the faculty and graduate students in the old Telecommunication and Film program at the University of Oregon, who constituted an intellectually vibrant, politically aware, and morally conscientious community of critical media scholars whose company I miss. My thinking about music video and media industries more generally has been greatly influenced by critical scholars including Dan Schiller, Herb Schiller, Vincent Mosco, Graham Murdock, Thomas Guback, Ben Bagdikian, and Ed Herman.

Several people at Westview Press were instrumental in seeing this book through various stages to its completion, most notably Gordon Massman, David Jenemann, Jane Raese, Linda Carlson, and Jim Grode. Everyone at Westview was always helpful, kind, and professional.

My mother, Deanna Banks, has been wonderfully supportive and understanding throughout this project. And finally, Mike Silverman has always been there for me, providing continual encouragement and constantly keeping me up to date with what and who was on MTV when I just could not watch it anymore.

Yet although I have been influenced by many, the arguments in this work are my own and I take responsibility for my occasionally less than flattering portrait of MTV, record companies, and the music video business.

Jack Banks

1

Constructing Video Dreams:
Music Video in a Commercial Culture

MTV: Music Television was launched in August 1981 as a twenty-four-hour cable program service presenting an endless stream of music videos, short visual productions featuring current pop and rock songs. As MTV's popularity increased throughout the decade, music video had a pronounced impact on popular culture in the United States, influencing most major media and stimulating demand for a wide range of consumer products. In the early 1980s, music video revitalized a troubled record industry by prompting renewed consumer interest in pop music and successfully developing several new recording acts such as Madonna, Boy George, Cyndi Lauper, and Duran Duran, who adeptly showcased their provocative visual images in this new media form. Music video has since become an indispensable means of promotion for recording artists, who are expected to have accompanying videos for their songs in order to become commercially successful.

MTV's influence gradually infiltrated traditional television shows on the commercial broadcast networks. *Miami Vice* (originally titled *MTV Cops* by network executives) prominently featured current pop music and adopted the flashy visual style of music videos. Even some network television news shows like *48 Hours* regularly presented stories that incorporated the pulsing music and frenetic editing characteristic of music clips.[1] Music video pervades theatrical films as well. Many motion pictures include musical segments that are self-contained music clips regularly excerpted from the film and played on MTV, whereas other music-oriented films like *Flashdance* and *Purple Rain* from the 1980s were described as extended music videos. Music clips featuring songs from a movie soundtrack and film excerpts that are played on MTV and other television shows have become an effective advertisement for current theatrical releases. As MTV and music video demonstrated their promotional efficacy, the advertising industry borrowed heavily from this cultural form to enhance the sales appeal of commercials.[2] Many commercials imitate visual techniques used in popular music videos and often are presented as ersatz music clips complete with dance routines and throbbing

1

music. Beyond its influence on various media, music video also stimulated consumer purchases in several markets, most notably in fashion apparel. MTV and
music videos frequently establish fashion trends by showcasing in music clips the
avant-garde clothing worn by performers, which provides a shopping guide for
style-conscious consumers. MTV's reach extended into the realm of politics with
its extensive coverage of the 1992 presidential campaign, which included interviews with prominent candidates including Bill Clinton.

The considerable impact of MTV and music video on American popular culture make this new media form a pertinent object of inquiry. This book examines
the historical development of music video as a commodity and the established
structure for the production, distribution, and exhibition of music video with
special emphasis on the premiere music channel, MTV. This historical and political economic analysis of the music video industry was prompted by the quite limited scholarly research of music video from this perspective. Most research on
music video is some variant of textual analysis. Quantitative empirical research in
the field of communications is preoccupied with content analysis of various aspects of music videos like the portrayal of sex and violence in music clips, whereas
cultural studies research emphasizes ideological analyses of music clips. These two
types of textual analysis are drawn from academic areas that adopt quite different
theoretical assumptions and research methodologies. Mainstream empirical research professes to be atheoretical, is grounded in positivist epistemology, and
relies on the methodologies of survey and content analysis. Conversely, critical research on music video from a cultural studies perspective is explicitly theoretical,
is grounded in a hermeneutic epistemology, and uses a range of methodologies
including semiotics, psychoanalysis, and literary analysis. In the sections that follow, I will review representative studies to illustrate the primary observations and
arguments made about music video from each tradition.

Quantitative Empirical Studies

Quantitative empirical studies often examine the gender and race of characters depicted in music videos and their attributes. Several such studies say that clips on
MTV strongly feature white male characters at the expense of women and minorities, who are underrepresented. Jane Brown and Kenneth Campbell report that 83
percent of all videos played on MTV during a two-day sample period in February
1984 featured white male singers or bandleaders.[3] White female singers or bandleaders were present in 11 percent of videos, and nonwhite singers or bandleaders
of either sex accounted for only 5 percent of videos. They conclude that "white
men, primarily by virtue of their greater numbers, are the center of attention and
power" in music video, whereas "women and blacks are rarely important enough
to be a part of the foreground."[4] Steven Seidman's review of MTV clips in February
1987 describes a similar pattern: Sixty-four percent of primary characters in the
clips were male and 36 percent were female. Where race was the measure, 89 per-

cent were white, dwarfing the 11 percent nonwhite characters.[5] The portrayal of minority groups probably increased somewhat in the early 1990s as MTV featured more rap music. Nancy Signorielli, Douglas McLeod, and Elaine Healy report that this composition extends to commercials on MTV. In ads on MTV examined in November 1991, 95 percent of characters were white, and males appeared somewhat more often than females, 54.4 percent to 45.6 percent respectively.[6]

White men are not only portrayed more frequently on MTV but in a more desirable manner, whereas women and minorities are represented as having derogatory, unflattering attributes. Women are depicted as sex objects in music clips more often than men. Barry Sherman and Joseph Dominick report that one-half of the women in music clips wore "provocative clothing" and only one-tenth of men were so dressed.[7] Signorielli et al. add that women in commercials on MTV were also dressed in skimpy clothing, but male characters almost always wore sexually neutral apparel. Music clips also depict women as submissive to men. Richard Vincent, Dennis Davis, and Lilly Ann Boruszkowski say that women were "put down" and "kept in place" by male characters in three-fourths of the music programs surveyed.[8] Seidman reports that music clips on MTV provide a caricature of traditional personality attributes for genders, where men are portrayed as more aggressive, domineering, and violent and women are more affectionate, dependent, and fearful. Music videos on MTV reinforce crude gender stereotypes for occupations as well. Men are almost always portrayed working in jobs that are stereotyped for males like firefighter, mechanic, and doctor. Men on MTV videos account for 94 percent of police officers and 90 percent of business executives. Seidman points out that this depiction distorts reality since women are employed in much higher proportions in many of these fields. Women are banished to occupations typecast for their gender like cheerleader, secretary, and librarian. All fashion models and telephone operators on the channel's music clips were portrayed by women. Racial minorities are similarly stereotyped into certain professions. Ninety-five percent of all nonwhite characters were lumped into six occupational categories, prominently including athletes, dancers, and entertainers.

Empirical studies also examine the portrayal of violence and sexual behavior in music videos because of public concern about this type of program content. Sherman and Dominick conducted a content analysis of music clips presented on three popular music video shows including MTV for two hours on Saturday mornings for a seven-week period, reporting that the depiction of sex in music videos was "more implied than overt."[9] Over half of all incidents of sexual behavior consisted of "flirtation and non-intimate touching," whereas "intimate touching" including caressing and stroking composed about 20 percent of sex depicted in music clips.[10] They conclude that the provocative appearance of half of the women present in music clips demonstrates the male orientation of this medium.

Sherman and Dominick report portrayals of violence in 56.5 percent of "concept" videos, productions that visualize a story or abstract theme, and an average of 2.86 aggressive acts present in videos with violence.[11] The authors say that the violence in music clips is comparable to traditional commercial television, noting George Gerbner's finding that 75 percent of prime-time television shows contain violent acts. Men committed almost three-fourths of the aggressive actions and constituted a slightly greater percentage of victims. About 90 percent of the aggressors and victims in these music videos were white. Brown and Campbell report that the white primary characters in music videos accounted for more than half of the observed antisocial behavior, including bodily assaults, physical threats, and verbal aggression.[12] Black characters were much less likely to be involved in such behavior, with black females least likely to be either aggressors or victims.[13]

Behavioralist communication research explores the potential effects of music video on the cognitive activity of young viewers. On the basis of a survey of college students, Rebecca Rubin et al. conclude that a person's "cognitive involvement" with music is greater when viewing video music than when simply listening to the audio version of a song on the radio or cassette player.[14] Conversely, Dean Abt worries that music videos "rob the imagination" of young people by offering preformed visual interpretations of popular songs.[15] Se-Wen Sun and James Lull's study of the viewing habits of high school students in San Jose, California, reports that the 80 percent of the participants who identified themselves as MTV viewers watched the channel an average of over two hours each day.[16] The authors conclude: "Young people watch an enormous amount of music video programming and they seem to enthusiastically accept the visual interpretations of songs that are provided, rather than create their own interpretations."[17] However, Sun and Lull note that adolescents are not passive viewers because their strong feelings about the music and artists likely influence their viewing experience.

Cultural Studies

Music Video as Consumer Culture

Cultural studies examine music video as an artifact of consumer culture. Ann Kaplan argues that *rock promos* is a more appropriate term for music videos because these productions are primarily advertisements commissioned by record companies to promote their artists.[18] She describes MTV as a continuous advertisement since all of MTV's programming consists of some form of commercial. Richard Gehr concurs, saying, "We refer to most TV as 'commercial'," but "only MTV can lay claim to that title because that is precisely what it is: ersatz commercials punctuated by 'real' ones."[19] Pat Aufderheide examines how music videos dissolve the traditional boundary between programs and commercials since music clips constitute both types of content.[20] Kaplan argues music video's dual role as advertisement and art encourages a perpetual conflict about the appropriate content of these productions.[21] Those involved in the production of music videos, including the musician, producer, and director, want to create an artistic work, but the record companies and MTV consider a music clip solely as a commercial to sell certain commodities, including itself.

Although video clips are made to sell compact discs and tapes, the promotional function of music video and MTV is much broader than being a simple advertisement for recorded music. Margaret Morse explains that rock video promotes a concept that can be used to sell a wide range of products:

> This concept can be used not only to promote (a) album and audio tape sales, but also (b) video tapes of itself, (c) the image of a rock star, (d) box-office and video tape sales of movies as well as soundtrack albums, and (e) products and services related not just to the music and performers, but also to the life-styles and world-view depicted in the visuals of the rock video.[22]

The most encompassing promotional objective served by music video and MTV is to advocate the viewer's embrace of consumerism as a way of life. Despite MTV's rebellious, irreverent image, Virginia Fry and Donald Fry argue that the program service promotes adherence to consumerism by presenting various cultural styles with associated products that the viewer is enticed to purchase.[23] The visual images of music videos serve as "markers" that position featured artists within a certain "stylistic community" with its own unique apparel and accessories.[24] The viewer can become a member of a desired style group like rap or grunge by purchasing the consumer products displayed in the music videos associated with a particular community. Fry and Fry say that young viewers develop their sense of self-identity through the acquisition of these goods providing group affiliation, and Aufderheide adds that the promotion of a personal identity that can be purchased is a primary function of rock videos.

Music video promotes consumerism through forms of emotional manipulation practiced in traditional advertising. Aufderheide explains that music clips cultivate certain mood states such as anxiety or dread, creating a sense of incompletion and lack that can be satisfied through the purchase of products displayed in the video. MTV as a program service also stimulates consumption through appeals to unrequited desire, according to Kaplan: "It evokes a kind of hypnotic trance in which the spectator is suspended in a state of unsatisfied desire but forever under the illusion of imminent satisfaction through some kind of purchase. This desire is displaced onto the record that will embody the star's magnetism and fascination."[25] Music video encourages the viewer to associate the purchase of consumer products featured in the clips with desirable emotions and values. Aufderheide says music video "equates the product with an experience to be shared, part of a wondrous leisure world,"[26] whereas Morse claims that music clips provide a magical link between featured commodities and the mythical values of rock culture, including creativity and self-determination.[27] Music video provides young viewers with the opportunity to "buy the illusion of freedom," says John Fiske.[28]

Although video music is a form of advertisement, Morse and Aufderheide maintain that music clips differ from traditional commercials. Although conventional advertisements offer the promise of a utopian paradise free of desire that can be obtained by buying a specific commodity, Morse says that videos provide the viewer with some immediate pleasure and cultivate a broader desire for fulfillment and control that can be exploited to stimulate demand for an entire range of consumer products.[29] Aufderheide concurs that music clips do not present an aggressive sales pitch for a particular product, but rather subtly place commodities within a consumerist milieu that comes to be perceived as a "natural" part of a viewer's daily life.[30]

Music video and commercials have a strong reciprocal influence, resulting in the increasingly similar appearance of both. Kaplan remarks that the provocative visual style of music videos, such as the presentation of visual non sequiturs, was derived from conventional techniques used in commercials, and Jon Pareles adds that the pace and structure of music clips is taken from advertising.[31] Kaplan also notes that the production arrangements for music video are similar to those of television commercials, where both are produced by a freelance staff and financed by a sponsor seeking to promote a product. As MTV and music video became more proficient at promoting commodities, the advertising industry began to incorporate elements of music clips in television commercials. Aufderheide observes that music video encouraged a more prominent use of pop music on the soundtrack for commercials, like an ad for Clairol Heated Rollers featuring bodybuilders moving to a pulsing rock beat. A 1988 survey of national television advertisements conducted by the American Association of Advertising Agencies reports that 72 percent of the ads featured music, an increase from 63 percent the prior year.[32] Television commercials increasingly used visual techniques prominent in music video, including *pushing,* a process that adds a grainy texture to film, and *matting,* a technique used to superimpose a person on a changing background.[33] More recently, a backlash occurred against commercials emulating music video when some advertising agencies became suspicious that this type of ad did not increase product sales.

Music Video as Postmodern Culture

Cultural studies also examine music video and MTV as a form of postmodernist culture. Although this is a nebulous concept, Kaplan explains that a primary feature of postmodernism is the emergence of a decentered consciousness that blurs traditional categories and questions established institutions.[34] Jean Baudrillard describes this state as an "implosion" of meaning characterized by "the defusing of polarities, the short-circuiting of the poles of every differential system of meaning, the obliteration of distinctions and oppositions between terms."[35] Kaplan says that young people in mature capitalist societies increasingly adopted this decentered perception of reality, attributing the development of this consciousness to such disparate forces as advanced technology, multinational corporate capitalism and increasingly sophisticated marketing strategies.[36] Baudrillard contends that an expanding mass media generates increasing amounts of information, contributing to the breakdown of conventional meaning.[37]

Kaplan says that MTV exemplifies postmodernism because the program service undermines established categories and boundaries, including different musical genres, art forms, and historical periods, and distinctions between high and popular culture.[38] MTV and music video incorporate material from an array of sources into a kaleidoscopic pastiche without acknowledging the conventional categories of this material. The channel subverts any aesthetic sense of history by indiscriminately mixing together material from film genres and art forms from various historical periods. MTV also repudiates linear conceptions of history, rejecting conventional distinctions between past, present, and future, instead placing itself in a timeless present. MTV's announcers rarely mention the time of day during their chatter between videos. The channel's around-the-clock presentation of widely diverse short clips with random content, and the channel's refusal to position itself from a particular perspective are claimed to contribute to the viewers' decentered experience. However, MTV's more recent movement toward a more conventional schedule of television programs with a finite length of time undercuts this argument to a certain extent.

Authors disagree whether the postmodernist nature of MTV and music video has a progressive or oppressive influence on viewers. Kaplan claims that the decentering process may release the viewer from the conventional codes of the dominant culture. This disorienting experience liberates the viewer: "In this view, then, the effacing of old boundaries . . . would be seen as exhilarating and freeing. MTV spectators would be seen as experiencing a healthy breaking of confining hierarchies and dichotomies, the new forms permitting new ways of seeing rather than enforcing old ones."[39] Kaplan says that postmodernist cultural forms such as MTV cultivate more creative people, less bound by tradition and more receptive to change. Other critics counter that MTV represents a co-opted form of postmodernism prone to place the viewer in a schizophrenic state, isolated in the present and unable to escape the dominant culture or develop a coherent, alternative worldview. MTV's postmodernism denies the ability for critical analysis of mainstream culture and the forms of oppression within society. David Tetzlaff declares that MTV allows no possibility for reflection, and Hanno Hardt says that the channel is indicative of "the absence of concrete forms of criticism" within capitalist society.[40] Tetzlaff describes MTV and music video as a self-contained world of "postmodern bourgeois consumerism" that contains appeals to sell products and denies the existence of alternatives beyond this consumerist milieu.[41]

Limitations of Textual Analysis

Although the studies just reviewed provide valuable insight into the nature of music video, most are confined to various types of content analyses, which provide an incomplete understanding of this cultural form. These works largely exclude direct examination of the social forces responsible for video music and how these forces influence music clips or account for their described content. For instance, several studies depict the consumerist ideology inherent within MTV and music video, but fail to examine how industry practices and operations may contribute to the incorporation of these ideological values within the productions.

Rather, both quantitative empirical and cultural studies research draw inferences about relevant social forces solely on the basis of their content analyses. Peter Golding and Graham Murdock's description of cultural studies accurately portrays this tendency in most research on music video: "Media artifacts are . . . regarded as texts, and the process of analysis consists of 'reading off' the layers of social meaning they contain, and then extrapolating outwards to the social relations involved in their production and use."[42] The studies cited previously provide numerous examples of this tendency to infer the strategic policies or actions of parties in the music video business solely from the author's content analysis of music clips. On the basis of their content analysis of sexual behavior in music videos, Sherman and Dominick conclude that MTV portrayed sexual encounters more frequently than other shows because the channel was trying to reach a young audience.[43] Similarly, Fry and Fry infer from their textual analysis of MTV alone that the channel vigorously pursued certain strategies to promote consumerism.[44] Tetzlaff also deduces from his reading of MTV that the channel's consumerist appeals were a direct result of corporate policy: "MTV has . . . sold skads of clothing, cosmetics, movie tickets and what not. The message is 'BUY!' and that's just what the kids are doing. The people who pay for cultural production are not stupid. If MTV didn't do what the capitalists in charge want it to do, it wouldn't be on the air."[45] None of these authors apparently investigated industry practices or MTV's corporate policies to support their claims. Golding and Murdock claim that this type of inference about social forces drawn solely from a textual analysis does not provide a competent understanding of the social context of production. "Extrapolations from cultural texts, no matter how subtle and elaborate, are no substitute" for direct examination of this social context.[46]

Although some studies provide limited analysis of certain social forces such as economics, this is ancillary to an elaborate textual analysis. For example, Kaplan's glance at the practices and operations of the video music industry is overshadowed by her detailed analysis of MTV as a postmodern cultural form.[47] According to Golding and Murdock, these studies provide "a highly asymmetric analysis in which an elaborate anatomy of symbolic forms sits alongside a schematic and incomplete account of social processes."[48] This current work attempts to redress this past imbalance by examining the relevant social forces involved in the historical development of music video as a cultural commodity, examining how forces such as economics, technology, and government have constrained and shaped music video.

The Political Economy of Communications

Political economy is a major area within the school of critical communications that embodies a skepticism toward major institutions like business and government and embraces a commitment toward greater equality and democracy in society.[49] Study of social forces that constrain and shape mass media is the province of political economy of communications. This scholarly area studies the allocation of scarce resources for the production and distribution of media products. Dallas Smythe's pioneering work says that political economy

> asks two related questions: 1) Who gets what scarce goods and services, when, how and where? 2) Who takes what actions in order to provide what scarce goods and services, when, how and where? The political economy of communications is the asking and answering of these questions with respect to the services and goods we have described above as constituting communications.[50]

Herbert Schiller chronicles the pervasive and growing inequities over access to information and cultural products due to the privatization and commercialization of information in broadcasting, libraries, government, higher education, and other realms of public discourse.[51]

Political economy also examines the inequities that persist in control and ownership of media institutions and how this may be related to broader inequalities within society. For instance, Herbert Schiller, Michael Parenti, Douglas Kellner, Edward Herman, and Noam Chomsky discuss how the same privileged economic class that controls wealth and power in society also possesses ownership of major media.[52] These authors examine how this media ownership serves to reinforce the existing class structure in the U.S. through the production and distribution of media content that encourages widespread consent to this social system despite its inherent unfairness. Eileen Meehan, Vincent Mosco, and Janet Wasko outline four basic concerns that guide political economic research: history, understanding the past development of media institutions; social totality, examining mass media within the context of society as a whole and its various interrelated institutions; moral philosophy, considering the morality of the practices and structure of mass media and the consequences for society; and praxis, an attempt to apply research to real life to contribute to a more just, fair society.[53]

This field offers a neo-Marxist economic analysis of cultural production, premised on Karl Marx's base/superstructure metaphor that contends a society's cultural production is structured and conditioned by economic relations.[54] Thus, an objective is to examine how economic forces constrain and shape the production of culture. Nicholas Garnham, Graham Murdock, and Peter Golding address how cultural forms are structured within capitalism. Garnham, who identifies his approach as "cultural materialism," explains that this perspective "entails focusing upon the irreducible material determinants of the social processes of symbolic exchange and the ways in which historically, within the general development of the capitalist mode of production, these processes have been brought within the sphere of commodity production and exchange and with what effects."[55] In other words, how has communication and culture been transformed by the structural demands of the market? Scholars from this tradition regularly criticize mass media research such as media effects and cultural studies scholarship that fails to undertake this economic analysis of cultural production as incomplete and idealist.

Political economy, in turn, is grossly caricatured by some cultural studies and mainstream theorists as economism for proposing complete and direct economic determination of culture. These critics assert that culture and ideology have a material dimension and a limited autonomy apart from any crude economic determination.[56] However, prominent political economic theorists like Murdock and Golding also reject any rigid economic reductionism, contending that the economic base does not dictate cultural form and content, but rather loosely shapes cultural products by exerting pressures and establishing constraints.[57] Yet although Garnham concedes that the mass media in capitalist societies have a degree of political and ideological autonomy, he argues that the ultimate determination of media content takes place within the economic base.[58] The control of resources is the most essential element involved in the process of cultural production. Cultural studies' work also differs from political economy by focusing more on audience reception of media content, emphasizing how people often decode content in oppositional, emancipatory ways. Although he acknowledges the ability of audience members to subjectively interpret media messages, Schiller stresses the difficulty of resisting the dominant ideas that are regularly emphasized in media content produced by culture industries.[59] A person who has always encountered the same underlying myths and values in the content of various media may be less likely to challenge that dominant perspective.

Adopting Garnham's cultural materialist approach, this work examines how video music as a cultural form is incorporated into the commodity production process and assesses the consequences of this. Considered is the extent to which economic imperatives constrain the form and content of music clips and influence the distribution and exhibition of music video. The analysis assesses the extent to which economic forces are a paramount consideration as predicted by the base/superstructure metaphor, and conversely, the extent of autonomy and "creative freedom" of cultural producers as emphasized by theorists who stress the relative independence of culture and ideology. Beyond direct economic considerations, this book looks at how other social forces, such as technology, government, and pressure groups, have also influenced the development of music video.

The Study of Corporate Activity

A primary focus of political economic study is the corporation involved in communication markets because of the central role of this entity in the production of media content. "The study of media economics should concentrate on the study of the organization and behavior of business enterprises," Douglas Gomery argues, "since they form the core economic institutions of the mass media industry in the United States."[60] Murdock explains that there are two primary approaches to the study of corporate activity: action-oriented approaches that examine the exercise of power by parties within the corporation; and structural analysis, which explores how corporate policies and objectives are constrained by the broader political and economic structure of a society.[61]

Action-oriented research focuses on the exercise of control and power by individuals within the corporation. Murdock identifies two levels of control within the corporation: allocative and operational.[62] Parties with allocative control shape the overall policy and strategy of a corporation, including plans for expansion into new markets or proposed retrenchment by closing down certain operations and laying off personnel. Operational control is a lesser degree of power that involves the implementation of policies established by those with allocative power. Individuals with operational control manage the daily operations of a firm and have a certain degree of flexibility, but their range of possible actions is circumscribed by broad corporate policy formed by others.

Structural analysis of the constraints limiting the actions of individuals within corporations depends upon the economic theory underpinning the study. Neo-Marxist analysis examines how the entire structure and dynamics of a capitalist economy constrains the actions of all individuals within a firm. Marx states that although capitalists occupy a privileged position, they do not have complete control over the economic system, comparing them to "the sorcerer who is no longer able to control the powers of the nether world whom he has called up by his spells."[63] The crisis-prone nature of capitalism restricts the range of policy options available to individuals who often form policies in reaction to economic developments that threaten a firm's future profitability. Garnham argues that the current state of capitalism is characterized by high levels of capital concentration in major industries and an insufficient quantity of investment outlets, driving capital in search of other areas for investment.[64] Within culture industries, this pressure encourages corporations to develop new media-related markets.[65]

Structural analysis of corporations premised upon neoclassical market economy theory stresses how firms are constrained by consumer preference. Proponents of this perspective say that the policies of corporate executives must be responsive to consumer demand for goods and services in the free market. This "consumer sovereignty" argument is often provided by academics and industry executives as a justification for the alleged abysmal quality of some media content, noting that companies simply give the public what it wants. Benjamin Compaine, a proponent of this perspective, comments that media critics

> seem least willing to accept the decision by "the people" in their choice of media content. These critics decry the low cultural level of so much of our television programming, for example, yet ignore that time and time again the mass public eschews the "quality" offerings of *Masterpiece Theatre* or the *MacNeil/Lehrer Report* for the *Dukes of Hazzard*.[66]

In his dissertation on the recording industry, Laurence Shore says that record companies advocate the consumer sovereignty argument in order to claim that they have no control over public tastes and that the commercial success of music is entirely dependent upon record buyers and radio listeners.[67] However, Shore counters that "the commercial restraints imposed on what music is made available and what is not place substantial limits on the claim of consumer sovereignty."[68]

Relationship Between Economic Function and Ideological Content of Commoditized Culture

Political economy also examines the relationship between the economic structure of media and the content of cultural products. Specifically, researchers investigate whether the ideological content of the media is consistent with the economic objectives of entities that control the media within a capitalist society, and if so, consider how such consonance is maintained. According to Murdock, political economy analyzes the relationship between media content and ownership using action-oriented and structural approaches.

Action-oriented studies, often termed *instrumentalism*, examine how capitalist owners of media actively manipulate their communication holdings to advance their best interests. Instrumentalist research adopts two different levels of analysis, focusing on the actions of an individual capitalist or the capitalist class as a whole. Instrumentalist analysis of media ownership at an individual level examines how specific owners intentionally influence the content produced by their media subsidiaries to promote their economic endeavors, or at the very least, not threaten or obstruct their business. For example, Richard Bunce reports that each of the U.S. commercial television networks refused to air a documentary, the *Pentagon Papers,* during the Vietnam War because the networks' parent companies feared that the program would imperil the lucrative defense contracts held by subsidiaries of all of these firms.[69] Martin Lee and Norman Solomon note that the television network NBC presented a documentary highly favorable toward nuclear power as an energy source, bolstering the economic interests of its parent firm, General Electric, which is deeply entrenched in the nuclear power industry.[70] The broader version of instrumentalist research investigates how media industries systematically advance the objectives of a dominant elite through the production of media content that cultivates consent to the prevailing inequitable economic structure, such as programming that celebrates the openness and fairness of the existing system while omitting embarrassing and disparaging news about corporations. Research from this perspective relies on content analyses to demonstrate that media content generally promotes capitalist ideology and denigrates oppositional ideas and movements.

Although there are documented instances of direct manipulation of media content by corporate owners, the instrumentalist approach is criticized for its attempt to explain the production or suppression of certain media content solely in terms of a conspiracy of capitalist owners who actively manipulate cultural products to serve their own interests. Rather, Murdock and Golding argue that the systematic presentation of media content amplifying capitalist ideological themes can be more adequately explained with a structural approach emphasizing the constraints on corporate activity imposed by the dynamic operation of the economy. According to Murdock, the increasing costs of the mass media exclude all potential participants from these markets except those parties with substantial capital resources.[71] For example, Smythe argues that the capital-intensive nature of mainstream film production limits access to this medium: "The sheer size of the investment required to produce 'colossal' features . . . designed to exploit the peculiar characteristics of new screen aspect ratios (e.g., Cinemascope) effectively limits access to the theatre market to the largest film producers and then only with the direct participation of banking interests."[72] Thus, firms most likely to control major media outlets are those that benefit most greatly from a capitalist economy and that would strongly embrace the ideological values associated with this structure. Conversely, parties most likely to oppose the inequitable distribution of resources in the economy generally lack the resources to operate major media outlets or produce programming, effectively excluding these groups from access to a forum in which to present their dissenting views to a large audience.

Murdock concedes that some cultural products, such as recorded music, have more modest production costs, making these media more accessible to a wider range of potential producers.[73] However, the necessity of adequate national distribution of media products, even those with lower production expenses, requires these producers' dependence upon large communication corporations that control distribution systems in these markets.[74] Shore's study provides support for this argument, contending that the extensive distribution operations of the major record labels owned by larger conglomerates maintain a great degree of control over the dissemination of recorded music throughout the world.[75]

Garnham criticizes these various approaches to study of the media for assuming that cultural commodities always promote capitalist ideological values: "Because capital controls the means of cultural production in the sense that the production and exchange of cultural production [become] the dominant forms of cultural relationship, it does not follow that these cultural commodities will necessarily support, either in their explicit content or their mode of cultural appropriation, the dominant ideology."[76] Rather, Garnham argues that the incorporation of culture within the commodity production process is a contradictory process where the economic and ideological functions of cultural products may be in conflict. Cultural products designed to generate profit may include content that is anathema to the expressed values of individual capitalists. However, content analyses demonstrating the relative lack of dissenting and oppositional views in various major mass media question the extent to which this contradiction is manifest in advanced capitalist societies.[77]

Trends in Ownership and Control of the Mass Media

A primary objective of political economic research is to depict current trends in the ownership of the mass media and examine the potential consequences of these economic developments for democratic communication within society. These studies assess the horizontal integration within a media market, which is a measure of ownership concentration in a particular medium. Murdock and Golding explain that this integration takes place "where firms acquire additional units at the same level of production,"[78] and Benjamin Compaine says that within media industries, "the most typical form of horizontal integration is that of a single firm owning more than one entity in a single medium."[79]

Research on this issue often concludes that there is steadily increasing concentration of ownership within media markets. Gomery reiterates the contention of media critics who claim, "The major film, newspaper and television companies number so few that their power is concentrated in the hands of a small number of owners."[80] Ben Bagdikian reports that by 1992, twenty corporations owned the majority of all major U.S. media, including newspapers, magazines, television, books, and movies.[81] This was a dramatic drop from 1981 when fifty large corporations held this dominant ownership of media. Bagdikian's study identifies and totals the number of companies with media operations that together constitute over 50 percent of each media industry comprising a "majority" interest in that market. On the basis of this criterion for measuring concentration, Bagdikian says that by 1992, eleven corporations accounted for more than half of all daily newspapers sold; two firms received more than half of the total revenues of the approximately 11,000 magazines in the United States; and three corporations with ownership of the major commercial networks possessed most of the audience and advertising revenue in the television industry.[82] In other media markets, a majority interest was held by four companies in theatrical film and five in book publishing. Bagdikian also says that media concentration greatly intensified over time, presenting the newspaper industry as typical of ownership patterns in all major media. He reports that 80 percent of daily newspapers in the United States were independently owned in the late 1940s, but by 1989, this same percentage of papers was now owned by large chains like Gannett.[83]

Concentration of media ownership is criticized for curtailing freedom of expression because this centralized control suppresses the presentation of a broad marketplace of ideas within society. Bagdikian argues that small, independent media outlets, which historically have presented a robust range of political, social, and cultural views and enhanced diversity within the media, gradually have been acquired or undermined by huge conglomerates. He derides these corporations as "a new Private Ministry of Information and Culture," which as a group tend to present similar homogenized views and ideas in their media outlets, omitting alternative perspectives. Critical theorists contend that centralized media ownership represents increasing control by the capitalist class of the means of ideological production in society.[84]

Vertical integration is another prominent trend in media ownership that Gomery defines as "the expansion of a business enterprise in gaining control of operations from the acquisition of fundamental raw materials through the sale of the final product."[85] Compaine notes that most firms are vertically integrated to some extent because these companies combine raw materials to create a good or service and market the finished product.[86] According to a Federal Communications Commission report, "vertical integration exists when an exchange that might have occurred by market transaction in a buyer/seller setting is handled administratively within a single 'firm.'"[87] In media industries, this integration occurs when a single company controls more than one stage in the production, distribution, and exhibition of a cultural product such as a film or record. Vertical integration can take place through direct ownership where a company owns subsidiaries at different levels of production or through a contractual agreement between companies with interests at various levels of production, such as affiliation contracts between cable operators and program services.

Gomery identifies two economic motivations that encourage companies to seek vertical integration. First, this integration allows firms to reduce costs because transactions are handled within a single entity, enabling the company to have smaller sales and accounting departments. Second, vertical integration provides a company with market control through guaranteed distribution and exhibition of a product. This type of integration is criticized because of the potential for anticompetitive practices by an integrated company. A firm with operations at different stages of production can take actions designed to undermine its competitors and enhance its dominance in a particular market. For example, a parent company with ownership interests in both local cable systems and cable program services can exclude competing program services from access to its own cable systems and provide its own services with the most desirable channel positions. Vertical integration in culture industries may also restrict freedom of expression and inhibit creative diversity in the media because integrated companies have an incentive to exhibit their own productions while excluding creative works by others. For instance, a major film studio that owns a theater chain may feature its own films at its theaters at the expense of productions by independent filmmakers, which remain ignored.

The theatrical film industry is a classic example of a vertically integrated media market. In the 1920s and 1930s, major Hollywood film studios that produced and distributed their own films acquired theater chains in order to provide guaranteed exposure for their productions. These studios were required to sell their theater interests as a result of court-ordered divestiture mandated in the Paramount decision in 1948, but some studios once again purchased theaters in the 1980s, reintegrating their operations and taking advantage of the lax enforcement of antitrust laws during the Reagan and Bush Administrations. Gomery notes that in the 1980s, studios also began to extend their vertical integration through acquisition of major television stations, providing another coveted outlet for exhibition of their films and television productions.[88]

Another prominent trend in media ownership is diversification. Since the 1950s, a continuous series of corporate mergers and takeovers shaped the typical modern corporation into a conglomerate, a parent company with subsidiary holdings in a range of different markets. Murdock identifies two types of conglomerate in media industries: the general conglomerate with media holdings secondary to interests in other industrial sectors; and communication conglomerates, whose principal operations are in culture industries with subsidiaries in various media markets.[89] He explains that corporations increasingly diversified their holdings because of a falling rate of profit in advanced capitalist economies.[90] Companies involved in less profitable industrial sectors diversified their operations to take advantage of relatively higher profit margins in other markets.[91] Diversified holdings also protect a company against a severe economic downturn in any one industry. Communication conglomerates can take advantage of their interests in various media through coordinated joint ventures between different media divisions, a strategy known as *synergy.*

This tendency toward diversification contributes to increasingly centralized control of media industries as relatively few conglomerates gain control in all major media. For instance, TimeWarner owns subsidiaries that are dominant in theatrical film, recorded music, magazines, and book publishing. Murdock claims that these conglomerates have "an unprecedented degree of potential control over the range and direction of cultural production."[92] Despite the name *diversification,* the actual result of this trend may be to curtail cultural diversity in major mass media. Bagdikian suggests that conglomerates tend to market the same concepts or artists in their various subsidiaries in a range of media.[93] For instance, TimeWarner can promote and sell cultural products featuring the artist Madonna in its music, film, magazine, and book subsidiaries simultaneously. This coordinated cross-media strategy limits the independence and autonomy of the individual subsidiaries. The units of a conglomerate in various media are also less likely to develop and promote a diverse variety of artists and concepts than if these subsidiaries were each independent media companies not affiliated with the same parent firm.

Corporations with media operations also have increasingly expanded internationally. These ventures include exports of cultural products, direct investment in foreign media industries, and ownership of media outlets in other countries. Companies in all industrial sectors, including culture industries, see foreign countries as lucrative new markets for products that are sources of revenues and profits. These foreign countries can be exploited as domestic markets become increasingly saturated. The U.S. film industry is especially aggressive in its development of the international market for American films. Thomas Guback argues that film studios have a strong economic incentive to distribute their productions in other countries.[94] The expenses involved in marketing a movie in other countries are minimal because the original costs of production have already been incurred, increasing the potential profits from foreign distribution.[95] Revenue derived from the international market also may compensate for losses from a commercially unsuccessful distribution in the United States. Other cultural products like popular American television shows are distributed in foreign areas for similar reasons. As firms develop their foreign operations, increasing concentration of ownership in some media industries results at a global level. For example, Shore contends that five transnational corporations control 70 percent of the production and distribution of pop music for the international market.[96] Bagdikian explains how the world's media are increasingly owned by a few transnational corporations like Rupert Murdoch's News Corporation, Hachette S.A. of France, Bertelsmann A.G. of Germany, and TimeWarner based in the United States.[97]

This international expansion contributes to a globalization of popular culture, where the same films, television shows, and recorded music become pervasive throughout the world. This global culture may undermine and erode the indigenous cultural identities of people in different societies that are inundated with increasingly homogeneous entertainment. Critical scholars like Herbert Schiller and Colleen Roach charge that there is a distinctly American cast to much of this global media, where Hollywood films, U.S. television shows, and music by U.S. pop stars like Madonna are dominant, leading to concerns about cultural imperialism with American ideas and values pervading other societies.[98]

The primary objective of profit maximization encourages media industries to adopt certain strategies as well. Firms continually attempt to develop new cultural commodities as well as new markets for products. Garnham contends that capitalists' strategies to exploit new products sometimes fail, such as initial efforts by RCA and Philips to promote the video disc as a consumer good, and other strategies evolve over an extended period of time, such as the existing distribution system for theatrical film.[99] Firms also try to distribute cultural products in a variety of media outlets in a coordinated strategy to enhance revenues. This "recycling" strategy is pursued most vigorously by Hollywood film studios that initially distribute their films in theaters. The films are then shown successively on pay-per-view television, home video, pay cable networks, network television, and finally are syndicated to local television stations as well as to other more specialized media outlets at various points along the cycle, like in-flight movies on airplanes.

Firms also try to maximize profits by reducing their expenses through attempts to reduce labor costs, increase productivity, and more generally strengthen control over the production process. Garnham argues that such attempts are more difficult in media industries than in other industrial sectors because of the precapitalist ideological values embraced by certain classes of workers in these fields emphasizing such ideals as creative freedom and artistic autonomy.[100] Gomery adds that media industries "hardly seem efficient enterprises," referring to the extravagant salaries of major film stars and the "limousine culture perks" enjoyed by certain employees at the commercial networks.[101] Despite such resistance, certain media industries are subject to increasing employee cutbacks and stringent cost-control measures.

A Political Economic Study of Music Video

This text considers how core issues confronted in political economy discussed previously are relevant in the music video business. As for concerns about corporate control, this book examines the exercise of power within record companies that finance the production of music videos and program services like MTV, which are primarily responsible for their exhibition. The policies and strategies of record label and MTV executives concerning music video are examined historically, considering both the exercise of allocational control by senior corporative executives and operational control by lower-level personnel. The influence these parties have on the content of music clips and how they act as gatekeepers determining which artists are featured in videos is also a topic of review. The consequences of these corporate policies are considered for recording artists as well as video clip producers and directors.

As for the issue of ideology, this work explores the relationship between the economic function of music video and the ideological content of music clips. Does the content of music videos reinforce the structure of commodity production that provides the economic base for this cultural form? Do the recurrent ideological themes of music videos advocate and celebrate the core values of a capitalist economic system, or at the very least, avoid a direct critique of this structure? If indeed there is a relative lack of oppositional and alternative ideas in music videos and program services, how is such dissent suppressed? Also considered is whether the development of music video as a cultural commodity created the possibility of an emergent contradiction between the economic function and ideological content of clips where music videos made for profit critique the very economic system that sustains them as a product.

Finally, the book investigates the extent to which the established trends in ownership of media discussed previously are evident in the emerging market for music video. To what degree is the music video business horizontally integrated at the levels of production, distribution, and exhibition? Of crucial importance here is the major record companies' control of music video production and MTV Networks' dominance in exhibition media for music clips. Vertical integration at the various stages of production in the music video industry is assessed, examining whether companies took advantage of this integration by engaging in anticompetitive practices. The cooperation between major record labels and MTV that created a form of vertical integration through contractual agreement is examined in detail along with the more recent attempts by the labels to create their own program service. Diversification by parent companies involved in music video is reviewed, with attention to whether these conglomerates developed "synergy" strategies involving joint ventures between their video music operations and other subsidiaries. Also examined is the tendency toward internationalization in the market for music video with the emergence of MTV program services around the world, perhaps contributing to a more homogenized global culture. The central imperative of profit maximization has shaped the music video business along with other culture industries. This book examines strategies adopted by record companies and program services to reduce expenses and increase revenues. Paramount in this survey of trends is an analysis of whether these economic developments have diminished the potential for diversity and freedom of artistic expression in music video.

The survey of music video is presented in two main parts, the first reviewing the historical development of music video as a business. Chapter 2 examines the early synthesis of recorded music and visual media and the creation of MTV, and Chapter 3 considers the growth of other video music program services. Chapter 4 explores the anticompetitive practices of MTV Networks that increased market concentration and cooperation between MTV's program services, major record companies, and cable systems. Chapter 5 surveys the growth of MTV's international programming and its contribution to a globalization of popular culture. The corporate acquisition of MTV Networks by Viacom and MTV's exploitation of ancillary markets is the subject of Chapter 6, which also reviews MTV's problems with sagging audience ratings and its current projects. Part Two explores the current structure of the music video industry, considering the various parties that shape and constrain the content of music clips. Part Two surveys the roles of the major entities involved in the production, distribution, and exhibition of music video: record companies (Chapter 7), video clip producers and directors (Chapter 8), and video music exposure media (Chapter 9). The conclusion in Chapter 10 considers the results of this historical study in the context of the theoretical framework presented in this chapter, assessing whether the existing business fosters or suppresses creative expression and cultural diversity in music video.

PART ONE

THE HISTORICAL DEVELOPMENT OF THE MUSIC VIDEO BUSINESS

2

The Early Years of Music Video

Early Combinations of Recorded Music and Visual Media

Music in Film from the 1920s to the 1960s

Video music clips shown on MTV are not a recent innovation, but rather the latest variation of the use of recorded popular music in visual media originally pioneered in the late 1920s and 1930s.[1] The film *The Jazz Singer*, starring vaudeville performer Al Jolson, which premiered in 1927, was not only the first motion picture with recorded audio but also the first film feature with a music soundtrack. This pioneering film was the precursor to different genres of films in the 1930s that featured music, such as the movie musical, which incorporated musical numbers into the narrative structure of the film. Busby Berkeley made films revolving around life on the Broadway stage using simple stories and elaborate musical productions. The Western, another film genre featuring music, would typically interrupt an action story to let cowboys perform country songs. Animated motion pictures of the period also made extensive use of music, such as Max Fleischer cartoons edited to songs performed by Cab Calloway and Louis Armstrong. Music was also prominently featured in "shorts," three-to-five-minute film clips starring vaudeville performers and vocalists known from radio.

Perhaps the closest historical ancestor to contemporary video music clips were "soundies," which became popular in the 1940s. Soundies were three-minute film clips that depicted musical performances and were played in nightclubs and diners. The clips were shown in Panorams, devices developed by the Chicago-based Mills Novelty Company that projected an image on a small plastic screen with a lens and mirrors. The Panoram used a closed loop film, which included about eight or ten soundies on each reel. People would deposit a dime into the Panoram and watch and hear a brief musical performance. As the new medium grew in popularity, several companies emerged that distributed a wide range of clips. These companies included Film Craft, R.C.M., and Minoco.

At the height of their popularity, top performers were featured in soundies, including bandleaders Duke Ellington and Louis Armstrong and singer Nat "King" Cole. Because of the small screen size, the soundies' visuals stressed extreme close-ups, portraying the artists lip-synching the songs on the soundtracks (usually with the visual and audio somewhat out of sync). Reflecting larger social divisions, the selection of music on the film reels was rigidly segregated into "white" and "Negro" performances so that a performance by a black artist like Cab Calloway would never be included on a reel with Caucasian performers.

Although soundies enjoyed brief commercial success, business and technical limitations as well as shifting cultural trends contributed to the medium's swift decline. Because of the distribution system and limited soundie production, machine operators were unable to change reels on the Panoram fast enough to feature current popular music on the reels, leaving the Panoram with yesterday's music unwanted by a fickle public. The projection reel format prevented selection of a specific artist, forcing customers to view the next soundie on the reel without knowing who the performer would be, unlike the more contemporary jukebox. The rise of the swing and big band era also favored the regular jukebox over the Panoram since people frequenting nightclubs would rather dance to the music of a jukebox than passively watch a performer on a screen. Although big band contributed to the decline of soundies, this genre's performers were prominently featured in more traditional motion pictures. These films had loose, simple plots that allowed popular swing performers to present their music in films (for example, Benny Goodman in *Hollywood Hotel*). Fifties' rock 'n' roll performers used film in a similar fashion (e.g., Elvis Presley in *Jailhouse Rock* and *Loving You*). Rock music was also integral to the narrative in many films like *Rock Around the Clock* and *Mister Rock 'n' Roll*. The Beatles continued this tradition in the 1960s, starring in the films *A Hard Day's Night, Help,* and the animated *Yellow Submarine,* all featuring their music and further enhancing their pivotal role within U.S. popular culture.

The Presentation of Pop Music on Commercial Television

Popular music has been a significant part of the programming on broadcast television since television's initial commercial development in the 1950s. One of the earliest commercial network television shows to feature popular music was *Your Hit Parade,* sponsored by Lucky Strike cigarettes. Like other early television shows such as *Amos 'n' Andy, Your Hit Parade* originated as a network radio show successfully making the transition to television. *Your Hit Parade,* a countdown show, presented the country's seven most popular songs of the week in reverse order. The songs selected for the show were not taken from any industry chart of popular songs, but rather were selected by Lucky Strike's advertising agency. The songs were performed by four band singers who carried out skits illustrating the lyrics. The show ran successfully on network television until 1959. It usually presented bland, inoffensive ballads appealing to a broad audience of all different ages without alienating key demographic groups, as did rock music in later years.

Network television infrequently presented programs in the 1950s featuring music that appealed primarily to younger viewers. Eddie Fisher, a bubblegum pop star with several hit records, was the first teen idol to receive prominent television exposure as the star of NBC's *Coke Time*. Elvis Presley's appearances on network television were much more controversial because of the raw sexuality of his performances. After establishing himself as a successful new star with a number of hit records, Presley began appearing on numerous variety shows including those hosted by Steve Allen, Milton Berle, and Ed Sullivan. Although Sullivan required that Presley be shown above the waist on his show, he was so impressed by the ratings of Presley's appearance that he regularly presented new pop music stars on his show to attract younger viewers.

In the late 1950s, the most prominent show featuring popular music was Dick Clark's *American Bandstand*, which premiered locally in Philadelphia in 1952 and became a national program on ABC in 1957. Pop stars like Fabian and Frankie Avalon lip-synched their songs and the studio audience danced along. In the 1960s, network television once again generated new excitement in rock by introducing the country to The Beatles and other English groups on variety shows and specials. The appearance of The Beatles on Ed Sullivan's show on February 9, 1964, was a milestone in this "British Invasion" that captured the attention of America's youth.

The networks tried to capitalize on this renewed popularity of rock music, while at the same time domesticate it and broaden its appeal in shows like *Shindig* on ABC and *Hullabaloo* on NBC. Both shows featured an awkward combination of soft rock music and Hollywood personalities such as Jerry Lewis and Zsa Zsa Gabor who had little or nothing to do with the music or its associated subculture. The shows, which premiered in 1964, featured performances by current soft rock musicians including The Righteous Brothers and Sam Cooke and a regular group of dancers performing to the beat of current hits (*Hullabaloo*'s trademark was the dancing "girl in the cage"). *Hullabaloo* and *Shindig* quickly faded in popularity and both were canceled in 1966. These shows rarely featured popular rock stars because network censors thought that Middle America would find contemporary hard rock and acid rock performers offensive. Also, the presentation of rock performers on shows hosted by non-rock television personalities like Jim Nabors was an odd combination that received mediocre audience ratings. These shows illustrated how network attempts to present the rock subculture in their programming were hindered by rock stars themselves, who were often perceived as too risqué and deviant for network television.

One solution to this dilemma was for television producers to create their own sanitized rock groups, purged of all the unconventional ideas about sexuality, drugs, and authority associated with this subculture, yet retaining a sense of innocuous "fun" in order to attract a broad audience. This was rock producer Don Kirshner's rationale behind his formation of The Monkees, a band specifically created for television. Four young men were hired as band members of this manufactured rock group that would star in their own television series *The Monkees,* featuring a wacky-yet-wholesome rock group obviously modeled after The Beatles. The selection of performers was unusual because none of them were musicians and the songs on their television show and records were initially performed by studio musicians. Yet, their lack of musical training did not prevent the commercial success of their television show, which received 20,000 fan letters a week, or their record albums, which sold 8 million copies in the initial four months after the debut of their show.

In the early 1970s, commercial broadcasters once again attempted to exploit rock music on television in several television series presented late at night. ABC introduced *In Concert* in November 1972, and NBC aired the *Midnight Special.* Television executives usually gave these shows a late time slot on a weekend night to attract younger people just coming home after an evening out. Musicians appearing on these shows would generally lip-synch their songs to taped music as had been done on *American Bandstand.* After a brief period of success, both shows experienced problems due in part to shifting tastes in music, which abandoned hard rock in favor of disco and middle-of-the-road music. Don Kirshner, The Monkees' creator, developed his own syndicated show featuring rock performers, *Rock Concert,* which was ultimately unsuccessful because the time lag between production and broadcast inherent in syndication at the time left the shows dated and unappealing to record chart-conscious viewers. All of these rock-oriented shows were gone by the mid-1970s.

For the remainder of the 1970s, rock music was relegated to occasional specials and featured performances by rock acts on shows like *Saturday Night Live,* targeted toward young viewers. Although the musical guests on *Saturday Night Live* in its prime in the mid- to late-1970s were usually signed to major record companies, the show occasionally featured alternative artists like Elvis Costello, the B-52s, Fear, and Captain Beefheart, which were rarely played on commercial radio stations with arthritic, stagnant rock formats. After network television largely abandoned the realm of rock and popular music in the early 1980s, syndication became the major sphere for music-oriented shows. The most successful syndicated effort was *Solid Gold,* a weekly show with respectable ratings that debuted in 1980 featuring a countdown of the week's most popular hits. The show's provocatively dressed "Solid Gold Dancers" danced to the music, while pop and rock stars lip-synched their hits. Casey Kasem also hosted a syndicated weekly show playing the week's top hits, which was a spin-off of his popular Top 40 radio show. A studio audience would dance along to current R&B and soul hits on *Soul Train,* a show that also featured popular African-American acts performing their latest releases.

The Awkward Mix of Pop Music and Network Television.   The attempts to introduce pop and rock music on commercial broadcast television were infrequent and often unsuccessful. This was partly due to the historical reluctance of rock stars to appear on television, much of which was based on financial considerations. Commercial networks generally paid musicians poorly for appearances on television programs, most often a minimum union scale payment, whereas concert tours paid much more. Also, performers and their managers were concerned that television appearances endangered the commercial success of their tours because people might decide to watch an artist on a television show for free instead of paying to see the artist in concert. Rock and pop stars, whose continued success was linked to a hip, youth-oriented image, also were concerned that appearances on Middle America–oriented network television could harm this image. An appearance on a variety show with Zsa Zsa Gabor or Don Knotts could be career suicide. Major rock acts would not perform on the *Midnight Special* after Helen Reddy was hired as the show hostess and more middle-of-the-road music was featured, because of fears that their images would be tainted.

Rock artists also shunned network television because of its history of censorship of music and visuals deemed offensive to its conservative sensibilities. Ed Sullivan, a classic practitioner of in-house censorship, not only demanded specific G-rated shots of Elvis Presley but also required The Rolling Stones to change the lyrics of "Let's Spend the Night Together" before allowing them to perform. Moreover, the constant battles with network censors on the *Smothers Brothers Comedy Hour* demonstrated network unwillingness to honestly represent a rock-oriented youth subculture out of fear of alienating its audience. Rock musicians preferred performing in venues like live concerts where their actions were not subject to censorious scrutiny (at least in the pre–2 Live Crew era). Finally, rock acts were repelled by the inferior sound quality of television, comparable to a cheap AM transistor radio, which diminished the sound of their music. The substandard sound quality was exacerbated by television production staff who had limited experience in audio.

When network television presented rock and pop music artists, the programming strategy of the networks demanded that these artists appear in programs that appealed to an undifferentiated mass audience and did not alienate any substantial part of this audience. These imperatives contributed to standardized program formats used by network executives to feature rock and pop stars and also determined which artists would (and would not) be given network exposure. Current artists often would be featured as musical guests in variety shows, which would be balanced with other non-music-oriented guests, comedy sketches, and a monologue by the host. Guests were selected for variety shows using a coalition-building strategy, having different performers appealing to different demographic groups to provide entertainment broad enough to assemble a mass audience. This search for mass audiences prevented networks from presenting music-oriented shows with performers all appealing to the same narrow demographic group, such as young rock fans.

Rock and pop stars infrequently hosted their own network series, but only certain performers were acceptable. Networks commissioned series starring performers with a clean-cut, wholesome image who presented bland, inoffensive

music. Pop musicians appearing on the network schedule included Glen Campbell, The Captain and Tennille, Dolly Parton, and Sonny and Cher. Television executives reasoned that such musicians could attract a large audience, in contrast
to more provocative rock stars, who might offend conservative viewers' moral
sensibilities and cause them to tune out. The network strategy of providing show-
cases for tame pop and rock stars was often unsuccessful because although these
mainstream performers were inoffensive, they were also perceived as boring and
mediocre by rock-conscious younger viewers who rejected these programs, thus
contributing to low ratings.

In general, commercial broadcasting's need to attract mass audiences largely
prevented the presentation of recording artists that appealed to smaller, narrowly
defined demographic groups. Prior to the 1980s, network television dominated
all commercial television, precluding any form of television "narrowcasting" that
might allow a hospitable forum for rock musicians. Radio remained the primary
electronic medium for providing exposure for pop and rock artists. Radio, unlike
television, offered specialized programming of interest to specific demographic
groups, which was ideal for the presentation of various genres of popular music.

The Birth of Music Clips: Promotional Films

A primitive form of the contemporary video music clip was developed in the
early 1970s and featured rock artists playing songs from recently released albums.
These filmed performances were commissioned by the major record companies
as a new promotional form to provide exposure for their recording artists. Record
companies were in the process of scaling back the expensive practice of subsidizing artists' concert tours and were exploring alternative, less expensive means of
promoting their artists. Promotional films were a relatively inexpensive way to
achieve this objective. The film clip of an artist's performance could be presented
in a variety of venues, such as in music stores, nightclubs, or as part of a paid advertisement on television, which hopefully would generate consumer interest in
the artist's latest release.

Major record labels with international operations generally produced music
clips for exhibition overseas rather than in the United States. Although radio was
the primary means of exposure for rock and pop musicians in the United States,
television played a much more prominent role in introducing new pop and rock
music in Europe. The United Kingdom and other European countries had public broadcasting systems with a limited number of radio stations and an even
more limited availability of radio programs featuring popular music. Those that
did feature current music had tightly controlled hit-oriented playlists that resisted
playing new or alternative music. Record companies (and musicians) found it
much more difficult to break a new song or artist on radio in England than in the
United States, which had a far greater number of radio stations playing more diverse music.

In contrast to American television's ambivalence toward pop music, television stations in the United Kingdom aired several shows featuring popular music that were a central forum for introducing new music to the public. These shows, most notably *Top of the Pops* and *Ready! Steady! Go!*, often presented short film clips of artists performing current songs. Record companies wanted to present film clips of their own artists on these shows since such exposure helped sell albums. Because of the importance of television for promoting recording acts in the United Kingdom and Western Europe, international record companies commissioned filmed music clips of their artists' recent releases and circulated these to popular European music television shows for airplay. These early clips were low-budget efforts that often involved no more than filming a group's concerts with one camera and editing the film into short productions featuring separate songs. The clips' content was often limited to simple scenes of rock stars performing their songs and did not include the elaborate visual illustration of stories or concepts characteristic of later productions. The first music clips usually were recorded on film rather than video because in the early 1970s video production was still prohibitively expensive.

Some early innovators of the music clip expanded the form beyond the original practice of passively recording performers in concert by such means as illustrating a story or concept in the clip or enhancing the song with special visual effects. Michael Nesmith, ex-member of The Monkees, was an innovator in music clips who produced an elaborate concept-oriented clip to promote his single, "Rio," in the overseas market in 1977. Nesmith also was an early advocate of video music, producing his music clips on videotape rather than film. He later produced *Elephant Parts,* one of the first visual albums, for the home video market. The album received a Grammy award for innovation in 1981. Nesmith predicted in a burst of hyperbole that the emergence of video records was "the single most important event in the history of the rock 'n' roll music industry—bigger than . . . Elvis Presley."[2] Another early pioneer in music clips was artist Todd Rundgren, who created Utopian Videos, which produced several short experimental music films with special effects for presentation on USA Network's music show, *Night Flight.*

MTV: The Novel Early Years

Political Economic Factors Contributing to the Development of a Music Program Service

Although music clips were being produced in greater numbers, American television stations rarely aired the clips as regular programming because commercial broadcasters sought mass audiences and these clips usually appealed to narrow demographic groups. The successful development and economic exploitation of certain communications technologies created the opportunity for the emergence of media outlets that could offer specialized programming such as video music. The growth of cable television in the early 1980s spawned the creation of specialized program services seeking certain groups rather than mass audiences. The concurrent development of satellite communications provided the means for program services to be transmitted to cable systems throughout the country. Home Box Office (HBO), the pay cable service owned by Time (now Time-Warner), pioneered this use of satellite technology in 1975 by leasing a transponder to nationally distribute its service via satellite. By the late 1970s, most cable services were distributed this way. The trend toward specialized programming was enhanced by the "upgrading" of existing cable systems throughout the latter part of the 1980s, providing substantial channel capacity beyond the original twelve channels usually offered, allowing for even more program services.

More specifically, the future embrace of video music was aided by technological developments in television audio that increased consumer interest in the presentation of music on television. Throughout the 1980s, many cable and broadcast television outlets began transmitting in stereo, and newer models of television sets received stereo signals that could be played through high-quality speakers, rather than through the six-inch audio boxes of older models. These developments led to programming that took advantage of the enhanced audio capabilities of television. MTV's self-promotions in its early years stressed the fact that viewers could hear it in stereo.

The development and commercial success of a program service featuring music video also was facilitated by general economic trends in the 1980s. In the post–World War II period, American industry was based on a mass consumer market with products designed for mass consumption. In order to stimulate broad demand for these products, advertisements stressed the general appeal of commodities and were presented in media with an undifferentiated mass audience, most notably network television and general interest newspapers and magazines. In the 1980s, this mass consumer market dissolved into a variety of specialized cultural niches. American industry shifted from the production and distribution of a few mass-oriented product lines to a wider range of specialized products targeted to specific demographic groups of consumers. Instead of a few main brands of consumer products like coffee, toothpaste, and jeans, companies increasingly market an infinite variety of these commodities with variations designed to attract every conceivable taste group.[3]

To competently promote these specialized products, American companies needed to develop advertising tailored to desired consumer groups and present these commercial appeals in media catering to these narrow audiences. This need contributed to the successful development of media that attracted these groups (such as cable program services), by providing these media with a valuable source of advertising revenue. Thus, the fragmentation of the American consumer market prompted a similar metamorphosis within American popular culture, shifting from mass-oriented media to more specialized media. In this context, a program service targeted to young people featuring popular music could be a lucrative enterprise, sought by advertisers wanting to reach these particular consumers.

Economic stagnation in the record business and industry dissatisfaction with commercial radio as a promotional forum also encouraged the ascendence of video music. Ever since the birth of rock 'n' rock in the mid-1950s, record industry sales grew consistently, about 20 percent a year for twenty-five years. Sales peaked in 1977 and 1978 with two huge hits, Fleetwood Mac's *Rumours* and the soundtrack from *Saturday Night Fever,* each selling more than 20 million copies.[4] After this prosperous period, the record industry slumped into a severe recession lasting four years. Retail sales dropped from 726.2 million records and cassettes in 1978 to 575.6 million in 1982.[5] According to the Recording Industry Association of America, industry gross revenues decreased from $4.31 billion in 1978 to $3.59 billion in 1982, even with rising record prices.[6] This sustained drop in sales forced record companies to cut back their operations dramatically. In 1982, CBS Records, the largest American record company at that time, closed ten of Columbia Records' branch offices and laid off 300 employees, 15 percent of its total staff.[7] The slump was attributed to a variety of trends including home taping of albums on inexpensive blank cassette tapes, young consumers' shifting preferences toward other media products like video games, and a generally sluggish economy. Music critics claimed that consumers were not buying recorded music because there was a lack of appealing artists and music during this period.

However, there was a consensus that increasingly conservative radio stations greatly contributed to the record industry's troubles. In the 1970s, radio stations with rock-oriented formats adopted highly restricted playlists that emphasized older, classic rock albums and largely refused to play new music. Thus, radio was not providing much exposure to new artists, which was considered necessary for commercial success. Because of radio's resistance to new music, record industry executives actively sought new means of promotion to provide public exposure for their new releases and new artists. Video music eventually emerged to serve this purpose.

Warner Communications Develops New Music Program Service

Warner Communications was the first company to take advantage of these conditions favorable to the development of video music. Warner was a media conglomerate with interests in theatrical film, recorded music, book publishing, and cable television. In 1979, American Express bought 50 percent of Warner's cable division, which was reorganized under the name Warner Amex Cable Communications.[8] Soon after, this company split into two divisions: Warner Amex Cable continued to be responsible for the operation of its cable companies, and Warner Amex Satellite Entertainment Company (WASEC) was created to develop specialized program services for cable. A small group of executives at Warner pursued the idea of creating a program service for cable television featuring music videos. In late 1979, John A. Lack, Warner Cable's executive vice president of programming and marketing, explored this concept. In 1980, Lack hired Robert Pittman, a radio program executive, as director of Warner Amex's pay-TV division, and both executives began to select a group of people hired originally to work on Warner's pay-TV service, The Movie Channel, to work on this new video music project. After extensively researching the possibility for success of such a new program service, executive officers in Warner and American Express agreed to fund this new project in January 1981.

Lack and other Warner executives were convinced a twenty-four-hour-a-day program service featuring video music was a promising idea for a number of reasons. Although the structure of cable television encouraged the development of specialized program services appealing to narrow demographic groups, no one had yet created a program service that would successfully attract teenagers and young adults. Lack noted that Warner itself had no programming of interest for this age group: Warner's Nickelodeon was a children's program service, and The Movie Channel was aimed at older adult viewers. Advertisers considered young people between twelve and thirty-four years old a coveted demographic group that was difficult to reach through traditional broadcast media because this age group did not watch much television. A channel that successfully attracted young people could draw sufficient advertising revenues to make the service a lucrative venture.

Warner executives reasoned that a music-oriented channel would attract a younger audience since rock music was a central element of a youth-oriented subculture. Further, the executives believed that a program service consisting of video music clips would be a cheap source of programming that could be built more quickly than any other proposed service. Also, Lack and Pittman felt their plan for a music video channel could take advantage of the pronounced recession in the recording business and radio's stodgy conservatism by creating new consumer excitement in rock music that would revitalize the industry. Pittman promised record labels that Warner's video music service would more effectively promote their artists than radio because Warner's channel would emphasize new music and emerging artists, eschewing radio's restricted classic rock formats.

Warner commissioned two early versions of a video music program before launching its twenty-four-hour program service. Both of these shows were analyzed to give Warner information about audience preferences and interest in video music. *Pop Clips,* Warner's first video music offering, which premiered in 1980, was a daily thirty-minute show presented on Nickelodeon. John Lack saw it as part of his objective to expand the audience of the children's network by adding music-oriented programming to draw teenagers. The show, produced by ex-Monkee Michael Nesmith through his Pacific Arts Corporation, had aspiring young comedians introducing video clips and featured a Top 40 format. *Sight on Sound,* the other precursor to Warner's music channel, was a daily ninety-minute show playing on Warner's famous interactive cable system, QUBE, in Columbus, Ohio. The show, presented without an on-air host, let viewers select videos through its interactive system. This service was the precursor to The Box, an interactive music channel that came to be one of MTV's most successful competitors.

Record Company Participation in New Music Channel. Before plans for a video music channel could be realized, Warner executives needed to get the major record companies to cooperate in the venture because the service would largely depend on the major labels that made these clips. Warner wanted the record companies to allow their video clips to be played on Warner's program for free. Pittman often argued that it was in the record companies' best interests to provide the clips without charge because clip exposure on a program was a valuable form of promotion that would sell their artists' music. As mentioned earlier, the major record companies had been producing video clips for the international market since the mid-1970s. The labels conceded that granting Warner access to these clips for exhibition on its program service would not require any additional expense on their part, but they were reluctant to give away program material without any compensation and doubted the promotional value of video.

Despite these apprehensions, most record companies making video clips permitted their free use on Warner's planned video channel. Record companies in the midst of a severe industry recession were desperate for any new means of promotion, however unproven, that might spark people's interest in their artists' music. The labels also reasoned that it was not practical to require payment since Warner's new venture had limited resources and would not be able to pay large sums for videos. Most record companies adopted the position that they would provide clips free while the channel was a fledgling, vulnerable enterprise, but would require payment after the service became profitable. This stance was not unanimous, however, as Polygram and MCA Records both initially refused to provide Warner with free videos.

Warner Conducts Extensive Audience Research. Marshall Cohen, vice president of programming, claims that the Warner program service, to be called MTV: Music Television, was "the most researched channel in history."[9] Warner executives commissioned a series of audience research studies to provide specific information about the prospective audience for MTV and their preferences about the music format for such a program service. Audience research from the *Sight on Sound* program on the interactive QUBE system revealed that the most common viewer of a video music program service was a teenage male from a middle- or upper-class household. In April 1981, WASEC surveyed 600 to 750 people in the desired demographic group aged twenty to forty, asking them about their musical preferences and what elements they would and would not like to see in a video music channel. The respondents were intrigued by music video but not sure what it was. According to Cohen, the survey revealed that the most likely viewer would be "the twenty-three, twenty-four-year-old educated, affluent, suburban viewer—that was essentially the profile of MTV."[10] The program service's format was designed to appeal to the tastes of this typical viewer, featuring video clips by artists preferred by this narrow audience. Warner executives used this research to develop a program service that would not simply play music but reflect the lifestyle of their target audience and become an integral part of their music-oriented subculture.

Pittman used this research to justify his claim that MTV should have a rock-oriented format, largely eschewing rhythm and blues. He reasoned that Warner's research indicated the average prospective viewer of MTV would be a suburban, white male with a strong commitment to rock music and an equally strong aversion to contemporary soul. MTV's playlist would pander to the ethnocentric nature of its core audience by playing almost exclusively white rock artists. According to him, the primary audience for black-oriented music was in major urban areas that were not yet wired for cable and thus unable to receive Warner's program service.

Premiere of MTV.   MTV: Music Television premiered on cable television systems on August 21, 1981, at 12:01 A.M. EST with a video of the song, "Video Killed the Radio Star" by The Buggles. The debut of the channel featured videos by artists such as The Pretenders, Todd Rundgren, and Pat Benatar, which were announced by an on-air host, Mark Goodman, a former New York radio disk jockey. MTV could be received in full stereo sound by hooking a viewer's stereo to a television set with a special adapter that Warner required all cable companies to provide. Advertising sales were meager, with only 30 percent of available commercial time sold to companies hawking products like current films, soft drinks, and clothing. Although no early ratings were available, MTV's premiere was carried by 225 cable systems in 2.1 million homes, and by the end of August, MTV was available in 2.5 million homes. MTV: Music Television was not offered on cable systems in New York or Los Angeles during its early years, contributing to a lack of national media attention to the new service.

Warner executives sought to establish a certain style and mood for MTV, distinguishing it from traditional television. Unlike commercial television's tightly structured shows, MTV would be "a channel with no programs, no beginning, no middle, no end," according to Bob Pittman.[11] MTV developed a non-cerebral approach to programming that "relies on mood and emotion rather than on the traditional television approach of story and plot."[12] MTV also tried to cultivate an irreverent, informal style that appeared to be unplanned and unscripted. The program service intentionally departed from the technical perfection of conventional broadcast television by having a messy, cluttered set and poor lighting and allowing the hosts to make mistakes on the air, all of which gave the channel a spontaneous, casual feel.

MTV featured on-air announcers called "vee-jays" (or "VJs"), a video age update of the abbreviation for radio's disk jockeys or "DJs." The vee-jays introduced video clips, interviewed music stars, presented music-oriented news and concert information, and provided general chatter about the pop music scene. The vee-jays were pivotal to conveying the channel's desired image of hip irreverence and relaxed informality. Vee-jays were chosen primarily for their ability to convey an amiable, inoffensive demeanor rather than their knowledge about music or interviewing abilities, both of which were criticized frequently as deficient. Vee-jay selections were also highly dependent upon audience research, which revealed targeted viewers' preferences for vee-jays (a black vee-jay was okay, but no beards were allowed).

In its early years, MTV largely consisted of an endless succession of video clips. This emphasis on music clips was a problem because MTV had a limited library of video clips—no more than 125 selections—at its premiere. Despite the cooperation of most major record labels, which allowed MTV access to their music videos, they did not have many videos to offer MTV since their production of video music was quite limited. MTV's Tom Freston recalled that MTV had so few clips in the beginning that it would play anything it received.[13] Many contemporary American rock acts did not have any music clips available when MTV began operation because video music was not considered a useful form of promotion in the United States in the early 1980s.

However, many English groups produced clips for exposure in the U.K. and European markets where television was more established as a way to promote recording acts. Given the paucity of available clips, MTV gave these productions by British artists heavy play on its schedule. Also, U.K. acts like Duran Duran, The Eurythmics, Thomas Dolby, Human League, and A Flock of Seagulls were well suited to a visual medium like MTV because they created visually provocative videos and constructed highly stylized images, which were incorporated into their clips. Music critics described these U.K. artists and other rock acts as part of a new trend in pop music in the early 1980s called (unimaginatively enough) "New Music." *New Music* was a vague, amorphous term subject to various definitions: The *Wall Street Journal* refers to New Music as "futuristic 'technopop' and a blend of rock, soul and reggae,"[14] and Robert Christgau of the *Village Voice* defines it as "all music deriving primarily from the energy and influence of the Ramones and the Sex Pistols."[15] Music grouped in this category usually featured a heavily synthesized sound and a danceable beat.

MTV's early emphasis on these British artists and other musicians relatively unknown in the United States placed the channel in the forefront of introducing new music to the public (the term *new* in the generic sense rather than the inspired name of a specific music genre). This emphasis on new British musicians prompted much interest in MTV and contributed to the success of these musicians in the U.S. market as well as a revitalization of the recording business. Ironically, despite MTV's heavy reliance on audience research, the decision to feature U.K. artists and new music was based more on the historical fluke of clip availability than research analysis. MTV could not feature many U.S. rock stars and groups favored by survey respondents because many had no videos available, so the channel featured new music out of necessity. Christgau remarked that if the major record labels would have made videos for current mainstream U.S. artists like Air Supply and Linda Ronstadt, MTV would have featured these mundane, stale performers and ultimately enjoyed much less popularity and missed its momentary cutting-edge impact on popular culture.[16]

Pittman estimated that video clips constituted about 80 percent of MTV's programming at its premiere. The remaining time was devoted largely to music news and promotional campaigns. The vee-jays would present current news in the music world twice each hour and pass along the latest concert tour information for current rock stars. The news was characterized by uncritical record industry boosterism that indulged in gushing, frivolous interviews with popular music stars. MTV also sponsored a series of contests prominently featured on the air that asked viewers to mail in postcard entries for a chance to win unconventional music-related prizes. The first contest, the "One Night Stand," was a typical MTV promotion that awarded a free luxury trip to see Journey in concert, a backstage interview with the group, and other prizes related to the contest theme.

MTV Stimulates Record Sales

Reports of increasing record sales at music stores soon after MTV's premiere demonstrated that claims by Warner executives about MTV's potential promotional power had not been mistaken. A *Billboard* magazine survey in October 1981 of record stores in certain cities with cable systems carrying MTV reported increased sales of records and tapes, which store managers directly attributed to MTV.[17] MTV's major impact was to stimulate sales of records by new artists featured on the channel. Bob Smith, manager of Peaches record store in Tulsa, Oklahoma, said, "I had 15 copies of The Buggles LP sitting in a bin for eight months. One of the videos MTV is showing is that group's 'Video Killed The Radio Star.' I sold out of that LP in several weeks."[18] Record stores began ordering additional units of a current release if the music was featured on MTV in a video clip. Industry analysts claimed MTV was also largely responsible for a significant increase in sales in major music chain stores, ranging from 5 percent to 30 percent in November 1983.

MTV's influence was especially noticeable for retail sales of albums by new artists featured on MTV who received little or no radio airplay. The Stray Cats was a new group playing "rockabilly" that Les Garland, then MTV's vice president of programming, said, "we stayed with and the record company believed in without much radio airplay at first. Their manager told me he even plotted their tour by the markets MTV serves, and they sold something like 200,000 records without any significant radio exposure."[19] Duran Duran was another group that became popular in many countries except the United States where it could not break onto commercial radio's tight playlists. After MTV placed Duran Duran's video "Hungry Like the Wolf" in heavy rotation, sales of Duran Duran's album jumped and the group finally received radio play, which helped further their American success.

An A. C. Nielsen study of MTV viewers in October 1982 provided further evidence of MTV's promotional influence, reporting that 85 percent of the 2,000 respondents in the intended demographic group watched MTV, and those that did viewed it an average of 4.6 hours a week. MTV clearly influenced viewers' music purchases since 63 percent of the survey respondents said they purchased an artist's album after viewing a clip featuring the artist's music. Record company executives came to believe MTV could create consumer interest in their artists' music. An Arista Records spokesperson described video clips as "an increasingly important sales tool," and Jack Chudnoff at RCA records proclaimed that "MTV does sell records."[20] By July 1982, Polygram Records was convinced of MTV's selling power and decided to change its policy to allow MTV free use of its clips, although MCA Records remained skeptical of video's potential and continued to refuse MTV free access to its videos.

MTV's Relations with Cable Companies and Advertisers

Despite increasing support from record companies, MTV still faced serious obstacles from cable companies in its early years. Cable operators, which provided MTV with its means of distribution, were reluctant to offer the program service on their systems. The limited channel capacity of cable systems was cited often by operators as the reason for their refusal to carry MTV as well as other specialized program services. This was often a legitimate excuse in early 1982 when 70 percent of cable systems in the United States were limited to twelve channels. Because of federal "must carry rules" requiring cable systems to carry all local broadcast signals within a certain distance from the cable transmission facility and other requirements to provide public access channels, cable franchises limited to twelve channels had few remaining slots for program services such as MTV.

However, Warner Amex executives were worried that cable operator reluctance to carry MTV went beyond technical limitations. They believed that many systems refused to carry MTV because the typical cable operator was from an older generation with a distaste for rock music who could not understand the appeal of a program service based on such music. This resistance to MTV presented WASEC executives with a dilemma since the channel was dependent upon cable franchises to reach viewers. For MTV to be a successful venture, it needed to rapidly increase its potential audience base to attract advertisers, yet in late 1982 the program service was still excluded from cable systems in major markets like New York and Los Angeles.

To circumvent this obstacle, WASEC executives commissioned a promotional campaign to convince cable companies to carry MTV. WASEC hired the advertising agency of Lois Pitts Gershon (LPG) to develop the promotion that was aimed at cable companies in New York and ten other major markets not offering MTV on their systems. Tom Freston, then MTV's director of marketing, targeted cities with a demonstrated interest in rock music: "We figured where we had the best potential penetration was in markets where rock and roll had the biggest share on the radio dial."[21] The promotion, which featured the slogan "I Want My MTV," encouraged rock fans to contact their local cable company and demand that MTV be offered. WASEC and LPG produced several television and radio commercials for the campaign, featuring popular rock stars like David Bowie and Pat Benatar saying variations of "I want my MTV. . . . Pick up your phone, call your local cable operator and demand your MTV." The advertisements were aired constantly in the targeted markets without MTV.

The campaign spurred broad participation from the public, which inundated cable companies with cards, letters, and phone calls telling the operators to carry MTV on their systems. This show of public support convinced multiple system operators (MSOs) that there was substantial community interest in the channel. Denise Bozi, promotion manager at Manhattan Cable in New York, said that the "I Want My MTV" campaign was "brilliant" and showed that the program service was "very viable."[22] The success of the promotional campaign as well as increasing publicity about the channel encouraged MSOs to add MTV to their systems, rapidly expanding MTV's potential audience base. In January 1983, Group W cable systems in New York City and Los Angeles began offering MTV, which was a major milestone for the program service. Gaining access to the country's two major media markets legitimized MTV as a truly national program service, rather than a primarily suburban phenomenon. MTV grew dramatically in 1983, reaching 18 million homes by that December, more than double the previous year, making it available to 22 percent of all U.S. homes with television.[23] In order to take advantage of MTV's newfound success, WASEC began charging cable operators that year for the right to offer MTV, which used to be provided free to cable systems.

MTV's rapidly growing subscriber figures helped major advertisers overcome their initial wariness of the program service. Jay James, a senior vice president for Doyle Dane Bernbach, which spent more than $2 million on MTV for advertising in 1983, explains that advertisers spent their budget primarily on established traditional media because most "are too conservative to look for the newest way to spend money."[24] However, advertising agencies gradually became convinced of MTV's ability to reach an elusive young audience. Advertisers were especially attracted to a survey conducted by Dresner, Morris, and Tortorello for Warner Amex and Pepsico describing the average MTV viewer as a twenty-three-year-old with a household income of $30,000 per year. *Fortune* magazine's award to MTV as Product of the Year attested to the channel's ability to deliver a desired audience to advertisers.[25] After the modest advertiser participation at MTV's premiere, the program service's advertising revenues grew significantly over the next few years. By June 1983, MTV sold advertising time to 140 companies representing more than 240 consumer products.[26] MTV was especially attractive for advertising clothes, selling time to sixteen companies advertising jeans by the end of that year.[27]

MTV's Exclusion of Black Artists

A persistent controversy in MTV's early years was the program service's virtual exclusion of black artists. MTV adopted a narrow rock music format with a playlist composed almost entirely of white rock acts. Initially, debate about this issue was confined to industry conferences and trade magazines where record industry executives reprimanded MTV for its refusal to air black videos. Nancy Leivska Wilde, director of Motown's Video operations, charged "MTV is just programming to the white rock 'n' roller,"[28] and Jeff Ayeroff at A&M records added caustically, "God forbid people should be exposed to blacks on cable."[29] Record companies' attempts to encourage MTV to air videos by black artists were motivated less by their executives' liberal convictions and more by the economic necessity of gaining valuable exposure for the labels' black acts. As Jo Bergman, video and television director for Warner Bros. Records, explained: "We're making clips on black artists but the trouble is getting black clips on TV."[30]

The general public became aware of this controversy in early 1983 when mainstream media began to address MTV's exclusion of blacks. Rick James, a popular black funk artist, focused attention on MTV's policies in a *Los Angeles Times* interview where he charged that the program service was racist for refusing to air videos by him or other black artists. He claimed that MTV refused to air black videos despite the proven commercial success of many black musicians:

> I'm just tired of the bullshit. I have sold over 10 million records in a four-year period ... and I can't get on the channel. I watch all these fluffed-up groups who don't even sell four records on a program that I'm being excluded from. Me and everyone of my peers—Earth, Wind & Fire, Stevie Wonder, the Gap Band, Marvin Gaye, Smokey Robinson—have great videos. Why doesn't MTV show them? It's like taking black people back 400 years.[31]

Rick James's accusations generated a flurry of attention in the general news media, leading ABC's *Nightline* to devote a program on May 13, 1983, to the topic of MTV's alleged racially discriminatory practices. MTV executives declined to appear on the show, which did include participation by Rick James, Casey Kasem, and Rick Dobbis of Arista Records. James stressed the importance of MTV exposure for black artists: "This show has a very strong impact on the market. . . . It means something for us to get our music to people, and it means something for us to get our visual concepts to people."[32] On ABC's newsmagazine *20/20*, Maurice White of Earth, Wind & Fire also claimed his group was banned from MTV: "I have trouble getting to play on [MTV]. Even though our music has broken all barriers, they consider our music R&B, so they say that they're only playing rock music, which I don't believe."[33] A spirited debate between MTV vee-jay Mark Goodman and rock star David Bowie about MTV's exclusion of blacks also received prominent media coverage. During one of MTV's celebrity interviews,

David Bowie began questioning the vee-jay about the lack of black artists presented on the music service.[34] Goodman lamely responded that most black music doesn't fit into MTV's "narrowcast" format, saying that viewers in Midwestern towns do not like black music.[35] Bowie argued that MTV and radio stations were morally responsible "to make the media more integrated."[36]

WASEC executives were unmoved by this increasing barrage of negative publicity about their treatment of black artists. A series of standard responses were always given to criticisms about MTV's exclusionary policy. Bob Pittman said on several occasions that most black music was not compatible with MTV's rock format: "Our position is that we play rock 'n' roll music. What we are doing is successful. We hope to find more black musicians doing rock 'n' roll and new music. It's not a color barrier—it's a music barrier."[37] MTV executives stressed that they did play those black artists who did fit MTV's sound, like the Bus Boys, a Los Angeles black rock act and Musical Youth, a British reggae group. Pittman also frequently tried to deflect responsibility for MTV's reluctance to air black artists by placing the blame on its ethnocentric target audience. He reasoned that MTV's viewers were primarily white teenagers in suburban and rural areas who were not interested in black music.

MTV's policy about black artists remained virtually unchanged until the program service became involved in a major confrontation with CBS Records over Michael Jackson, a major CBS recording artist.[38] Jackson released a hit album, *Thriller,* which reached the top spot on the *Billboard* charts in February 1983. CBS Records commissioned an elaborate video for "Billie Jean," a single from the album, which captured the number one position on the *Billboard* "Hot One Hundred" chart on March 5, 1983. CBS wanted Jackson's video to receive extensive play on MTV to expand the album's crossover appeal into the album-oriented rock market. MTV refused to air Jackson's video, citing the standard reason that his music did not fit MTV's particular format. After repeated attempts to persuade MTV to air Jackson's video failed, CBS president Walter Yetnikoff allegedly threatened to take away all of the company's video clips from the channel, an especially potent threat since CBS record labels' share of the record market was 25 percent.[39] A CBS boycott would deny MTV video clips from many popular rock stars including Billy Joel, Journey, and Pink Floyd. MTV ultimately relented, adding Michael Jackson's *Billie Jean* video to its playlist on March 2.[40]

Despite numerous accounts of the showdown detailed previously, both CBS Records and MTV deny that CBS threatened to pull its videos or that MTV capitulated to CBS's demands.[41] Rather, WASEC executive John Sykes claimed that Jackson's *Billie Jean* became such a huge crossover hit MTV could not ignore it, and moreover, the song fit MTV's rock-oriented format (despite earlier assertions that it did not).[42] Regardless of exactly how the *Billie Jean* video made it onto the MTV playlist, the fact that it was accepted was a milestone for videos by black artists. The success of Michael Jackson's album and the favorable reception accorded his *Billie Jean* video contradicted MTV's conventional wisdom that the video channel's predominantly white rock-oriented audience would reject music or videos by black performers. The phenomenal success of Michael Jackson demonstrated to MTV executives that black artists could be successfully incorporated into its playlist. Although black artists remained underrepresented on the channel in the mid-1980s, MTV slowly began to accept videos by black artists with crossover hits perceived to fit into the MTV "sound," like Prince, Eddy Grant, and Garland Jeffreys.

MTV's Corporate Activities Through 1984

MTV underwent a corporate reorganization in February 1984 when its parent company, Warner Amex Satellite Entertainment Company, was dissolved and its assets were transferred to a new company, MTV Networks, which was incorporated. MTV Networks was owned entirely by Warner Amex Cable Communications until August 1984 when it completed a public stock offering of one-third of the company's common stock, raising about $70 million.[43] MTV executives decided to undertake the stock offering because it needed the revenues to pay off bank loans and provide the company with funds for contracts with major record companies providing MTV with exclusive access to some of the labels' videos (discussed in Chapter 4). Warner Communications and American Express jointly held the remaining two-thirds ownership through their subsidiary Warner Amex cable. Because of certain provisions of the stock offering stipulating reduced voting rights for the publicly owned shares of common stock, Warner Amex retained 90.7 percent of MTVN voting power even though it only owned 66.1 percent of the capital stock outstanding.[44]

In 1984, MTV reported an annual profit for the first year since its debut. The video service had had heavy losses each prior year. Denisoff said MTV's total losses between 1981 and 1983 were $33.9 million; however, *Time* magazine estimated much higher losses for MTV during this period, exceeding $50 million.[45] MTV Networks reversed this trend in 1984 with an annual profit of almost $12 million made possible by a dramatic jump in the company's total revenues to $109.5 million, more than double the previous year.[46] The increase was due to growing advertising revenue and cable operator license fees instituted in 1984. The following year, the new MTV Networks company was bought by the media conglomerate Viacom, an acquisition discussed in Chapter 6.

Expanded Record Industry Involvement in Video Music

The U.S. record industry began to recover from its extended recession in 1983 when retail sales rose by 5 percent over the previous year to an estimated $3.8 billion and continued its rebound in 1984 when sales exceeded $4 billion, matching the industry record set in 1978.[47] Many observers credited MTV and video music with stimulating much of the industry's success by igniting consumer interest in new recording artists that were ignored by radio. Steve Mitchell, buyer for the

Sound Warehouse, claimed "MTV has opened up our business to sell a more diverse group of artists."[48] Moreover, MTV encouraged radio to become more receptive to new music as well. Radio stations with rock and Top 40 formats expanded their playlists to include music by artists introduced on MTV. Richard
Neer of WNEW-FM in New York acknowledged that "seeing a new act on MTV
that isn't in our rotation makes it a little easier for us to expose them because of
the built-in audience."[49]

Although MTV's impact was considerable, it was not solely responsible for the
industry resurgence.[50] The record companies' recovery coincided with an overall
growth in the general U.S. economy, providing young people with more disposable income to buy records. Technology was also a contributing factor, as the
widespread popularity of the Sony Walkman and boom boxes dramatically increased sales of cassette tapes. Video games, which cut into record industry sales,
became yesterday's fad and many young people returned to buying albums and
tapes. The phenomenal success of Michael Jackson's *Thriller* was also cited as a
key factor in generating new excitement in pop music (although his success was
magnified by prominent MTV exposure).

Yet MTV received much of the credit for the industry's good fortune. In January 1983, the industry trade magazine, *Billboard,* began printing a weekly "Video
Programming" chart that presented MTV's current playlist and praised the network's "success in exposing and helping establish new and developing acts."[51]
MTV received additional accolades from the National Association for Record
Manufacturers, which gave the service its 1984 Presidential Award for its role in
reviving the industry.[52] The channel received so much favorable publicity by 1983
that the conventional wisdom held that video music was no longer an option, but
a necessity for commercial success. Record industry executives began to claim that
an artist's song needed an accompanying video clip in order to be a potential hit.
Moreover, record labels considered airplay on MTV essential for a video clip to
effectively promote an artist. Len Epand of Polygram Records claimed "if you're
not on MTV, to a large share of consumers you just don't exist."[53] The importance
of video music was evident by the increasing number of hit songs on the record
charts with videos. Whereas only twenty-three of the top 100 hit singles listed in
Billboard's "Hot 100" chart had accompanying videos in May 1981, the number
of singles with videos increased to fifty-nine by May 1983 and jumped even further to seventy-six in May 1984.[54]

Increased Record Label Investment in Music Video

As MTV increased in prominence, record companies came to favor video music
over live tours as a way to promote their artists. Prior to MTV's debut, record
companies scaled back their practice of financially subsidizing tours because of
the industry recession as well as the belief that the limited public exposure derived from touring did not warrant the expense. The advent of MTV accelerated
the labels' curtailment of their funding of touring as label executives discovered

video music could provide broad exposure of their artists at a cost much less than that incurred by live tours. Further, a video clip played on MTV could be viewed by millions of potential record buyers, while live tours might reach several hundred thousand people at best. In 1983, Gil Friesen, president of A&M Records, said the label's budget for tours was "exactly half" of the budget four years ago.[55] In 1984, recording artist Joe Jackson claimed that "two years ago, four times as much record company money was spent on support for tours as on videos; that ratio has now reversed, which, incidentally, isn't helping live music much."[56] Concert promoters worried that the increasing popularity of video music at a time of diminishing label support of live performances would severely diminish future tour revenues.

The enhanced credibility of video music as an effective form of promotion led major record companies to dramatically increase their investment in video music. Most record labels gradually established divisions to coordinate the production of video clips for their artists and the distribution of these clips to major exposure outlets, such as MTV. Most of these music video divisions did not produce the clips themselves, but instead commissioned production firms and directors to make a music video for a certain budget set by the label.

As the demand for video music grew, record companies underwrote a growing number of video clips to successfully promote their artists. *Fortune* estimated that the record companies commissioned about 2,000 clips in 1984 at a total cost of $100 million, which was three times the quantity of clips produced two years earlier.[57] Further, the average cost per video clip increased dramatically during these years. Whereas the average four-minute video cost about $15,000 to produce in 1981, this rose to $25,000–$35,000 in 1983 and still further to $40,000–$50,000 in 1984.[58] The budgets for video clips featuring major recording artists frequently topped $100,000. The video for Madonna's hit, "Like a Virgin," was filmed on location in Venice at a cost of $150,000, and Lionel Richie's "All Night Long" video, including forty dancers, cost $100,000.[59]

As these costs continued to rise, the major labels worried how they could recover their expenses in video production and distribution. Video clips produced no direct revenue for the labels at that point because the videos were provided free to MTV and other exposure media. The companies claimed that the escalating costs of video could diminish their profit from retail sales of their artists' products. The cost of the clips produced solely for their promotional value were deducted out of gross revenues from retail sales before profit was calculated. High video costs meant that the associated record needed to sell an increased quantity of units before the album could be considered profitable. Don Dempsey, then senior vice president and general manager of Epic/Portrait/CBS Associated Labels, argued, "If you add [video expenses] to the production cost of a record and normal marketing expense, it's caused us to raise the break-even point on records," estimating that the extra sales required to break even on a record by a new act might be up to 50,000 units.[60] Although videos were widely credited with increasing retail sales of artists' records, the labels claimed that the increasing expense of a video clip might at some point outweigh the benefit of the additional sales generated by the clip.

Record companies took certain measures to recover their expense on video clips and protect their profit margin on product sales. The actions taken by CBS Records (now Sony Music) were typical of the major labels.[61] Before CBS would commit itself to a video clip, it would try to get some confirmation from radio and MTV that they would play the single and the corresponding clip. If radio and MTV were pessimistic about the chances of airplay, CBS might dump the video at the storyboard stage, cutting its losses. CBS also instituted provisions in its recording artists' contracts requiring the company to be repaid for promotional expenses on video production out of the artists' royalties received from retail sales.

Record companies also tried to recover their investment in video music by attempting to convert the video clip from a promotional device for records into a retail commodity in its own right. Encouraged by the widespread penetration of VCRs and the growth of the home video market, many of the major labels established their own home video divisions, such as CBS/Fox Home Video, in order to market and sell video clip compilations as a retail product. Yet, despite a few notable exceptions, the commercial potential of this market initially proved to be quite limited. "The Making of Michael Jackson's *Thriller*," including the fourteen-minute *Thriller* clip as well as other Jackson clips, was very successful, selling 800,000 copies by September 1984.[62] Yet, this music video was perceived as a special case due more to the phenomenal popularity of Michael Jackson.[63] A more typical best-seller for the video music genre in the early 1980s was Picture Music International's *Duran Duran*, which sold around 50,000 units in the United States. Still, the average video music title sold an even less impressive 5,000 units and rarely exceeded 10,000 units. The video music portion of the home video market was severely limited—only 4 percent of videocassette sales and rentals in 1984.[64]

Given the relative inadequacy of these various approaches for generating revenue from music video clips, the record labels began to reconsider their policy of providing the clips free to exposure media, including MTV and other music television shows discussed in Chapter 3. Some record labels began to charge television shows fees to pay for their expenses on video clips. In May 1985, CBS instituted a payment plan to charge all outlets for the right to exhibit its videos. The plan imposed a flat monthly rate that varied according to the format and length of the video show. Herb Rossin, spokesman for UHF video music station WLXI in Greensboro, North Carolina, claimed that the proposed monthly fees for half-hour and one-hour shows ranged from $500 to $1,000, and twenty-four-hour services would be required to pay $2,000 a month.[65] The WEA Record Group, including the Warner Bros., Elektra, and Atlantic labels, soon followed the policy of CBS Records by announcing its intent to charge for its videos starting November 1, 1985.[66] The policy assessed a general "service charge" to cover the companies "out of pocket expenses" such as "tape stock, duplication, handling and shipping" and also an additional "programming" fee for "hit" videos.[67] The remaining labels said they would either study the issue (MCA and RCA Records) or institute their own fees in the future (Polygram Records).[68]

Most television shows were fiercely critical of the proposed charges. Many claimed that these fees would imperil music video shows because stations could not pay the charges, and others complained that license fees were repugnant because the videos were just commercials for record company products. Initially, most shows refused to pay and dropped all video clips distributed by labels charging fees from their shows. The main target of the clip boycott was CBS Records because it was the first major label to introduce a comprehensive license fee plan and its charges were considered to be unreasonably high. CBS promotion executives estimated that about 80 percent of video clip shows stopped airing clips from its affiliated labels after the company unveiled its fee plan.[69] Other music programs complied with the CBS plan, and still another group negotiated agreements with CBS, offering advertising time to the label instead of cash payments. However, some outlets simply dropped their video music shows altogether. The increased expenses were especially difficult for local shows to continue since local productions usually operated on a limited budget. In 1986, record label executives acknowledged this fallout of clip shows, but claimed that limited exposure of their clips on select media outlets was more desirable for promotion anyway because oversaturation of a clip played everywhere could undermine its promotional value since people would quickly get bored with often seen videos.

In sum, the institution of license fees advanced two related record company objectives about video clips. The fee plans created a revised perception of video as a legitimate form of programming in its own right with value rather than simply a free promotional device used to sell records. The license fees also increased the record labels' control over distribution of the clips, allowing the labels to restrict access of their videos to select exposure outlets like MTV. MTV Networks also benefited from these license fees because they undermined many of MTV's competitors that were unable or unwilling to pay for clips. When the fees were first introduced, *Variety* predicted, "The general consensus is that only the financially strong will survive in the music video TV arena once the diskeries begin to impose charges for the promo clips," most notably MTV Networks, which could rely on the deep pockets of its parent company.[70]

Some label executives said that the rising expenses associated with video music compelled record companies to develop these new strategies to generate revenue from the exploitation of video clips. However, the labels' policies can be better understood within the context of cultural producers' historical tendency toward product recycling. Media companies generally attempt to recycle their products in as many forums as possible to maximize their profit. For example, Hollywood production companies will recycle films in a variety of media including theatrical exhibition, home video, cable, broadcast television, and so on. The production company recycles programming because once the initial expense of a production is incurred, costs for future exploitation of the product in other media are minimal. Similarly, once record companies finance videos for promotional purposes, the labels try to exploit the video in as many additional sites as possible. Thus, the companies can not only use the videos to expose their artists but sell the videos as programming to program services and as a retail good to consumers in the home video market.

3

The Growth of Other Video Music Program Services

After MTV had been operating for a few years, several other program services were launched, seeking to capitalize on MTV's success. Such programming was especially attractive in early 1984 because of the low cost and high yield of video music. The initial popularity of video clips assured a satisfactory audience and hence advertising revenue, and the clips were provided by the labels in the early 1980s for use free of charge so expenses were minimal.

The emergence of alternative outlets for video music besides MTV Networks' offerings was heralded as an opportunity for a broader range of musical genres and styles to be presented on television. MTV was often charged with presenting a quite narrow segment of music largely confined to white rock acts, excluding all music falling outside the boundaries of its restrictive format, most notably music by black artists. Critics voiced concern that if MTV were to remain the primary source of exposure for video music, artists that did not meet the arbitrary standards of this one entity could be effectively excluded from television. Some record industry executives hoped that the development of other viable program services might encourage a pluralistic market where video music deemed unsuitable in one forum would be appropriate in others. The variety of outlets might conceivably break the monolithic style of music presented on MTV.

The most direct challenges to MTV were plans for full-fledged national music program services. Three parties announced their intention to launch twenty-four-hour daily video music programming in 1984 and 1985. Each of these potential competitors sought to distinguish its program service from MTV's offering in roughly similar respects. All claimed their services would eschew video clips with gratuitous sex and violence so prominent on MTV, instead featuring more "wholesome" videos suitable for family viewing. These competitors also rejected MTV's "narrowcasting" program strategy, claiming they would play a broader range of pop music, which would include music by black artists largely banned from MTV at that time. Although each service wanted to compete with MTV, all had difficulty surmounting the industry's "Rule of One," which held that there was only sufficient consumer interest to sustain one program service for each type of specialized programming. Following this conventional wisdom, cable operators offering MTV were reluctant to add a second video music service, citing insufficient subscriber interest to support two music channels. Further, each competitor claimed MTV's special relationship with major record companies (discussed in Chapter 4) made it difficult for competitors to gain access to current hit videos by popular artists.

Cable Music Channel

In August 1984, cable industry entrepreneur Ted Turner became the first to announce plans for a rival video music channel. Turner characterized his project as not simply a business venture but rather a moral crusade designed to humble MTV, a program service he denounced as a depraved and corrupt influence on young people. Turner sought to provide cable operators with a wholesome alternative to MTV, which he claimed would "stay away from the excessive violent or degrading clips to women that MTV is so fond of putting on."[1] Turner's challenge to MTV was also partially prompted by his company's recent success over another cable program service, Satellite News Channels, a product of ABC and Westinghouse, which failed in its attempt to compete with Turner's Cable News Network (CNN). Turner decided to launch his new music service at this time because many of MTV's affiliate contracts with cable operators expired and were being renegotiated, providing an opportunity to encourage cable operators to replace MTV with the new Turner channel.[2]

Turner sent a letter dated August 7, 1984, to more than 8,000 cable operators announcing his company's intention to launch an as yet unnamed rock music video service to begin operation December 5. The video service would be provided free of charge for five years to cable operators that committed to carry it before August 24. The tepid response of cable operators fell far short of Turner's goal of having 10 million subscribers at the channel's premiere. Despite early claims from Turner Broadcasting Systems (TBS) of reaching 2.5 million subscribers, a TBS stock prospectus revealed that the service received commitments from cable companies serving only 400,000 households. Cable companies were skeptical of the new service, belatedly titled the Cable Music Channel (CMC), doubtful the industry could support two music services. Industry analysts became even more skeptical of Turner's venture because of his company's habit of providing inconsistent and inaccurate information about CMC's programming and subscriber base. The service emulated the radio format of contemporary hits radio emphasizing current hit pop singles, while banning the "offensive" videos shown on MTV. The service sought a broad target audience of people in the twelve to thirty-four age group, with a special emphasis on viewers over twenty-five.[3]

While CMC was never perceived as a credible competitor to MTV, Turner's service caused two problems for MTV. Turner's announcement of the new service coincided with MTV's stock offering, which was noticeably hurt by the disclosure. The 5.1 million shares of MTV stock were expected to sell at between $16 and $18 a share, but news of Turner's new venture pushed the price down to $15 a share, costing MTV Networks between $5 million and $15 million.[4] Further, Turner's new service put MTV at a disadvantage during its contract negotiations with cable operators. MTV wanted to institute licensing fees for the right to carry the program service, which had been free, but Turner's offer of a free service for five years forced MTV Networks to accept lower license fees.

MTV Networks reacted to Turner's challenge by taking actions designed to maintain its dominance in video music. MTV quickly announced its intention to launch a second music video channel, Video Hits One (VH-1), at the beginning of January 1985, which would target the same older demographic group sought by CMC. MTVN had long planned to develop such a second service but Bob Pittman acknowledged that Turner's venture forced the company to accelerate these plans.[5] In order to ensure access for this new service, MTVN negotiated contracts with cable companies, providing VH-1 free to companies that carried MTV, hoping that cable operators would carry its own new service instead of Turner's.

The Cable Music Channel failed quickly. On November 28, TBS announced that its music service would be discontinued after only five weeks in operation and its assets sold to MTV Networks. TBS was unable to persuade enough major MSOs to offer the Cable Music Channel and thus could not attract advertising, given its paltry audience. *The Economist* attributes CMC's failure to MTV's overwhelmingly dominant position in the market as well as the poor relations Turner had had with cable operators ever since he raised license fees for his other service, CNN.[6] MTV's exclusive contracts with record companies denying competitors access to current hit videos was also mentioned as a contributing factor in CMC's demise.

However, the decision to end CMC was largely dictated by outside financial institutions that provided TBS with substantial bank loans. Although Ted Turner was often portrayed as a swaggering, individualist capitalist who directly ran his own company, TBS was in fact a highly leveraged company subject to very restrictive loan covenants, limiting the company's autonomy. The long-term debt of TBS grew dramatically during the early 1980s, increasing Turner's dependence upon lending institutions.[7] Despite Turner's moral condemnation of Warner Communications as a "sleazy" company playing "dirty videos,"[8] TBS's lenders forced him to talk to Warner Amex to discuss the possible merger of Turner's news services with MTV's music and children's services.[9] When Warner Amex president, Drew Lewis, and Turner failed to reach an agreement and Turner decided to pursue his proposed video music channel, financial institutions strictly limited his losses on CMC to $1 million in 1984, $7.5 million in 1985 and $5 million in 1986.[10]

TBS needed to spend much more than this to develop a strong competitor to MTV. A TBS prospectus acknowledged that losses would exceed these limits: "The company presently anticipates that Cable Music Channel will lose in the range of $5 million to $10 million in its first year of operation and may continue at this level thereafter."[11] Further, as mentioned previously, MTV lost between $33 and $50 million or more before it became profitable in 1984.[12] CMC would be unable to generate this magnitude of revenue on its own for several years because the service was provided free to cable companies and advertising revenues were minimal due to poor subscriber figures. Turner had no other choice but to discontinue the channel.

After CMC's failure, MTV purchased its assets in an action the *Wall Street Journal* described as "more a mercy killing than anything else."[13] MTV Networks agreed to pay Turner $1 million and purchase $500,000 worth of advertising on Turner's other cable program services. In exchange, MTV received a satellite transponder, the rights to CMC's name, and its list of subscribers, which Pittman indicated would be helpful in "converting CMC subscribers to VH-1 subscribers."[14] Whereas Turner lost about $1.5 million on the CMC venture, the acquisition helped MTV Networks become even more firmly entrenched as the unchallenged leader of national video music programming and facilitated the expansion of the company's offerings with VH-1.

Discovery Music Network

Two weeks before Ted Turner announced his ill-fated venture, plans for another video music service, the Discovery Music Network (DMN), were unveiled in July 1984 with much less fanfare. Discovery was developed by Glen Taylor and Karen Tyler, founders of the Financial News Network (FNN). Taylor abruptly resigned as chairman of FNN before the cable service went public in July 1982 after the *Los Angeles Times* reported allegations that he sold unregistered stock and was investigated by the IRS for paying income taxes on only two occasions between 1968 and 1979. DMN's founders, much like Turner, wanted to create a sanitized alternative to MTV. Taylor and Tyler claimed there was a potential older audience for a music video program service that was not served by MTV's youth-oriented format and risqué videos. Tyler, DMN's president, said Discovery would not "program the heavy-metal sound, violence or heavy sex. We want to be more an uplifting entertainment channel." Discovery sought to attract viewers in the twenty-four to forty-five age group, specifically targeting housewives during the day and younger adults in the evening. The service intended to play an eclectic mix of music from various genres, while avoiding clips considered to be in poor taste.

Discovery planned to debut in December 1984 as a direct competitor to MTV, but DMN executives could not persuade many cable companies to carry the service. Because of this resistance, Discovery altered its distribution strategy, abandoning attempts to become a cable program service and instead assembling a network of UHF and low-power broadcast television stations that would circumvent the recalcitrant cable operators. Discovery still encountered many problems that repeatedly delayed its expected debut date. Although DMN executives estimated that $10 million was needed at minimum for Discovery's operation during the first year, Taylor was unable to obtain commitments for even half this amount. Further, Discovery was concerned that MTV's contracts with record companies providing exclusive rights to some videos would prevent the service from playing popular songs. DMN filed a lawsuit against MTV and the record companies for alleged antitrust law violations, which ultimately had no effect on MTV's contracts with record labels. The program service was never launched, leading *Billboard* to report in May 1988 that "Discovery . . . never got off the ground."[15]

Hit Video USA

Despite the dismal performance of CMC and Discovery, Constance and Mark Wodlinger made yet another attempt to develop a full-fledged competitor to MTV. On July 12, 1985, their company, Wodlinger Broadcasting, started a modest local music service on a low-power VHF station in Houston, Texas. The company president, Mrs. Constance Wodlinger, wanted to develop an alternative to the standard fare of network reruns on independent stations. The program service, TV5, included interview segments with artists along with currently popular and classic videos. In December, the company expanded to a national program service distributed via satellite for cable television. This service, Hit Video USA, was launched December 16, 1985, retaining the contemporary hits format of its local predecessor, TV5. Hit Video USA played Top 40 videos without excessive sex or violence.

Hit Video USA had little support from cable operators at its debut. No cable systems in major markets were offering the Wodlinger service after it was in operation for a month. The Wodlingers attributed their service's problems to MTV's anticompetitive practices, including franchise contracts that discouraged cable operators from offering a competitor's video music service and MTV pacts with record labels that denied Hit Video access to popular videos. Hit Video pursued Discovery's strategy of filing an antitrust lawsuit against MTV to void these agreements. Despite Hit Video's initially poor showing, the channel was moderately successful by April 1987 when it was carried on 120 cable systems as well as some broadcast stations.[16]

The Wodlingers altered their distribution plans for the service in early 1988 because of the limited potential for additional cable subscribers.[17] Hit Video USA was discontinued as a twenty-four-hour cable program service and converted into programming for broadcast stations, offering seven hours (later increased to ten hours) of daily video music shows to broadcasters. Each hour of programming contained ten minutes of ad time, half of which was provided to the broadcaster, who could choose how many hours of Hit Video USA it wanted to air. After this shift to broadcasting, the service was available on fifty-seven stations in January 1990, giving it a potential audience of 37 million. Hit Video USA expanded internationally with agreements to provide programming in fifteen countries and held negotiations to introduce the service in about twelve others.

Hit Video USA suffered increasingly serious financial problems, leading to the channel's demise. In 1988, Wodlinger's company lost a line of credit from its major bank and had substantial financial losses for the year.[18] Constance Wodlinger claimed that the continuing lawsuit filed against MTV drained the financial resources of the company and was responsible for the losses. Hit Video USA hit bottom on October 4, 1990, when the company shut down transmission of the domestic service and fifteen employees were fired. The international programming was continued with a limited staff.[19] Hit Video was hurt by a steep decline in the number of TV stations carrying the service: Only thirty-two stations carried any portion of the service in October 1990, a drop of twenty-five stations since January. Local stations were replacing music videos with movies to increase ratings, a program shift that also spelled the end of *Night Tracks* on WTBS. Increasing the financial strain, both Hit Video USA and the local stations were unable to sell ad time during the show. After Hit Video USA was shut down, the parent company, Wodlinger Broadcasting, was sold and the only properties Constance Wodlinger retained were the name Hit Video USA and the logo.[20] She attempted a modest comeback in April 1991 by preparing pilots for four shows featuring music videos for syndication in the cable market, despite much skepticism about this project. The major labels regretted the death of Hit Video USA because it was the major alternative to MTV and presented videos not seen on its more well-known competitor. The loss of Hit Video USA consolidated MTV's dominance of national music video exhibition.

MTV's Sister Service VH-1: Video Hits One

MTV Networks eventually adopted the strategy of its competitors by launching a second music video service that would appeal to an older adult audience having an interest in video music, but who were repelled by the heavy metal featured on MTV. MTV announced plans to launch a second service, Video Hits One (VH-1), in late August 1985, about two weeks after Turner made known the plans for his own video music venture. The timing of MTV's announcement led to speculation that the primary purpose of VH-1 was to sabotage Turner's plans and prevent the emergence of any full-fledged competitor to MTV. Pittman acknowledged this in his discussion of in-house research on the viability of a new service: "We polled our affiliates and found that while almost no one was going to drop us, Turner could get 15 million subscribers in two years as a second music service. We thought, shit, if there's that big a market, we should be the second service, not him."[21] The VH-1 service was used as a barrier to prevent any direct competition to MTV. As Pittman pointed out, potential competitors such as Turner were "relegated from fighting MTV to fighting VH-1."[22] Fredric Dannen remarked that this strategy reinforced MTV's monopolistic dominance in the market, much like HBO's creation of its companion service, Cinemax, did in pay cable.[23]

MTV Networks tried to develop a program service that would attract somewhat older, more affluent people who did not normally watch MTV. MTV was successful but still unable to persuade some of the nation's most prominent advertisers to buy spots on the channel because MTV's audience was mostly people between eighteen and thirty-four, an age group with limited disposable income that was not of much interest to companies advertising "big ticket" items like luxury cars, major home appliances, and furniture. MTV wanted to tap in to this lucrative source of advertising by launching a channel targeted toward a wealthier, older audience that bought these "big ticket" products.

MTVN estimated that the cost to develop VH-1 would approach $7 million, much less than the total cost to establish the company's other program services.[24] MTV could greatly contain expenses for VH-1 by taking advantage of what Pittman termed his company's music video *infrastructure*, which provided VH-1 with already established sales, research, programming, and marketing departments. MTV also acquired the assets of Turner's defunct CMC, which provided VH-1 with essential resources for developing a program service such as a satellite transponder and subscriber list. VH-1 was expected to operate at a loss for a long time because advertising revenues were limited and the channel was offered free to cable operators who carried MTV.

VH-1 premiered January 1, 1985, and was carried by 215 cable systems with a subscriber base of 3.4 million. Pittman boasted that "of the top 20 MSOs (Multiple System Operators), we were launched by 18."[25] The service adopted the "adult contemporary" format of radio that focused on easy listening music from various genres and omitted the hard rock and heavy metal that older audiences often found offensive. The original vee-jays included popular New York radio personalities Don Imus and Scott Shannon as well as John "Bowser" Bauman, the keyboard player for Sha Na Na. VH-1 presented music by inoffensive, middle-of-the-road artists like Alabama, Chicago, Elton John, Diana Ross, and Barry Manilow. About one-third of the videos played on VH-1 featured black musicians, including Rick James, who was finally represented on an MTVN channel after a long dispute with MTV, which refused to play his videos.[26] Some saw the prominence of black videos as an attempt to draw the audience of Black Entertainment Television (BET), which relied heavily on videos by black artists.

Television reviewers depicted the service as boring video valium. *Newsweek* critic Cathleen McGuigan's skewering attack is typical:

> VH-1's programming is a mishmash of soft rock, oldies, soft country, Sinatra, and soft rhythm and blues. Mostly, this diet of music is so bland that viewers might snooze through it if someone like Imus didn't occasionally jolt them into semiconsciousness by suggesting between videos that John Denver be sent up on the space shuttle—and kept there.[27]

Within the record industry, VH-1 was viewed as the dumping ground for videos not trendy or stylish enough for MTV, and musicians hated having their videos played only on VH-1.[28] *Billboard* magazine's video editor Steve Dupler questions the economic viability of a music service for older viewers, saying, "The idea of getting 45-year-olds to watch music videos is a flawed one."[29]

Advertisers were similarly skeptical of VH-1 in its early years. An article in *Advertising Age* pessimistically headlined "MTV's New Music Network May Prove Tougher Ad Sell," reported advertising executives' apprehensions about the ability of VH-1 to reach its intended mature audience.[30] Despite this concern, VH-1 gradually attracted an increasing number of national advertising accounts with major automobile companies and film studios especially well represented. Advertising revenue for VH-1 increased steadily each year, rising from $2 million in 1985 to $11.5 million in 1988.[31] VH-1 demonstrated its promotional value to record companies and retailers soon after its premiere. *Billboard* reported in February that although VH-1's impact was regional and erratic, the service prompted interest in artists featured on the channel and encouraged music sales.[32] However, record company executives had conflicting views on VH-1's selling power. Whereas some attributed the commercial success of artists like Anita Baker and Julia Fordham to the heavy play of their videos on VH-1, other label executives said radio was responsible for these artists' hit records.[33]

VH-1 expanded its potential audience faster than expected during its first year, more than tripling its initial subscriber base to 11 million by the end of 1985. The channel continued this rapid increase throughout the remainder of the 1980s, reaching an estimated 34.4 million households by 1989, although the average viewing audience declined slightly from 82,000 viewers on an average day in 1988 to about 65,000 viewers in 1989.[34]

MTVN executives overhauled VH-1 in 1987 to increase the channel's popularity with its intended target audience. VH-1 replaced all of its vee-jays, changed its visual presentation to feature stylish computer graphics, and abandoned its sedate soft rock format, dropping all country music and "easy listening" artists like Julio Iglesias. The channel's revamped format appealed to the baby boom generation with 1960s rock, nostalgic video clips, lifestyle information, and comedy programs. Although VH-1's ratings remained stagnant, the format changes strengthened the channel's identification with the "Big Chill" generation, making it attractive to advertisers seeking this age group. VH-1's ratings slide continued into the early 1990s, prompting the channel to change direction once again. The channel inaugurated a new format in September 1990 with the slogan "The Greatest Hits of Music Video," playing almost exclusively current hit videos by top artists like Madonna and Bruce Springsteen along with well-known popular videos from the 1980s. To make room for these hits, VH-1 curtailed its play of new artists and avant-garde videos. "We're not interested in developing the obscure and less-known artist," proclaimed Juli Davidson, VH-1's vice president of programming, "our job is to bring familiar hits and videos from solid emerging artists to the audience."[35] Record labels were dismayed by the change. Clive Davis, president of Arista Records, suggested that VH-1's programming stifled creativity and fresh innovation in music. "VH-1 has abdicated its potential as an alternative by becoming the easy-listening equivalent of a classic rock/oldies station."[36] The format shift led to a chilling effect on the labels' production of videos for aspiring artists in the adult-contemporary genre played on the channel.[37]

VH-1 tried to further establish its identity by launching a campaign about environmental issues, a major concern of its baby-boom viewers. The promotion, including short film clips featuring stars like Sting and Jeff Goldblum offering their views on the environment, had a decidedly activist edge with the channel endorsing the grass-roots organization Greenpeace rather than the more staid Sierra Club. The channel's 1992 *World Alerts* campaign presented short segments on issues like the greenhouse effect and global warming. Although taking a partisan position on a political issue like the environment was a potentially risky venture, Andrew Grossman notes that it certainly was not as divisive as other possible issues like abortion.[38] In its quest to attract viewers and shape its identity, the channel also focused more on personalities in its programming. By July 1993, the channel offered an aerobics show with model Rachel Hunter and programs hosted by Dr. Ruth Westheimer, Peter Noone, and Tom Jones.[39] VH-1 still remains an anemic sister to MTV, ranked the sixteenth most-watched major cable service in terms of subscriber households, whereas MTV held the number eight position at the end of 1991.[40] However, the channel steadily gains new subscribers. It was available in 47 million households in the second quarter of 1993, an increase of 3.7 percent over the same period in the previous year. In early 1995, VH-1 changed its format once again to attract somewhat younger viewers in their late twenties and early thirties, deciding to abandon its older baby-boomer audience, which it had catered to in the past with nostalgic music and programming. The channel will now present more current popular music by acts like Sheryl Crow and the Counting Crows, deemphasizing play of classic videos.

The Box

The Box differs from other music services because it is a pay-per-view offering. Although the service is usually available on basic cable for no extra monthly charge, viewers pay to see certain preferred videos. Viewers program The Box by calling a 900 number to request videos for a charge of $1.75 to $3.00 per music clip. The more people who request a particular video, the more likely it will be played. Viewers choose from a list of 200 to 450 videos clips whose titles are scrolled across the bottom of the screen. Andrew Orgel, the network's president, says that the "viewers pay for the privilege to control their television sets."[41] The Box, based in Miami, was launched nationally by the Video Jukebox Network on March 6, 1989. The channel is partially owned by some prominent media-oriented companies: Newhouse Broadcasting Corporation and Equity Associates together own 27 percent of the network's stock and Tele-communications (TCI), headed by cable magnate John Malone, controls about 10 percent of the company's stock in exchange for a $5 million investment. TCI's involvement provides The Box with easier access to TCI cable systems.

In contrast to MTV, which lately is airing more conventional television shows without music videos, like game shows, talk shows, and forays into animation, The Box presents nothing but music clips twenty-four hours a day. The channel has a rough, bare-bones style, airing video clips without any on-camera video jockeys or much of the overheated promotional flourish associated with MTV. The videos played on The Box on each cable system are determined by the 900 number calls to the channel in that system's particular geographic area. The viewer response created a largely urban and rap music format for the network since these are the types of videos most often requested.[42]

The Box has cultivated a reputation for developing new artists that do not get played on other more well-known channels like MTV. The channel gave heavy airplay to *Ice Ice Baby* by Vanilla Ice and *Knockin' Da Boots* by Candyman when these artists were still largely unknown, nurturing public interest in the acts.[43] The Box also played early videos by Naughty By Nature, Jodeci, EMF, and Gerardo, leading the network to claim that its initial support helped these artists become successful. This music service is more adventurous and daring than some of its competitors, playing videos that are rejected by these other services for violating their standards. Madonna's risqué black and white video, *Justify My Love,* rejected by MTV for its depiction of bisexuality and partial nudity, was prominently featured by The Box, leading to thousands of requests for the video.[44] The channel also agreed to play Garth Brooks's *The Thunder Rolls,* even though it was refused by both Country Music Television and the Nashville Network. Despite the network's success in carving a distinct niche for itself, The Box's Les Garland claims it is kept at a permanent disadvantage because of MTV's arrangement with the major labels, giving MTV exclusive access to popular videos by top stars for up to six months, preventing The Box from airing these clips.

The major record labels are impressed with The Box because of its active role in breaking new acts and hence regularly provide the channel with videos for their signed artists and as of November 1991, also started advertising on it. The channel's viewership is also growing. In March 1991, The Box reached more than 12 million subscribers and was carried on 147 cable systems and low-power television stations in seventy-five geographic areas.[45] By February 1992, the network increased its subscribers to 13 million homes and began to expand internationally that March, airing in 72,000 homes in the United Kingdom.[46] If its presence in England proves lucrative, the channel plans further expansion throughout Europe. The Box suffered some financial problems as its revenues in the third quarter of 1991 fell 2.6 percent from the same period in the prior year.[47] MTV reacted to the growing prominence of The Box by more aggressively featuring interactive programs such as *Dial MTV,* where viewers request videos.

Black Entertainment Television

Of the several cable program services with nonmusic formats, Black Entertainment Television (BET) likely has the greatest commitment to video music. BET's emphasis on music videos featuring black artists provided an important forum for black musicians denied access to MTV in its early years. On August 8, 1979, Robert L. Johnson, the founder and president of BET, announced his intention to create a black cable network. Johnson sought to develop a program service that would become the primary source of entertainment and information for black Americans. He said that his objective was "to show there is another way to make television for an audience that's been denied its culture in a real sense."[48] The service's philosophy was "to provide programming that reflects the black cultural experience in fact or in fiction, and programming that features blacks in leading or dominant character roles."[49]

Prior to his involvement in this venture, Johnson was a lobbyist for the cable industry, serving as vice president of government relations for the National Cable Television Association. While at this job, Johnson established contacts with key executives in the cable industry who provided him with invaluable assistance in launching and expanding this new program service. Johnson says that John Malone, president of TCI, was especially helpful in getting the network started: "About April 1979 I borrowed $15,000 from a local bank, told the boys at NCTVA that I would try a new venture, then I went and talked to John Malone at Tele-Communications Inc. about my concept. He said he would invest in it, he put up half a million dollars, and that's how I got started."[50] USA Network head, Robert Rosencrans, also arranged for Johnson to get access to three hours each week of USA Network's satellite transponder time. With this corporate help, Johnson launched BET on January 25, 1980, in 350 markets, reaching a potential 3.8 million subscribers. BET's original schedule was quite modest with only two hours of programming on Friday nights at 11:00 P.M. EST featuring black collegiate sports and various specials. BET gradually expanded its program schedule, becoming a full fledged twenty-four-hour daily program service on October 1, 1984.[51]

As BET expanded, video music became more prominent, with music clips saturating much of the service's added airtime in shows like *Video Soul* and *Video Vibrations*. After becoming a twenty-four-hour cable service, BET provided up to eighteen hours of daily video music programming, later cutting back to ten hours a day by early 1990. The channel also offered programs featuring specific genres of black music, including the *Bobby Jones Gospel Show, Rap City*, and the *Black Showcase*, presenting jazz. Johnson outlines his reasons for BET's extensive commitment to video music: "First, music is a very important part of black entertainment and culture. Second, black artists wanted a broader outlet for their videos. So, we made a heavy commitment, which was fine, because it's such good programming for us."[52] BET's spotlight on videos by black artists led *Channels of*

Communication to describe the service as a "Black MTV." Johnson takes credit for
the increased opportunities for African-Americans in music video: "We have created a whole black video music industry for producers, artists and directors as a
result of our commitment."[53] In October 1993, BET announced plans to considerably expand its interest in music video by launching The Cable Jazz Channel, a
twenty-four-hour program service featuring "wall-to-wall" jazz.[54]

Yet despite BET's emphasis on music, Johnson describes his service as a general
television network that presents a wide range of shows of interest to black America. Besides music videos, BET also presents standard television offerings with a
black perspective including sports, news, sitcoms, religious shows, talk shows,
films, and cartoons. BET also airs many program-length advertisements like *Can
You Beat Baldness?*, which bring in a substantial portion of BET's revenues.

Johnson claims that BET's growth was impeded by the racist practices of cable
operators in primarily white suburban and rural areas, which were reluctant to
carry BET. He depicts these operators as "telecommunications slumlords" who
benefit economically from black subscribers while refusing to serve these viewers
in their program offerings.[55] Cable operators respond that Johnson used heavy-
handed coercive tactics to force BET onto cable systems. The impasse was averted
in 1984 when HBO purchased a 16⅔ percent interest in BET, a share equal to each
of the service's other partners, TCI and Taft (now Great American). As part of its
agreement with BET, HBO took control of the service's marketing operations.
HBO, with its extensive resources and dominant position within the cable industry, was quite successful in expanding BET's subscriber audience from 7 million
in 1984 to 21 million in 1989.[56] However, BET has often been unable to reach its
intended African-American audience because cable systems in some major cities
with large black communities are older with limited channel capacity and frequently do not carry BET full time.[57]

BET's two primary sources of income are advertising revenue and license fees,
both of which have been increasing steadily, enabling the service to become a
profitable venture as of 1987. BET is an attractive site for advertisers seeking to
reach the black consumer market with specialized products such as Mattel Toys'
black Ken and Barbie dolls and black-hair care products. BET's prominent advertisers include leading corporations like Proctor & Gamble, General Motors,
and *Time* magazine. Yet, BET's major source of advertising revenue is derived
from general interest program-length ads estimated to have been $8 million of
the service's total net ad revenues of $13.3 million for 1989.[58] Johnson also dou-
bled license fees from 2.5 cents to 5 cents per subscriber in 1989, increasing affiliate revenues to $10.2 million that year.

In response to pressure from cable operators, BET announced plans to reduce
its emphasis on program-length ads as well as video music and increase the quantity of traditional television shows oriented to a black audience. BET became
profitable so quickly because of its heavy reliance on these long-form ads and
video music involving minimal expense. BET demonstrated its commitment to

providing more traditional television programs in 1989 with the opening of its new high-tech $10 million production studio in Washington, D.C., built to produce shows in-house for the network. In September 1989, BET launched eight new series, including two talk shows, *Our Voices* and *Teen Summit*. BET also signed a contract with Tim Reid of *Frank's Place* and *WKRP in Cincinnati* to produce dramas for the network. Johnson hopes to benefit from the increased profile and success of African-Americans in Hollywood and lure this talent to BET to produce dramas, comedies, and music shows for the channel.

BET's audience has grown briskly, with a 15 percent increase in viewers during the first three months of 1991 over the same period for the previous year, while ratings for MTV and VH-1 declined 9 percent and 13 percent, respectively.[59] Yet despite these encouraging signs, Johnson believes that MTV's ultimate objective is to steal BET's audience for music videos by introducing new programming and engaging in anticompetitive practices. MTV premiered a new show, *Fade to Black,* in October 1991, featuring up-tempo urban music by black artists such as Bell Biv DeVoe, Guy, and Whitney Houston, and already was airing *Yo! MTV Raps.* Some record labels suggested that MTV's underlying strategy in presenting these shows was to develop a strong black audience that would be in place when MTV launched two new planned music channels at the end of 1994, one of which was expected to feature urban black music, directly competing with BET.[60] MTV has since delayed these plans. BET's friction with MTV is compounded by MTV's exclusive contracts with major record labels. BET is increasingly angered by MTV's exclusive access to videos by popular black artists, denying BET the right to air these clips for a lengthy period. Johnson finds this practice intolerable since BET has always supported aspiring black artists, whereas MTV only features black artists once they are popular, and in its early years largely banned videos by black performers altogether. This conflict reached a peak in the summer of 1991 when BET held a twelve-day boycott of videos by artists signed to MCA Records when MTV was granted exclusive rights to a video by MCA's rap group Heavy D. & the Boyz.[61]

The Nashville Network and Country Music Television

Whereas BET provided a forum for black artists largely excluded from television in the early 1980s, The Nashville Network (TNN) fulfilled a similar function for country and western musicians. TNN, a twenty-four-hour cable service, offers a range of shows featuring country music and entertainment, including concerts, talk shows, variety specials, and sitcoms. TNN's early efforts to increase its emphasis on video music were frustrated by the initial lack of clips. C. Paul Corbin, TNN's director of programming, recalls: "In country, we [had] a very light supply of music videos when we started. The whole marketplace was about 50 videos at that point and they used to be mainly the music and having the camera shoot birds, trees and streams."[62] As production of country videos grew, TNN devoted more of its programming to videos, adding two new shows, *Country Clips* and

Video Country in January 1985, and further increasing its play of music video to thirty hours a week by 1991.[63] TNN's audience expanded along with its embrace of music clips, having the fourth highest audience ratings for basic cable channels in December 1991.[64] Country Music Television (CMT), another network playing music clips twenty-four hours a day, emerged as the primary alternative to TNN for country music on cable. The service reached 15 million households by November 1991, primarily in the South, targeting somewhat younger viewers than TNN targeted.[65] Unlike other programs focused solely on hits, CMT provides ample exposure to aspiring artists whose videos receive heavy play. CMT expanded abroad, launching Country Music Television Europe, which was available in 5.8 million homes throughout the United Kingdom and continental Europe by August 1993.[66]

When TNN enhanced the profile of music video in the mid-1980s, most record company executives were initially skeptical about the service's promotional value, claiming that country videos did not increase retail sales of records as did videos by pop and rock artists. However, the increased visibility of country music on cable by the early 1990s made the labels more optimistic about the promotional value of video shows, encouraging a dramatic increase in video production for country artists. Record companies rely on video to promote artists like Lyle Lovett and k. d. lang, who have been ignored by more conservative country radio stations.[67] Lang's breakthrough in 1987 came when TNN began playing her video *Hanky Panky,* produced by her independent label.

WTBS's *Night Tracks*

Although Ted Turner's Cable Music Channel was a spectacular failure, his company's more modest venture into video music became an established feature for several years on his "superstation" WTBS, an Atlanta broadcast station carried on most U.S. cable systems, showing old movies, network reruns, and sports. Lynch/Biller Productions convinced Turner executives that a video music program on weekend nights would broaden their audience and draw teenage viewers, attracting new advertisers seeking to reach this age group. On June 3, 1983, WTBS launched *Night Tracks,* its video music show with computer graphics and off-screen announcers, airing Friday and Saturday nights for several hours. The show's producers, Tom Lynch and Gary Biller, rejected MTV's narrowcast format, presenting a broad range of pop music, which included black and country artists excluded from MTV. *Night Tracks* eschewed the dark, moody quality of much video music in order to create a show that a promotional advertisement described as "bright, upbeat and fun."[68] The "fun" did not include videos with excessive depictions of sex or violence, consistent with Turner's publicly stated moral sensibilities.

Night Tracks received consistently respectable ratings throughout its history with an audience share often rivaling MTV's. Yet some attributed *Night Tracks*' substantial audience to the pervasive reach of WTBS, available in 44 million homes, which constitutes 93 percent of households with cable and 50 percent with a television set.[69] WTBS added the companion hit-oriented countdown shows *Power Play* (later named *Power Play Dancin'*) and *Chartbusters* in May 1984 and by November 1988, *Night Tracks* expanded to fourteen hours of weekly programming. The late 1980s turned out to be the zenith for *Night Tracks*, which later faltered due to waning viewer interest. WTBS gradually cut back on its music video programming, reducing *Night Tracks* to six hours a week and replacing the clip shows with movies. Despite a last-ditch effort to save the show by changing the format in July 1991 from Top 40 to alternative modern music, *Night Tracks* was canceled the following June to make way for more movies.[70]

Video Music Shows on Commercial Broadcast Television

Traditional broadcasters also began using video clips in their programming as video music became more popular. The networks experimented with video music in various ways, but the only established long-running show featuring videos on network television was NBC's *Friday Night Videos*. NBC needed a fast replacement for its failing comedy show *SCTV* that would reach a young audience on late Friday evenings. In June 1983, NBC quickly assigned David Benjamin as the show's producer and just one month later, *Friday Night Videos* premiered as a ninety-minute video clip show following Johnny Carson. The show featured well-known television personalities as guest hosts and mainstream pop designed to appeal to NBC's mammoth audience. After a long run, the program was finally canceled in October 1993 due to poor ratings.

Video music's impact on local broadcast stations in the mid-1980s was much greater. By September 1984, six UHF and low-power television stations adopted a video music format, playing videos twenty-four hours a day, and up to thirty stations were expected to begin full-time video music programming by the end of that year.[71] Broadcasters launching new UHF and low-power stations saw a music format as a popular alternative to the usual fare of independent stations dominated by network reruns, syndicated shows, and old movies. A music format was also financially attractive because start-up and operating expenses were minimal. A station presenting only video clips needed far less staff and production facilities than a station with conventional shows. Programming expenses were limited because videos were provided free at the time. KMSF-TV, a UHF station in Sanger, California, was launched with a music format at a cost of only $1.5 million, and WLXI-TV, another UHF video music station in Greensboro, North Carolina, premiered March 5, 1984, and showed a profit by early September.

These new video music stations attempted to distinguish their programming from MTV by cultivating a local character, presenting videos for the local community rather than a national audience. Gary Smithwick, president of UHF station WLXI in Greensboro, said that "we see ourselves completely different from MTV. Anything you offer nationally has to be very finely tuned to a narrow part of the audience. We want to have personalities [that all] local people can relate to. Local news. Local weather."[72] Rick Scott, general manager of UHF music station KRLR-TV, also emphasized this local perspective: "Our 'vee-jays' are live and that enables us to talk specifically about Las Vegas."[73] These local music stations often promoted video clips of local bands and emphasized play of local favorites.

Due to music video's growing popularity, broadcasters formed their own trade association at the National Association of Broadcasters convention in early 1984. A primary objective of this new group, the Association of Music Video Broadcasters, was to attract new advertisers for their stations. As more stations adopted a music format in the mid-1980s, these broadcasters expressed a heady optimism about the future of local music video television. John Garabedian, who planned to begin his own video music station in Massachusetts, forecasted that "there will be at least one video music television station in every market in the country within the next three to five years."[74] Such predictions proved much too optimistic as MTV's monopolistic policies, record company demands for fee payments, and shifting public tastes contributed to a swift decline of the local twenty-four-hour music format in the late 1980s.

4

Monopoly TV: A History of MTV's Anticompetitive Practices

MTV's premiere in 1981 sparked public fascination with music video and was considered partially responsible for a resurgence of the record business in the mid-1980s, which had undergone a prolonged recession. As discussed in Chapter 3, the popularity of music video led other companies to launch full-fledged cable music channels like the Cable Music Channel (CMC), Hit Video USA, and The Box. Other cable channels heavily featured certain genres of music like Black Entertainment Television's (BET) focus on black artists and The Nashville Network's (TNN) emphasis on country music. Music on cable became increasingly pervasive.

MTV responded to this burgeoning diversity of music programming by adopting anticompetitive policies to undermine these new services and regain monopoly control over the market for music video programming. MTV's systematic long-term plans to exert dominance over this field are examined in this chapter. MTV's primary means to achieve this control were through contractual agreements with the producers of music clips, the major record companies, and with the cable companies that presented the program service on their systems. This survey of MTV's policies illustrates the tendency of media companies to seek forms of vertical integration between production, distribution, and exhibition of media programs to maintain control over a particular media market and undermine possible competition, suppressing the diversity of available program content.

MTV Exclusivity Agreements with Record Companies

As several potential competitors to MTV emerged, MTV executives worried about protecting the channel's dominance in the market for video music programming. In a confidential memo written in 1983, MTV executive Bob Pittman proposed a corporate strategy designed to undermine competing video music services and consolidate MTV's monopolistic control. In his memo, Pittman depicts MTV as a product distributor serving as the intermediary between a producer, the record companies, and a retailer, the cable systems. He explains, "the traditional solution for the distributor to protect his business is to lock up the shelf space and/or lock up the supply of the product."[1] Pittman planned to do both by encouraging cable operators to carry only MTV's music service and negotiating contracts with record companies giving MTV exclusive rights to the most popular music videos, denying these to MTV's competitors.

MTV sought these exclusive rights during negotiations with record companies in 1984 concerning proposed license fees for videos. Ever since MTV's premiere in 1981, record companies made clear that they expected MTV and other program services to pay fees eventually for the right to their videos. The labels reluctantly waived these fees during MTV's early years because at the time, MTV was a struggling neophyte incurring heavy losses without the resources to pay hefty license fees. The record companies granted MTV free access to their videos during this period, claiming they wanted MTV to succeed because of its proven promotional power, but vowed that when MTV became a profitable enterprise, they expected to be compensated.

When MTV first reported profits in 1984, the record companies were anxious for MTV to start paying license fees and began negotiations with the channel toward this end. MTV executives conceded it was inevitable the service would have to pay for videos, but insisted on exclusivity provisions as a condition of these payment agreements. In April 1984, Bob Pittman said that without these guarantees of exclusive access to videos, "we're not prepared to pay for them."[2] He explained that MTV was not trying to institute a monopoly in video music exhibition, but rather sought to "make sure at MTV that we have a few points of differentiation" from other services.[3]

MTV's first proposed agreement with a major record label was with Capitol/EMI. On December 1, 1983, the channel offered to pay Capitol $1,250,000 over three years and give it free advertising spots.[4] MTV would get exclusive use of 35 percent of Capitol's video clips for thirty days, with two-thirds of these videos selected by MTV and the other third by Capitol. The exclusivity provisions were broadly defined to cover "all forms of television programming."[5] Capitol ultimately rejected the proposal, but the terms of the deal became the prototype for future agreements with other record companies.

In June 1984, MTV announced that it had reached agreements with four major record companies: CBS, RCA, MCA, and Geffen.[6] An additional agreement with Warner record labels Elektra and Asylum reported in August 1984 gave the music network exclusivity rights with companies responsible for 40 percent of all videos produced in the United States.[7] Polygram signed a similar agreement in September 1984, as did the remaining Warner labels, including Atlantic, the following September.[8] It is quite likely that independent label Chrysalis also had a pact with MTV because videos featuring some Chrysalis artists in 1984 were presented as

MTV exclusives.[9] Capitol Records, which originally rejected MTV's proposal, finally signed an agreement by 1986.

Terms of Exclusivity Contracts

Official information about the MTV agreements is limited because MTV and the record companies were unwilling to discuss the pacts' terms, most likely due to confidentiality clauses.[10] MTV provided some very general discussion of the agreements in official corporate documents. In a 1984 stock prospectus, MTV estimated it would pay $4,575,000 for the year for exclusive access to some clips from the original four companies signed to exclusivity agreements.[11] Ken Terry noted in *Variety* that MTV's later agreements with Polygram, Capitol, and the Warner labels would likely double this amount.[12] In MTVN's Form 10-K to the Securities and Exchange Commission (SEC) for 1984, MTV provides the following discussion of the pacts:

> The Company has concluded agreements with five record companies for terms not exceeding three years which, in exchange for cash and in some cases advertising time, will assure the continued availability of such companies' music videos, assure MTV that the videos are not available for any other television exhibition earlier than their availability to MTV and provide some videos for exclusive periods on MTV.[13]

The following year, the Form 10-K to the SEC for Viacom International, the company that acquired MTV Networks in 1985, repeated the extracted description verbatim, except that now MTV had agreements with eight record companies.[14] Viacom's Form 10-K for successive years entirely omitted the number of agreements.[15] The company's 1991 Form 10-K did reveal that certain contract provisions did extend to MTV's sister services VH-1, MTV Europe, and Nickelodeon, which would "assure the availability of such companies' music videos for exhibition on MTV and, in some cases, on MTVN's other basic cable networks."[16] However, the exclusivity stipulations appear to apply only to MTV.

Trade journals *Billboard* and *Variety* reported more specific information about these agreements' terms by relying on industry sources, often unnamed. According to *Billboard*, CBS, which produced about 200 video clips a year, received $8 million from MTV over a two-year period, an amount expected to fully cover CBS's expenses for video clip production.[17] RCA and MCA each received about $2 million for the full three-year span of their contracts with MTV.

The CBS Records agreement was typical of the other labels' contracts.[18] Under the CBS deal, MTV could choose 20 percent of the company's annual video clip production for its exclusive use. CBS had the right to place another 10 percent of its own videos on MTV's playlist in either light or medium rotation, although Lawrence Fox, a broadcast industry attorney, claimed that MTV was obligated to play videos chosen by labels only twenty times a week.[19] These percentages were standard provisions of the five initial record company contracts. The mutually beneficial arrangement allowed MTV to pick video clips featuring hit singles and major recording stars for its exclusive use that would likely increase its ratings, and record companies could get guaranteed exposure for their new artists that might not otherwise receive airplay.

The length of time MTV had exclusive use of its chosen clips ranged from one week to one year. In most cases MTV's exclusive use of the clip was for thirty days, but some videos' period of exclusivity was shorter.[20] However, Fox and Mark Potts of the *Washington Post* state that MTV had exclusive use of clips for at least thirty days, and in some cases, from six months to one year.[21] The videos could be shown on most music video shows like NBC's *Friday Night Videos,* after 30 days.[22] These videos could not be aired on competing music video networks for six months to a year after premiere on MTV. Fox explains that the longer exclusivity periods applied to services that programmed over twelve hours of music videos each day, which would apply to many of MTV's potential competitors, including Discovery, CMC, and Hit Video USA.[23] This provision raised charges that MTV's objective in these agreements was not simply to reserve popular videos for itself, but to undermine any direct competition.

Recording Artists and Exclusivity Contracts

The record companies' ability to grant MTV exclusive access to videos was limited in some instances by the labels' contracts with their artists. The labels could not control video clips by artists whose contracts granted them ownership rights to their video clips, such as Madonna and Hammer. Miles Copeland, manager for the Police, said that their record company could not grant exclusive rights to videos featuring the Police without the group's approval.[24] However, *Billboard* notes that artists who owned their own clips were under "considerable pressure" from their labels to grant MTV exclusivity.[25] More successful recording artists often retained rights to their videos because of their substantial economic clout, whereas the labels usually controlled the rights for videos by new and aspiring artists who signed contracts favoring record company interests because of their weak bargaining position. Videos by less established artists were often granted to MTV on an exclusive basis, even if the artist opposed this arrangement. Martha Davis of the Motels objected to MTV exclusives of her group's videos, explaining "Many groups do not receive MTV. Personally, I would like those locations to get a chance to watch my new single."[26]

Established recording stars were often reluctant to grant MTV exclusive access to their videos on terms proposed by their labels and MTV. Despite Warner Brothers' pact with MTV, Warner recording star Prince demanded that his videos for "Kiss" and other singles be released to black music video program services like BET and *Hit City* at about the same time they premiered on MTV.[27] Michael Jackson's manager arranged to have videos from the singer's album *Dangerous,* including the initial eleven-minute clip for the single "Black or White," to be premiered simultaneously on the Fox Network, BET, and MTV on November 14,

1991.[28] Major stars like Bruce Springsteen, The Rolling Stones, and Madonna insisted that the period of MTV exclusivity for their videos be limited to thirty days, rejecting more elaborate pact provisions for exclusive periods of six months to one year.[29] Janet Jackson's deal with A&M Records and MTV provided MTV with an exclusive of her videos for usually only a weekend or a week at most. Her brother Michael typically gives MTV exclusive use of his videos for only one day before they can be shown elsewhere. Bob Pittman claimed that artists' ownership of their own videos and reluctance to allow extended exclusivity did not dilute the effectiveness of the label contracts: "If an artist owns their own video, if we cut a deal with them separately, we don't have to count it as one of the videos we have an exclusive under record company deals."[30]

Another aspect of the exclusivity pacts affecting the recording artists concerned revenues MTV was to pay to the labels for access to the videos. Musicians expressed dismay that these contracts included no provisions to pay artists a portion of the revenue the labels would receive. The labels were the sole financial beneficiary of the pacts because the companies generally owned the rights to the videos, even though many artists were still required to repay a substantial portion of the production expenses of the video clip from the artists' royalties derived from sales of their records associated with the clip.[31] Antony Payne of GASP! Productions, a video clip production firm, said these unfavorable pact terms would encourage artists to arrange their own independent financing for their videos to maintain ownership rights.[32] However, Pittman countered that few recording artists retained ownership: "As people's contracts came up, I find most record companies buying up rights to their videos."[33]

Contracts Create Vertical Integration Between MTV and Record Labels

MTV and the record labels publicly acknowledged that a primary objective of these accords was to gain a measure of joint control over the emerging distribution system for clips. These agreements created a degree of vertical integration by forging links between the production of clips (commissioned by labels) and an important stage in the distribution of clips through exposure media (MTV). This integration was established by contractual agreement rather than common ownership, although when MTV was partially owned by Warner Communications through Warner Amex, vertical integration through ownership existed between MTV and Warner Brothers. In his 1984 letter to stockholders, WCI chairman Steven Ross said that Warner exploited this integration to promote Warner Brothers recording artists such as Prince by providing these artists with prominent airplay on MTV.[34]

This vertical integration led the labels and MTV to jointly decide the primary means of distribution for about 30 percent of the video clip production by the record companies. This 30 percent portion was especially important because it included the clips featuring recording artists considered to be most popular (MTV's 20 percent) and most promising (the labels' 10 percent). The contracts allowed the labels and MTV to provide exposure for any label's video clip that they wanted without any say from the public. These companies wanted to establish an integrated system that clearly avoided the laissez-faire distribution system that had developed earlier in the music business, where commercial radio and record labels were relatively independent from each other. Bob Pittman said that MTV wanted to make sure music video did not repeat the patterns of distribution of that market, which had no clear mechanism to provide guaranteed airplay of the labels' product.[35] The labels depended upon radio for exposure, but radio would not always play their new artists' material unless it suited their own separate interests, which hinged upon presenting music that would increase audience ratings.

Pittman said that MTV was "trying to find a new [distribution] model beneficial to us both. . . . Record companies have had no access to radio—they couldn't count on access."[36] These contracts were a way record companies could get exposure for their artists while also ensuring the stability and strength of MTV. The contract provisions requiring MTV to play certain videos selected by the labels led Peter Hall of the *Village Voice* to question whether MTV would become "Monopoly TV, a powerful promotional tool that is contractually obligated to roll whatever product the [labels'] A&R departments favor, regardless of whether the audience agrees."[37]

These agreements created a formal structure for a type of "payola" arrangement where media outlets agreed to play certain artists requested by the record companies in exchange for certain favors, much like illegal payola in radio. Underground payola was common in the 1950s when labels would covertly pay radio station disc jockeys a sum of money or goods and services to play records of new artists that the label wanted to promote. Such covert transactions were condemned and ultimately prohibited by Congress in its adoption of Section 508 of the 1934 Communications Act.[38]

The cooperation between MTV and the major record labels encouraged a top-down popular culture where companies controlling the production, distribution, and exhibition of music clips collaborated to shape and direct popular tastes in music in a manner that promoted their own respective economic interests. Through their collusion, MTV played videos that promoted major label artists and cultivated audience interest in the styles and genres of music primarily distributed by these record companies. In this sweetheart deal, considering the preferences and wishes of the public became less important than the project of shaping demand for cultural products in ways intended by the major labels and their parent conglomerates.

Media companies responded that their own policies were dictated by consumer decisions in the free marketplace: MTV gave the public what it wanted on the basis of ratings, and record companies developed plans on the basis of recorded music sales. Yet this was true only to a certain extent. Exposure media like radio, and now

MTV, play a major role in limiting the range of music choices that people hear on a regular basis and thus channel the public's music preferences in certain directions. The practice of payola was condemned and prohibited in commercial radio in large part because of this cultural gatekeeping role performed by radio. It was believed that radio should be independent of record companies so that radio stations would make unconstrained, autonomous decisions about what type of music they felt people wanted to hear, rather than presenting music that the labels wanted people to hear. The ban on payola was intended to make radio stations' first allegiance to the public, not to record companies' promotion departments.

Yet in these exclusivity agreements, MTV and the record labels restored payola-type agreements, where the primary goal of the program service was to push the record labels' product rather than truly understanding and responding to the desires and wishes of its audience. Moreover, this collusion squeezed out alternative styles of music and recording artists, since most of these pacts were with major record labels that focus more on conventional, mainstream music. Smaller, independent record labels that cultivated and nurtured new, off-beat music styles and acts were largely ignored.

Although payola schemes in radio were outlawed following highly publicized scandals in the 1950s, critics allege that the major and independent record labels remain involved in illegal payola to get commercial radio stations to play their artists. Fredric Dannen's *Hit Men: Power Brokers and Fast Money Inside the Music Business* provides a scathing indictment of this industry, claiming that the major record companies rely on a group of unscrupulous and criminal independent promoters. Dannen claims a loose confederation of large promoters called "The Network" colluded to divide the nation into geographic areas with each organization granted an exclusive franchise for a certain area.[39] The major labels paid these promoters more than $10 million a year to get exposure for their artists on radio. To achieve this goal these illicit promoters allegedly bribed radio station program directors and executives with cash, prostitutes, cocaine, and other drugs to play specific new releases by record label artists. The Justice Department conducted an investigation of illegal practices by these companies, which lasted several years, culminating in a 1990 trial in Los Angeles and indicting two top promoters in the record business, Joseph Isgro and Ray Anderson. Although the major record labels proclaimed their innocence and ignorance of illegal activity by promoters, Dannen claims that they benefited by getting invaluable exposure for their artists and shutting out smaller independent record companies unable to afford the large fees of these promoters, consolidating the majors' hold over the industry.

With the increasing popularity of music video in the 1980s, the record labels wanted to develop a legitimate and legal form of "payola" with MTV to give the labels guaranteed access for their videos. The labels and MTV came to adopt a practice where MTV played specific clips requested by the labels in exchange for the benefits of exclusive play of other clips that would hopefully boost the video

network's ratings and increase advertising revenues (not to mention preclude direct competition). The labels and MTV could formally adopt such payola-like
agreements because the Communication Act's Section 508 only applied to broadcast outlets and not to cable, a prime example of uneven regulatory policies. This
was clearly demonstrated when Richard Benjamin, producer of NBC's *Friday
Night Videos,* stated that his show could not sign MTV-like exclusivity agreements
because the FCC would consider such deals payola and NBC affiliates would be
in danger of losing their licenses.[40] The cable industry's relatively unregulated status allowed the music network to make these more structured arrangements with
the record companies.

   The exclusivity pacts between MTV and the record labels were consistent with
the historical attempts of companies engaged in cultural production to achieve a
substantial degree of vertical integration to ensure their products' guaranteed access to major exhibition outlets. In the 1920s and 1930s, major film studios
bought theaters for guaranteed exhibition of their films. Although Hollywood
film production companies were forced to divest their theater holdings in the
Paramount decree in 1948, these companies have restored large-scale vertical integration in recent years by acquisition of theater chains. Television producers
similarly enter into long-term contracts with commercial networks in order to
ensure exhibition of their shows. Record company integration with programming
services is simply an extension of this established corporate practice. The record
companies were prone to adopt strategies similar to those in related media sectors, given that the labels' parent companies were entertainment conglomerates
with holdings in these other culture industries with long traditions of vertical integration, such as MCA with its interests in recorded music, film, and television.
MTV attempted to defend its contracts with record labels by referring to this
long-established practice in a statement that asserted "exclusivity [is] a common
and accepted feature of entertainment-industry contracts."[41]

   In fact, MTV's parent company, Viacom, practices this form of vertical integration both through contract and common ownership throughout its various
subsidiaries. Viacom's recent purchase of Paramount Communications creates
special opportunities for access to the studio's films on its pay-per-view and pay
cable channels, Showtime and The Movie Channel. In May 1995, Showtime Networks acquired exclusive television exhibition rights to Paramount Pictures feature films. Further, these program services aggressively sought contracts with
other studios for exclusive rights to show their films in the pay cable market. In
1989, Showtime Networks signed an agreement with Walt Disney Pictures for exclusive pay cable rights to its films, adding to previous similar agreements with
Tri-Star Pictures, Orion Pictures, New Line Distribution, and Polygram Investments.[42] Viacom's broad strategy then was not only to have a guaranteed stream
of programming, but to have exclusive access to those programs produced both
in-house by Viacom subsidiaries as well as by outside companies: Where Show-

time Networks does this for theatrical films, MTV Networks does it for music videos.

Reaction of Record Labels and Television Shows to Contracts

MTV pacts with record labels as well as the video clip access fees discussed in Chapter 2 emerged from a controversy within the record industry about how the labels should most effectively use video clips to increase revenues and profits.[43] The MTV-label exclusivity deals divided record company executives over whether the video clip was purely a promotional device whose expense was recovered through the additional music sales it stimulated, or a commodity capable of generating revenue in its own right.[44] This industry conflict split record company executives in the business departments from those in the production and promotion departments. Business executives warmly embraced the MTV pacts and the idea of selling exclusive rights to the clips because the revenues would cover their video production costs. Further, exclusive showing on MTV would provide the needed exposure to market the videos clips themselves as a retail commodity. Promotion and marketing executives strongly disagreed, arguing that exclusives undermined the promotional value of clips because they were seen in fewer places by fewer people, making them less able to promote sales of an artist's music.

MTV's competitors criticized the pacts as an attempt by the channel to strengthen its monopoly over video music exposure media. David Benjamin, producer of NBC's *Friday Night Videos*, claimed that "MTV wants to end competition. . . . [It] wants to own rock and roll." "MTV is cutting us and all other music programs off from the superstars," said Dain Eric, program director for the ill-fated Discovery Music Network, "and that makes it very hard to compete."[45] Mike Green, vice president and general manager of the Video Music Channel, a full-fledged regional program service, added that the pact "smacks of restraint of trade" and appeared to be an attack on all long-form program services competing with MTV. Green was concerned that the pacts would exclude his channel from all of the most current and popular videos needed to build an audience.

Moreover, he argued that gaining access to certain video clips after the period of exclusivity lapsed would be of limited value because about two months after the clip is released, the accompanying album has fallen from the charts and both the record and its related video lose much of their popularity. Video clips of old songs have little power to attract the steady audience necessary for a program service to attract sufficient advertising. These competitors also claimed that the pacts harmed the recording artists and ultimately the record companies because granting exclusives on MTV limited the clips' promotional value. The exclusivity agreements, these shows argued, would severely limit exposure of videos featuring artists' recent releases and possibly undermine album sales.

Video music program services had several reactions to the exclusivity pacts. These shows were forced to alter their programming to compensate for the loss of the exclusive videos. Some shows planned to increase videos featuring new artists.[46] Since videos of most current top hits would become MTV exclusives, WTBS's *Night Tracks* decided to play videos of songs ranked lower on the record charts that were still available to all services.

BET offered a much more aggressive response. In August 1986, it announced plans to ban all videos by certain record labels in retaliation for exclusives granted to MTV for videos by popular black artists.[47] BET's action was prompted by MTV exclusivity on current video clips by Profile's Run-D.M.C. and A&M's Janet Jackson. BET protested the thirty-day exclusive period on these clips by immediately dropping all videos by Profile artists and threatening to do the same for A&M artists. Jeff Newman and Jamie Brown, coproducers of BET's music show, *Video Soul,* were offended by exclusives for artists that BET had supported before these artists achieved success. Brown voiced resentment, commenting that "it seems artists get to a certain level with the aid of the exposure of our show and then get pulled away from us."[48]

The severe decline in video clip shows in the late 1980s appeared to vindicate critics' predictions that the exclusivity contracts would contribute toward strengthened MTV dominance of the market for video music programming by undermining potential competitors. However, the actual impact of the pacts on competitors remains unclear because there were a variety of factors that hindered the growth of video music programs. Yet, it seems clear that the pacts' most devastating impact was upon full-fledged video music program services that planned to directly compete with MTV. Turner's Cable Music Channel lasted only about a month and eventually was absorbed within MTVN, and the Discovery Music Network was stalled indefinitely. Although Hit Video USA lasted longer, it was a marginal service, at best able to reach only a minor fraction of the audience for MTVN services, and ultimately failed as well.

The threat posed by the exclusivity pacts apparently thwarted potential competitors by increasing the difficulty of acquiring capital for such a project. Mike Green, for example, sought to expand his successful regional Atlanta-based service, the Video Music Channel, into a fully national video music channel to be distributed by United Satellite Corporation (USC). Unfortunately, since the exclusivity pacts had gone into effect, five potential investors declined to provide him with funding to undertake this expansion. Green claimed that the major reason he could not get financial backing was the potential investors' awareness that these pacts would exclude popular video clips from the Video Music Channel and decrease its chances of attracting an adequate audience. "It takes us out of a real competitive position nationally," said Green.[49] Seth Willenson, vice president of programming for USC, agreed, adding that unavailability of hit videos by major artists would make it difficult for USC to help any party establish a competing video clip service.

Antitrust Action Against MTVN

The exclusivity contracts as well as other alleged monopolistic practices by MTV were subject to numerous legal challenges and investigations that examined whether MTV had violated applicable antitrust laws. The first such challenge to the MTV pacts was mounted by Discovery Music Network, which filed a suit in Los Angeles federal court September 19, 1984.[50] DMN's representatives argued that MTV had arranged these deals to stop direct competition from Discovery or any other long-form video music program service, protecting its monopoly. Discovery accused MTV of "pernicious, predatory and anti-competitive" activities that restrained trade by trying to prevent DMN and other video program services from access to current video clips released by major record companies.[51] The Discovery suit charged that "music video clips involving major recording superstars from the music industry will not be available to plaintiff and other competitors" during the six-month period MTV got exclusive rights to the clips.[52]

Discovery claimed it would be unable to run a program service without these current music videos because these clips featuring top hits by popular artists generated most of the public interest in video music. Discovery representatives maintained that access to the clips after the six-month period was little consolation because it could not attract an audience with out-of-date videos. Dain Eric, program director for Discovery, said "seeing how the average life expectancy of a hit record—and therefore a hit video—is two to four months, those videos don't do us any good after a year."[53]

Discovery charged that MTV took advantage of its established position in the video music programming field and its influence with record labels to undermine any potential competitor. Eric said DMN filed suit because "we felt that MTV was trying to lock out any full-time competition. . . . MTV saw full-time competition coming, and they wanted to prevent that."[54] He observed that both DMN and Turner's Cable Music Channel were planning to commence operation when MTV began soliciting exclusivity deals with major labels. The suit claimed that MTV used its influential programming service as an offensive weapon to prevent any services from competing with it. According to the suit, MTV and its owner at the time, Warner Amex,

> have used and abused their monopoly power obtained or gained in one market (the music video programming market) to obtain an unlawful competitive advantage in another market (the distribution of music videos produced by the major record companies) for the purpose of eliminating competition in that other market.[55]

The Discovery suit portrayed the record companies as unwilling victims of the pacts, claiming that MTV "coerced and intimidated" the labels into accepting the exclusivity agreements, which would ultimately cause the labels and their artists economic harm by limiting the potential audience for videos and thus curtailing their promotional value. MTV blandly responded that the Discovery suit was "totally without merit," while Bob Pittman attempted to defend the pact, claiming, "Exclusivity is absolutely a part of the television industry."[56]

MTV and Discovery agreed to an out-of-court settlement in January 1988 in which MTV paid what it described as a "nominal fee" to Discovery.[57] A spokesperson for Discovery's attorney, Joel Bennett, claimed that the payment "basically covered all Discovery's legal fees."[58] Although the settlement terms were not revealed, Bennett's spokesperson said that the accord was "highly unlikely" to affect the contracts.[59] Although Discovery was unable to end the MTV pacts, the channel's founding executives were probably anxious to end litigation since Discovery was a moribund project.

Wodlinger Broadcasting, owner of another full-fledged competitor, Hit Video USA, and local Houston outlet TV5, filed a second antitrust suit against MTV and its parent company, Warner Amex, in the U.S. District Court of Texas on October 10, 1985, seeking $205 million in damages for economic harm caused by MTV's monopolistic practices.[60] The Wodlinger action reiterated the central charge of the Discovery suit, claiming that MTV's exclusivity contracts with record labels constituted unlawful restraint of trade prohibited by the Sherman and Clayton Acts as well as Texas antitrust laws. The suit charged that the pacts "deny competitors access to vital, unique, and otherwise unavailable materials, namely the choicest music video clips of most major record companies."[61] Constance Wodlinger claimed that MTV was increasing its exploitation of the exclusivity pacts in a deliberate attempt to undermine competition:

> When we went on the air on July 12th, there were six to eight exclusives that we couldn't play. Currently, there are twenty, which indicates that MTV has elected to escalate their use of the exclusivity agreement in an attempt to cripple the programming of the local video stations. Half the current hits we can't play and won't be able to for six months.[62]

The Wodlinger action made additional allegations about MTV's attempts to deny its competitors access to cable systems.[63] The suit charged that MTV negotiated contracts with cable operators that discouraged access to competitors by including "tie-in" provisions that stated that if cable companies wished to add a second music video service, the new service must be MTV's VH-1. The Wodlinger action also accused MTV's parent company at the time, Warner Amex, of refusing to offer TV5 or Hit Video USA on its cable systems in the Houston area and coercing other systems in that area to reject the services. Finally, the suit claimed that MTV tried to prevent the Wodlinger services from "access to advertising coverage on many of the channels carried" by these cable systems.[64]

MTV provided little official response to the Wodlinger action beyond a brief comment by an MTV spokesperson characterizing the suit as "absolutely without merit."[65] Viacom International, the successor corporate parent of MTV, presented a terse review of the Wodlinger suit in its 1987 Form 10-K to the SEC with no rebuttal to the charges except the statement that "the Company intends to defend the action vigorously."[66] Despite Hit Video USA's desire to abolish these exclusive deals, the Wodlingers settled with MTV out of court in February 1989.[67] Constance Wodlinger claimed that the lawsuit drained the finances of the company, contributing to a severe cutback in the channel's operations and programming in early 1988, which was later to be shut down completely. Wodlinger met with Viacom's Sumner Redstone in a private meeting in the fall of 1988 where they settled their dispute in an agreement that neither will discuss, although the exclusivity pacts were not likely addressed in this deal since they remain unchanged.[68]

The Wodlingers' allegations also prompted investigations by the Federal Trade Commission (FTC) and the Federal Communications Commission (FCC). Mark Wodlinger met with several members of Congress to discuss the exclusivity pacts as well as MTV's attempts to prevent Hit Video USA from getting on cable systems. Consequently, in March 1987, five U.S. senators and a Houston congressman requested that the FTC investigate whether MTV used illegal means to obstruct the Wodlingers' service.[69] In the FTC complaint, the Wodlingers charged that MTV not only denied their program service with access to videos but also conspired with cable companies to prevent Hit Video USA from gaining access to cable systems. The FTC investigation, which began April 1987, is described in Viacom's 1987 Form 10-K to the SEC as an "informal inquiry to determine whether the Company's practices in the solicitation of cable television system operators to carry MTVN's services constitute anti-competitive acts or practices."[70] Wodlinger sought an FTC investigation in addition to the initial suit because of his belief that the commission inquiry would be relatively swift compared to a civil suit, which could take years to resolve. Wodlinger also filed a complaint about MTV's exclusive agreements with the FCC, but that commission's investigation was terminated in May 1987 "for lack of a basis to proceed further."[71]

The Antitrust Division of the U.S. Department of Justice also launched a civil investigation of MTV's exclusivity pacts in August 1984, to determine if MTV and the record labels had violated federal antitrust laws.[72] The Justice Department's preliminary action was termed an *informal inquiry* to ascertain whether there was sufficient evidence of antitrust violations to file a suit against MTV and the labels. Although the Justice inquiry commenced at roughly the same time that Discovery Music Network filed its suit against MTV, a department spokesperson said that their investigation was parallel with the Discovery action, but not instigated by it.[73] In response to the probe, an MTV spokesperson reported, "We have received a routine inquiry from the Justice Department and we are cooperating fully. We are confident that our agreements with the record companies do not violate the antitrust laws. In particular, we believe the exclusivity provisions are appropriate and valid—exclusivity being a common and accepted feature of entertainment-industry contracts."[74] The inquiry ultimately did not affect MTV's practices and the Justice Department never filed a suit against MTV. Moreover, none of these legal challenges and investigations had any effect on MTV's contracts with the record companies and they still remain in force, allowing MTV to continue its exclusive premiere of videos.

MTV and Record Labels Renew Contracts

MTV and the major labels continually reevaluate their commitment to these exclusivity agreements as the pacts expire and are considered for renewal. The increasing number of alternative outlets for video music and MTV's declining ratings (discussed in Chapter 6) led some of the major labels to reconsider whether these pacts were in their best interests.[75] CBS Records president, Al Teller, publicly questioned the promotional value of video for its artists, and CBS refused to allow its clips to be used on MTV's syndicated show, *Top 20 Countdown.*[76] Some executives suggested that the pacts were no longer needed because they were originally intended to help a young fledgling MTV achieve success as an established national service promoting record label artists, which it has since done.

Yet other label executives keep their eyes on the money that these contracts generate. "When you spend $50,000 to $200,000 on a video and you have an opportunity to make money back on it, any revenue is a plus," says Steve Stevenson, Warner Brothers' director of music video promotion. The labels realize that the millions MTV pays them each year pays for much of their own production expenses. Also, they love the promotional flourish and constant showings that MTV grants videos picked as exclusives, which some feel more than make up for the possible lost exposure on other less well known programs. A music clip selected as an MTV exclusive gains a certain cachet and prominence, which labels believe help promote the act and the album.

MTV also reexamined these pacts. In May 1986, Bob Pittman said that negotiations with the labels about renewal of the pacts would be postponed until MTVN's new owner, Viacom, assessed the value of exclusives. Pittman said that the pacts were "costing us a lot of money. . . . Viacom is wondering whether that may not be a wonderful source of cash for other ventures."[77] Despite these reservations, MTV Networks signed multiyear extensions of its exclusivity contracts with A&M Records and all of the Warner affiliated labels in 1986.[78] In July 1991, all major record labels had exclusive contracts with MTV Networks except Virgin, Mercury, and PLG. Estimates offered during that year for MTV's annual payments to the labels ranged from $10 to $15 million.[79] By 1994, some record labels discontinued their exclusive agreements with MTV, including RCA and MCA, but Island, Elektra, Atlantic, Virgin, and Geffen Records still had MTV-only videos. Some record companies dropped the MTV contracts in part because of plans to launch their own program service, described later.

Recent Attacks by The Box and BET

Two of MTV's major competitors recently launched a renewed attack on MTV's deals with the labels: the Video Jukebox Network's The Box and Black Entertainment Television (BET). Les Garland, who moved from MTV to The Box as its vice president of programming, now suddenly complains about these contracts that deny the channel certain videos for up to six months. Garland argues that these contracts are not fair to The Box, because his network makes the effort to nurture and develop new acts by playing their videos while they are still unknown.[80] MTV's increasing emphasis on hit songs by well-known artists and "lifestyle" programs that ignore music altogether exclude videos by aspiring musicians. But once these acts gain a wider audience as a result of The Box's efforts, MTV decides to use its arrangement with the record companies to take future videos by these artists exclusively. Garland says that this happened both with the artists Kris Kross and Gerardo, where The Box played their first video, and after they received more attention, MTV claimed exclusive rights for their second videos. The Box executive claims that these exclusives are harmful and unfair to The Box since it did the groundwork to create an audience for the musicians, to the artists who are denied exposure on The Box, and also to the audience that is not allowed to watch popular videos unless it turns to MTV.

Garland also raises the disturbing possibility that MTV's true goal is to create a "monopoly" over music video by combining these record label pacts with an ambitious plan for expansion. MTV sought to expand to three separate channels in the United States by the end of 1994: the original MTV and two new channels each featuring a specific genre of music, one channel rumored to play black urban videos. Garland claims that these three channels along with VH-1's adult contemporary format would give MTV Networks an impressive degree of control over music video presented on television. Since MTV gets exclusive rights to major label videos, MTV would be in the position to extend its "monopoly" over a wider range of music presented on television and determine what acts get extensive play. Current videos by popular artists of any music genre may only be seen on an MTV channel, enhancing MTVN's role as a cultural gatekeeper. Aspiring artists may also find it difficult to get played in this brave new MTV-world of choices since the original MTV and VH-1 both tend to ignore new artists in favor of familiar faces and established hit songs. For these artists, Garland suggests, the MTV "monopoly" may become a "roadblock." Although MTV delayed its plans to split into three channels because cable systems did not have the room for additional services, the company may return to this plan in the future as more systems greatly expand their channel capacity.

Johnson's BET launched a more forceful attack on the MTV–record label deals through high-profile boycotts, immediately getting the labels' attention. The exclusive deals generally prevent BET from airing a video selected by MTV for thirty days.[81] BET tangled with record labels before on this issue, but decided to embark on a more intensive campaign against these pacts in 1991, taking on labels that granted MTV exclusives for popular artists. In the spring, BET dropped all Columbia label artists from its channel for two weeks in reprisal for MTV's exclusive of C&C Music Factory's video, *Things That Make You Go Hmm,* and the following summer boycotted MCA Records for twelve days over an MTV exclusive for Heavy D. & the Boyz' video *Now That We've Found Love.*[82] A similar action against Capitol Records for a Young M.C. music clip was averted through negotiations.

Johnson's goal was to break MTV's lock on videos. "We will not tolerate their use of monopoly power," he said.[83] "This is the closest thing to a declaration of war that we've had with a competitor." BET wanted the record labels to discontinue these MTV pacts when they expired, or at least see that they were "renegotiated so that we're not hurt," explained BET's Jeff Lee, vice president of programming.[84] Each of these boycotts, threatened or carried out, was called off when the respective label agreed to do so, considering BET's needs for videos by black artists featured on the channel.[85]

Although bound by these contracts, the labels tried to work out possible compromises to satisfy BET, like Columbia's plan to provide the channel with an alternate version of a clip for a song, so that when MTV got exclusive rights to a particular video, BET received another clip featuring the same song. Capitol Records tried this approach for Hammer's *Here Comes the Hammer* clip, where BET got an exclusive to the original clip taken from a production for home video and MTV received a newly produced eight-minute version of the song. This strategy did not satisfy BET, as it claimed the label had promised them a sole exclusive to the song.[86]

Despite their tepid attempts to be accommodating, the major labels generally defended their MTV deals, saying that MTV's audience and promotional power were much greater than BET's.[87] The labels claimed MTV's overheated fanfare and publicity for its exclusives generated more public attention for an album and act than did play on BET. Some labels said that MTV was justified in having exclusives because it paid millions to the record companies yearly for the rights to videos, whereas BET paid little or nothing for the videos it aired. Said one label executive, "BET can't demand the same respect as MTV unless they're coming to the party in some way. They never pay us anything. We make videos specifically for BET that we probably wouldn't be making if it weren't for the money we get from MTV."[88] BET responded that it did not have the clout or financial resources that MTV did to pay that kind of money. Even with record label grousing and the continued existence of these contracts, BET's hardball tactics got the record labels' attention much more effectively than reasoned arguments by competitors and critics that were presented in the trade press.

Label Payola Agreements with Other Music Programs

More recently, record companies are making payola-like deals with other music program services besides MTV to get guaranteed exposure for their artists. For instance, labels pay a fee between $550 to $650 for each clip they want played on College Music Video, a monthly three-hour program that features alternative and hip hop music and is seen on about 190 stations nationally in 1995. The president of the service, Robert Artura, openly admits that "the music mix is dictated by the labels who buy the time."[89] Record labels that want to see their artists' video clips featured on the weekly program, *End TV*, must pay a $5,000 fee to the program owners. *End TV* plans to debut in late 1995 on broadcast television stations in major cities including Los Angeles, New York, and Miami. Record labels especially seek play on The Box channel because of its impressive success in establishing new artists like Mary J. Blige and R. Kelly. To make sure their artists are played, record companies take advantage of the channel's pay-per-video system by flooding The Box's telephone lines with requests for current clips by these acts. The labels hire teams of callers to request certain videos they want shown, a practice called "jackin' The Box" inside the industry. The more calls that The Box receives for a clip, the more likely it will be played, hopefully creating a buzz about the featured artist. Tommy Silverman of Tommy Boy Records describes this tactic for getting video play as "very big, all-pervasive" in the music business although few record companies admit that they are "jackin' The Box."[90] This is a very expensive promotional strategy since each call to the 900 number charges $2 to $3 to the caller's telephone bill.

The practice is a form of payola since the revenues from these calls go directly to The Box, so that in essence, record labels are paying the program service to play their videos. The Box is fully aware of the record labels' actions and actually encourages the practice by selling cards to label executives that allow a certain number of 900-number calls. The channel also offers special package deals where the label pays a certain fee to receive guaranteed play of videos that it wants shown during a two-week period along with commercials for the labels' latest videos.

Whereas this payola provides advantages for both the record labels and The Box, it is The Box's viewers that are shortchanged and deceived. The Box presents itself as a program service that lets its viewers select what videos are played through their calls. The slogan of the Box is "Music Television You Control." Yet the collusion between The Box and record labels suggests that the amount of control viewers actually exert over the channel is quite limited. Record labels are greatly influencing the music that gets played on the channel—much as they do on other services like MTV.

Major Labels Create Own Music Video Channel

The major labels' cooperative relationship with MTV in the 1980s clearly provided these record companies with a reliable national forum for hawking their artists' music. Indeed, MTV's emphasis on acts signed to major record companies is so extensive that many independent labels deride MTV as a "major label only" channel, which rarely plays videos by their bands.[91] Yet, recently the majors indicated that they are unsatisfied with their current degree of control over music video programming and are taking various steps to launch their own music channel. In early 1994, four of the six major labels developed plans to start their own global music video service, which would directly challenge MTV.[92] The original backers for this proposed channel were TimeWarner, Sony, Polygram, and EMI Music, companies that collectively supply 63 percent of music videos shown on MTV.[93]

The prototype for this operation was to have been Viva, a cable music program service in Germany that began in December 1993.[94] The four major labels previously mentioned and Frank Otto, a businessman with holdings in German radio, are all equal partners in this venture. Viva was prompted by the lack of videos by German artists played on MTV Europe, which focuses more on American and U.K. pop acts. If Viva is successful, the labels hope to expand the channel to other parts of Europe and Asia. Ultimately, if Viva's partners proceed with their plans to develop a global service, it will directly challenge MTV's empire. In early 1995, four major labels purchased one-half ownership of Star TV's music service, Channel V. The Channel is available throughout Asia and will compete with MTV Asia and MTV Mandarin.

These companies announced plans in 1994 to compete with the original American MTV by launching a music video channel in the United States. The new major label service would be able to get immediate access to an ample portion of U.S. cable systems because of the involvement of TimeWarner, which is the second largest cable system operator in the United States, serving more than 7 million subscribers. TimeWarner, as a major media conglomerate, would then be able to provide guaranteed promotion for its artists, using its various subsidiaries. Warner Music would produce a music clip for its artist and the clip would be shown on the new label music channel, which would in turn be presented on a TimeWarner cable system. All of this could be coordinated at corporate headquarters to nurture and shape public demand for Warner artists without having to rely on any outside media outlets.

Bertelsmann Music Group, the German media conglomerate that owns RCA Records, and Telecommunications, the major U.S. cable multiple system operator, also announced plans in September 1993 to launch a channel that would present music videos and sell merchandise through a toll-free telephone number.[95] However, Bertelsmann and TCI abandoned this venture in early June 1994 and by the end of that month Bertelsmann had decided to join the consortium of major labels planning their own music channel. With the addition of Bertelsmann, this new music cable channel would be jointly owned by five record labels that together have overwhelming dominance of the international recording industry, controlling 80 percent of the $11 billion global market for recorded music in 1994.

The major labels have several possible reasons for announcing these plans. Some see the disclosure of these ambitious ventures as a thinly veiled threat to MTV to encourage the channel to be more compliant and yield to demands for better financial terms in their deals with the network.[96] The labels want to be paid substantially more for rights to their videos, especially since MTV has become more successful. MTV and its sister station, VH-1, were expected to have revenues of $395 million in 1993, a 22 percent increase over the previous year.[97] These companies believe that their videos are in large part responsible for MTV's prosperity and want to be compensated for this. As MTV's success grows, the labels also may seek to become part owners to share in its wealth and more directly shape its programming. These record companies may believe that threats of a new global competitor would intimidate MTV and Viacom, making them more willing to consider these proposals for increased fee payments and ownership bids. However, this hope seems slender given Sumner Redstone's penchant for complete domination over Viacom subsidiaries, demonstrated in his unwillingness to share control of Paramount in that recent acquisition.

The major labels also are considering global ventures because they may be dissatisfied with the current degree of vertical integration they have in this market. The MTV deals provide these companies with certain integration through contractual agreement where MTV provides some guaranteed access for their productions. Yet this type of integration is imperfect: MTV is not completely submissive to the labels' wishes and has certain economic interests that diverge from these companies. For instance, MTV's need for higher ratings led the channel to expand its nonmusic programs: Almost 25 percent of its schedule is devoted to shows without music clips, and about 50 percent of the prime-time block is nonmusic programming, like talk, news, and comedy shows. This gradual decline in music disturbs the record labels since the music clips promote their acts, hopefully increasing music sales. In October 1994, MTV president, Judy McGrath, tried to address this concern by announcing a corporate reorganization designed to increase the emphasis of music on MTV and refute "the perception that we're not paying attention to music and that music is not important to us."[98] Still, the labels remain dissatisfied with MTV's play of music, but they cannot directly affect MTV's policies since the channel is owned by another company.

By creating their own worldwide music video channel, the labels would achieve complete vertical integration through ownership, producing the video clips, and exhibiting them on their own program service. This would give the labels direct control to promote their acts however they wish without the autonomy of an independently owned service. The plan is somewhat analogous to the Hollywood film studios' purchase of theater chains to show their own films, and even more similar to the studios' aborted attempt to launch the pay-TV movie channel Premiere to provide a showcase for their productions on cable. As with other instances of vertical integration in media industries, a label-owned video music channel would raise the possibility of anticompetitive practices that could diminish diversity in music. The Viva-like channel might only air the music videos of artists affiliated with these five companies, excluding music by acts signed to other labels, especially independent record companies with limited clout and resources.

Moreover, apprehension about free competition and diversity is even more warranted because five of six major transnational record labels plan to cooperate on this global project. These companies could collectively pull their videos from competing music video program services like MTV, although label executives deny any plans to do this. A global music channel owned by these companies could also be consciously used to cultivate and craft worldwide interest in their labels' acts, at the expense of emerging musicians not fortunate enough to be signed to one of the Big Five. MTV's Tom Freston raises a disturbing possibility, suggesting "you've got to wonder whether this is going to become the OPEC of the music industry"[99] (although his self-serving comment is rather hypocritical since MTV actively collaborated with these companies in agreements blasted by competitors as equally anticompetitive).

This potential for collusion among major record companies prompted the Antitrust Division of the U.S. Justice Department to launch a preliminary investigation into the proposed venture in July 1994 to determine if the label-owned channel would lead to "anti-competitive practices in the music-video industry."[100] The Justice Department wanted to know if the record labels would use their control over the supply of programming to undermine competitors, notably MTV. MTV in particular is worried that the labels acting in unison might decide to either raise the license fees for rights to their videos or just deny MTV access to the videos altogether. Either course of action would cripple MTV since it gets two-thirds of its videos from these five record labels that are partners in the channel. The labels respond that MTV and VH-1 so dominate music video programming that there is a need for alternative media outlets that play music clips.

The record companies pushed back the launch of the channel to 1995, attributing the delay to the government probe and a lack of available space on cable systems. In public the labels say they are committed to the channel, but behind the scenes some executives had second thoughts about the project, dreading a protracted and expensive legal battle. In early 1995, the labels were enmeshed in an internal debate over the best form of vertical integration to ensure guaranteed access for their videos and promotion for their artists: They may either go ahead with direct integration through ownership by having their own channel, which can focus on their own artists, or the labels may abandon the project and return to a form of collusion with MTV, working out some deal to get their artists featured prominently on a regular basis. In the United States, the labels seem to be moving toward the latter option for the moment. In July 1995 these companies decided to drop plans for a music channel in the United States. However, Brett Atwood reports in *Billboard* that most of the participants in the abandoned project, including Warner Music Group, EMI Music, and Polygram, may be developing alternate plans to launch a U.S. music video network in 1996.[101] Polygram's joint ownership with MTV of its Asia services in 1995 demonstrates that some record labels are still willing to collaborate with MTV Networks. Either way, the major labels with or without MTV will be able to shape and direct the flow of music on television to nurture audience interest in popular music however they want, likely leaving smaller independent record labels out in the cold.

MTV Attempts to Coerce Artists

For videos by recording artists not bound by the exclusivity pacts, MTV used coercive tactics to persuade the artists to give the channel unconditional allegiance over other competing services. Several artists and program services alleged that MTV repeatedly threatened to curtail its exposure of artists who gave video clip exclusives to competitors. David Benjamin, producer of NBC's *Friday Night Videos,* claimed artists would reluctantly refuse to give his show an exclusive for fear of reprisals from MTV: "Artists come to me and say, 'We'd like to give you this video, but MTV says if they don't get it first, they'll never play any of our videos again.' I tell them, 'Don't risk your career, give it to them.' . . . They are bullies, showing utter disregard for the art."[102] Les Garland, while at MTV, issued the following veiled warning to artists who appeared to lend credence to Benjamin's claim that MTV did indeed punish artists who granted other services video clip exclusives: "We have difficulties when a group shows its loyalties are not with MTV. We have to have the chance to get it first. We're doing the groups a favor by playing their videos."[103]

MTV allegedly punished The Rolling Stones and Billy Joel for allowing their clips to be premiered on other video clip shows.[104] After MTV said it would require editing for the Stones' new video, *She Was Hot,* the video was played first on *Friday Night Videos,* which offered to play the video in its original form. After the video premiered on the NBC show, MTV added the Stones' clip in "light" rotation for three days before it was dropped. Although The Rolling Stones' management angrily charged that MTV's treatment of the video was designed to punish the group, MTV responded that the clip was pulled because the Stones' album became less popular. After Billy Joel's clip for "The Longest Time" premiered on NBC's *Today Show,* MTV refused to air the video for about a month. Joel's management said that MTV's action was in retaliation to the video's debut on NBC. This sort of intimidation is more effective on new and emerging artists than established recording stars because musicians that are less well known are more dependent upon MTV for national public exposure.

MTV's competitors charged that the program service used its coercive practices to ensure that it received exclusive rights not only to an artist's new videos but to personal appearances by the artist as well. Mark Wodlinger repeatedly claimed that MTV would blacklist the videos of artists who granted interviews on Hit Video USA.[105] Prior to the debut of the ill-fated Cable Music Channel, John McGhan, vice president of programming for the service, also alleged that MTV discouraged artists such as Rod Stewart, Billy Ocean, and the Thompson Twins from appearing in station identification (ID) spots for Turner's channel.[106] According to McGhan, "they won't do IDs for us because Les Garland has told them that if they participate for Ted Turner in any way, shape or form they're going to be cut off at MTV."[107] A spokesperson for Garland denied charges that he intimidated artists in this manner, although his statement about artist loyalty appeared to entail an implicit threat of punitive action against artists who appeared else-where. In retrospect, Garland's actions at MTV seem ironic given his later con-demnation of this very type of behavior when he moved to VJN.

MTV Attempts to Control Access to Cable Systems

MTV's monopolistic practices extended to attempts to dominate access to cable systems. MTV sought to establish entrenched vertical integration through contrac-tual agreement "downstream" with cable operators as well as "upstream" with record labels and artists in order to establish its guaranteed access to all stages of production and distribution of video music. Conversely, MTV sought to exploit this entrenched vertical integration at all levels to undermine potential competitors.

MTV Networks' strategy to assure its dominance in the programming market was outlined in Pittman's 1983 confidential memo referred to earlier, which said that a service in MTV's position should "lock up the shelf space and/or lock up the supply of the product."[108] Whereas the latter objective was accomplished through exclusivity agreements and informal coercion as reviewed previously, Pittman sought to achieve the first goal, locking up the "shelf space," through con-tracts with cable companies. In 1984, when MTV decided to institute license fees, the company negotiated franchise agreements with cable operators offering dis-count rates for long-term commitments to their service. MTV's Pittman wanted to establish multiyear contracts with cable systems because he predicted that MTV would "be most vulnerable to competition from new entrants over the next five years."[109] MTV promptly signed long-term contracts with the two largest cable companies in the United States in 1984, Tele-Communications and Ameri-can Television & Communications (ATC).[110] These extended franchise agree-ments guaranteed MTV's long-term distribution and increased cable operators' reluctance to add a competing music service.

The alleged provision of these contracts, requiring cable companies to offer VH-1 if the operator wanted to offer a second music video channel, served to make cable system access even more difficult for potential competitors. Constance Wodlinger claimed that these contracts prevented Hit Video USA "from doing business with 80 percent of the nation's cable systems" and forced the channel to abandon cable and attempt to distribute its programming via broadcast television before shutting down entirely in October 1990.[111] "It's unfortunate that the na-tion's cable operators are prevented from having a choice in music video net-works," Wodlinger said.[112] These provisions were unsuccessfully challenged in the Wodlinger lawsuit discussed previously. Some cable operators acknowledge that MTV Networks has continued to pressure them to carry VH-1 as a condition of gaining access to the more popular MTV service. In 1995, Wayne Vowell, general manager of Scripps-Howard Cable of Sacramento, admits: "I had to take VH1 to get the MTV channel."[113]

Although MTV never confirmed the presence of this mandatory provision, the contracts were widely acknowledged to offer VH-1 free to cable systems carrying

MTV, which at the very least, provided a strong incentive for the operator to add this service over a competitor. This vigorous promotion of VH-1 in franchise agreements was perceived as a direct attempt to deny cable access to MTV's expected full-fledged competitors, Discovery, CMC, and Hit Video USA, all of which had tried and failed to offer "adult contemporary" music formats similar to VH-1.

MTV also tried to prevent a competing video music service from acquiring access to cable systems through legal action involving the FCC.[114] In 1985, MTV filed a petition to prevent WWHT, a local UHF station with an all-video music format, from being carried on New York area cable systems. In the petition, MTV requested that the FCC waive the application of the "must carry rules," which required cable systems to carry all local broadcast stations within a certain distance of the system's transmission facility. David Horowitz, chief executive officer of MTV Networks at the time, claimed that the company did not file the petition primarily because the station had a music video format, but rather "that petition was motivated by a desire to keep the channels of distribution open for our program services."[115] When the petition was filed, FCC officials said that it was unlikely the must carry rules would be waived because of the absence of strong UHF signals in the areas involved. Given MTV's history of anticompetitive practices, it seems unlikely that WWHT's music video format was not a primary consideration motivating MTV to file the FCC petition, as claimed by Horowitz.

However, MTV likely had broader reasons for this action, which went beyond an isolated attempt to prevent one UHF station access to cable systems. After the Cable Music Channel failed to compete directly with MTV as a twenty-four-hour cable service, MTV's other potential competitors, Discovery and Hit Video USA, modified their distribution strategies to seek coverage on UHF and low-power broadcast stations instead of cable systems. Both services reasoned that distribution via broadcast stations rather than cable would circumvent MTVN's stranglehold on cable system access, which had caused CMC to flounder. Moreover, if Discovery and Hit Video USA were presented on local broadcast outlets, these services would be able to gain access to cable "through the back door" because cable systems in these areas were required to carry these stations under restrictive "must carry rules" that were in effect in the mid-1980s. Given this background, MTV's petition could be perceived as a preliminary attempt to undermine its potential competitors' "back door" access to cable systems.

Finally, besides attempts to manipulate cable operator contracts and government regulation to increase its audience at the expense of competitors, MTV could always rely on its direct vertical integration with cable systems owned by its parent companies to serve this purpose as well. Since its inception, MTV was a subsidiary of a media conglomerate that also owned cable systems offering program services like MTV to its subscribers. This ownership of both programming and cable systems provided MTV with guaranteed access to the systems owned by the parent firm. Within the cable industry, this cooperation between a company's media "software" (programming) and "hardware" (distribution system) is a common practice, as explained by Peter Falco, a media analyst from Merrill Lynch: "It is clear . . . that big cable system operators from Time on down to second-rung operators like Cablevision are increasingly using their cable systems as preserves for programming services in which they have an interest."[116] This common ownership allows the firm to provide preferential treatment of its own programming on its systems. Conversely, program channels not owned by the company that directly compete with its own offerings may be banned from its system, only partially presented during certain hours, or given substandard contract terms.

MTV has always been affiliated with large cable multiple system operators (MSOs) throughout its history. From 1981 to 1985, MTV was owned by Warner Amex Satellite Entertainment Company (WASEC), whose parent companies, Warner Communications and American Express, also owned Warner Amex cable, which was the sixth largest MSO in 1984 with 1.2 million subscribers.[117] This vertical integration provided MTV with an important base of guaranteed subscribers during its early fledgling years when advertising was limited, viewers were indifferent, and good music clips were scarce. From 1985 until the present, MTV has been owned by Viacom and is the flagship service within the subsidiary MTV Networks, which also owns the other music video services VH-1 and MTV Europe, and Nickelodeon, a children's network with some music clip shows. The parent, Viacom, also owned cable systems under its division, Viacom Cable Television, which was approximately the fifteenth largest MSO in the United States, with about 1,087,000 subscribers at the end of 1991.[118]

Viacom's policy is to take advantage of its integration by carrying its numerous program services on its own cable systems, stating in the company's 1991 10-K report to the SEC, "the Company offers the Company's own basic programming services, as well as such third-party services as CNN, ESPN and USA Network."[119] Although there is no systematic evidence showing a pattern of exclusion of program services that directly compete with Viacom services, The Box has noticed that it is not welcome on Viacom systems. In March 1991, Viacom had not put The Box on any of its fourteen cable systems, which seems to be more than a coincidence.[120] Viacom cannot plead limited channel capacity for banishing The Box since it says with pride that only 12 percent of its cable subscribers receive service on a system with thirty-five channels or less. Clearly Viacom seems to reserve its channel capacity for program services like MTV, which it owns, ignoring services like The Box no matter how intriguing, adventurous, or cutting-edge their programming may be. Viacom sought to sell off its cable systems to a minority-owned business affiliated with Telecommunications (TCI), a major MSO. The company made this deal to take advantage of a substantial tax break for selling media outlets to racial minorities, but was thwarted in February 1995 by the Republican-controlled Congress's proposal to repeal the policy.[121] Viacom ultimately did sell its cable systems to TCI in 1995. Viacom will probably rely more heavily on a policy of collusion through contractual agreement with major MSOs like TCI to get guaranteed access for its programming. This strategy seems likely given the increasing cooperation between Viacom and TCI on proposed joint ventures in 1994. In May 1994 Viacom's chief executive, Frank Biondi, disclosed that the company was negotiating a series of different links between the two companies.[122]

Ironically, although Viacom apparently used vertical integration in cable to advance its own economic interests at the expense of competitors, the company cries foul when others do the same. On May 9, 1989, Viacom filed an antitrust suit for $2.4 billion against Time (prior to the TimeWarner merger), charging that Time's cable systems under its subsidiary American Television & Communications (ATC) refused to carry Viacom's pay-TV services Showtime and The Movie Channel (TMC) while promoting its own Home Box Office (HBO) service.[123] Yet Viacom seemed to give The Box the same brush-off on its own services. Viacom's lawsuit also charged that Time's HBO had tried since 1980 to coerce non–Time-owned cable systems to exclude Showtime in contract negotiations. Viacom's outrage seems rather hollow given that Constance Wodlinger claimed that MTV manipulated its contracts in a similar way to exclude Hit Video USA and other music video shows from cable.[124] Despite the ample hypocrisy, Viacom settled the suit, with the newly merged TimeWarner agreeing to pay Viacom $75 million and cooperating in a joint marketing campaign to make Showtime more competitive on TimeWarner systems.[125]

∾   ∾   ∾

MTV has clearly demonstrated a consistent history of aggressive collusion with major record labels and cable operators to secure its own monopoly control in the field of music video programming. The channel wants to do whatever it takes to shut down competition and become the only music clip show around. MTV's executives conspire with record companies to get exclusive rights to the hottest videos by popular artists, knowing that other shows may not survive without these clips. Besides these agreements, many artists and agents fear giving exclusives or interviews to other programs because they know MTV punishes artists that do not show allegiance. In its dealings with multiple system operators, MTV uses its contracts as a weapon by stipulating provisions discouraging cable systems from carrying music shows not owned by MTV Networks. And despite numerous lawsuits and government inquiries, MTV's anticompetitive practices continue unchecked. These policies raise disturbing concerns about the degree of unrivaled control MTV has over popular music presented on cable television because aspiring artists might be excluded from cable television altogether if they are not featured on an MTV program service. The major record labels benefited from these deals with MTV because they received guaranteed exposure for their acts on MTV through a legal form of payola. Yet this cozy arrangement shows signs of deteriorating as the labels take steps to launch their own music program, strengthening their vertical integration and giving them even greater control over the flow of music on television. However, what seems certain is that either separately or in collusion, the record companies and MTV Networks will act as gatekeepers largely deciding which musicians are featured on cable television—and which artists are excluded.

5

MTV and the Globalization
of Popular Culture

Like other media companies, MTV Networks has expanded its operations globally, launching derivatives of MTV, including MTV Europe, MTV Asia, and MTV Latino, in other countries and regions. This international expansion of MTV's services raises perennial concerns about U.S. cultural influence abroad since MTV's programs mostly play artists from the United States and the United Kingdom, often giving scant attention to indigenous music and only showing local artists if they mimic American-style rock. This chapter examines the history, operations, and programming of MTV's various international services, giving special attention to the proportion of regional and foreign music presented. MTV's strategies in its overseas operations are reviewed, most notably its attempt to foster and exploit an international youth culture. MTV hopes to shape a global audience of young people that will be sought by transnational advertisers wanting to reach this group. Finally, alternatives to MTV are explored like Canada's MuchMusic, which attempts to preserve the country's indigenous music.

Corporate Incentives to Develop International Markets

MTVN's launch of music program services in other countries is the company's most extensive attempt to develop ancillary markets related to the original American MTV. Tom Freston, the president of MTV Networks, stresses the importance of MTV's international expansion, saying, "Our goal is to be in every home in the world."[1] MTV Networks also has ambitious plans to export versions of MTV's sister services VH-1 and Nickelodeon to other countries. This expansion exemplifies the natural tendency for U.S. companies with media interests to expand to other countries after the U.S. market has been saturated, relying more on foreign markets for future growth. International operations often account for more than 50 percent of total revenues of media conglomerates. Freston reports that MTV

Networks received about 25 percent of its revenue from international sources in 1994 and expects this proportion to reach 35 percent to 45 percent over the next five years.[2] Companies also export programming because most production costs are already paid and additional distribution costs are minimal, increasing potential profits.

American cable program services aggressively pursued international expansion for these reasons. MTV, CNN, and ESPN were among the first U.S. cable networks to establish their programming in Europe in the late 1980s, and by October 1991 several other services had plans for overseas expansion as well, including the USA Network, CNBC, and The Family Channel. Exporting program services can be a lucrative project because programming expenses are limited and other countries offer a new audience that can generate additional advertising revenue and subscription fees.

These other countries are especially attractive to program services like MTV because many Western industrialized areas including Europe are still in the early stages of getting hooked up to cable, providing opportunities for growth. In Europe in 1992, the number of homes wired for cable grew 10 percent over the previous year, to 33 million.[3] Such growth led MTV's Tom Freston to proclaim, "Europe is the last great frontier in the TV business, the last big game to be played."[4] Further, these program services, including MTV, can be readily exported by taking advantage of political movements toward privatization and deregulation of many media systems in Europe and other regions.[5] Many countries now allow privately owned foreign services to be carried on their media systems for the first time. A recent boom in satellite communications made it easier for U.S. program services to export their programming to Europe and other areas for distribution to cable systems and individual households with satellite dishes. Cable program services also shifted their attention abroad as the U.S. market became less lucrative. Recent changes in federal regulation of cable systems, placing limits on rates, made it more difficult for program services to charge higher subscription fees, curbing potential profits. Established major cable services also found growth in the United States tapering off as most areas of the country now have cable available and these services are fully distributed on existing cable systems. In 1993, Hilary Condit, a Viacom spokewoman, reported that MTV was "pretty much at full distribution in the U.S." Since almost all households with cable were receiving MTV, she conceded that the slight increase in subscribers for that year "may be a natural plateauing" for the music channel.[6]

Despite this trend toward expansion, cable program services face certain obstacles when trying to move into other countries. Some nations have protectionist measures limiting foreign programming because they wish to preserve their own culture and do not want to be overwhelmed with American ideas and values inherent in this foreign media content. Countries in the European Community, especially France, frequently voice concern about imported Hollywood films displacing their own film industry and diminishing their own cultural distinctiveness. U.S. program services are also hindered by the different economic practices of European cable companies. Although American services like CNN and MTV receive a substantial part of their revenues from subscription fees paid by cable operators, European cable companies are reluctant to pay such fees, which is a recurring source of tension between programmers and operators. Finally, U.S. program services seeking to expand throughout Europe face skepticism from financial analysts who claim there is a limited market for pan-European advertising, suggesting that most advertisers target specific countries or geographic areas.

MTV Europe

Of the several versions of MTV produced around the world, MTV Europe is the most elaborate and successful venture. MTV Europe was launched August 1, 1987, with 1.6 million subscribers in fourteen European countries when Elton John threw the switch at a nightclub in Amsterdam starting the first video, Dire Straits' *Money for Nothing*. The format of MTV Europe is similar to its American predecessor with on-air VJs introducing videos, music news segments, and flashy promos. At its launch, MTV Europe competed with Rupert Murdoch's Sky Channel and the Super Channel, program services widely available throughout Europe, which both had music video shows along with more traditional television fare like sitcoms and dramas. The channel's debut was viewed skeptically because music shows on these European services had been somewhat unsuccessful.[7] Further, some questioned whether enough potential advertising revenue existed to support pan-European services like MTV Europe.

Viacom originally owned about 25 percent of MTV Europe, with British Telecommunications holding another 25 percent and Maxwell Communications Corporation, controlled by the late British publisher Robert Maxwell, owning the remaining 50 percent. Both of the U.K. partners have since sold their shares to Viacom, giving it complete ownership. British Telecom sold out in February 1990, followed by Maxwell in August 1991 for $65 million in order to pay off the extensive company debt left amid the disarray caused by the founder's death.[8] MTV Europe, based in England with a staff of around 150, moved its headquarters to studios in Camden Lock, London, in July 1993. The new facilities provide MTV with two studios to produce live shows and concerts.

Despite its claims of featuring European music, MTV Europe mostly presents music clips of American and British artists, calling into question just how "European" the channel really is. The spotlight on U.S. and U.K. acts reinforces the dominance of these acts throughout the continent, consigning indigenous artists to the margins of popular culture even within their own countries. MTV Europe executive producer Brian Diamond conceded that two of every three videos presented on MTV Europe are by Anglo-American artists, and an August 1991 survey of the channel's weekly playlist revealed that only about 15 percent of its airtime was devoted to European artists.[9] MTV Europe's chief executive officer, Bill

Roedy, claims that the channel provides somewhat more exposure for European artists, saying that 25 percent of the artists on the playlist were by Continental acts in March 1992.[10] MTV Europe's high-profile show featuring the week's top 20 videos is also regularly top-heavy with American and British artists. The channel imports several programs from the American MTV like *Yo! MTV Raps,* showcasing U.S. artists. MTV Europe's Anglo flavor is not confined to the music clips, as almost all programs are presented in English and the vee-jays speak English as well. MTV Europe does not have any local or national "cut-ins," used by other services where more local programming is presented during certain segments instead of the pan-European program feed.

Stylistic differences exist between the American and European MTV, although there is no consensus on what these are. MTV executives say that MTV Europe is somewhat more adventurous, playing a more eclectic, diverse range of alternative music than the U.S. MTV, which has a more conservative playlist of established acts.[11] MTV Europe claims to feature emerging artists more frequently because European youth are more receptive to hearing new acts. Yet a *New York Times* review of MTV Europe presents an entirely contrary characterization of the channel, depicting it as less "vibrant" and more stodgy than the American version.[12] The *Times* reports that the European channel relies on more conservative, middle-of-the-road artists like Phil Collins and Rod Stewart and classic rock by acts such as David Bowie. The channel generally excludes louder, heavy metal acts like Poison and Motley Crue, which are popular in the United States but lack a following throughout Europe. MTV Europe also displays rampant commercialism in its programming, which surpasses even the American MTV, with show titles named after prominent sponsors, including the *MTV Coca-Cola Report* and *The Pulse With Swatch.* Some nonmusic shows do confront pressing political and social issues relevant to the channel's young audience. In April 1993, MTV Europe presented the show *The Unity Weekend,* which explored concerns about ethnic cleansing and neo-Nazi movements, in a studio debate with celebrities and experts.[13]

The major record labels appreciate MTV Europe for promoting their acts throughout Europe, and the channel congratulates itself for breaking certain new artists like Roxette and Dr. Alban. However, there are tensions: Record companies outside of the United Kingdom complain that the channel plays few French, German, Italian, or Spanish acts, instead favoring Anglo artists.[14] MTV Europe's Roedy responds that MTV does play some Continental artists, but emphasizes American and British acts because that is what the audience wants.[15] He refers to a survey commissioned by the channel reporting that 76 percent of their German audience believed that MTV Europe played enough music by German artists. Yet simply saying "we give the people what they want" does not address how MTV may play a more active role in cultivating desires for U.S. acts in the first place.

MTV Europe is embroiled in a conflict with record companies over royalty fees for videos. The channel objects to the collective licensing system used in Europe to determine royalties to be paid for the right to air the record companies' videos. MTV Europe is required to go through a central body, Video Performance Limited, which licenses videos for most record companies and establishes standard royalty fees.[16] In 1993, MTV Europe sued this body in the United Kingdom, arguing that the system was monopolistic, forcing MTV Europe to pay exorbitantly high fees for videos. MTV Europe further stated the system should be abolished, allowing MTV to negotiate video rights individually with each record company.[17] The record labels oppose this move because it would likely lead to much lower license fees. Partly as a result of these tensions with MTV Europe, four multinational record labels created their own music video program service, Viva, in Germany in December 1993.[18] Although this conflict has not been resolved, Sony Music reached a separate accommodation with MTV, announcing in November 1994 the signing of a global licensing agreement that provides MTV with rights to Sony music clips on all of its services around the world.[19]

MTV's reach throughout Europe is expanding steadily, although its growth was hindered initially by the limited penetration of cable throughout Europe. In December 1988, 13 million households on the Continent were wired for cable, representing only 10 percent of homes with television in that region.[20] Further, MTV Europe's publicity campaigns were thwarted by a lack of available advertising time on other television stations to promote the service because of prohibitive government policies. MTV Europe resorted to persuading rock stars like Sting to present a half-hour of the program service on big screen television at live concerts instead of an opening act. Despite the obstacles encountered, by March 1993 MTV Europe's subscriber base increased 38 percent from the previous year to 46 million homes, having more than 8 million subscribers in Germany alone.[21] The channel has crafted a loyal audience of young people between sixteen and thirty-four in thirty-one countries.[22] Roughly three-quarters of European households receive MTV Europe through cable television, and a small portion of its audience views the channel via direct broadcast satellite or terrestrial broadcast television in some areas. MTV Europe is transmitted on rented transponders on Europe's Astra satellites.

Uneven construction of cable systems throughout Europe continues to dampen MTV Europe's expansion in certain areas. MTV thrives in countries with elaborate cable penetration like Germany and the Netherlands, but is seen by relatively few in countries with limited cable, notably Spain, Italy, and France, where less than one million households received the channel in 1992.[23] People in areas without cable can still receive MTV Europe and other program services if they buy a satellite dish, but this still remains prohibitively expensive for many. Ironically, even though the channel is based in London, MTV Europe's presence in the United Kingdom is limited because the country has few cable systems. Most of the 3 million who can watch MTV Europe in the United Kingdom do so through satellite receivers. Roedy's priority is to increase subscribers in these countries so that the channel becomes a truly pan-European service. MTV Europe is also moving beyond its namesake continent, with current service in Israel on cable and plans to operate in Lebanon and Nigeria.

MTV Europe only gets 10 percent of its revenue from subscription fees from cable systems, the remaining 90 percent from advertising sales.[24] This is quite different from the American MTV and other U.S. cable channels, which get a much larger proportion of their revenues from license fees paid by cable companies. Many cable systems and all individual viewers with satellite receivers received MTV Europe free as of November 1992. MTV's signal is unscrambled so that anyone with a satellite dish capable of receiving transmissions from Astra satellites can view the channel. MTV Europe's professed goal is to make all cable systems pay license fees for the right to carry the channel, but it acknowledges that only about one-half of the companies do so. MTV Europe was willing to let cable systems have the channel free in its early years while it was still developing an audience, but now pressures cable systems to pay. Although MTV's Roedy says confidently, "eventually everyone will be paying," the channel faces persistent conflicts with cable operators unwilling to pay, since European cable systems historically received programming free.[25] MTV Europe's most serious confrontation has been with cable operators in the Nordic region, which resisted MTV's demands for license fees.[26] In 1992, MTV Europe discontinued all of its contracts with cable systems in Sweden, Finland, and Norway and in March, the channel was dropped entirely from Norway after cable systems there were unable to reach an agreement with MTV over fees.[27]

Despite these disputes, MTV Europe claimed to be profitable for the first time in 1992, confounding pessimistic critics that questioned its ability to survive. During 1992, MTV Europe claimed to receive $60 million in revenues annually from 2,000 advertisers, including Wrangler, Pepsi, and Sony.[28] MTV Europe's objective is to create an audience throughout Europe that advertisers can reach to market their products across the continent. Advertisers like the German company Braun took advantage of this broad reach by making a generic ad for its appliance products to be seen all over Europe.[29] Yet, skeptics claim that few companies have sufficient resources to market their products simultaneously across an entire continent.

Media companies use MTV Europe to coordinate their marketing campaigns for new releases in films and music in Europe. Hollywood film studios, the largest advertisers on the channel, uses MTV to help establish a single release date for new theatrical films in Europe, with a simultaneous marketing campaign in European countries, which includes prominent ads on MTV. The major record labels, also heavy advertisers, have similar objectives, placing ads on MTV Europe to have a synchronous release of new albums by major artists in European countries. "There's no question record companies now take a great deal more care about coordinating pan-European releases since the advent of MTV Europe," concedes Muff Winwood of Sony Music.[30] These orchestrated pan-European campaigns on MTV promoting new films or albums treat Europe as an undiffer-entiated mass that can hopefully be herded to see a new film or buy a new com-pact disc promoted by an entertainment conglomerate. The one-size-fits-all ad-vertising is relatively uninterested in the distinctions or cultural differences of various countries, but simply seeks to sell a product on a regional basis.

Expansion in Eastern Europe and Russia

MTV Europe is taking full advantage of the collapse of the Soviet Union by ex-panding into Eastern Europe and Russia, bringing the milieu of consumerism with a rock beat. MTV's programming promotes materialistic fantasies that were staunchly condemned in the prior regime but today promote the acquisitive val-ues of the region's unbridled market economy. Bill Roedy, the chief executive of MTV Europe, who was also an U.S. army officer based in Italy as part of NATO, recognizes the irony of his current job, saying, "now I'm selling rock 'n' roll to the same audiences we once pointed missiles at."[31] Roedy also clearly understands the powerful ideological capabilities of Western popular culture that may surpass even the threat of blunt military force. "I used to say that had we spent all the money we invested in the Cold War on satellite TV and music, the Cold War would have ended a lot sooner."[32] Such observations recall Louis Althusser's dis-tinction between ideological state apparatuses (ISAs) that socialize people to ac-cept dominant value systems and repressive state apparatuses (RSA) that use coercive force to maintain order. Roedy seems to acknowledge that ISAs like the media are often more successful instruments of social control than RSAs like the military or police.

MTV's increasing presence in Eastern Europe paralleled the steady dismantling of communism in these nations in the late 1980s. MTV Europe began broadcast-ing its service to hotels in East Berlin just two days before the Berlin Wall fell.[33] By January 1990, MTV was available in limited areas of then East Germany and the company was negotiating with government officials to obtain partial carriage of the service on the country's sole national television channel.[34] The issue was rendered moot by the nation's absorption within the Federal Republic of Ger-many, which received the entire MTV service. After ample negotiations, MTV made modest incursions in other regional countries by January 1991, reaching 266,000 households in Hungary and a total of 212,000 homes in former Czecho-slovakia, Yugoslavia, Poland, and Romania.[35] MTV is even seen today in war-rav-aged Croatia, where a viewer called the service to request a video, asking them to get it on the air quickly because she was worried she might get shot soon.

Yet this sanctioned presentation of MTV on sporadic cable systems and televi-sion stations accounts for only a fraction of MTV viewers in Eastern Europe. Most people watch MTV through unauthorized means by directly pirating the unscrambled program signal carried on the European Astra satellite. Poland alone has more than one million dishes that can pick up MTV Europe, which clearly influences the music scene there.[36] Independent radio stations like Radio Zet in

Warsaw and Radio Fun in Cracow feature music on MTV's playlist, airing more rap in particular. Leszek Stefiej, a cofounder of Radio Zet, praises MTV effusively, saying "MTV is the only reason most people buy satellite TV. It's the only way people here have to keep up with the music."[37]

Yet praise for MTV Europe is far from unanimous as some in Eastern Europe raised concerns about U.S. and British music overwhelming their own culture and supplanting local musicians. Milan Smid, a media buyer from CSSR-TV in former Czechoslovakia, was skeptical of MTV's presence and a proposal by it and Super Channel, another satellite program service, to coproduce music videos with local organizations. "I fear a one-way street from West to East," he worried. "I don't think it's acceptable to be on the receiving end of so much Western music." However, such fears were voiced less often following Eastern Europe's embrace of a market economy.[38]

In the Baltic region, Lithuania's exposure to MTV Europe has been intricately bound up with geopolitical events and its turbulent relations with the erstwhile Soviet Union. Troops from the Soviet Union broadcast MTV throughout Lithuania after invading the country in January 1991.[39] The army took over the state-run TV station and aired MTV Europe for about six months, pirating the satellite signal. MTV tried to stop Lithuania from illegally showing the service, according to Tom Hunter, vice president of MTV's international programming, who said the company "asked them to turn it off, but when we found out the person in charge was a colonel in the Soviet Army..."[40] The Soviets continued to show MTV until the "Second Russian Revolution" led to the reinstatement of the independent Lithuanian government. Although many viewers wanted MTV back, MTV was not shown because the nation's media could not afford the price for the rights to the service, providing the country with an object lesson in the economics of cultural capitalism, where media products are available only to those that can purchase them.[41]

MTV gained increasing exposure throughout Russia as well between 1989 and 1994. In 1989, MTV reached an agreement with Gostelradio, the state agency in charge of all Soviet radio and television broadcasts, to begin a modest program exchange the next year.[42] The program service debuted throughout the greater Soviet Union on October 12, 1990, in an abbreviated format with a one-hour weekly show taken from two programs on MTV Europe, *The European Top 20 Countdown* and the *Party Zone*.[43] The hour of MTV was presented as part of a popular youth-oriented show titled *ViD*, an acronym for "Glance and Others" seen in 88 million households each week.[44] Andrei L. Rrazhash, director of *ViD*, gushed about MTV, saying "MTV's influence on our youngsters is enormous. It shows them new images, new ways of life, and the spirit of a society with much more freedom."[45] The potential influence also extended to ideas about consumerism. The MTV show had eight minutes of advertising per hour, becoming the first regularly scheduled program on Soviet television to ever have commercial sponsors. Companies including Benetton, Wrangler, L.A. Gear, and Renault advertised on the show even though their products were not available within the Soviet Union. The goal was to cultivate viewers' desire for these products and the lifestyle they represented, to increase possible future sales when these companies established their operations in the area. MTV's Tom Freston explained, "these advertisers are clearly seeking to increase awareness in anticipation of getting into a very major market."[46]

Yet as political and economic turmoil intensified in the region, Western sponsors dropped out of the program and MTV was presented on Soviet television commercial free. In March 1991, the program also switched to the American version of MTV resulting from copyright disputes involving MTV Europe. After the dissolution of the Soviet Union, MTV became more prominent on Russian television. In 1991, as Russia moved to embrace a capitalist economy, Leningrad launched private commercial television, including MTV Europe as the only non-Russian channel.[47] The city leaders of Leningrad praised MTV as a way for Russians to learn about Western culture, leading one to speculate about just what ideas and values a new viewer might glean from MTV. MTV seeks to expand its presence further, planning to debut a Russian program service.

MTV's expansion throughout Russia and Eastern Europe also helps the transnational record labels by promoting an interest in the American and British music marketed by these companies globally. All of the major labels expanded their activities in this region since the collapse of the Soviet Union. Most labels operate in Eastern Europe through licensees, local companies that are granted permission to market and distribute their signed artists' recorded music. As the labels grow in this region, MTV is likely to play a major role shaping popular interest in their wares. Yet, given MTV's inclination in its various services to emphasize U.S. and U.K. artists, this may limit exposure and publicity for home-grown acts in Russia and other regional countries.

MTV Australia and MTV Japan

MTV Australia is a more modest version of MTV that premiered on that country's National Nine Network in April 1987, airing six hours a week Friday and Saturday nights. MTV boasted that its Australian show was the most popular program on the continent, reaching more than 7 million homes, and it did have higher ratings than four local video shows in 1991.[48] Yet Tony Mitchell counters that MTV is watched less than *Rage,* an all night music video show presented by ABS, an Australian network.[49] MTV is more sensitive to the local music scene in Australia than in some of its other versions. MTV Australia plays music clips from Australian bands almost one-half of the time and has local personalities as hosts.[50] MTV executives may take greater care to respect indigenous music in its programming because Australia is particularly concerned about a cultural invasion by American artists, prompting government policies to nurture Australian musicians. Australia also has long had a vibrant music scene, nurturing local bands from the Easybeats in the 1960s to Men at Work in the 1980s, which received heavy play on the original American MTV in its early years. MTV likely plays some Australian acts on its services because they sing in English and the style of rock is fairly compatible with MTV's music format. MTV's major competitor, *Rage,* achieved notable success by playing a broad range of videos by independent local acts, encouraging MTV to do the same.[51] Mitchell reports that MTV plays few videos by black or non-Anglo Australian musicians and none by Aboriginal bands, but concedes that music by white American and Australian acts dominates *Rage's* playlist as well.

MTV has been far less successful in Japan than in other areas, having been canceled by two Japanese television networks for lack of audience interest. TV Asahi carried MTV for a few hours each week from 1984 to 1988, when it was first dropped, later reemerging on the Tokyo Broadcasting System (TBS) as a magazine-style show combining material from the American MTV with clips of Japanese artists.[52] TBS also gave sparse program time to MTV, airing the service a total of five hours a week at various times between midnight and 6 A.M. and drawing a meager audience of 100,000 households.[53] TBS canceled MTV at the end of June 1991 due to an unresolved dispute with the parent MTV, which wanted more program time in more desirable prime-time hours, a demand the Japanese network refused, claiming that MTV was unable to draw a sufficient audience in that time period. MTV Japan's failure was attributed to a crowded field: Japanese television had several other more successful music video shows such as *Space Shower* and *Sony Music TV,* a weekly program featuring the record labels' own artists. MTV's emphasis on American artists was also perceived as a failing because Japanese often prefer their own national artists over foreign acts, unlike other countries such as Germany.[54] A new offering, Music Channel, was conceived to fill the void left by MTV, established by Pioneer Electronic Corporation, TDK Corporation, and Tokyo Agency, an advertising firm. These companies negotiated with MTV to receive the Japanese broadcast rights to the U.S. version of MTV and resurrect its presence in Japan. Music Channel began operation in 1992 as the latest reincarnation of MTV in Japan, playing mostly foreign music.[55] By October 1994, Music Channel's performance was mediocre: Only 850,000 subscribers received the service on cable in a country where 99 percent of the 42.5 million homes had color television sets, and its influence in the music scene remained marginal.[56]

MTV Asia

MTV's parent, Viacom, became partners with Hutchvision, a satellite operator based in Hong Kong, to establish MTV Asia, which would be shown throughout the Far East.[57] For MTV, this project would enhance the program service's global reach. "Launching MTV in Asia is key to MTV's vision of being the world's premiere outlet for rock music and pop culture programming," explained MTV's

Sara Levinson.[58] This region was especially attractive for MTV because it included several countries like India and Indonesia that were increasingly open to commercial media ventures. MTV Asia was carried on Hutchvision's Satellite Television Asian Region Service (Star TV), the first pan-Asian satellite service with a transmission area covering forty countries and a population of over 2 billion.[59] MTV became one of five channels on this service, which also included news from CNN and BBC and sports. MTV Asia had a modest audience of about 500,000 when it was launched in September 1991 with the debut music clip of "Wild in the Snow," by Chinese rock artist Cui Jian, a popular performer in China whose songs deal with the loss of freedom. The service was promoted about a month before its launch on the MTV Roadshow, a two-hour program featuring music from the channel, which toured ten cities throughout the region, including Seoul, Taipei, Bangkok, and Manila.[60]

MTV Asia grew rapidly, reaching 13 million subscribers by July 1993 and developing a strong following of young people in Taiwan, Hong Kong, and India. The program service receives more than 350 calls a day from viewers, most from Taiwan and India, but also some from the People's Republic of China.[61] Most of India's viewers are in major cities where about 20 percent of the population lives.[62] In 1993 each of these three countries had about one million satellite receivers, with an annual increase of about 20 percent. Other countries in the area, Thailand, South Korea, and Hong Kong, have similar yearly growth.[63] China officially claims to have about 40,000 satellite dishes, but the actual number of dishes is believed to be up to ten times as many.[64] MTV and Star TV are officially banned in countries like China, Singapore, and Malaysia, but anyone with a satellite dish can receive the signal. China's government outlawed the sale and possession of satellite receivers by ordinary individuals in October 1993, but does not actively enforce this action.[65]

MTV sought to present itself as fostering global cultural diversity in music. "Our intention," claimed Star TV deputy chairman Richard Li, "has always been to offer a window to the world to artists in Asia and the Middle East, while at the same time creating an opportunity for audiences in the region to experience the talents of artists from around the globe."[66] Yet in its first year, MTV Asia did more of the latter, primarily presenting music clips from Western and U.S. artists. Roughly 90 percent of the music presented on MTV Asia was by U.S. and U.K. musicians like Paula Abdul, Phil Collins, and Michael Jackson; only a minimal 5–10 percent of its programming was devoted to Asian artists from the region.[67] MTV claimed that it played so few Asian videos because few were available. Most countries in the region had no music video production and the most India could contribute were musical excerpts from Hindi movies that were often in poor condition.[68] After the launch of MTV Asia, the situation improved as local record companies began to pay for the production of music clips for some of their artists; for instance, Magnasound India paid $5,000 to make a video for a Hindi rap musician. MTV now says that as much as half of its programming is devoted to Asian artists during certain times of the day.[69]

MTV Asia says that it tries to present programming that reflects the culture of its audience, a difficult task since the transmission area of the program service has spanned forty-two countries, twenty-one major languages and eight major religions.[70] Some question whether MTV is able to do this, one major transnational record label executive commenting that MTV Asia "is run almost entirely by expatriates, who are technically excellent, but who don't always seem to understand the various cultures well."[71] MTV segmented its programs according to time zone, targeting certain programs to a particular country during prime viewing hours in that area when young people in other countries were less likely to watch. For instance, MTV would air *Gone Taiwan* in the afternoon in Taiwan to attract Taiwanese teenagers while young people in India were still in school. MTV also started presenting videos in regional languages to attract specific national audiences, debuting in November 1993 a top 20 video countdown show of Mandarin-language videos popular in Taiwan and China.[72] Star TV also planned to offer Cantonese language broadcasting of MTV's music videos in Hong Kong in 1993 until government apprehensions about the company's foreign ownership delayed this action.[73]

MTV featured indigenous artists from major Asian countries, creating much popularity and success for these acts. Yet MTV Asia generally does not present artists that simply play traditional music from their native culture. Instead, MTV chooses to spotlight acts that combine elements of Western musical styles and genres with this indigenous culture, a practice very evident in the Indian acts shown on MTV. The Indian musician Khalid who plays Western style rock was introduced on MTV, prompting record sales of 150,000 albums, impressive sales for that area.[74] Indus Creed was featured after the band changed its focus from local ethnic music to a mixture of Western and native instruments.[75] Other fusion artists played on MTV Asia were Baba Seghal, India's first rap performer, and Apache Indian, which combined Bhandra, an Indian music genre, with reggae. MTV's choice of bands extends the historical pattern of cultural fusion of foreign Western music and indigenous Indian music genres that previously resulted from British colonialism. This synthesis of Western and Asian styles was also reflected in MTV Asia's VJs, the program hosts who were all Asian or part Asian. The VJs would present a breezy, offbeat Western style silliness while toning down the irreverence of American MTV hosts in deference to more authoritarian Asian cultures. Many VJs are also bilingual; Nonie Tao, host of MTV's *Most Wanted* show alternates easily from Mandarin to English with a Californian accent.[76]

Despite the multicultural style of MTV Asia, the program executives maintain that they are respectful of the host cultures of their audience and self-censor their programming to avoid insult or ridicule of these cultural traditions or values.[77] Nonetheless, some nations in the region like China and Singapore remain sufficiently wary of MTV Asia's content to forbid its distribution (even though illegal satellite reception exists).[78] Other countries that allow MTV, like India, still have reservations about its impact on the values of its young people. There is concern that a consumerist lifestyle glorified on MTV will subvert traditional cultural values.[79]

MTV Asia attracted both multinational and national advertisers seeking to reach Asian youth between twelve and twenty-five. This age group was targeted by MTV's programming with a total of forty five advertisers as of February 1993.[80] Multinational corporations, including Coca-Cola, Nike, and Levi Strauss, that were advertising on other MTV services followed the channel to Asia. For these companies, advertising on MTV was part of their strategy to develop a global market of young people for products like soft drinks and jeans. Record companies also took an interest, seeing MTV Asia as a forum for selling music in that region. Polygram Taiwan signed an advertising contract for $500,000 as part of a promotional campaign directed at China.[81] Besides direct advertising, MTV Asia's heavy play of videos by Western artists signed to major labels helped nurture and cultivate popular interest in these artists' recorded music. MTV's presentation of the video for Whitney Houston's "I Will Always Love You" helped make it the best-selling song in Asian history.[82] Some companies like Hindustan Lever, which sells products only in India, also advertised on MTV Asia to develop a national market. Other firms like Hong Kong's Giordano clothing, which tries to sell jeans in ads prominently featuring Chinese backpackers, advertise to reach a more regional audience. Local advertisers are less drawn to MTV, preferring traditional broadcasting for reaching a more specific audience.[83]

Rupert Murdoch purchased almost two-thirds of Star TV in July 1993, making a $525 million investment in the company.[84] The purchase was part of Murdoch's strategy to have a global television distribution network giving his media empire, News Corp., the ability to reach most of the industrialized world simultaneously. Besides Star TV, Murdoch owns the Fox TV Network in the United States and Sky Broadcasting Corporation, which presents satellite programming throughout Europe, and recently purchased an interest in an Australian television network. The purchase of Star TV created problems for the service in Hong Kong because the government there was disturbed by the prospect of Star TV being foreign owned, leading to a reevaluation of its transmission license and a delay in its plans to begin Cantonese language broadcasting.[85] In May 1994, MTV ended its partnership with Star TV, announcing plans to launch two twenty-four-hour MTV channels in Asia that it would solely own. "We feel the timing is right," said MTV's Tom Freston, "for us now to independently own and operate our business in Asia as we do in the U.S., Europe and Latin America."[86] MTV Mandarin debuted April 21, 1995, as a program service presented in Mandarin Chinese that is available primarily in Taiwan, Hong Kong, and China through an encrypted satellite signal.[87] The second service, a reborn MTV Asia, was also launched as an English-language channel broadcast to households in India and Southeast Asia. MTV's advertising for the channels claims that they will have "more localized programming than ever before."[88] Both of MTV's new Asian channels were picked up by Singapore Cablevision on June 1, 1995. In April 1995, MTV and Polygram announced a partnership to jointly own the new MTV Asia services and share the financial risk of the undertaking. Although the companies say that MTV is in charge of programming, Polygram will likely insist on using the program services to some extent as a promotional forum for the label's artists like U2 and Sheryl Crow.

After MTV severed its ties with Star TV, the Murdoch-controlled company changed the name of its music service to Channel V and increased its emphasis on local Asian artists. Channel V has two signals, Mandarin- and English-language programs, each reaching the same respective areas as MTV's planned services. Nicky Loiterton of Channel V says that the Star TV offering is more responsive to its viewers: "MTV is global, we're for Asia. . . . The difference between us is that MTV tells its audience what it wants. We let the viewers tell us."[89] Yet this claim deserves scrutiny given the purchase of one-half of Channel V by four major international record companies on January 6, 1995. Sony, EMI Music, BMG, and the Warner Music Group, four of the companies that plan a U.S. music channel, each bought a 12.5 percent share of Channel V totaling $30 million.[90] Despite Channel V's assurances of independence, it seems likely that these four major record companies plan to use this Asian program service as a vehicle to promote their own artists. Given its new owners, Channel V may indeed "tell its audience what it wants," namely the products of these four transnational conglomerates, whereas artists signed to local record companies will be ignored.

MTV in Latin America

MTV's presence in Latin America began modestly with *MTV Internacional,* a one-hour weekly show hosted by Daisy Fuentes, presented in Spanish and shown throughout the region via syndication as well as to Latino audiences in the United States on the Spanish language Telemundo network. Despite its Latino format, the show initially emphasized English-speaking videos, playing 70 percent of clips in English and only 30 percent in Spanish.[91] The producer, Barbara Corcoran, explained that the show primarily played English videos at its premiere because there were few Spanish-language videos made at the time. As more higher quality Spanish music clips were produced, the show shifted to a 50–50 mix of English and Spanish videos. By 1991, about 20 percent of the videos presented were by popular American artists like Madonna.[92] The playlist is varied and multicultural including such diverse Latino music as folk rock from Santo Domingo, guitar singers from Buenos Aires, and Chicano rap artists from East L.A. Keeping with its young, hip image, the show adheres to a "No Julio" policy, refusing to play videos by Julio Iglesias whose traditional ballads attract older audiences. *MTV Internacional* reached 10.6 million homes by August 1991, but contended with an increasing number of competing music shows like *Tu Musica* and *Bailando,* broadcast on the Univision Spanish-language network.[93] MTV also confronts extensive piracy in this region, according to Corcoran: "Beyond just stealing the signal, we've had people using our logo and creating their own shows."[94]

MTV Brazil was a more elaborate program service launched in that country in October 1990. The American presence in this MTV is strong, as most video clips played are by U.S. artists and many of the shows are imported from the original American MTV including *Yo! MTV Raps, Buzz,* and the video countdown shows, which also highlight U.S. acts.[95] Yet the channel, which has Brazilian VJs, does give some attention to its national music culture, airing some videos by popular Brazilian artists and planning a show, *Demo,* which would present certain music clips submitted by local Brazilian acts.[96]

MTV's most ambitious project to date in Latin America is MTV Latino, a full-fledged program service premiering October 1, 1993, which seeks to reach young people between twelve and thirty-four throughout the continent. At its debut, MTV Latino was available in about 3 million homes in twenty countries and territories including Mexico, the Caribbean, and Central and South America as well as parts of the United States with large Latino populations.[97] MTV says that 70 percent of the channel's viewers are in Argentina and Mexico, countries with more established cable systems. Although the VJs speak in Spanish, once again 70 percent of the videos presented are by English-speaking artists.[98] Tom Hunter, an MTV vice president, gave a familiar explanation for this imbalance, saying "there's not a lot of videos being done in Spanish, but as we've gone into each new region, video production has increased, and we hope that will happen again in Latin America, particularly in the U.S."[99] MTV's Sara Levinson says that the network wants to eventually have about 50 percent Latino music depending on audience preferences.[100] However, MTV Latino does not intend to play indigenous regional music like salsa, banda, or merengue, whether or not videos are made, a decision that annoys local and regional record companies that want a major media outlet like MTV to play native music.[101] Hunter responds to this criticism saying that MTV Latino "is about rock and pop. . . . We feel we should confine ourselves to MTV-style artists," identifying such Western acts as Bon Jovi, Depeche Mode, Peter Gabriel, Aerosmith, Madonna, and Michael Jackson.[102] The channel continues to follow this policy: Eight of the ten top music videos played on MTV Latino in December 1994, which received heavy exposure, were English-language songs by major label Anglo-American and U.K. artists including Sting, Bon Jovi, Nirvana, Aerosmith, and Madonna.[103] In 1994, the service generally played four English-language videos for every one Spanish-language clip, far below MTV's supposed objective of parity between these two types of videos.[104] MTV Latino will present some Latino acts, but only those with crossover appeal and that incorporate Western style rock into their music like Maldita Vecindad, Soda Stereo, and Caifanes, whose video for "Aqui No Es Asi" was one of only two Spanish-language songs in the channel's top ten at the end of 1994. MTV Latino plans to add more Spanish-language programming on the channel, but some of this will simply be shows from the U.S. MTV that are dubbed in Spanish, like *Beavis and Butt-head*. MTV Latino's advertisers are similar to those in other MTV services, which seek a global audience of young people to buy their wares. The advertisers, says Hunter, "are the usual suspects in the categories we've been very successful with around the world—movies, beverages, jeans, sneakers, candy."[105]

A major focus of MTV Latino will be Mexico, where about 800,000 homes received the channel at its premiere. This was not the first time Mexicans could view an MTV program, as the American MTV was originally offered on Cablevision, a Mexican cable company, in 1986.[106] However, MTV was dropped from the system allegedly because the Mexican president's wife objected to the excessive sex and decadence depicted on the channel, fearing it would encourage promiscuity and immoral behavior.[107] The American MTV resurfaced on another cable system, Multivision, which was less susceptible to government influence. The new MTV Latino offers the appearance of a more culturally indigenous program, although the emphasis on English-speaking American artists undercuts this impression. Mexico's Televisa network seeks to offer some substantial competition for MTV, planning to launch two Latino music channels, La Puerta and Nuestra Musica.[108]

MTV's International Youth Culture

MTVN's most far-reaching strategy for its program services is the attempt to develop and exploit an international youth culture. MTV executives acknowledge the skeptical industry argument that indigenous cultural differences of people from various countries could undermine the success of a program service designed for an international audience. Yet, MTV claims that young people from disparate countries are part of an emerging international youth culture that transcends any national cultural identity. MTV sees pop music as a key element in this culture, constituting a common denominator of youth in all countries. An MTV executive referred to the company's internal research, which concluded that although there were cultural differences among European countries, "young people around the world tend to be interested in the same kinds of things, and that includes music and television."[109] Thus, it was argued, the presentation of music on television would be an ideal form of programming heartily embraced by young people in all cultures throughout the world. "Music is the global language," proclaims the channel's Sara Levinson. "We want to be the global rock 'n' roll village where we can talk to the youth worldwide."[110] Tom Freston's characterization of this transnational youth relies heavily on a shared affinity for popular consumer products: "This is the first international generation. They wear Levi's, shop at Benetton, wear Swatch watches and drink Coca-Cola. This is not to say there aren't cultural differences, that the French aren't different from the Germans. But a French teenager and German teenager are much more similar to each other than they are to their parents."[111] Freston believes that there is a "world pop culture and sensibility among 12–34 year olds" who "have a viewpoint, attitude, consumer habits that have been shaped by the last 25 years of technology."[112]

Yet Freston's description of this youth culture seems based solely on the value of consumerism, where young people define themselves purely in terms of what they purchase whether it is Levi's jeans, a Benetton sweater, or a Swatch watch. And MTV's music videos and promotions tend to encourage this commoditized conception of self. "What bothers me about MTV is it represents consumption as identity," worries communication professor Pat Aufderheide, "the way that you define yourself as a consumer. The way that you become real to yourself is by purchasing the right song, assuming the right attitude."[113] MTV encourages young people around the world to embrace a consumerist way of life, rejecting alternative values, traits, or traditions as a part of their self-identity. MTV presents a blizzard of appealing consumer products both in traditional commercials and the music videos themselves that entice young viewers in the United States, South America, Asia, and Europe with a homogeneous, consumerist lifestyle.

Encouraging young people to accept this acquisitive culture serves MTV's economic interests. MTV wants to provide a program service that will attract the world's youth in order to assemble a receptive, pliable worldwide audience that can be sold to transnational advertisers seeking to reach this demographic audience on a global basis. A program service successfully targeting youth throughout the world would be much sought after by advertisers seeking to expand their share of the world market for specific consumer goods of interest to youth, including jeans, designer clothes, watches, and soft drinks. Moreover, such a program service could benefit these advertisers and itself by attempting to subtly define this transnational youth culture—and one's inclusion within it—in terms of the acquisition of fashionable consumer products advertised on the service, much as Freston does.

MTV's Global Advertisers

Coca-Cola is particularly aggressive in using music video as a vehicle to promote global sales of its soft drinks among young people. The company paid $1 million in 1986 to acquire the sole sponsorship rights to the *World Music Video Awards*.[114] The show was truly global since Rupert Murdoch's News Corporation aired the program on his various media outlets around the world, including the Fox Network in the United States and satellite Sky Channel in Europe. William Lynn, Coca-Cola's vice president for corporate media worldwide, was ecstatic, saying "it has the opportunity to be a major TV event and to pull together the world's youth, as Live Aid did."[115] Hoping to leave no doubt about Coca-Cola's participation, the show was called *The Coca-Cola World Music Video Awards* and the Coke logo was placed on all promotional materials for the show. More recently, Coca-Cola signed an agreement in January 1992 with MTV and CNN to place ads on its various program services reaching viewers in 100 countries on six continents.

MTV's Harvey Ganot described the deal as "a pioneering effort by Coca-Cola. . . . Coke is ubiquitous and it makes sense for Coke to try this type of thing."[116] Clearly Coca-Cola considers music video programs and MTV in particular as a desirable forum to shape young consumers' desire for its products on a global scale.

Cultural producers like Hollywood film studios and major record labels that seek to develop global markets for their wares increasingly use MTV to coordinate and organize their marketing campaigns for films and recorded music on a global basis. Both the studios and labels want to move toward releasing and distributing new products simultaneously around the world, eliminating the traditional lag between a debut in the United States and other countries. For instance, new Hollywood films that premiere in the United States are often shown in Europe or Asia several months later. The studios want to use popular global media like MTV to promote a new film around the world through commercials and related music videos featuring songs from the soundtrack and clips from the movie playing simultaneously on all of MTV's sister services. Then, people around the world would ideally be primed by this global campaign in which MTV figures significantly to go see these movies at their local theaters. At this point, the Hollywood studios are in the early stages of engineering this calculated global operation by using MTV Europe for promotions to synchronize the release of films in Europe with their U.S. debut, eliminating the past lag time.

Major Record Labels' Global Marketing Campaigns

The transnational record companies also want to establish this coordinated global marketing effort debuting new albums by their superstar artists everywhere concurrently. This desire to develop a more integrated global market is heightened by the increasingly centralized control of the record business by six transnational conglomerates like Germany's Bertelsmann and Japan's Sony, which perceive this market in worldwide terms and further have the extensive, far-reaching resources to pursue this grand objective.[117] These record labels now pursue centralized strategies to market a new album worldwide in a coordinated manner. For example, at EMI, dozens of executives from around the world meet for strategy sessions where the company tries to figure out how to market EMI's artists' compact discs and cassettes in thirty-eight countries from Europe to the Far East. Jim Fifield, the president of EMI Music, a division of Thorn-EMI, claims that his company as well as the other majors are becoming more adept at this effort:

> Each of the multinational companies is getting increasingly more efficient at exploiting music globally. For instance, we can now pick a date and release a superstar album in dozens of countries simultaneously and successfully coordinate a marketing plan with common advertising and video and packaging all over the world. That didn't go on five years ago. It's a completely different ball game now.[118]

Rudi Gassner, president of BMG Music International, agrees that as the record business seeks to develop sales, overseas companies will adopt more global marketing campaigns. The labels also seek to develop international marketing campaigns for their video music titles. Adrian Workman established a worldwide market for BMG videos, selling these in more than thirty countries.

The record labels have made significant progress toward having more simultaneous marketing campaigns. For example, there used to be a nine-month time lag for U.S. albums to be released in Hungary. Now, the labels have adopted a single worldwide release date for albums to be sold everywhere, like Prince's *Diamond and Pearls* and Simply Red's *Stars*.[119] The major labels want to eliminate this time lag because the delay encourages illegal piracy of popular albums in regions outside the United States. The pirates sell unauthorized copies of the album in areas where the authentic record label version is not yet available. In order to have this coordinated marketing and stem piracy, the record companies establish a presence in countries either by negotiating a licensing agreement with a local company to manufacture and distribute their albums or by opening their own branch office to perform these tasks.

The labels are more interested in developing a global market for recorded music in part because the U.S. business is somewhat stagnant, whereas sales outside of the United States are expanding rapidly. In contrast to worldwide sales that grew 10.2 percent in 1990 over the previous year to $24 billion, U.S. shipments of recorded music fell 11.08 percent for the first half of that year.[120] According to the Recording Industry Association of America (RIAA), the U.S. market remained sluggish in 1991 when unit sales of recorded music including compact discs and cassettes dropped 7.5 percent over the previous year to 801 million from 866 million in 1990 (although actual sales for 1991 rose 4 percent).[121] The U.S. share of the global market for record sales has shown a long-term decline expected to continue for some time. The International Federation of the Phonographic Industry (IFPI) reported that the U.S. portion of recorded music sales dropped from 34 percent in 1986 to 31 percent in 1991 and was expected to decline still further to 24 percent by 2000.[122] The United States is no longer considered the primary market for the major record labels as sales in other regions continue to increase relative to the United States, especially the European Community, which accounted for 35 percent of recorded music sales in 1991, surpassing the United States.[123] This changing composition led the record labels to enhance their global marketing campaigns outside of the United States. As EMI's Jim Fifield says, "executives aren't just thinking about getting albums on the [U.S.] *Billboard* chart anymore."[124] Instead, the six major labels expect to be marketing planetary hit albums by the year 2000.[125]

In this brave new world of music, the United States is distinctive not as the primary market for sales, but instead as the major producer of music. A majority of the world's music sold in the global record business is by English-speaking

American artists. The dominance of U.S. acts extends far beyond their home country as 60 percent of the $18 billion sales in 1991 outside of the United States was from sales of music by U.S. acts.[126] The major labels consider it essential to maintain their U.S. subsidiaries largely to supply the rest of the world with music by American acts. Al Teller, chairman of the MCA Music Entertainment Group, explains that "in order to keep feeding the overseas infrastructure that the conglomerates have put in place, it's imperative to have a healthy American record operation. American rock and pop music are by far the biggest sellers overseas."[127] Michael Dornemann, chairman of the Bertelsmann Music Group, concurs, saying, "the U.S. is very important because it is here where you have the talent and here where you have the trends."[128] This raises the concern that the record labels' primary strategy in this global market is to continue to shower American music on the rest of the world rather than foster a reciprocal multicultural exchange. Other label executives say they hope to introduce the U.S. public to music from other countries in their promotions. Yet, Teller's and Dornemann's remarks seem to support the apprehensions of many developing countries about becoming inundated with American music and other cultural products.

Global Cooperation Between MTV and the Labels

MTV has been crucial in helping the major record labels exploit this global market for music, which is heavily dominated by American music. Although MTV seeks to depict music in general as an integral part of an international youth culture that it presents on its global program services, the company refers more precisely to a very narrow, restricted portion of the world's music. MTV's focus is confined largely to certain genres of pop and rock music produced and distributed by the major transnational record companies. A *Billboard* survey of the U.S. MTV program service discovered that almost all of the videos played in a sample twenty-four-hour period were by artists distributed by the major record labels.[129] Further, the survey of other MTV services discussed in this chapter illustrates that most of these programs strongly feature popular Western acts signed to the major labels. These sister services are likely to rely heavily on videos of artists signed to major transnational record companies given MTV's longstanding cooperation with these labels (discussed in Chapter 4).

In this regard, MTV plans to cooperate with the major record companies to coordinate promotion strategies on a global scale for the labels' recording artists. As Lee Masters, executive vice president and general manager for MTV and VH-1, explains, "We are planning to have 'planetary premieres,' in which we will premiere a clip simultaneously in all countries that we're in at once, and really do a job in marketing or breaking an artist worldwide."[130] This nicely parallels the major labels' desire to have integrated worldwide marketing campaigns with new albums released simultaneously throughout the world. MTV and the record companies then can shape the contours and direction of popular music globally by featuring certain selected artists (usually American or British) in new videos that are prominently played on the MTV services.

A One-Way Flow of Music and Culture

Cooperation between MTV and major record labels prompted concern that the channel's emphasis on U.S. and U.K. artists signed to these labels may exacerbate the global dominance of music from these Western countries at the expense of artists from other regions. MTV may intensify the one-way flow of music and popular culture from these Western nations to other countries, eclipsing and marginalizing indigenous music. MTV's play of major label artists may also strengthen these transnational companies by stimulating sales of their artists' recorded music, while undermining local and regional record companies whose artists are often denied this valuable exposure. MTV Europe is criticized by local record companies outside of the United Kingdom for ignoring French, German, Italian, and Spanish artists, instead devoting most of its time to English-speaking Anglo acts.[131] A similar complaint is made against MTV Latino, which plays 70 percent English-speaking music clips in a Spanish-speaking region. MTV's Tom Hunter admits that the channel will not play regional music because it does not fit in with the "MTV style." MTV Asia, also prominently featuring American acts, only seems to play Indian artists if they adopt Western music genres like rock and rap.[132]

The introduction of MTV along with other satellite program services into some countries previously sheltered from Western media also raises concerns about the values and ideas presented in the content. In India, for instance, this programming prompted a controversy about whether the consumerist values celebrated in the shows and commercials should be embraced in Indian society or rejected as incompatible with traditional beliefs and values. Rajiv Desai, a spokesman in India for Star TV, which carries MTV, claims that satellite television in the country marks "the dawning of a global consciousness" in India that will encourage more demands for consumer products.[133] He claims that a younger generation exposed to these shows will reject the socialist political orthodoxy of their parents. "Now, his children are going to say, 'I want to go the Mediterranean, I want fast cars.'"[134] However, Mehesh Praad, India's Secretary of Information and Broadcasting, counters that these programs foster unattainable consumerist fantasies, claiming that satellite TV is "giving [poor people] dreams which cannot be fulfilled. It can create social tensions."[135] Ads for overseas vacations and fast cars become somewhat irrelevant and counterproductive in countries that struggle to feed their population. In the past, the public broadcasting network in India has prohibited ads for products like jewelry, to quell divisive values of greed and acquisitiveness. In contrast, MTV actively promotes such feelings in commercials and video clips featuring luxurious consumer products. India worries about the corrosive influence of this programming on its society, says Praad: "Our own so-cial ethos, our cultural values—we would not like them to be subverted."

MTV executives claim to be sensitive to the cultures of their host countries by censoring program content that would challenge the core values of these cultures. For instance, Darren Childs, MTV's programming director in Hong Kong, ex-plains that MTV Asia attempts to respect the region's faiths. "It is really a simple question of being sensitive to religions. For example, we wouldn't show slaugh-tering a cow in India or nudity in Muslim countries."[136] MTV Asia enforces these standards in large part to avoid a political backlash against the program service in these countries that might lead to its banishment.

MTV rejects charges of cultural imperialism saying that its program services instead foster a robust cultural diversity of American rock combined with the in-digenous music of the host country. Tom Hunter claims that MTV programs have a mix of local music and international hits, such as MTV Europe, which is pre-sented in English but plays many videos by British and European singers signed to independent labels.[137] MTV's Tom Freston says that "MTV would never work if you just took music tailored to the American audience and put it into a differ-ent country. It requires some significant changes. Yes, the music is always rock-and-roll based, but the selections are different country to country."[138] Yet this means that MTV still presents primarily U.S. acts but varies their play from coun-try to country. A majority of clips on many MTV services are by U.S. artists signed to major labels. Moreover, the channel often ignores local and regional music, only playing indigenous artists if they perform within the rock genre. And, as Freston concedes, "Rock, at its roots, is an Anglo-American art form."[139]

Alternatives to MTV

There are alternatives to MTV around the world that attempt to preserve and pro-mote a country's own artists and musical culture, most notably Canada's Much-Music. MuchMusic is a cable program service that cofounder John Martin de-scribes as a "mainstream rock 'n' roll station" with specialized programs like *RapCity, Soul in the City,* and the country tinged *Outlaws and Heroes.*[140] The channel actively features Canadian artists, exceeding government regulations that require at least 30 percent Canadian music, not a difficult task according to exec-utives, given the abundance of talented Canadian musicians like Bryan Adams, k.d. lang, and Rush.[141] MuchMusic, owned by CHUM, is a successful venture that changed from a pay-TV operation to a basic cable service in 1989 and also launched a sister service in Quebec, MusiquePlus, a French-language channel whose music playlist has a greater French and European influence.[142] The channel strongly supports local music video production by subsidizing a fund to produce videos for Canadian artists called VideoFACT, the Video Foundation to Assist Canadian Talent. MuchMusic allocates 5 percent of its revenues to this fund, with contri-butions of more than $500,000 a year.[143] Independent Canadian artists submit a storyboard and detailed budget for a prospective video to VideoFACT, and if approved, MuchMusic pays for half of the production budget. By late 1989, 219 videos were partially financed through this program, including a video for k.d. lang.

Canadian record companies, most of which are subsidiaries of multinational firms, also underwrite the production of videos for possible airing on MuchMusic or other national shows like CBC-TV's *Dan Gallagher's Video Hits* and *Good Rockin' Tonight*. Canada had extensive music video production in 1992 although budgets for music clips were rather meager, with an average of $30,000 to $40,000, somewhat less than budgets in the United States.[144] Don Allen of Revolver Films said that budgets were half what they were in the late 1980s, forcing producers to make exciting, provocative videos for less.[145] The budgets for videos financed by regional and national record labels that are independent are much smaller than those underwritten by the major transnational record companies. However, these independent labels receive funding from VideoFACT and the Foundation to Assist Canadian Talent on Records, part of the federal government's Sound Recording Development Program.

The Canadian government remains firmly committed to policies designed to nurture Canadian artists and curb U.S. influence in the realm of music video. Besides content regulation requiring program services like MuchMusic to present a certain proportion of Canadian music in its programming, the Canadian Radio-Television and Telecommunications Commission (CRTC), the primary regulatory body for the country's electronic media, also enforces a preference for Canadian music video program services over American programming. In June 1994, the CRTC issued a ruling declaring that the U.S. service Country Music Television (CMT) that was available in Canada would be replaced with a domestic service playing country music called the New Country Network (NCN). CMT filed a petition with the Canadian Federal Court of Appeal in November 1994 to challenge CRTC's decision, but the court upheld the ban and the new Canadian service took CMT's place the following January.[146] The New Country Network plays about 30 percent videos by Canadian artists in each twenty-four-hour period. CMT retaliated against its dismissal by banning Canadian artists that do not have contracts with U.S. record labels from its own program service in the United States and Europe. Tony Gottlieb of the record label 1-800-COUNTRY based in Nashville claims that the ban unfairly discriminates against independent record labels since artists signed to huge conglomerates with U.S. subsidiaries are exempt: "The CMT decision is clearly biased in favor of large companies."[147] The Nashville Network, a U.S. program service featuring country music that is still available in Canada, is not taking part in the boycott. In May 1995 the U.S. government threatened to retaliate against Canada if it does not restore CMT, by implementing trade sanctions against several Canadian businesses operating in the United States, including Cineplex Odeon Corporation, a theater chain based in Toronto, and the cable service MuchMusic. MTV is also not welcome in Canada, a source of irritation to the channel's Tom Freston: "It's easier for us to operate in Vietnam and Lebanon that it is to operate in Canada. Canada's about the only country in the world we have a problem operating with."[148]

Jamaican television also provides prominent exposure of music clips for its local musicians. Since 1987, a majority of music clips on television present the music of Jamaican artists whereas only 20 percent to 40 percent of clips aired feature international music.[149] This emphasis on indigenous music is due primarily to the policies of the Jamaica Broadcasting Corporation (JBC), the operator of the country's national television station, which has been committed to emphasizing local musicians and nurturing the country's rich musical traditions such as reggae. The JBC established a committee including members of the Jamaican Federation of Musicians and JBC executives to develop guidelines for the selection of music clips to be aired on the station. Prominent among these guidelines was a desire to present more clips by local artists.

A cross-cultural study of popular music around the world conducted by the International Communication and Youth Consortium (ICYC) research group found uneven support by national television in various countries for music clips by local musicians. The ICYC study, which relied on data from personal interviews with 220 local musicians from eight countries and eighteen case studies on music industries in different countries, found that some countries like Nigeria and Jamaica with a rich history of indigenous popular music provide heavy play of their artists on television.[150] Television stations in these countries often use music clips as a filler between programs. Yet musicians in South Korea say television stations in that country rarely if ever present local performances. Television in the Netherlands offers some shows with local musicians, but music featuring local acts is overshadowed by a much greater emphasis on international music by a ratio of five to one. The Italian program *Videomusic,* operating for several years as a terrestrial service, presents a mix of national and international videos.[151] In general, a substantial portion of the musicians interviewed for the ICYC study were involved in music video production: "Over half the Hungarian and Dutch musicians, about one-third of the Americans and Nigerians, and roughly a quarter of the Canadians and Jamaicans had made videos."[152] These music clips were usually produced on very limited budgets and rarely aired on television. Instead, the videos were made solely for promotional purposes and sent to record labels in hopes of getting a recording contract.

The primary emerging threat to MTV's dominance of global music video programming is not alternative national programs, but instead far-reaching plans by the major transnational record labels to develop their own global music video channel. Viva, a German-language music service, was launched by four of the six major labels in Germany in December 1993 and was available to 90 percent of the 1.3 million cable households by February 1994.[153] TimeWarner, Thorn-EMI, Sony Music, and Polygram decided to create Viva in part because of their dissatisfaction with MTV Europe, which played few clips by German artists that the labels wanted to promote.[154] Although Viva promised to feature German artists, the channel's playlist for the first few weeks played only two German acts out of fourteen in the heavy rotation category, the rest being familiar U.S. and U.K. acts played on MTV.[155] These labels also sought greater control over the distribution and exhibition of their music clips. In late 1994, the record labels' Viva channel was collaborating with other prominent national music television stations in Europe, France's MCM service, the Scandinavian channel Z-TV, and Italy's *Videomusic,* to share programming and resources to more directly challenge MTV Europe's success on the Continent.[156]

After Viva's premiere, these labels began talks about expanding their foray into music video programming to develop a global music video service that would directly compete with MTV.[157] In February 1994, the same four record companies along with Ticketmaster, the ticket sales agency, announced they would combine their resources again for a music video program service in the United States to compete with the American MTV and VH-1.[158] Another major label, Germany's Bertelsmann, joined this consortium of record companies as a part owner of the new service in June 1994 after its own joint venture with Tele-Communications to launch a channel combining music video and home shopping was abandoned.[159] (The plans for a U.S. music channel were dropped in 1995, although some major labels including Warner, EMI, and Polygram may try again to create a music video network in the United States in 1996.) These major labels are also trying to gain control of major exposure media by purchasing large shares of existing music channels. In January 1995, four major record companies purchased one-half equity in Star TV's Channel V in Asia and the labels TimeWarner and Thorn-EMI each made bids for 25 percent to 30 percent of the Italian program service *Videomusic.*[160] Despite the growing mutual antagonism, record companies are not opposed to direct collusion with MTV services when it suits their purposes: Polygram's purchase of part of the new MTV Asia services in April 1995 provides the label with a reliable platform to promote its artists throughout this continent into the twenty-first century. This pattern of acquisitions may prompt a growing concentration of control over existing major music channels throughout the world by major record labels and their parent transnational conglomerates.

ᨈ   ᨈ   ᨈ

As MTV continues to expand, concerns about its contribution to a one-way flow of music and culture grow more urgent. MTV's networks lavishly play and promote U.S. and U.K. artists, giving scant attention to local musicians in the countries where MTV is offered. MTV Europe, the most successful and far-reaching of MTV's international services, features American artists in two of every three clips it plays, giving European acts as little as 15 percent airtime. MTV only appears to play music clips by native artists if they parrot Western genres of rock, jettisoning indigenous musical styles. Moreover, MTV increases the clout and cultural power of major transnational record companies by largely limiting its playlist to artists affiliated with these labels. Such a playlist undercuts regional and local record companies unable to promote their own acts on the channel. Smaller record companies in Latin America and Europe complain that MTV does not play their artists' music (although independents in the United States make a similar charge, suggesting that MTV in the United States and elsewhere only plays music affiliated with major labels). Beyond music, MTV's programming is permeated by a relentless commercialism that attempts to nurture an international youth culture based on ideals of consumerism (buy these clothes, buy that compact disc to define your self-identity), contributing to an erosion of indigenous culture, values, and traditions.

Fortunately, some countervailing trends have led music video program services to provide modest exposure for local and regional musicians outside of the United States. As music video becomes more popular, local record companies fund the production of music clips for their artists although their meager financial resources limit the number of clips they can make. Once music video production for local acts blossoms, MTV plays some of their clips—as long as the artists conform to U.S. rock music styles. The emergence of other music video programs besides MTV also provides an alternative forum for indigenous artists' clips. Public policies in a few nations such as Canada, requiring a certain proportion of native artists to be presented on media outlets, further ensures that home-grown musicians will be featured there.

Despite the obvious benefits MTV provides the transnational record labels, these parties' relationship is complicated. There is cooperation between the record companies and MTV to promote these labels' signed artists on a global basis as MTV heavily plays these acts' videos, presents their concerts, and features them in contests and promotions. MTV also helps to undermine possible regional competition to the major labels by ignoring offerings from local record companies. Yet the large record companies seem irritated by MTV's periodic modest displays of independence from them: In the United States the labels are worried by MTV's decreasing play of music videos in favor of traditional programs without clips, like game shows and talk shows, whereas in Europe these companies are dismayed by MTV Europe's challenge to the established collective system for licensing videos that may lead to decreased royalty payments to them for exhibition rights. The record labels are also uncomfortable with MTV's swaggering dominance in music video programming: BMG filed a complaint with the European Commission in 1994 claiming that MTV used this control over programming to retaliate against the company by banning all videos by BMG artists on MTV Europe during a dispute over royalty fees between MTV Latino and BMG.[161]

Yet the underlying reason for the major labels' discontent with MTV may be the limited control they possess over the program service, leading major labels to launch their own music video channel. Whenever possible, large cultural producers like record companies and film studios seek direct control over the distri-

Promotion Department
5500 Central Avenue
Boulder, Colorado
80301-2877
Telephone 303 444-3541
Fax 303 449-3356

A Division of
HarperCollins*Publishers*

▰ WestviewPress

Here is your complimentary review copy:

MONOPOLY TELEVISION: MTV'S QUEST TO CONTROL
THE MUSIC

JACK BANKS

PUBDATE: June   5, 1996   (hc) $ 69.00
                                   (pb)   19.95

Critical Studies in Communication & in the
Cultural Industries

To Order: P.O. Box 588 • Dunmore, PA • 18512-0588 • 1-800-331-3761 bution and exhibition network to guarantee sufficiently broad exposure of their product. Governments periodically restrict such direct control through owner- ship because of the potential for anticompetitive practices, such as the U.S. Jus- tice Department's decision requiring film studios to sell their theater chains in the late 1940s. However, a global trend toward deregulation of media industries pro- vides an opportunity for cultural producers to acquire and create exhibition out- lets without state interference, regardless of the consequences to cultural diversity or open competition. This may have prompted four of six major record labels' plans to create their own music video channel, Viva, to provide a showcase for their own music in Germany with the ultimate objective of expanding this ven- ture into a global music service. Here, the record labels would be able to promote and publicize their music however they desired without having to contend with MTV as a semi-independent intermediary.

The ultimate success of this venture is uncertain though, because although the labels control access to music clips, MTV is already firmly established in many countries with a core audience for its programming. Further, despite the deregu- latory mood, the grandiose plan may arouse some governments' apprehensions about the legality of this scheme under existing antitrust provisions, since the la- bels would be in a position to promote only their music while excluding other record companies' acts. MTV complained to the European Commission about Viva, charging that the labels' ownership of the channel provides it with an un- fair advantage over MTV since the labels control the production of videos. MTV also sued five record companies and a performance rights organization, claiming they act as a cartel establishing excessively high fees as a group for MTV's access to videos. As discussed in Chapter 4, the U.S. Department of Justice began inves- tigating the major labels' plans to launch a music video channel in this country in July 1994, examining if the proposed channel would prompt anticompetitive practices by the labels.

MTV exemplifies the growing globalization of popular culture and moreover is a key agent fostering this trend. Large cultural producers of various media (the- atrical film, television, and recorded music) seek global audiences for their offer- ings. MTV's worldwide network of services encourages the emergence of this global market both through its program content and advertising. In terms of pro- gramming, music video clips presented on MTV are a hybrid of film, television, and music, so that the clips themselves can promote these cultural products glob- ally. For instance, music videos often feature songs from film soundtracks in- cluding short clips from the film in the video. The film-related video played con- currently on MTV's services shapes and nurtures audience interest in the film everywhere MTV is shown. For record companies, MTV's play of certain genres of Western popular music helps create a global audience for this music. Music video is at its core a type of advertisement for cultural products: films, film soundtracks, recorded music, live concerts, fashion apparel depicted in the clip, and even the music clip itself as a home video retail product. Omnipresent play of music videos on MTV (and elsewhere) shapes global demand for this array of products. Certainly globalization strategies did not originate with MTV: Film studios, television producers, and record labels have been pursuing global markets for some time. But MTV clearly advances such trends.

Besides the videos, conventional ads on MTV's services serve to promote a more integrated global market for consumer goods targeted toward young people. Coca-Cola, for example, uses advertising on MTV and music video shows to reach this worldwide audience of young people to attempt to shape demand for its soft drinks. MTV's plans to develop an international youth culture based on consumerism provide a receptive audience to advertisers seeking to sell their products to upscale youth everywhere. With the demise of the Soviet Union, MTV has become part of the vanguard in incorporating this region into the emerging global market, preparing the way for manufacturers that wish to expand their operations there. MTV's programs and advertising act to create desire and anticipation for consumer products before they are actually available, in regions recently converted to a capitalist economy so that demand for products will exist when companies start selling in these areas. Companies advertised on a version of MTV in the former Soviet Union even before their products were available there for this reason. As mentioned earlier, MTV began transmission in the former East Germany just as the Berlin Wall fell, MTV made inroads throughout Eastern Europe as these countries were embracing a market system, and it became the first non-Russian channel introduced in Leningrad when the city introduced commercial television. Clearly MTV and music video are influencing the emerging global economy as well as the contours of a global popular culture—what remains uncertain is the role played by MTV in molding a global consensus about the shape of this economy and culture.

6

MTV's Corporate Intrigue and Sagging Ratings

Corporate Acquisitions of MTV Networks

Viacom's Purchase of MTV Networks

MTV Networks has always been a subsidiary of a major media conglomerate. This chapter examines Viacom, the current parent firm of MTV, and how it influenced MTV's strategic policies about its program services and related ventures. Despite the success of MTV Networks in the early 1980s, its original parent companies, American Express and Warner Communications, sought to sell the company in 1985. In September, a group of investors dominated by top MTV executives tried to purchase the company, but were outbid by Viacom International by $80 million.[1] Viacom, a conglomerate with interests in television production and syndication, radio and television stations, and cable programming and franchise systems, sought deeper involvement in specialized cable program services. In November, it acquired two-thirds interest in MTV Networks with its three basic cable program services from Warner Communications, which earlier had bought out American Express's interest. In this transaction, Viacom also purchased from Warner the one-half interest in the pay movie services, Showtime/The Movie Channel, which Viacom did not already own. Viacom purchased the remaining one-third equity interest in MTV Networks from publicly traded shares in March 1986. Press reports estimated that Viacom paid Warner $690 to $694 million for the entire purchase, although Warner Communications' 1985 annual report said that Viacom paid "$510 million in cash and short-term notes, plus additional consideration."[2] Viacom borrowed extensively to finance the purchase, leaving the company with a long-term debt of $1.1 billion at the end of 1986.[3]

The purchase agreement included a provision protecting MTVN's and Showtime/TMC's program services from future competition by Warner. Viacom's Form 10-K to the U.S. Securities and Exchange Commission (SEC) for 1985 vaguely alluded to provisions for cooperation between Warner's cable systems and Viacom's newly acquired program services, most likely providing terms for guaranteed distribution of the services on Warner's franchises for a limited time.[4] Viacom also disclosed that Warner agreed not to compete with "the subscription pay and basic cable businesses of S/TMC and MTVN for a period of three years after the closing."[5] This was not a problem for Warner at the time because after Viacom's purchase, Warner's only remaining cable interests were its franchise systems. However, after this three-year period, Warner became a direct competitor of Viacom in cable programming when it merged with Time. TimeWarner's HBO competes with Viacom's Showtime/TMC in the pay cable market and its Comedy Channel briefly challenged Viacom's HA! before the two firms merged their services into the jointly owned single offering, Comedy Central.

After acquiring the program services, Viacom restructured its corporate organization by creating the Viacom Networks Group, comprising the seven basic and pay cable program services of Showtime/TMC and MTVN. The acquisition greatly expanded Viacom's cable holdings, making the company one of the largest owners of specialized cable program services. The purchase also created a significant degree of vertical integration between programming and distribution through Viacom's extensive cable system holdings. This integration provided Viacom with guaranteed substantial distribution of its program services, including MTV and VH-1, because the company was the tenth largest multiple system operator (MSO) in the United States in 1988.[6] Viacom can also use its extensive domestic and international television syndication business to distribute the programming of these services in many other forums.

Sumner Redstone's Acquisition of Viacom

Two years after purchasing MTV Networks, Viacom itself was acquired by Sumner M. Redstone through his closely held company, National Amusements, which owns a chain of movie theaters in the United States and United Kingdom. Although Viacom is a publicly traded company, Redstone's National Amusements owns an overwhelming 83 percent of Viacom's stock.[7] Redstone, the chairman and controlling shareholder of National Amusements, purchased Viacom in a leveraged buyout for $3.2 billion in June 1987, thwarting a failed attempt by high-level Viacom executives to buy the company for $2.9 billion.[8] Redstone convinced a consortium of banks to lend him $2.1 billion to finance the acquisition.[9]

The bank loans, mainly high interest junk bonds, plunged Viacom even further into debt with a long-term debt of almost $2.2 billion in 1988, more than double the amount owed the previous year.[10] The loans had restrictive covenants greatly circumscribing Redstone's control over broad corporate policy and largely prohibiting further acquisitions by Viacom.[11] Redstone once remarked that the only action he could take without bank approval was to change the pronunciation of the company name from VEE-ah-com to VY-ah-com. Further, the banks loaned

Redstone the sum on the condition that his company repay $450 million in interest payments within two years.[12]

Favorable business conditions enabled Redstone to raise needed cash to meet Viacom's immediate financial obligations and eventually renegotiate better loan agreements. After cable subscription rates were deregulated in 1987, the market value of cable systems greatly increased so that Viacom could sell its Long Island and Cleveland systems for more than twice their 1985 estimated value.[13] Viacom also owned the syndication rights to the extremely popular television show, *The Cosby Show,* which generated millions of dollars of revenue from local television stations. Further, Viacom was helped by MTV Networks, which became quite profitable. The substantial increase in revenues allowed Redstone to renegotiate Viacom's bank loans in 1989, signing a ten-year unsecured bank agreement for $1.5 billion with better terms that lowered interest rates and removed the more severe restrictions on corporate policy, giving Redstone greater control over Viacom. In January 1992, Viacom revised its credit agreements, increasing the company's line of credit and delaying principal loan payments until 1995.

Yet despite Viacom's increased revenues and Redstone's enhanced power, the company is still deeply in debt and its activities are closely monitored by lenders. The company had a hefty total debt of $2.3 billion in January 1992.[14] If Viacom's fortunes should change and its cash income sharply decline, the company's banks would likely reestablish a tight rein over its affairs. Moreover, Viacom's highly leveraged position makes the company less likely to finance MTV Networks' expansion plans should this division become less profitable. However, this scenario has not occurred as MTV Networks remained "one of Viacom's best-performing sectors," according to *Billboard,* with revenues of $394.8 million in 1991, an increase of 14 percent over the previous year.[15] Redstone appreciates MTV's financial importance to Viacom, conceding, "I still don't like the music [on MTV] but I've become enamored of the economics."[16]

Viacom made its largest acquisition ever purchasing Paramount Communications, another media conglomerate, on March 11, 1994, for about $9.7 billion in cash and stock.[17] Paramount's board of directors accepted Viacom's offer in February after a protracted, acrimonious five-month takeover battle with QVC Networks, the home-shopping channel run by Barry Diller, which also wanted to buy Paramount. Viacom originally agreed to a friendly takeover of Paramount the previous September, which Diller's QVC contested with a counteroffer, leading to a series of lawsuits, corporate maneuvering, and escalating offers, ultimately forcing Viacom to pay $2 billion more than its original offer for the company.[18] The merger made Viacom the second largest media conglomerate in the United States after TimeWarner. Most prominent among Paramount's wide assortment of holdings were its film studio, Paramount Pictures, book publisher, Simon & Schuster, Madison Square Garden, the New York Knicks basketball team, and the New York Rangers hockey team. Viacom had two main allies in its takeover bid that contributed to the purchase price in exchange for shares in the company: Blockbuster Entertainment, the video rental chain, offered $1.8 billion, and Nynex, the Bell Telephone company serving the Northeast, pledged $1.2 billion for the acquisition.[19] Viacom later acquired Blockbuster and its chain of video rental and music stores. To reduce the bloated debt it had incurred from the acquisitions, Viacom sold off parts of Paramount that did not fit with its vision of becoming an integrated media conglomerate, most notably Madison Square Garden and the sports teams, which were sold to ITT Corporation in 1995.

The extended battle for Paramount sharply depressed Viacom's stock, diminishing the value of the company. Viacom's class B nonvoting shares were $28 the day the merger was announced, a drop of almost 53 percent from September 11, 1993, when Viacom revealed its original offer.[20] Sumner Redstone's own holdings in Viacom shrunk from $6.6 billion before the merger attempt to $2.85 billion after it succeeded. Redstone alienated some powerful figures in the course of this merger, notably Marvin Davis, the chairman of Paramount, who was excluded from takeover plans after QVC's hostile bid and forced out of the company, and John Malone, the head of the largest U.S. cable company, Tele-Communications, who was sued by Viacom for Tele-Communication's alliance with QVC. Redstone dominates the new merged company, controlling 61 percent of shareholder votes, and installing Frank Biondi as the firm's president and chief executive in 1987.

Soon after the merger, Viacom abruptly fired Simon & Schuster's flamboyant chairman, Richard Snyder, raising the issue of the autonomy of former Paramount subsidiaries. Although Viacom blandly said that Snyder was let go because of incompatibly different management styles, critics suggested that the major reason for Viacom's disapproval was Snyder's staunch independence.[21] A Viacom advisor said the company objected to his attitude toward the parent firm, which was "Let me run the place, see you next year."[22] Viacom wanted a more compliant, submissive executive who would implement the parent firm's directives without dissent.

Viacom planned to mandate more cooperation among its own divisions and the various subsidiaries of Paramount through joint ventures and cross-media promotions. Viacom plans to take advantage of its newly diverse interests in film, publishing, cable television, and broadcasting to produce more coordinated campaigns to market a concept, artist, or program affiliated with the company's subsidiaries. Moreover, these "synergy" plans are likely to involve MTV, already established as a major promoter of various media products. For instance, MTV can heavily play videos featuring songs from the soundtrack of Paramount films with clips from the movie to entice MTV viewers to go see it. The film might also be featured on MTV's movie show, *The Big Picture* or *The MTV Movie Awards,* or VH-1's *Flix*. A current young hip author for Simon & Schuster might be given extensive airtime on MTV's news and talk shows or VH-1's entertainment shows. After the Paramount takeover, Viacom executives were anxious for MTV to develop films for Paramount's studio and books for Simon & Schuster that would appeal to the channel's young audience.[23] The additional acquisition of Blockbuster provides even more possibilities for coordinated cross-media promotion strategies. Blockbuster's chain of video rental and music stores can be used to sell a variety of MTV Networks' products. Beavis and Butt-head video games are prominently featured in Blockbuster stores and MTV-related compact discs and cassettes can be given prime display space in its retail music outlets. MTV and VH-1 can also promote certain acts in their programming that are featured in Blockbuster music stores to increase sales. Viacom formed a task force in December 1994 to consider launching its own record label, which would take this synergy in the music business a step further: Viacom could sign its own recording acts, feature them on MTV and VH-1, and promote their releases in Blockbuster music stores, the third-largest music retailer in the United States.

After purchasing MTV Networks, Viacom directly influenced the broad corporate policy of the company by encouraging it to exploit ancillary markets related to its video music programming, including program syndication, home video sales, licensed retail products, and international program services.[24] John Reardon, past president of MTV, depicted the role of ancillary activities using an analogy: "I like to think of MTV as the hub of a wheel—the strength, the core of the structure. Each spoke radiating off that hub is either a business or a potential new business that relies upon the hub for its strength."[25] Viacom executives often sought to develop these ancillary markets by applying its long-established, strategy of synergy, where a media product is developed jointly by corporate divisions in different media markets. For instance, programs produced by MTV Networks for presentation on MTV could be syndicated to other markets by Viacom Enterprises, its program distribution subsidiary. In its 1985 annual report, the first after MTV's purchase, Viacom emphasized this sort of cooperation, reporting: "MTV: Music Television and Viacom Enterprises are collaborating on syndication in early 1986. . . . *MTV Top 20 Video Countdown,* a weekly series, is being sold jointly on a barter basis by MTV Networks and Enterprises. . . . More such joint projects between MTV Networks and other Viacom operating units are planned."[26]

This synergizing strategy was made possible by Viacom's involvement in a variety of related media markets as well as the company's vertically integrated structure, active in all stages of program production and distribution. After Redstone's acquisition of the company, this policy was also strongly advocated by Frank Biondi, Viacom's chief executive officer, who promoted more active cooperation among subsidiaries and plans for joint ventures by these divisions. Biondi revealed that in 1994, Viacom executives developed more than 140 ideas for projects involving coordination among the company's various subsidiaries. Only five or six of these have been publicly revealed.[27] Stuart Rossmiller, director of Fitch Investor Services, reported that Viacom's subsidiaries are indeed becoming more integrated. "You are now looking at a company where the three moving parts, MTV, Blockbuster and Paramount, are being coordinated."[28]

MTV also increasingly develops and markets a wide range of retail products that feature the channel's logo and personalities, hoping to trade in on its hip cachet. MTV wants to do for teenagers what the Walt Disney Company accomplished with younger children, using trademark characters to spin off endless consumer goods targeted to its loyal audience. Yet, whereas Disney markets clothing with Mickey Mouse's smiling face and home videos of classic movies like *Cinderella* for young kids, MTV sells video games featuring Beavis and Butt-head overcoming obstacles through the use of bodily gases and considers publishing a sex manual for teens. The channel sells a series of *MTV Party to Go* compact discs and cassettes that include music played on the channel. MTV began peddling products in February 1995 through its new mail order publication, the MTV Merchandise Catalog, which features products like CDs from its *MTV Unplugged* performances, videos from its programs, video games, coffee mugs, and T-shirts promoting such shows as *Headbangers' Ball*. In yet another example of synergy, the catalogs will be distributed in Viacom's Blockbuster music and video rental stores. MTV is also developing home-shopping programs to sell these licensed goods on its own services. Also on the drawing board in 1995 is a proposed tourist attraction in Manhattan with a Beavis and Butt-head ride.[29]

Viacom's aggressive demand for MTVN to develop ancillary markets was prompted by several factors. Viacom's particular media holdings naturally encouraged such exploitation because its subsidiaries could easily cooperate with MTV Networks in joint ventures to develop new markets. Yet, Viacom also wanted to pursue this policy because its takeover of MTV and later acquisition by Redstone left the corporation deeply in debt and quite anxious for its subsidiaries to cultivate new sources of revenue to help pay off its loans. The additional debt taken on after the Paramount acquisition increased this need for quick cash. Further, MTV Networks needed to develop other areas because the company's primary business in U.S. cable programming was reaching a plateau as most of the country became wired with cable.

The Decline of Video Music in the Mid-1980s

MTV Ratings Decline

After MTV's launch in August 1981, public interest in the program service and video music increased steadily until 1985 when the widespread infatuation with this new media form abruptly subsided. The severe decline in MTV's 1985 audience ratings led industry analysts to speculate whether music video was to be a short-lived fad and MTV 1984's "Cabbage Patch doll."[30] MTV's ratings peaked in the last quarter of 1983 with a 1.2 rating, representing an audience equivalent of 1.2 percent of all households able to receive MTV at that time.[31] The channel's ratings remained consistently strong throughout 1984 with an average rating for the year of 1.0, equivalent to 246,621 television homes.[32] In a letter to *Rolling Stone*, Bob Pittman boasted that "no basic-cable network had a higher rating than MTV in any quarter except the first quarter of 1984."[33]

However, this heady success was cut short the following year when A. C. Nielsen's ratings for MTV plunged dramatically to a 0.6 rating for MTV for the fourth quarter of 1985, representing a decline of more than 30 percent of MTV's audience from the previous year.[34] Even more alarming, MTV lost much of its core audience, losing 20 percent of eighteen- to twenty-four-year-old viewers and 25 percent of twelve- to seventeen-year-olds.[35] MTV challenged the Nielsen ratings, claiming that its survey methods underreported the channel's audience by excluding large groups of MTV viewers in such places as college dorms and bars. The program service's ratings remained stagnant at 0.6 from 1986 to 1989 with minor variations, although the total number of subscribers able to receive the service steadily increased throughout the late 1980s. The ratings decline had an immediate and sustained impact on MTV's advertising revenue, which dropped from $74.4 million in 1985 to $71.4 million in 1986 and still further to $65.7 million in 1987.[36]

MTV's problems were attributed to various causes. Some suggested that video music was simply a short-lived fad and that MTV's drop in ratings demonstrated waning interest in this novelty. MTV executives and others claimed that viewers were repelled by the channel's increasingly conservative programming. Whereas MTV featured new music by unknown artists with unique visual styles in its early years, the channel played more Top 40 music as it became more successful. MTV's playlist increasingly resembled that of commercial radio, which ironically MTV had derided for its stale sound several years earlier. Tom Freston conceded that "MTV had become boring."[37] A general slump in the recording industry also affected MTV. The Record Industry Association of America (RIAA) depicted sales for 1985 as "flat," with a 4 percent decline in records and a modest 2 percent increase in cassettes shipped to retailers from the previous year. The sluggish sales and lack of any blockbusters hurt music video shows, which depended on the record industry's offerings. Further, many new artists that MTV had heavily promoted in its early years and helped make video stars, including Duran Duran, Culture Club, and Adam Ant, were declining in popularity by 1984, and the channel had no new acts to take the place of these fading stars and sustain viewer interest. MTV also sorely missed Michael Jackson's favorable influence on the channel, which achieved its highest ratings during late 1983 and early 1984 when it was playing Jackson's wildly popular video, *Thriller*.

MTV's Strategies to Revitalize the Channel

MTV developed several strategies to stem the ratings slide. In October 1985, MTV launched a "multimillion" dollar advertising campaign with the slogan, "Some People Just Don't Get It," replacing the original refrain of "I Want My MTV!" The campaign was based on a series of commercials with the new slogan featuring comical characters who expressed their disapproval of MTV, including a television evangelist, a conservative businessman, and a Soviet official.

MTV executives modified the channel's music format on several occasions. These repeated music playlist shifts vacillated between total rejection or ecstatic embrace of heavy metal, hard rock, and more pop-oriented Top 40, as the channel attempted to find a desirable music mix that would attract viewers. When MTV's ratings declined in early 1985, Bob Pittman announced that the channel would sharply curtail play of heavy metal, deriding this genre as uncreative and "a quick, crass, easy buck for record companies."[38] In October 1986, MTV sought to restore its image as a "leading edge" rock music station by increasing play of new rock acts and eliminating softer pop and rock music by artists like Paul McCartney and Lionel Richie, shifting that music over to VH-1. By 1987, MTV moved away from Top 40, and heavy metal was back as the channel's most favored genre with groups such as Cinderella and Poison receiving massive exposure on MTV. An MTV executive said that playing Top 40 and soft rock music alienated its viewers and "damaged its credibility with its core audience of rock 'n' roll fans."[39]

Despite MTV's much-publicized return to an exclusive rock format, the channel began introducing Top 40 dance music into its playlist and launched *Club MTV,* a daily dance music show, by late 1987. MTV's format gradually shifted once again to embrace current top hits. The program service drastically cut its playlist to feature extensive play of a limited number of hit videos by popular artists like Madonna and Janet Jackson. By 1990, although MTV played more than 300 different video clips each week, only about thirty of these videos, usually featuring popular acts, received two to six plays each day.[40] MTV's Abbey Konowitch explained, "We want to bet on the winning horses. We want to get behind those that can sell millions. We want to get behind those that will be big stars."[41] New and emerging artists became a casualty of MTV's contemporary hits format, as videos by these aspiring artists received light play at late night hours. Major record labels were irritated and confused about MTV's frequent changes, leaving them unsure about the channel's actual format.

The program service also altered its programming strategy for presenting video clips. Since its debut, MTV had adopted a radio-style format in which random music videos were played continuously throughout the day. In 1988, MTV abandoned this approach and instituted a "dayparting" format, where videos were segregated according to musical genre and presented in distinct programs at different times of the day according to viewer habits.[42] For example, videos featuring dance music were included in *Club MTV,* the channel's dance show, which aired in the early afternoon when young girls were watching. Other specialized programs included *Yo! MTV Raps* and the *Headbangers' Ball,* featuring heavy metal video clips. MTV's Konowitch said that the specialized shows presented at specific times let viewers watch their own musical preferences.

MTV's dayparting format was part of a broader movement away from Bob Pittman's original conception of MTV as a nonnarrative, continuous flow of programming and toward more conventional television programming with shows of certain defined lengths. Although video clips increasingly were presented in genre-specific shows, MTV also began to present other programs without video clips like the comedy shows *Monty Python's Flying Circus, The Young Ones,* and *The Monkees.* MTV produced more of its own non-video clip programs, including the successful off-beat game show, *Remote Control,* and the *MTV Half-Hour Comedy Hour.* The channel developed programs based on mutations of traditional television genres such as news, sitcoms, talk shows, or game shows that captured MTV's hip and irreverent style. MTV increased its production of new shows with little or no video music, spending about $60 million on new programming in 1990.[43]

Although MTV embraced more conventional shows to increase its ratings, the programming shift was prompted by other considerations as well. Television shows with a certain length and a structured beginning, middle, and end are more attractive for advertising since these programs generally draw viewers for the entire length of the show. In contrast, MTV's original programming, consisting of an endless stream of video clips, encouraged viewer "grazing" habits, where one would watch a few video clips and then switch to another channel. This viewer grazing intensified with the widespread diffusion of remote controls and was a source of concern to MTV's advertisers who feared that grazing viewers were not watching commercials. One of its newer shows, *Beavis and Butt-head,* actually performs the "grazing" for the viewer by showing the characters watching brief excerpts of music clips and mock television shows, aimlessly changing channels with their remote control. The more conventional programs also let MTV syndicate its shows like *Remote Control* to other media outlets, a major goal of its parent firm, Viacom.[44] Finally, MTV was concerned when some record companies announced their intention to decrease video clip production (discussed later in this chapter). Faced with a possible cutback, MTV sought to develop alternative sources of programming to fill its schedule. As MTV continued to introduce new programs, the record companies worried that it was decreasing its emphasis on music video and thus diminishing the promotional value of the clips for the labels.

The channel made other changes to improve its sagging ratings, including firing all of the original five vee-jays whom MTV's Lee Masters described as "symbolic of no change."[45] The vee-jays were replaced by new personalities, including Julie Brown, a British black woman who previously hosted a morning U.K. television show, and Kevin Seal, a performer with a permanent smirk. The program expanded its music news coverage, hiring permanent news announcers and launching a daily news show. MTV also changed its visual presentation, abandoning studio sets in favor of shots of the vee-jays matted onto constantly shifting bizarre backgrounds. The channel's changes had mixed results: Although the audience decline was halted, MTV's ratings roughly stagnated at 0.6 throughout the rest of the decade.[46]

Record Label Decrease in Video Music Production

In early 1986, the diminished interest in video music extended to the record labels, several of which planned to reduce their video music production in response to the "production excesses" of prior years.[47] Alvin Teller, then president of CBS Records and a frequent critic of MTV, said, "This beast was out of control. I was looking at a ton of money being spent on videos, many of which were no good."[48] Many labels discontinued the practice of automatically providing videos for all of their artists. Instead, record companies would only commission video clips for acts likely to get on MTV and a few other major programs. For those artists granted video clips, the record companies began to limit the number of videos produced from an act's current album. Record labels also implemented more stringent constraints on expenses by limiting budgets for video clips, which had already been stagnant for the last few years. This retrenchment was not unanimous though, as RCA Records and Warner Brothers said there would be no production cutbacks at their labels.

Some record labels said that despite their investment, many videos did not provide the expected promotional benefits for new artists. Amy Stanton, A&M Records' associate video producer, explained that her label was becoming more selective in commissioning videos because, "In the past, we've wasted a lot of money on videos that didn't work and didn't help sell records, and we obviously want to avoid that this year."[49] The inferior, shabby quality of many videos being produced made the labels reluctant to continue funding them. The failure of the retail market for music videos also contributed to the record labels' reluctance to continue financial support for a product that was generating little or no direct revenue.

The labels' cutback can be viewed as part of a comprehensive strategy to rationalize their investment in video music in order to increase their long-term profit and create a stable market. The record companies limited the supply of videos while simultaneously exploiting this finite number of clips more thoroughly in many venues. This strategy limited production expenses and enhanced direct profits generated through program license fees and retail sales of clip compilations as well as indirect profits from the clips' promotional value encouraging sales of related music products. This practice of limiting production costs while exploiting a product in primary and ancillary markets through product recycling is an established policy of cultural producers, most notably Hollywood film studios and television production companies.

Despite earlier declarations of cutbacks, the record labels remain firmly committed to video music. In 1994, record companies claimed to spend about $150 million a year on clip production. Record label reliance on music video is so extensive that video clips are considered a necessity for a record to achieve commercial success in the pop market. While eighty-two of the top 100 current hits listed in *Billboard*'s "Hot 100" record chart had accompanying videos in May 1986, a period when some labels were more skeptical of video, this figure rose to ninety-seven of the top 100 hits with videos by December 1989.[50] In 1989, some record labels like Chrysalis Records and Motown Records, with reputations for aggressively cultivating and promoting new artists, expanded their video music departments to help establish their emerging acts.

Resurgence of MTV

MTV successfully revitalized itself, enhancing both its financial position and its prominent role within American popular culture. Although the novelty of music video is surely gone, MTV has survived. The major record labels still consider MTV to be the single most important media outlet for promoting new artists and selling compact discs and cassettes. In 1993, Capitol Records executives said that the debut albums by acts Blind Melon and Radiohead became successful largely because of their exposure on MTV and regional video music shows.[51] The labels also continue to believe that MTV helps their established stars. Jeff Gold, A&M Records vice president, claimed that his label sold "millions more Janet Jackson records" because of the channel's heavy play of her videos.[52] MTV and its sister services retain impressive power to influence the direction of music by what videos they decide to play. Yet some labels worry that this influence stifles diversity within popular music since MTV has a rather narrow playlist of videos featuring popular songs by established artists, ignoring music clips by emerging acts signed to independent record companies.

MTV's ratings remain stagnant. In February 1993, MTV was available in 57 million households but had an average audience of 0.5 percent of these, or less than 300,000 homes.[53] MTV still draws a young audience as one-third of the channel's audience are adolescent viewers between twelve and seventeen and 55 percent of the audience are eighteen- to thirty-four-year-olds.[54] In late 1992, MTV's audience dropped by 17 percent, some attributing the decrease to the loss of women viewers repelled by the channel's emphasis on rap and heavy metal music, not to mention these genres' videos' often demeaning, degrading images of women.[55] MTV's total subscriber growth has tapered off considerably compared to its sister services. In early 1993, MTV's growth slowed to 4.1 percent over the previous year to 57.4 million homes, whereas VH-1's reach grew 6.1 percent to 47.2 million and MTV Europe leaped 37.5 percent to 44.7 million homes.[56] MTV's sluggish expansion over the past few years occurred because it has already saturated the U.S. cable market.

MTV Networks, including MTV, VH-1, and MTV Europe, has growing profits and revenues, becoming an important financial center for its parent firm, Viacom. MTV alone increased its revenues to $411.4 million in 1991, 18 percent over the previous year. Sixty-two percent of this increase was due to advertising sales and 31 percent was attributable to increases in affiliate fees from cable companies.[57] Major advertisers also demonstrated their commitment to MTV and its related services over the long term, with Proctor & Gamble signing a deal in 1990 with MTV Networks for $50 million in advertising sales.[58]

In its programming, MTV continues to move toward a more conventional schedule with traditional television-style programs. Besides an attempt to stop viewers' "grazing" habits, these shows are part of MTV's strategy to expand beyond music clips to become a complete "lifestyle" network for the young, presenting programming on a range of topics of interest to its audience. MTV Networks now spends about $150 million a year on new programming for its services, developing new series and specials.[59] MTV produces all of its own programming in its own facilities with low-cost talent and production staff. MTV and Viacom avoid standard Hollywood practices that lead to higher expenses by not using more costly talent agencies, production companies, or writers employed by Hollywood film studios and television networks.[60] If actors or performers demand higher salaries, Viacom and MTV are likely to replace that talent, as Viacom did with the star of the syndicated series *Superboy* a few years back. MTV Networks also economizes by repeating its programs frequently, leading Mike Rubin of the *Village Voice* to complain that "not only are most of these offerings bad, they're rebroadcast and recycled constantly; a typical programming day has nearly as many reruns as Nick at Night."[61] MTV also launched a new company, MTV Productions, that will develop new programs for syndication on traditional broadcast television and feature films for theatrical distribution.

The channel received widespread publicity and hefty audiences for some of its recent shows like *Unplugged,* a series of concerts by musicians using acoustic instruments without electronic amplification. Ironically, the show's popularity stemmed in part from a backlash against heavily produced acts like Milli Vanilli, which had a distinctive image in music videos played on MTV, but little or no authentic musical talent. The shows spawned several successful *Unplugged* albums by artists like Eric Clapton and Mariah Carey, featuring music from their concerts. *The Real World* is a real life soap opera in its third season featuring seven people from diverse backgrounds who live together in an apartment with ever-present cameras recording all their actions. A different group of roommates in their twenties is assembled each year and the show has shifted its locale annually, inhabiting apartments in New York City, Los Angeles, and San Francisco so far. Early on, the show featured a fair amount of voyeuristic sexuality, with ample shots of women jiggling in tank tops, but more recently was commended for a sensitive portrayal of an HIV-positive gay man's life and relationships.

Beavis and Butt-head is an animated series that received much notoriety in the press for its depiction of two teenage male morons who watch music videos and make lurid, inane remarks and sounds. The show is frequently mentioned as a classic example of eroding public taste in the United States and gained attention for encouraging young viewers to imitate actions portrayed on the show, like setting fires or being cruel to animals. In one tragic incident, a five-year-old boy in Moraine, Ohio, set a fire killing his two-year-old sister, his mother claiming that he started using matches after regularly watching *Beavis and Butt-head,* whose characters frequently talked about playing with fire.[62] MTV denied responsibility for these copycat acts, but did decide to air the show later in the evening and remove all references to fire. As for special events, MTV continues to heavily promote its awards shows, having Roseanne host its eleventh annual *MTV Video Music Awards* in 1994 and cultivating tie-ins with theatrical films in the younger *MTV Movie Awards*.

The channel still rotates its VJs to keep in touch with its young viewers, firing Martha Quinn (again) and Julie Brown for being over thirty and replacing them with younger personalities like Karyn Bryant, Adam Curry, and Steve Isaacs, who themselves gave way to names like Kennedy, Duff, and Bill Bellamy. To attract viewers the channel emphasizes personalities in its shows, like Cindy Crawford in the fashion-oriented *House of Style* and Jon Stewart, who hosted a talk show before leaving MTV to offer his show on broadcast television through syndication. Pauly Shore, who hosted the summer show *Totally Pauly*, was a frequent presence on MTV until he also left to pursue movies, after his moderate success, *Encino Man.* Known for calling attractive women "nugs," Shore's segments on MTV involved stunts like going up to a woman in a bar saying "I like your cones, I think they're really cool."[63] Dan Cortese, a reporter for MTV Sports, was known primarily for his "BK TeeVee" commercials for Burger King, which tried to make The Whopper hip and stylish for the MTV set.

MTV expanded its news department over the past several years with reports on current events in music, popular culture, and politics of interest to MTV's young audience. Although it stumbled in 1989 with a daily thirty-minute show, *News at Night,* which was canceled after six months, the channel still presents a daily ten-minute show, *The Day in Rock,* and a thirty-minute weekend wrap-up, *The Week in Rock,* with anchors Kurt Loder and Tabitha Soren. These shows provide a mixture of record company boosterism, relaying fluff about an artist's latest video or album, and more penetrating analysis of issues affecting the young like AIDS, sexuality, hate crimes, and homelessness. These social concerns are also infrequently addressed in more depth in MTV "rockumentaries," which apply music video's frenetic visual style to a newsworthy topic. MTV increased its news programs in part because these provide a more respectable image to the channel for large "blue-chip" companies, which were reluctant to advertise on the channel in the past because they did not want their corporate image to be associated with the sexually explicit videos MTV usually shows.[64]

In 1992, MTV News for the first time had extensive coverage of the U.S. presidential campaign with its own unique, irreverent style, such as sending rocker Ted Nugent to cover the Republican convention. MTV News followed the progress of the campaign, which included Tabitha Soren's interviews with George Bush, Bill Clinton, and Al Gore. The channel sponsored a series of "Choose or Lose" meetings between viewers and presidential candidates, the first of which featured ninety minutes of Bill Clinton answering questions from young people about issues like AIDS and gay rights. MTV's executives claimed that the channel's extensive coverage encouraged young people to become engaged in politics after a prolonged period of apathy. "I'd like to think that MTV is helping to make politics cool again," said Tom Freston, in a self-congratulatory burst.[65] MTV's Judy McGrath pointed to a 20 percent increase in voting by eighteen- to twenty-four-year-olds in the 1992 election, reversing a twenty-year decline, suggesting that MTV's "Choose or Lose" campaign was partially responsible.[66] MTV became acknowledged as a political force during the campaign season with Al Gore saying at the MTV Inaugural Ball, "Thank you, MTV! Thank you for winning this election. You did it!"[67] Critics express mixed opinions about MTV's new political beat: MTV received some praise from the traditional news media, winning a Peabody award for its campaign coverage, yet others dismiss its superficial, frivolous reports. Christopher Georges also claimed that MTV's coverage was blatantly biased toward the Democrats, providing complimentary reports on Bill Clinton, while highlighting flaws and failures of the Bush Administration.[68] Yet for all its irreverent flourish and jazzy visuals the coverage could be considered profoundly conservative and establishment-oriented by confining its attention to the two traditional political parties and one billionaire independent, largely ignoring alternative parties and movements, much like the traditional U.S. news media.

MTV's perpetual changes in programming and music are not simply an attempt to increase its ratings but also intended to enhance its identification with young people in its target audience. MTV constantly tries to feature personalities, music, and "lifestyle" shows that appeal to teenage and college-age viewers. In this strategy, MTV refuses to "grow older" with its audience as it ages, but constantly reorients itself to what is hip for today's young, discarding viewers in their thirties who are turned off by the cutting edge of youth culture—they are shuffled over to the less rambunctious VH-1. MTV's constant play of Nirvana and its heavy coverage of Kurt Cobain's death can be seen as the program service's attempt to identify with the young, labeled by the media as "Generation X." MTV used the importance of Cobain to young people as a way to try to establish itself as the voice of this generation. After Cobain's demise, MTV continually replayed Nirvana's "Unplugged" concert, the band's videos, and MTV News reports on the tragedy to fuse a connection between the symbolic importance of Cobain, hyped as "the poet of his generation," and MTV.

MTV Networks' Future: Multiplexing, Home Shopping, and Videos for Tots

MTV and its parent companies are developing several strategies to extend and expand its music video programming to larger audiences, hoping to gain even greater control over this market. MTV announced plans to split its single program service into three separate channels with distinct music formats. The cable industry refers to this type of expansion as "multiplexing," after the multiplex theaters that offer several films in one establishment. MTV and other cable services like HBO, Showtime, and ESPN are taking advantage of technological advances in cable and satellite communications to multiplex their programming: Transponder compression would allow MTV to transmit three program services via satellite transponder in the space of one without additional cost, and upgrades to fiber optics provide more cable systems with greatly expanded channel capacity to carry additional MTV channels. "Television is fragmenting just like radio," said MTV's Freston. "This is a move on our part to specialize and then sell a larger combined audience to our advertisers."[69] MTV planned to begin a trial run of expanded offerings on selected Cablevision systems in Massachusetts in late 1993. Cable systems would be offered the current MTV service and two new channels with specialized music formats, one of which was expected to adopt a contemporary black music format competing head on with BET.[70] MTV presents specialized shows featuring black genres of rap, dance, and up-tempo R&B, which may be a prelude to a full-fledged MTV sister service. VH-1 may also eventually expand to three channels as well, presenting various music formats of interest to its older audience.[71] This strategy reflects the growing fragmentation of popular music and culture, prompting increasingly specialized program services reaching ever more narrow audiences. Moreover, the plan is a clear indication of MTV's desire to control the entire spectrum of popular music presented on television. MTV Networks put its multiplexing plan on hold by 1995 because it could not persuade cable operators to carry these new program services due to a lack of available space on their systems. MTV may likely return to this plan for expansion for itself and VH-1 in the near future as more cable systems are renovated to greatly increase channel capacity.

Viacom continues to develop traditional broadcasting operations that provide the opportunity for future cross-promotions with MTV Networks. In 1995, Viacom owned three AM and nine FM radio stations and five television stations. Viacom's Paramount Pictures subsidiary also launched a new commercial network, United Paramount, on January 16, 1995, with two nights of programming including the science fiction show *Star Trek: Voyager*. Despite initially mediocre ratings, UPN plans to increase its program schedule to more nights of the week. As Viacom continues to explore possible strategies for "synergy" among its various subsidiaries, these broadcast properties could be used as a forum for promoting personalities, shows, and featured musical artists from MTV Networks' program services. MTV and VH-1 contests and promotions might be hawked on Viacom radio stations. Artists currently hyped on MTV or VH-1 might get played on these stations as well. UPN and Viacom television stations could become regular outlets for shows made by MTV Productions.

Viacom is also aggressively developing interactive video systems to be a major player in the emerging "information superhighway," experimenting with a more interactive cable system in Castro Valley, California.[72] Viacom plans for MTV to have a prominent role in this emerging two-way system, prompting experiments with a more interactive version of MTV where viewers choose what videos they want to see and what programs they would prefer, like *Beavis and Butt-head* or *House of Style* ("none of the above" will not likely be an option). In 1993, MTV announced it was developing more interactive programs soliciting greater viewer involvement, perhaps in part to challenge The Box, whose format and revenues rely entirely on viewer response. In July 1995, Viacom's Paramount Television Group announced the creation of Paramount Digital Entertainment to develop programming for on-line computer information services like America Online and the World Wide Web. The programming will initially be limited to text, graphics, and some audio, but later expand to full-motion video. Such a service may become yet another forum for promoting personalities and shows from MTV and VH-1 as well as a site for marketing consumer products with the MTV logo.

MTV Networks also developed new music video shows on its children's network, Nickelodeon, to appeal to its youngest viewers. An example is *Nick Jr. Rocks,* which premiered in 1991 presenting videos for two- to seven-year-olds. The show provides a forum for music clips featuring children's music, a growing market being developed by the major labels. Some companies like Warner, A&M, and Disney in particular have a catalog of music videos for children that can be shown on Nickelodeon's programs. The channel is encouraging the labels to produce more videos for children and to have established adult artists star in new videos singing familiar children's songs. Nickelodeon executives hope to socialize its youngest viewers into a consumerist mentality early on so that they will be faithful consumers of music products later in life. "Kids have brand identification that's different from their parents that starts at a very early age," says Geraldine Laybourne, president of Nickelodeon/Nick At Nite. "Though it's a bit of a stretch, Sting could benefit down the road from a 2-year-old seeing him sing 'Farmer in the Dell.'"[73] MTV Networks hopes that such programs will help train young viewers to be receptive to advertising for recorded music both on Nickelodeon and later on MTV when they get older. MTV is apparently unconcerned about the ethics of manipulating impressionable young viewers in this manner. Nickelodeon's plans appear to be part of a broad strategy by MTV Networks to present cradle-to-grave music video for viewers: Nick Jr. for toddlers, MTV for teens, and VH-1 for thirty-somethings. Perhaps a channel for seniors is on the horizon.

MTV Networks is also taking seriously the dismissive comment of some critics that MTV is basically just a home-shopping club offering products for the record labels. The company is considering launching a bona fide home-shopping channel in 1995, which would be "a natural extension of MTV," according to Michael Seymour of Saatchi and Saatchi.[74] MTV's channels have all tried to cultivate and nurture a consumerist milieu in some form; MTV itself presents lifestyles and group identities that can be purchased by its viewers. An MTV shopping channel would simply be a more direct reflection of that underlying objective. The proposed channel would appeal to various demographic groups and have specialized programming targeted toward these audiences. As a trial run of this project, MTV Networks produced its own shopping program, *The Goods,* featuring products like souvenirs from The Rolling Stones' latest tour, which airs sporadically on MTV, VH-1, and Nickelodeon, preempting regular programming on these services whether the viewers like it or not. Another of MTV's home-shopping shows (which it prefers to call "electronic retailing") was the *Beavis and Butt-head Mega Model Jam* hawking such must-have items as a $90 denim jacket, $60 hockey jersey, and $40 backpack, all prominently featuring the likeness of MTV's resident cartoon morons.[75] These shows blur the line between entertainment and advertising by adding celebrity interviews, live music, comedy, and a hipper-than-thou MTV style along with the sales pitch. Besides MTV, several other program services surfaced combining music video with home shopping. MOR Music, launched nationally in September 1992, is a music channel with a conservative format eschewing gratuitous sex and violence that lets viewers purchase albums through the mail. QVC's sister shopping channel, Q2, says it will use music videos to help sell products, and the record label Bertelsmann planned a combination music video and home-shopping channel in a joint venture with the cable giant Tele-Communications, which has since been abandoned. Clearly these companies recognize music videos as an effective, thinly veiled advertising appeal.

MTV is a growing colossus expanding in all directions with increasing dominance over music on television and potentially great influence over its narrow demographic audiences, shaping and molding their very cultural self-identify. The company is in the early stages of expanding the number of its own services, creating an MTV2 and MTV3 through its multiplexing strategy with MTV Networks' VH-1 close behind. These services featuring different genres of music may increase MTV's control over music on cable and threaten the survival of the remaining national alternatives to MTV like BET, which plays black genres of music. Viacom's broadcast stations and UPN service conceivably may further increase the parent company's dominion over music offered on a cable system television and radio.

Nickelodeon's plans also highlight another path of expansion, creating music programs and channels for different age groups from the very young on *Nick Jr. Rocks* to the middle-aged on VH-1. MTV Networks also seeks to expand the reach of influence over the demographic audiences targeted by its channels. The original MTV has moved beyond simply playing music videos and now seeks to become a complete "lifestyle" program service for teens and college-age viewers, presenting a full slate of programs covering all aspects of their lives, including fashion, entertainment, politics, and sex. Such an all-encompassing mandate may allow MTV to subtly shape and define what constitutes youth identity, rather than just reflect it. MTV's consumerism-as-identity encourages viewers to define themselves in terms of consumer products featured on the channel's programs, which can be easily purchased. MTV's tentative foray into a home-shopping channel targeted to specific groups represents the culmination of this objective: Not only will MTV define what's hip, depicting essential accessories to a group identity, but it will sell it through an 800 number shown on your screen. The launch of MTV Productions will extend MTV-style programs to broadcast television and theatrical films, while MTV's numerous services like MTV Europe, MTV Asia, and MTV Latino export MTV's influence on popular culture and music globally. MTV is everywhere.

PART TWO

THE STRUCTURE OF THE MUSIC VIDEO BUSINESS: FORCES THAT SHAPE MUSIC CLIPS

7

The Record Companies' Role in Video Music Production and Distribution

Video Music Incorporated into Record Companies

As video music gradually became an institutionalized part of the record business, the major labels incorporated this cultural product into the permanent organizational structure of their companies. At some labels, video music operations were subsumed within preexisting departments such as at A&M Records where video music was managed by the label's marketing department. Video music is often assigned to the label's promotion department since music clips are perceived foremost as an effective way to promote their artists. Other labels, like Polygram, established separate divisions with the sole mandate of developing video music. As music clips gained stature, some record labels shifted toward this latter approach, rather than treating video as an ancillary function of other departments. For example, Atlantic Records consolidated its video music activities into one area in 1987.[1]

Music video functions at the major record labels can be divided roughly into three areas: production, promotion, and retail distribution. Some labels combine these areas into a single centralized department, like Polygram Music Video, which produces and distributes music programming for television and home video, whereas other labels disperse these operations into different divisions.

Label divisions with responsibility for video music production oversee the making of video clips for their artists. Record labels primarily finance the production of videos, but try to recover all or part of this expense from their artists by deducting a contractually agreed upon portion of the artists' royalties from sales of their albums. The labels act as a selective "gatekeeping" force in the production of videos by deciding which of their artists will be featured in music clips and which songs from the artists' albums will have accompanying videos. Record companies often simply coordinate clip production by hiring outside directors and production firms to produce the clips. Label executives commission a production company to make a video for a current single released by a label artist for a certain predetermined budget. The record companies control the content of the actual videos, often requiring the producer to incorporate a particular concept or visual style into the clip.

Some record companies produce their own videos. Picture Music International (PMI) is the in-house video production company for Capitol Records, which makes a substantial portion of clips for Capitol and EMI America artists. Major labels with their own video production units give record companies extensive vertical integration for music video, comparable to their interests in audio-recorded music because they have almost complete control over all stages of the production and distribution of video music. Some labels prefer their own production facilities because the arrangement reduces dependence on outside firms and allows greater control over production expenses.

Video promotion departments use video clips to get favorable public exposure for their artists. These divisions distribute a label's video clips to music program services and also plan marketing campaigns for artists that often include promotional contests on MTV or other major music television shows. These executives make arrangements for their label's artists to be guests on major exposure outlets like MTV or BET and develop short promotional spots featuring the artist to air on these services.

Most major labels use their extensive distribution systems to distribute videos as well as audio music products. As the market for music video grew more successful in the late 1980s, some labels established divisions to develop the retail market, such as CBS Music Video (CMV), which began releasing titles under its own name in 1988 and was later renamed Sony Music Video.[2] There are four general types of music-related titles in home video: the vidclip compilation, which consists of an artist's music clips for various songs; a concert film of an act performing live; a documentary featuring an artist or musical event; and music-oriented films like *Purple Rain*. In this market, the major labels take advantage of their status as subsidiaries of media conglomerates by developing music video titles in cooperation with the parent company's established home video division. For example, MCA Records frequently cooperates with MCA Home Video by producing videos that the record label can use for promotional purposes and that the home video division can sell in stores.

Record Label Video Production Dependent Upon Exposure Media

The record companies' funding for videos for certain types of music depends upon a music genre's current prominence on major exposure media, most notably MTV. When establishing their video music budgets, record companies take into account the degree to which a broad genre of music is given exposure on popular music shows. In MTV's early years when the program service featured "New Music" techno-pop and heavy metal, record company executives generally provided artists from those genres with generous levels of funding for videos. Conversely, artists from genres that received little or no MTV play during the early 1980s, most notably music by black artists, received much less record company support for videos because the labels believed that these videos would not get enough exposure to justify the expense of production. Dan Daid of Capitol Records said then that "one of the problems with black videos is that you are limited to where you can show them."[3] At the time, Warner Brothers commissioned videos for only a few black artists with crossover appeal like Prince and The Time, which were accepted on MTV because of these acts' funk-rock sound, which attracted rock fans as well as a rhythm and blues (R&B) audience.[4]

As MTV shifted its emphasis to different genres of music, record companies reevaluated their funding policies for videos for artists. In the late 1980s, MTV played more videos by black artists while cutting back its airplay of heavy metal. MTV's format change and the growth of other exposure media for black artists such as BET directly affected label video production policies as video budgets for clips by black artists blossomed, whereas funding for heavy metal clips was sharply curtailed. By 1992, the major labels increasingly relied on music video to promote artists in the rhythm and blues and rap genres because they were impressed with the ability of music television programs like *Yo! MTV Raps* to provide publicity for these acts.[5]

Video Clip Promotion

The labels' general objective with videos is, of course, to increase the retail sales of their artists' music through widespread distribution of the artists' videos on music television shows as well as other sites for potential exposure like nightclubs and music stores, which display music clips on monitors. However, the record companies use videos in more specific ways to help develop their artists. Video clips establish and cultivate a certain image for an artist. Video producers attempted to develop a wholesome, clean-cut image for the pop group New Kids on the Block through their videos, whereas Bryan Adams's videos were designed to endow the performer with a tough, manly character. Videos are used to modify an established performer's public identity as well. Madonna regularly reinvents her persona through her videos, becoming at various times a trashily dressed boy-toy, a reincarnated Marilyn Monroe, a rebellious Catholic, a high gloss "Vogue" model, and a sexually provocative dominatrix.

A primary function of videos is to introduce a label's new talent to the public. Music videos are not expected to boost sales of new acts immediately, but rather are used as part of a long-term promotional strategy designed to familiarize consumers with emerging artists. "It's a development process with new artists," explained Peter Baron, manager of video services at Arista Records.[6] "You don't have to necessarily go for the home run the first time up. You just try to successfully build an image [for the new artist] over a period of time." However, this strategy is often undercut by the increasingly hit-oriented major program services like MTV and VH-1, which limit exposure for new music by unknown artists. Videos are used to make commercial radio more receptive to playing certain songs by label artists. When radio stations refuse to play a current single by an act, record companies often heavily promote the video for the single, hoping that prominent play of the clip on major exposure media will encourage radio stations to add the single to their playlists. MTV's frequent play of New Music in its early years persuaded radio programmers to add songs by these artists previously excluded from radio. The labels continue this strategy with some success. In 1989, Robin Sloane, Elektra Records' vice president of video, reported that a video commissioned for the heavy metal group, Metallica, which received extensive exposure on MTV, resulted in play on Top 40 radio stations. Sloane acknowledged that the radio play for Metallica, which was initially ignored by radio, was "based entirely on the video."[7]

Promotion departments that distribute video clips to television shows developed several strategies to heighten their clips' promotional efficacy. Most importantly, executives provide MTV with copies of recent videos and vigorously lobby the channel to add these to its current playlist. Video play on MTV is considered crucial because the channel is the most important element in the promotion campaign for many of the labels' mainstream rock and pop artists. Labels also distribute their videos to several regional and local program services that help establish a new act. Promotion executives also selectively distribute videos for certain genres of music to video shows that feature these specialized genres, like programs on the cable services The Nashville Network and Black Entertainment Television. The labels limit distribution of their clips to certain favored shows because of the fear of overexposure, worrying that excessive television play of a video clip might diminish public interest in an act. Celia Hirschman, president of Vis-Ability, an independent promotion firm, adds that in order for video music to be effective, the clips are complemented by a marketing campaign where promotion personnel "set up interviews, arrange album giveaways, cut video IDs for the individual shows."[8]

Role of Exposure Media in Record Label's Promotional Strategy

Music programs like MTV have a symbiotic relationship with the record labels, which generally encourages them to cooperate in promotional campaigns for their artists by providing regular airplay of videos by record company acts. The clip shows and the record labels have a common interest in promoting videos by popular artists. Frequent airplay of videos of hit songs can increase the television show's audience ratings and ultimately expand advertising revenues. MTV's ex–senior vice president Abbie Konowitch explained that the channel heavily promoted videos and personal appearances by Paula Abdul because growing public interest in her music and videos enhanced MTV's image as well. "Her success is our success," noted Konowitch.[9] Similarly, for the record company, broad exposure of a video can help create an audience for a label's artist and increase sales of the artist's music.

However, the ultimate objectives of the program service and the record label are not synonymous and at times lead to divergent, conflicting interests that impede the label's promotional strategies. Exposure media outlets need programming that will get high audience ratings to increase advertising revenues, whereas the record companies seek public exposure for their acts. The conflicting nature of these objectives is most pronounced for music videos by unknown and emerging artists. Major program services are reluctant to play videos by new artists because these clips are unlikely to attract a large audience. In fact, in recent years major exposure media like MTV shifted more toward video play of hit songs by established artists while shunning videos of new artists. One anonymous label executive complained, "I can name a whole bunch of bands in '89 that we made videos for and had high hopes for, and we were very disappointed in [MTV's] lack of support."[10] This aversion to new music creates a perennial predicament for the labels who seek to provide their new artists with opportunities for exposure.

The exclusivity pacts between the record labels and MTV provide the record companies with a partial remedy for this lack of exposure because MTV must play some videos by artists specified by the labels. These contracts give the major record companies guaranteed exposure for some clips by new artists that might not get played otherwise. Yet despite these contracts, the labels have limited control over exposure media for video music. The contract provisions only require MTV to play a limited number of videos selected by the record company, generally 10 percent of the label's annual video output. Further, MTV only provides relatively light airplay of these required videos. Moreover, since the contracts are only with MTV, the labels have no formal influence over the playlists of other major exposure media like BET or syndicated shows. The lack of control may be the underlying reason why several major record labels developed plans to launch their own music channels where they could completely control the choice of videos presented.

The labels' relationship with video music shows is somewhat analogous to their relationship with commercial radio broadcasters in that radio stations are dependent upon programming provided by the labels, but cannot be compelled by the labels to air specific songs or artists (except through illegal payola schemes). Because of this limited influence, the labels developed a "lobbying" strategy for video clip shows similar to their approach for radio. The labels' video promotion departments frequently contact programmers at major program services. The promotion people provide the shows with copies of recently released clips by their artists and constantly try to persuade program services to add the videos to their regular playlist. MTV's Konowitch received an average of 140 telephone calls a day from record company executives trying to get MTV to play videos of certain new songs or artists.[11] The label executives and artists infrequently stage publicity events at the program services to encourage the clip show to air a certain video. Epic Records sent its entire New York staff to the MTV offices wearing hard hats and personalized T-shirts in order to get the channel to play a video by the label's new group, Danger Danger. Konowitch recounted another occasion when Gene Simmons from Kiss came to his office "wearing kneepads and wanting to know, 'who do I have to blow to get my videos played?'"[12]

Video Replaces Touring in Promotional Strategies

Before MTV, the record labels regularly financed tours for their new artists to cultivate a following. In the 1970s, record companies often required artists to do a series of live performances concurrently with the release of a new album to increase sales of the artists' records in a local area. However, by the early 1980s the major labels largely stopped subsidizing tours, leading Larry Fitzgerald, a manager of Toto, to say, "The term 'tour support' really doesn't exist anymore."[13] Record labels became skeptical about the promotional benefits of tours and questioned whether live performances really increased record sales. Label executives' enthusiasm for tours was also dampened by rapidly increasing tour expenses and mediocre concert attendance, which limited revenues. This disenchantment with tours combined with the growing popularity of video music gradually led the major record labels to favor video music over live tours as a way to promote their artists. Eddie Rosenblatt, president of Geffen Records, praised videos, saying, "The good news is that a band that used to go on the road for six weeks and play in front of 10,000 people now can have a video on MTV and immediately be seen by millions of kids."[14]

In the early 1980s, concert promoters predicted gloomily that music video would eventually undermine touring by artists. Music consumers, it was argued, would prefer to watch their favorite artists on television in the convenience of their own homes rather than pay to see a live concert. However, program services such as MTV did not adopt an adversarial approach to tours, but rather developed a supportive stance toward live performances by actively promoting tours by featured artists. MTV, VH-1, and other services publicize upcoming tours through on-air promotions and special programming involving the artist. MTV regularly develops extensive campaigns for U.S. tours by popular acts that include frequent mention of concert dates, heavy play of the artists' videos, live reports by the veejays from the concerts, and other programming featuring the artists. For instance, MTV and VH-1 gave extensive publicity to The Rolling Stones' 1994 Voodoo Lounge tour, incessantly hawking concert souvenirs in home-shopping programs.

The growing prominence of video music did have an impact on artists' live performances, but not in the manner predicted. Music video did not destroy concerts, but instead influenced the form and content of actual performances. Pop stars attempt to replicate the imagery, special effects, and choreography of their videos in live concerts. Madonna and Michael Jackson both stage elaborate concerts that recreate prominent scenes from their videos. These attempts by artists to make concerts resemble their video music productions make some live performances more rigidly structured and preplanned, draining the concert of any potential spontaneity. Artists make use of their videos in various ways within their concerts, such as presenting music clips in lieu of an opening act. The centerpiece of the stage for concerts by Duran Duran, a group whose commercial success was largely created by video music, was a $300,000 "video wall" consisting of forty-nine video monitors that played segments from the group's videos during the performance. Jon Pareles observes that video music had a pronounced impact on concert audiences as well as the actual tour performance, remarking that audiences at concerts by artists who are known primarily for their videos behave passively as if watching television.[15]

Record Companies and Artists

Artists' Contracts with Record Labels

As music video grew in importance, provisions concerning this type of production were incorporated in contracts between record labels and recording acts. These provisions let the labels recover their expenses on video production from the recording artists promoted by the music clip. This section examines some basic features of recording contracts and how these relate to music video. Although contracts vary substantially, there are a few standard provisions. Contract terms largely depend on the artist's relative commercial success at the time of negotiations. New, unknown artists usually sign "standard agreements" heavily weighted in the record label's favor. Jeff Berke, an attorney specializing in music and entertainment law, claims that in the typical contract, "the record company promises little, charges all expenses back to the artist, grants itself the sole option to decide whether the agreement will continue, and often won't even guarantee the release of the first record."[16] New artists generally accept the label's terms because they are anxious to get any recording contract and often lack financial resources to hire a competent attorney and manager who might get them more favorable terms. Conversely, more established artists are in a better bargaining position because the labels want to retain acts with a proven record of commercial success. Moreover, recording stars can hire adept representation to get better deals.

Two provisions of recording contracts apply to music video: artist royalties and recoupment of label expenses. The royalty rate determines the gross revenues an artist receives from disc and tape sales. The artist's royalty is a percentage of the retail sales of their music products. For example, for a cassette priced at $9.98, an artist with a 10 percent royalty rate would receive a gross royalty of $0.998 from the retail sale of each cassette. The royalty rates for different recording formats vary, with compact discs having a lower royalty rate than cassettes. The royalty percentage for artists increases with their degree of commercial success: New and mid-level acts receive about 12 percent to 14 percent, and superstars get from 16 percent to 18 percent, although some successful artists have even higher rates.[17] Madonna's 1992 contract with TimeWarner reportedly gives her a 20 percent royalty rate along with a $5 million advance for each of her next seven albums.[18]

Recording artists do not receive all of their royalties because labels deduct the album's production and promotion costs from the musician's gross royalties. The artist's actual income from album sales, the net royalties, is any amount remaining after these debts are subtracted from gross royalties. Some artists and industry lawyers complain that the record labels drastically inflate the costs of marketing and promotion, and overcharge recording artists for this expense.[19] Also contested is the record label's ownership of the album: Even though the artist pays the record label back for all expenses through these deductions, the label still usually retains ownership, which some artists believe rightly belongs to them. Because of the high costs of producing and marketing an album, the artist may not receive any income from royalties even if an album sells 100,000 copies.[20] In 1991, *Variety* reported that record labels spend on average $150,000 to $200,000 to market an album and pay from $50,000 to $100,000 for a video to promote a single from the album.[21] This is in addition to the album's production costs, which average almost $250,000.[22]

Record labels try to recover their expenses on video music by incorporating the costs of video production into this conventional structure of recording contracts. In mid-1983, the major record companies began including clauses in contracts that deduct a portion of the cost of video clips from the artist's future gross royalties derived from sales of the album related to the music video.[23] The actual percentage of the cost of the video clip deducted from the artist's royalties varies greatly. Steve Manger of the law firm Shapiro and Steinberg, whose clients include Fleetwood Mac, disclosed, "We've negotiated agreements ranging from no recoupment to 50 percent. The record companies sometimes will recoup 100 percent, depending on who [the artist is]."[24] The major record labels generally try to recover at least 50 percent of video production costs.

The party that initially pays for the production usually owns the music video. When the record company finances a music video, it owns the production and keeps all profits derived from the future exploitation of the clip. Yet, the record companies claim exclusive ownership rights to a video even after they recover production expenses by withholding artists' royalties. Some claim that the record company does not deserve sole ownership because the artist paid for part or all of the production costs through these royalty deductions.

The record labels make money from these clips that they own by charging television shows license fees for the right to exhibit their videos and selling the clip as part of a compilation in the home video market. The record companies made no provision for sharing the revenue from these license fees and home video sales with their artists even though the musicians partially financed the videos. The record labels' increasing revenue from music clips that was not shared encouraged some artists to stop relying on the labels to finance their video clips and instead pay for the productions themselves. Musicians who finance their own videos and retain ownership can lease the music clips to their labels for promotional purposes and also receive income from retail sale of clip compilations. Yet although ownership is advantageous, new artists often lack the money to pay for their own productions and continue to rely on record labels to finance them.

Influence of Video Music on Artists' Careers at Record Companies

The increased prominence of music video and MTV also influenced the record company's criteria for signing artists to recording contracts, emphasizing the importance of a musician's visual appearance. Since MTV gained widespread popularity, the major record labels tend to sign artists with an attractive image. Dan Beck of Portrait Records acknowledged that "Cyndi [Lauper] was signed because she'll be a great film performer."[25] Other popular performers like Madonna and Grace Jones were granted contracts because of their provocative visual appearance. Conversely, artists with musical talent who lack a visually appealing image are less likely to receive a contract. "I have two bands that I'm managing that would have been signed four years ago," explains Larry Mazer, manager for heavy metal groups Kiss and Cinderella.[26] "Now nobody will commit. The labels tell me that they won't get on MTV." MTV itself is biased against videos with unattractive performers, admitting that it refused to play a video for "Woodgoblins" by Tad, a hard rock guitarist, partly because Tad was judged to be too ugly.[27] The channel is also less likely to play videos by aging rock performers, favoring the young, pretty, and beautiful that are more photogenic.

Once an artist is signed to a label, the prospective commercial success of an artist increasingly depends on an act's visual image; musical talent becomes a less important consideration. Stephen Holden, a *New York Times* music critic, reports that seven of the best-selling recording acts from 1988 to 1990 became successful in large part because of their appealing music videos, naming New Kids on the Block, Bobby Brown, Paula Abdul, Hammer, Milli Vanilli, Madonna, and Janet Jackson.[28] Joe Jackson, a musician who is deeply disillusioned with music video, says that the stress on video devalues the musical abilities of artists: "Things which used to count, such as being a good composer, player or singer, are getting lost in the desperate rush to visualize everything. It is now possible to be all of the above and still get nowhere simply by not looking good in a video, or, worse still, not making one."[29] Holden concurs, saying "the wedding of pop music and video has shifted the balance of power between a song and the image of its performer," where the latter is now paramount. Yet although music video certainly helps develop an artist's image, clips are not always essential for success. Three songs from Garth Brooks's album, *Ropin' the Wind*, reached the top of *Billboard*'s country music singles charts even though Brooks made no videos for these songs.

Performers with minimal technical skill or musical talent are able to create hit songs with an attractive video and assistance from an adept producer. Any deficiencies in an artist's vocal or instrumental performance can be remedied through extensive audio mixing by studio engineers. Pat Aufderheide notes that Madonna's vocals are heavily processed by a production staff to enhance her own "reedy" voice.[30] A former MTV video jockey, J. J. Jackson, cynically suggests that the visual appearance of artists is so important to MTV viewers and record buyers because this audience is relatively unconcerned about the artistic merits of a musician's work. "Whether you're talking about Bon Jovi or Sting, they just want to know: 'Is he pretty?'"[31]

The rise and fall of the pop group Milli Vanilli dramatically illustrates the increasing importance of visuals and relative insignificance of an artists' musical abilities in popular music. The overwhelming success of Milli Vanilli's debut album, which sold more than 6 million copies was largely attributed to the group's attractive presence in videos. Abbey Konowitch, formerly of MTV, explains that Milli Vanilli's video, *Girl You Know It's True* was added to the channel's playlist while the group was still unknown: "We played it three or four times a day and made them stars. Milli Vanilli in an interview said they feel seventy to eighty percent of their success was attributable to MTV."[32] Yet, after the group sold millions of albums and was awarded a Grammy for best new artist of the year, Milli Vanilli was exposed as a fraud that did not sing or play any of their own material. Milli Vanilli achieved commercial success largely on the basis of their stylish looks and dancing abilities, which were elaborately displayed in the group's popular videos. Until their deception was uncovered, the group's lack of talent was no barrier to their success in the record business.

Although the record labels publicly condemned this particular ruse, the importance of video music combined with enhanced audio engineering capabilities encouraged the development of a new division of labor in the music industry in some instances where off-screen studio musicians create a song that is lip-synched by camera-ready performers who appear in the video. Numerous instances have been reported in recent years where successful recording acts were accused of not actually singing their own songs. Underpaid background vocalists charge that their voices were used for the lead vocals for songs credited to other performers in the spotlight. Martha Wash, a full-figured former member of the Weather Girls, accused several groups of using her voice for the lead vocals in songs without giving her appropriate credit or financial compensation. In each of these cases, the videos for these songs featured an attractive performer lip-synching Wash's lyrics. Music clips for C&C Music Factory presented faux lead singer Zelma Davis mouthing Wash's words, and Katrin Quinol performed in music clips for the dance group Black Box, although the songs were again sung by Wash.[33] Paula Abdul and New Kids on the Block, performers that relied on appealing videos for their success, were both accused by associates of not singing many of their own songs, but instead having anonymous vocalists perform them.[34] Both acts denied the charges. Many allegations of lip-synching involve recording artists from the dance music genre, which can be traced back to its historical antecedent of the 1970s, disco music, where producers regularly created short-lived one-hit acts from anonymous studio vocalists. However, music video, with its emphasis on visual presentation and image, further weakened the importance of authenticity in popular music, prompting a growing number of acts where attractive performers mouth the singing of uncredited vocalists who stand in the shadows because they lack an acceptably alluring image.

The heavy media attention to allegations of lip-synching led to a public backlash, with a lawsuit filed against Milli Vanilli for deceiving their fans, and state governments introducing bills that would require the disclosure of lip-synching in concerts. Some industry observers claimed that people were repelled because lip-synching and producer manipulation betrayed music fans' trust in performers who were supposedly expressing their own feelings and ideas in music. Ironically, MTV, which initially encouraged the growth of this practice through its emphasis on image over substance, exploited this backlash and the growing public preference for authentic recording artists in its programming. The channel launched the hugely successful series of *Unplugged* concerts where artists perform without any electronic amplifications or enhancement to showcase their natural musical talents.

Music Video at Independent and Major Record Labels

Music video today has become institutionalized as a necessary form of promotion for recording artists that cultivate an audience for the act's music. This requirement of music clips to showcase artists reinforces the relations of power between the half-dozen major record companies that overwhelmingly dominate the music business and independent labels who operate on the fringes, producing artists whose music is either too specialized or avant-garde for the majors, which primarily seek mainstream blockbuster artists. Major record labels are generally considered to be vertically integrated companies with their own self-contained production, manufacturing, and distribution operations, whereas independents usually only have production operations, contracting with other firms to provide the remaining industry services. However, the actual definition of an "independent" record label is somewhat open to question. Quality Records' Russ Regan defines an independent as "a label that isn't distributed by the majors. It's strictly a question of who distributes."[35] Yet there are variations of independent labels that do not meet Regan's definition, such as an independently owned record company that produces its own albums but is distributed by a major record label like Warner or Polygram. Many independents like Delicious Vinyl sign these distribution agreements because the majors have extensive distribution networks that can ensure widespread exposure for a label's product and placement in retail stores that the company could not achieve on its own.[36] The independent often loses a measure of autonomy in such deals, giving the major control over the marketing and promotion of artists signed to the smaller label.

Independent record labels have historically played a vanguard role, cultivating and introducing music genres and artists into popular culture. Most new styles and genres of music in the past several decades emerged from independents. In the 1960s, the first songs by The Beatles to be released in the United States were from an independent Chicago label, and in the 1970s and 1980s small labels were a major force in the alternative music scene, promoting artists in punk, new wave, and rap before majors had any interest in these areas. Yet although independents pursue cutting-edge music, the major record companies market more mainstream, conservative music to attract a broad audience. These majors do not want to sign acts that have moderate sales, but instead seek to promote a few superstar artists that will have hit albums on a regular basis. As their distribution systems grew more elaborate, the majors raised the minimum standards for successful albums from sales of 100,000 albums to more than a million. As a result, most of the labels' resources go to signing lavish multimillion dollar contracts for their established artists like Madonna, Janet Jackson, and Whitney Houston. This financial outlay for a few stars means that less money is available for nurturing unknown artists with unconventional styles. Stephen Holden points out that the money spent for Janet Jackson's contract with Virgin Records for $32–$50 million for her next three albums would pay for contracts for 100 new recording artists. By contrast, independents have much more modest goals for their acts and actively develop unknown artists. Tommy Couch, the president of Malaco Records, a small label that features Southern soul and blues, explains, "the majors are not built around making records that are profitable with sales in the 50,000 unit range but we are and we make out well on that kind of scale."[37]

In the past decade, independents were threatened by a strong movement toward concentration of ownership in the record business as many prominent labels were acquired by majors, giving these large companies greater control over the range of popular music. A&M Records was acquired by Polygram in October 1989, Geffen Records was bought by MCA Records in March 1990, and in 1992, Britain's Thorn-EMI, owner of Capitol and Chrysalis, purchased Virgin Records, known as the last big independent.[38] Other established independents like Enigma and Coyote failed, unable to compete with the majors' extensive promotion and distribution apparatus. The failure of Rough Trade, an independent music distributor, in May 1991 was especially devastating to independent record labels, which relied on the company's distribution system to get their albums into music stores.[39]

As a result of a series of acquisitions and company failures, the record business became highly centralized, with six major record labels (each owned by multinational conglomerates) that were responsible for 93 percent of all albums released in the United States by 1991.[40] These six companies are Sony Corporation, which purchased CBS Music and its associated labels from CBS, including Columbia and Epic; MCA, which Seagram Company (best known for its liquor and beverage businesses) controlled after purchasing about 80 percent of the company from the Japanese electronics firm Matsushita in 1995; Polygram, owned by Philips Electronics N.V., based in Holland, which owns A&M, Mercury, and Island; EMI, a subsidiary of Thorn-EMI P.L.C., owner of the Chrysalis, Capitol, and Virgin labels; BMG, owned by Bertelsmann A.G., the German publishing company that purchased RCA Music from RCA and also holds Arista; and Warner Music, a subsidiary of TimeWarner, the only remaining U.S.-owned major record company, which controls the Warner, Atlantic, Elektra, and Sire labels. These six companies now have near complete dominance over popular music, demonstrated by the almost total hegemony of major labels over popular album and single charts. Tommy T.'s single "One More Try" on Quality Records was notable in February 1991 for becoming the first record to be distributed by an independent to reach the top 10 on *Billboard*'s Hot 100 Singles chart in over two years.[41]

Industry critics complain that the acquisitions and concentration stifle the creativity and artistic expression within the record business that thrives at independent labels. David Geffen, who sold his own label to MCA Records, derides the impersonal bureaucracy of the industry today. "It's starting to be like the movie industry now. All that's left now in the movie world is a bunch of faceless conglomerates, and the result is that there aren't many good movies being made anymore, are there? I'm afraid it won't be long before the music industry ends up the same way."[42] Some record producers worry that most of these mammoth companies are controlled by people with minimal knowledge of record production, with one executive revealing that "four of the six heads of major record companies have little or no background in the business."[43] *Billboard* magazine, certainly no radical critic of the industry, argued in an unsigned editorial that the takeovers threaten the enterprising development of new artists and emerging music styles.[44] *Billboard* pointed out that most of these acquisitions of independents placed major conglomerates deeply in debt, which discouraged them from taking creative risks on unknown artists or music. Because of this debt, the major labels become more preoccupied with launching blockbuster hit albums by established stars to increase short-term profits rather than developing new artists. The labels seem to be following this strategy, cutting back on record contracts for new artists in early 1992, while continuing the practice of signing established artists like Madonna and Janet Jackson to lavish multiyear contracts. The major labels also encourage these successful artists to produce albums that are collections of potential hit singles tailored for radio play rather than an artistic thematic statement.

When a major label buys an independent, executives often claim that the acquired label will remain autonomous, yet surviving independent labels suggest the opposite is true. Once a smaller label is purchased, the company often no longer aggressively pursues new talent with unconventional music styles. John Salstone, co-owner of M.S. Distribution, argues that independents like Motown acquired by majors are largely decimated:

> When these independent labels go to the majors, history has shown that the majors are not interested in the label itself, nor in the people who own and run the label. They're interested in the successful artists with proven track records who are selling a lot of records. . . . Once they get those artists and milk them, then the label falls to the

wayside. Where is Motown today? Where is Casablanca? ABC? All of these were once really viable labels. When they're ready to cash it in, so to speak, then indie labels will make their deal with the majors. But I think that if they want to make their mark and continue to break new artists and be vital, then they'll maintain their independence.[45]

Even though they dwarf independents in power and financial resources, the major labels are often less willing than their smaller counterparts to support artists who present controversial ideas in their music. Whereas independents usually champion and protect their acts' freedom of creative expression, major labels often retreat cowardly from any criticism of their artists' music from special interest groups. All of the major labels buckled under to pressure from the Parents Music Research Center (PMRC) and state governments to place warning stickers on albums for explicit lyrics, which was derided by some artists as an insidious form of censorship. An incident involving the rap performer Ice-T illustrates how major labels fail to stand up for individual artists as well. Ice-T and TimeWarner, the parent company of his record label, were harshly criticized by some law enforcement officers, members of Congress, and Los Angeles politicians for Ice-T's song "Cop Killer," which was perceived as a call to murder police officers.[46] Even though Ice-T claimed that this was a misinterpretation of his song, which actually dealt with issues of police brutality and racial prejudice, an organization of law enforcement officers sponsored a boycott against TimeWarner for its sales of the album that included the song. TimeWarner eventually canceled Ice-T's record contract, most likely because the corporation decided the artist's right to freedom of expression was less important than the company's profits. Ice-T explained that "dropping me was the corporation's decision. And I'm not gonna attack them either because I understand it was about dollars and cents."[47] The performer clearly realized he was being punished by TimeWarner for expressing certain objectionable views, saying "anybody who is black has to be prepared for situations like with me when their agenda runs counter to the system."[48] He might add that TimeWarner is an integral part of that system.

Under attack from right-wing critics headed by William Bennett for selling rap music with explicit lyrics, TimeWarner's Chairman Gerald Levin signaled that the company would practice more heavy-handed in-house censorship of its artists. Speaking to an annual shareholder's meeting in May 1995, Levin said that he had directed company executives to enforce standards for its music and to balance artistic expression with corporate responsibility. Yet in contrast to TimeWarner's craven actions, small independent labels, especially those featuring hip-hop and rap, defend their artist's rights to express views that may be offensive or controversial. However, as major labels continue to devour these smaller labels, fewer forums remain for artists to express oppositional views through their music.

There are various reasons for the demise of truly independent record labels and increasing dominance of major labels owned by larger conglomerates. At a more general level, media critics like Ben Bagdikian demonstrate that there is a movement toward centralized control by a few large corporations in all media markets, including the record business. As of 1992, only twenty corporations owned a majority of U.S. mass media outlets, a decrease from fifty corporations in 1981. Within the music industry, independents are at an extreme disadvantage because they lack the financial resources of the majors to promote and market their artists to get exposure for acts on a national basis. "We're outmanned," says Cory Robbins, president of Profile Records. "The major labels have 20 promotion people to every one we have. They can go and get 150 [radio] stations on a record the first week."[49] Independents lack clout with program directors at radio stations, making it difficult to get their artist's music played. These labels also do not have the majors' elaborate distribution system, which makes it hard to get their albums carried in music stores. The economic recession in the early 1990s harmed independents that were less able to survive during lean periods than the major labels because they lacked the financial reserves of these larger competitors. The industry's conversion from vinyl records to compact discs also was difficult for independents because of the higher manufacturing costs of the new format. Finally, when independents were able to surmount these various obstacles and develop new successful artists, major record companies would usually swoop in and acquire the record label or buy up the record contract of the label's successful acts. Gerard Cosloy, comanager of Matador Records, an independent label based in New York, describes the major labels as "vultures," saying "they're eager to step in and take the lead from the indies."[50]

The Challenge of Music Video for Independents

In this environment where independents struggle to survive, music video presents certain advantages as well as obstacles to these smaller companies as a form of promotion. Although several independents use the video form in an innovative, creative manner, providing valuable exposure for their artists, the costs of video music production create problems for these labels. The average cost of a music video commissioned by major record companies is about $60,000, which is far more than smaller independents can pay. Many independents lack the financial resources of the major labels to underwrite the expense of video music production and distribution on a regular basis. Yet, the conventional wisdom of the industry holds that clips are generally necessary to develop a commercially successful song or artist. Without the competent production and distribution of video clips, the artists of independent labels may not receive the essential exposure needed to generate public interest in an act. Thus, the necessity of music video creates a dilemma by increasing the minimum promotion budget for an act, which independent labels may be unable to afford.

Some independents confront this dilemma by producing videos with a limited budget. The Independent Label Coalition, a trade association with the objective of developing alternative approaches for independents to promote their artists, aggressively pursued the production of low-cost videos. Jeannie Hance, director of creative services for the Coalition, explained that the organization would contact aspiring film producers and directors who might be interested in making videos with limited funds as a way to become established in the music video field.[51] Hance said, "we think there may be some film people who would be challenged by the restrictions of low budgets and the artistic freedom they'd get working outside a major label."[52] According to speakers at a new music seminar, videos can be produced for under $15,000 by using a variety of cost-cutting production techniques.[53]

Since 1992, independent labels more aggressively pursued the making of low-cost videos to promote their artists, underwriting an increasing number of music clips. Mammoth Records made eight clips in 1992, an increase from only two the previous year, and Earache U.S., another independent, commissioned fifteen videos between June '91 and June '92, an increase from only six the prior year.[54] As the quantity of their clips grew, the budgets further shrank. Music videos made by independent labels now have minuscule budgets between $1,000 and $6,000. "Most of our clips are made for between $2,500 and $6,000," says Jim Welch, president of Earache U.S. "That's nothing when you compare it to other people's video budgets, but we've found that you can get the same amount of play no matter how much you spend as long as it's a cool video."[55] Music clips for Touch and Go Records cost even less, an average of $1,000 to $1,500, a modest budget made possible because the label solicits novice directors to make their productions for a minimal fee. The label's president, Cory Rusk, explains, "we go out and find people who have recently graduated from film school or people who are trying to make a name for themselves in the video world."[56] Despite the minimal budgets, the independents must still pay additional costs for duplication and shipping, which increases their outlays.

Yet even when independent record companies are able to finance and produce a video for an aspiring new artist, these labels have difficulty receiving exposure for clips on major outlets, notably MTV. MTVN is highly integrated with the major labels through contractual agreements that provide guaranteed access for the majors' popular and emerging acts. Besides these pacts, MTV has a conservative programming policy that primarily features established acts already signed to major labels. MTV and other prominent national program services are also less likely to play the low-cost videos made by the independents because these often have a primitive, raw production quality that is perceived as too unpolished for commercial television, even though the videos may be highly creative and innovative. MTV and its sister service VH-1 prefer to play videos with higher budgets that come from the major labels because these clips usually have higher production standards and a more glossy "professional" visual appearance, even though the content may be trite and banal.

As a result of these factors, almost all video clips presented on MTV, the premiere showcase for music video, are by artists signed to major record companies. According to the results of a *Billboard* survey, of the 131 artists featured by MTV in one twenty-four-hour period, only two clips featured artists signed to independently distributed labels: James Brown with Afrika Bambaataa by Tommy Boy records and Johnny Winter of Alligator records.[57] In the mid-1990s, MTV occasionally plays videos by independent labels on its specialty shows featuring a certain type of music like rap or alternative rock. Also, MTV's play of a music clip for the band Offspring signed to the independent label Epitaph was a notable exception to its "majors only" policy, which led to their album's commercial success. However, representatives of independent labels say that in general MTV rarely plays their videos, preferring to showcase major label artists exclusively. Ron Resnick, executive vice president of the record label Sleeping Bag, complains, "we have seven active rap acts on the label now, and during the past 14 months five of them have gone top 30 or better on *Billboard*'s black album chart. But getting the videos played is next to impossible."[58] "It would be wonderful to be on MTV," concurs Bruce Duff of Triple X Records, "but there are a million reasons for them not to play us."[59] Bryan Turner, president of Priority Records, the independent label best known for the rap group N.W.A., charges that MTV only plays videos of artists with major labels because of the channel's cozy arrangement with these companies where MTV plays new artists signed to a major in exchange for exclusive videos by their established artists. "It's all too conveniently becoming a major only situation," says Turner. "It's financial reasons that's allowing them to play major label stuff. A major says to them, 'Here, play this and we'll give you an exclusive on our video by Sinead O'Connor,' or whoever."[60]

Turner took his grievance with MTV one step further, distributing a press release charging MTV with censorship for refusing to play any music clips by the label's acts.[61] Turner was especially outraged by MTV's rejection of a clip for the group Low Profile allegedly because of the depiction of drug paraphernalia. The clip included a scene of a person opening a packet of a substance resembling crack. Yet Turner claimed that the actual reason for MTV's rejection was the close-up shots of Presidents Reagan and Bush in the video, reinforcing the contention of the lyrics that the policies of these administrations were to blame for the disenfranchisement of young blacks and their increasing use of drugs. Turner implied that MTV was unwilling to present a provocative video that challenged establishment policies. Moreover, he condemned the channel for not confronting the drug crisis in America, saying, "I see this as blatant censorship. Every day, the television screen is bombarded with stories about the drug crisis. Here's a band trying to say something powerful about the subject, and it's turned away by the very outlet most likely to reach young people."[62]

The almost complete exclusion of independent labels' artists from MTV's playlist is a powerful impediment to the independents' marketing strategies because of the video channel's unparalleled clout in the industry. If MTV refuses to play an act's video, that artist may have difficulty reaching a national audience. Moreover, music stores may be unwilling to stock titles by acts signed to independent labels until they see the acts on a prominent national outlet like MTV.

Monica Lynch, vice president of Tommy Boy Records, complains, "It's getting to the point where retailers now think that having your videos listed on MTV's rotation chart gives a record credibility—and they may not decide to order until the clip goes into regular rotation."[63] Thus, by excluding music clips from smaller independent labels, MTV helps to keep these independents in a marginal position in the record business, while the products of the major record labels are incessantly promoted on the channel.

However, although independent labels are usually unable to get their videos played on MTV, they often have better success with regional and local music video shows that are more willing to air their clips. Bruce Duff of Triple X Records says, "every now and then we get one on [MTV], but if they don't play it, we'll get 80 other local and regional shows, pools, and other national outlets."[64] Many independents rely on video promotion companies to get their clips played by these music shows. Caprice Carmona, the head of the promotion firm Sudden Impact, claims a high success rate for airing low-cost videos, saying "Urge Overkill, Afghan Whigs and Mudhoney have all gotten played at over 90% of the outlets serviced and each was made for about $2,000."[65]

So independents are able to underwrite the production of some music clips on limited budgets, but cannot afford to make more expensive clips with high production standards that are usually played on major outlets like MTV. These labels are able to get modest airplay for their clips on local television shows, yet are rarely able to get their music videos presented on MTV. MTV and its sister service VH-1 primarily feature artists from major labels, keeping independent label artists at a constant disadvantage since these channels are the primary vehicles for national exhibition of music clips. Thus, the incorporation of music video within the music business as a means of promotion has largely served to reinforce the existing power relations between independents and majors. The production and exhibition of music video supports the dominance of major labels, which get extensive national promotion, whereas smaller independents are kept at the margins, their few music clips getting limited exposure for their artists in isolated communities and subcultures.

The added expense of music video production and distribution also raises the total costs for marketing an artist, which creates financial problems for cash-strapped independents, who previously only worried about paying for the production of their artists' albums and minimal promotion costs. By contrast, the major labels with their extensive financial resources can easily finance music videos as part of their promotional campaign for artists. Thus, the costs of video music enhance the control of the majors at the expense of the independent by escalating even further the costs for marketing an artist and album to a level only these conglomerates can afford.

8

Video Clip Producers and Directors

The two parties that actually make video music clips are the producer and director. The producer handles all of the business aspects of a production. This person manages all expenses for the production including employee salaries and payments for sets, costumes, and equipment. The two groups managed by the producer are creative personnel like performers, writers, film editors, directors, and production assistants, and technical staff such as camera operators, audio engineers, lighting directors, and stagehands. The producer can be a full-fledged company involved in many projects like commercials and theatrical films, or an individual who produces and directs the video clip singlehandedly.

The video clip director transforms a script or concept and the accompanying song into a short production. Millicent Shelton, a music video director for many rhythm and blues (R&B) and rap artists, says "one of the chief responsibilities of the director is to convey the idea [of the music clip] to everybody around you so that your dream can happen."[1] The director visualizes a proposed script by providing a detailed description of a scene sequence. After this preliminary planning, the director oversees the making of the music clip by coordinating the performers in front of the camera, including the featured musicians, and the production crew behind the camera. In music clips with larger budgets the director usually works within a production company under the supervision of a managing producer, whereas in more modest productions, one person produces and directs. Record companies see the director as the primary creative force behind music videos. According to Paul Flattery, head of the production company, Split Screen, "The videoclip business is one of the few where the director is seen as the auteur—and they do have the dominant creative input."[2]

Music Video Clip Producers

Large Production Companies

The most prolific makers of music clips are large production companies that specialize in music video. Some of these firms are independently owned and produce videos for several record labels on a freelance basis, like Propaganda Films and Limelight Films and Video, whereas others are owned by record companies and produce videos for their own labels (as well as other labels), including EMI's Picture Music International and Island Records' in-house video production studio. Production companies not directly owned by record labels still have long-term relationships with the major record companies that regularly commission these firms to produce their clips.

These companies generally have low overhead and a minimal administrative staff because their operating income is limited by the labels' stringent video clip budgets, which often barely cover production expenses. Alex Omeltchenko, head of Pendulum Productions, complains that "many labels don't understand there's no such thing as profit in video production companies. We don't make a profit, we just make money to cover overhead."[3] The meager production budgets also help ensure that these music video–oriented production companies remain non-unionized. Producer Lenny Grodin says that the paltry clip budgets prevent production companies from paying union scale wages and offering benefits required by union contracts, making video producers "scabs of the highest order."[4] John Marsh, producer for Casey Movies, agrees that the stingy record label practices fostered the development of a "non-union, unregulated, cutthroat" music video industry and says he would "like to see union scale tied into budgets."[5]

Most production companies that make music videos in the United States are in either Los Angeles or New York, the bicoastal centers for most television and film production. Locating in Los Angeles is advantageous for production firms because most of the major record labels are based there, providing closer contact with executives that hire companies to make clips. Some producers like Lenny Grodin of GPA Films prefer New York because as Grodin claims, "it's a better place to shoot than Los Angeles. There's less of a hassle, the police are free, you don't have to pay for a permit, and you get at least as good a deal here on services as you can in L.A."[6] Globally, London is a major center for music video production. Several large music video production companies have divisions in London, including EMI's Picture Music International. U.K. firms became established in video music before American companies because British record labels relied upon video clips as a primary means of promotion some time before their American counterparts made a significant investment in this new cultural product.

Propaganda Films is the largest and most prolific company in music video, making about 150 clips in 1990.[7] The founders and cochairs of Propaganda, Steve Golin and John Sighvantsson, met while studying at the American Film Institute in Los Angeles and gained extensive experience producing music videos at other production companies. Propaganda grew into a large enterprise with ninety-five staff members by May 1992 and branched out from music videos to feature films, producing Madonna's documentary *Truth or Dare* and David Lynch's *Wild at Heart.*[8] Yet Propaganda's main focus remains music video, and the chairs say their company is focused on making clips that meet the needs of the record labels. The company primarily uses its own in-house directors for productions, having a stable of young, acclaimed directors like David Fincher who made clips for Madonna's "Vogue" and Don Henley's "End of the Innocence." Alex Melnyk, head of Propaganda's music video division, says the company constantly seeks to develop fresh, talented directors for music videos, who can progress to feature films and commercials. Propaganda, which has a reputation for financial stability, will only agree to make videos for record labels with budgets that include a 15 percent markup over production costs.

Picture Music International, another large established production firm, was established in 1983 by its parent company, Thorn EMI, a British consumer electronics and music conglomerate, and has since established offices in New York, Los Angeles, and London, producing hundreds of video clips for rock acts including David Bowie, Duran Duran, and the Stray Cats. Picture Music has an administrative infrastructure that supports a group of permanent and freelance directors who are hired to make specific music clips for the firm. The company coordinates plans for the production of videos and oversees production expenses for equipment and personnel. For one typical video for Billy Idol, Picture Music employed more than forty people for two weeks and paid for the costs of video shoots, set construction, and transportation of the entire production staff to Los Angeles where the clip was taped. Music videos constitute most of Picture Music's production, but the company expanded into related production areas, producing commercials for Sony, RCA, and Coca-Cola as well as sales presentations for JVC. Mark Levinson, the president of Picture Music, explains, "We see rock videos as just a springboard for a broader business."[9]

Large production companies whose primary specialties are in other areas like commercials or film occasionally make music videos, for example, Lucasfilm Commercial Productions, a company owned by director and producer George Lucas. Lucasfilm, which usually makes commercials, began producing some music clips in early 1991, including Paula Abdul's clip for "Rush Rush." Lucasfilm is selective about what projects it accepts, doing only about six music projects a year with larger budgets—at least $100,000.[10] Although music videos are not very profitable for the firm, directors at Lucasfilm are drawn to the creative freedom of this form.

Smaller Production Companies

Smaller firms owned by a sole producer or a partnership of a few producers also make video clips as well as related types of production. For example, Ken Walz is a producer based in New York who has made over 100 video clips since the late 1970s for artists like Cyndi Lauper, but has since shifted his focus more toward commercials and industrial films because of the greater financial rewards in those production areas. Pam Tarr is the owner of Squeak Productions, which makes both music videos and commercials. Even though Squeak does more music clips, commercial work accounts for about two-thirds of the firm's gross income because, according to Tarr, "commercials are simply more profitable. I don't think anybody's getting rich off of music videos."[11] She is willing to accept production assignments for music clips with rather limited budgets, but only under certain circumstances. "The other day we got a video with a budget of $15,000 and that was OK because the label person [was realistic] and could work with those limitations," Tarr says.[12] "It's tougher if you have a low budget and the [lead musician] has bad skin, the wardrobe is important, and he can't move so you have to surround him with dancers."

Finally, some music clips are produced by aspiring video or film producers trying to establish themselves in the industry. These novice producers are often recent film school graduates who finance their own work as well as produce and direct the clip almost singlehandedly. These self-produced clips usually have an extremely limited budget, forcing the producer to cut costs to an absolute minimum, using whatever means available. Jim Hershleder, who made a video for Island Records artist Peter Himmelman for less than $6,000, explained that he was able to produce his clip so cheaply by "calling in assorted favors from friends" such as camera and equipment loans.[13] Phil Mailard of Shoot til You Drop Productions pursues every possible avenue for props and scenery for his music clips, saying, "I've done videos where I robbed my mother's bedroom for stuff and she called the police."[14]

Music Video Clip Directors

Music video directors have varying degrees of experience and prestige in this field, which roughly determine the extent of creative autonomy and financial support each director will be accorded. Directors fall into three general categories, each with a different level of status and related magnitude of creative control and production budgets: the superstar, the professional, and the novice.

The director with the greatest degree of status, the superstar, is not a full-time music video director but rather is established in a related production area like television commercials or films. Several successful Hollywood film directors have made video clips, including Brian De Palma, Martin Scorsese, and John Sayles, as has Bob Giraldi, the prolific director of well-known television commercials such as the Miller Lite ads. While the superstar's work in his or her primary field is more financially lucrative, this director is attracted to video music because of the unprecedented degree of creative autonomy permitted (to this director at least). Giraldi appreciates the artistic freedom of music videos compared to the tightly controlled content of television commercials. He especially enjoys making music videos because "there's no time limit and there's no technique limit. It's totally open."[15] This successful director usually makes one or a few videos for established rock stars with budgets ranging from $100,000 on up. The superstar is not usually subject to the stringent budgetary restrictions imposed by the record labels because this director often works directly with the established recording act, who pays for the video. All of Giraldi's videos were commissioned by major stars like Michael Jackson.

Ranking considerably below the superstar in terms of status is the professional. Unlike with the successful film director who dabbles in music video, directing clips is often a full-time occupation for the professional. This director either works through one of the major production companies or his or her own smaller firm. These directors have established reputations with major record labels for completing video clips before deadlines and within predetermined budgets, and thus receive regular assignments from label executives. The professional generally directs videos with tightly limited budgets, which average $60,000 and often must pay for any expenses over that allocated budget. A director's financial compensation for directing a video is similarly limited. Producer Lenny Grodin estimates that a director's fee for three weeks' work on a completed video is in the range of $5,000.[16] This fee is usually 10 percent of the overall budget for the clip. Moreover, the director is generally not entitled to any royalties made from broadcast license payments or future sales of the video clip in the home-video market. Because of the limited income derived from music videos, directors often expand into more lucrative areas of production, like commercials. The professional's creative control is limited by record label executives who often require certain content and visual styles to be incorporated in the clip.

Millicent Shelton is an example of an accomplished professional who is perhaps best known for her videos for the female rap group Salt-N-Pepa, including "Expressions" and four versions of "Let's Talk About Sex." Shelton studied at the New York University graduate film school and held a succession of jobs leading to music video, including second assistant cameraperson on a shoot and production assistant on *The Cosby Show*. Her first low-budget music video gained the favorable attention of Warlock Records, which hired her to make a music clip for "Free South Africa" for a modest $8,000. Even though that video never aired, she began making videos for Salt-N-Pepa, establishing a trademark style of bright colors, quick cuts, and hip street fashions in her videos. Shelton gets ideas for the look of her productions from European fashion magazines and volumes of still photography. She has achieved a level of success in the industry, allowing her to reject certain unpalatable job offers. "I don't want to do a video for $20,000, and I don't want to do a video about women's butts," Shelton says firmly.[17] Yet as one of the few successful African-American women directors in the business, she faces the twin obstacles of racism and sexism. Even though she would like to make videos for a diverse range of artists, Shelton is usually only offered productions for black artists at lower budgets, a common experience encountered by black directors. As for her gender, she faces entrenched sexism in the male-dominated industry. "People think you slept with somebody or that there's some male figurehead telling you what to do," she says. Shelton cut her hair short, explaining "I had long hair, but people always thought I was one of the dancers or somebody's girlfriend."[18]

The novice, the director with the least degree of status, has little or no formal experience directing music videos and usually both directs and produces clips. The novice makes videos on a very limited budget, far below those allocated to a more experienced director. Although average budgets for videos are roughly $50,000 to $60,000, first-time directors make videos for $30,000 to $50,000 or even much less.[19] The novice also accepts a lower director's fee for producing the video in exchange for the opportunity to become established in the industry. To demonstrate their proficiency, these directors may even finance their own videos and take a major financial loss on the production. Although it is difficult to break into this competitive market, record companies infrequently commission aspiring directors for their videos because these beginners are considered more economical to use than established directors.

Music Video Production as a Transitional Occupation

Music video is widely considered to be a transitional role for most directors and producers. Many directors who enter the industry making video clips expect to move into other, more lucrative fields of production. Jon Roseman of the London-based video production company JRTV claims that directors generally do not want to continue making video clips indefinitely, saying bluntly, "If a video director's still doing only clips after five years, he's a failure."[20] Moreover, although the creators of music video enjoy the challenge of working in this area, most become frustrated with the limited budgets and substandard working conditions such as tight deadlines and nonunion production crews. Directors and producers who become established with music video can increase their income dramatically by moving into commercials, television shows, and films. Some continue to make use of their background in music video by specializing in "long-form" music productions such as music-oriented television specials or theatrical films.

Major film studios and independent film companies consider video clip directors to be a prime source of new talent for theatrical films, hiring some to direct productions with only a year's experience. Several film directors had their start in music videos, including Russell Mulcahy, Julien Temple, Paul Justman, and Steve Barron, director of Michael Jackson's *Billie Jean* video. Mark Robinson, another new film director with a music video background, says that film companies seek video clip directors because of their industry experience, saying "They constitute a talent pool of guys who are trained with guns to their heads as opposed to film school. We're talking actual hands-on stuff where if, in fact, you're given x amount of dollars and if, in fact, you deliver it for $10,000 more, it comes out of your pocket. You learn real quick what you can and cannot do."[21] Film companies also like video clip directors because the studios primarily make films for a young audience and these clip directors work in a medium that captures the attention of this desired demographic group. Scott Rosenfeld, coproducer of the film *Roadhouse*, actively sought a director with a video background for this reason, observing, "the industry perceives these directors as people who understand what kids want."[22] He says that because rock video directors are skilled at entertaining teenagers, film companies are more likely to hire these video makers than novice directors with a different background. "Documentary filmmakers," he notes, "don't even come close to getting the shot that the guys with a couple of rock videos get."[23] Some film critics worry that the studios' increasing use of video clip directors may enhance the importance of visual style in theatrical motion pictures at the expense of traditional narrative elements such as plot and character development.

The Music Video Producers Association

In 1984, video clip producer Lenny Grodin organized the creation of the Music Video Producers Association (MVPA) to create general standards for the industry that would establish better working conditions for producers and encourage record labels to increase clip budgets. The MVPA, a coalition of thirty producers in 1985, sought to act as a liaison between video producers and the record labels to discuss the producers' concerns about industry practices. Clip producer Ken Walz comments that producers can effectively voice their grievances to the record labels only through an organized group like the MVPA because "that's the only way we'll get anywhere."[24] Walz claims that individual complaints by producers are ineffective because the labels "will inevitably feel that if you don't want to do it, there are plenty of others standing in line."[25] However, producer Jon Roseman argues that intense competition in the market prevents video clip directors from working together through organizations such as the MVPA. "I'd like to see an association," Roseman said, "but we're so paranoid and competitive it just won't happen."[26]

The association continued to lobby for better financial arrangements and budgets for producers, issuing a set of recommended guidelines in 1986 for its members and record companies to abide by in contract negotiations with each other.[27] The group tried to establish policies about payment arrangements for videos, fees for concept proposals, and the bidding process for selecting a production company. The MVPA hoped to discourage the record companies' common practice of soliciting concept proposals for a video from several production companies simultaneously, deceiving these firms into believing that they each had been awarded the production. Under this proposed "firm bid plan," record labels would pay 50 percent of the budget for a video soon after a deal was made with a producer, dissuading labels from making false promises to several production companies for the same music clip. These policies were only recommended to production companies and record companies, calling into question their effectiveness since they could be ignored without consequence.

In 1991, the MVPA had forty-two members and claimed to represent companies responsible for 90 percent of music video production in the United States.[28] By this time, the association was more vigorously complaining about the record labels' declining budgets, unfair contracts, and unprofessional payment practices for videos. The MVPA was especially dissatisfied with the standard 15 percent allotted profit margin or "markup" in the music clip budgets. "No other industry works on a 15 percent margin," said Michael Hamlyn, then MVPA president.[29] "With that low a markup, the minute business starts going down, people start falling out." Because of this, Hamlyn said that the MVPA would be "strongly encouraging" its members to seek 20 percent profit margins.[30] Because the group is a trade association rather than a union, the organization only recommends such actions, but cannot collectively bargain for its members to establish standard policies. MVPA also proposed resolving disputes between record labels and production companies by an arbitration committee, but Pam Tarr, the MVPA's West Coast chairperson, claimed "the labels aren't interested."[31] More generally, both Hamlyn and Tarr admit that their group's proposals for better pay and working conditions can be easily dismissed by the record labels because of the large number of producers competing for projects. "The labels know we're pretty darn hungry for work and that they can push us pretty far," says Tarr.[32]

Record Label Contracts with Video Clip Producers and Directors

Record company executives hire producers and directors to make video clips for specific songs by label artists. In the early years of the video music industry, business practices were not firmly established regarding the process for selecting a production company or the standard terms of a contract between the label and producer for the production of a video clip. Producer Ken Walz described the video music field as "an outlaw industry with no guidelines as to methods of operations. Whatever style of operation worked for us and was acceptable to the record companies, was the one which was used."[33] Record labels commissioned videos and negotiated arrangements with production companies on a case-by-case basis. In 1994, directors and producers still described the music video business as an informal one with few rules or guidelines. Although there is no consensus between labels and producers about business arrangements for video clip production, certain general trends have emerged. The labels often solicit bids from production companies for video clips using a method called "fixed bidding," where the label establishes a set budget for a particular clip and then requests production companies to submit a script providing a detailed description of their proposed concept for the video.[34] The record label ideally reviews the submitted scripts and selects one company to produce the video on the basis of their proposal.

However, producers object to how record companies conduct this bidding process. Lenny Grodin argues that the record label practice is "unethical" because the labels appropriate ideas provided by production companies without paying for them.[35] According to Grodin, the labels "can read a dozen good treatments, hire one person, and then suggest elements that they've picked up from other treatments."[36] Director Kevin Kerslake filed a lawsuit in March 1994 against the band Nirvana and the late Kurt Cobain for this practice, claiming that Cobain stole many of his ideas in the clip of the song "Heart Shaped Box," directed by Anton Corbijn and made for Geffen/DGC video.[37] Music clip directors claim that instances like Kerslake's happen all the time. Jon Roseman adds that production companies often submit a script for a video solicited by a label and hear nothing from the record company until "we see it on TV and there's an idea we submitted."[38] Production companies oppose this bidding process because they must prepare time-consuming, expensive script proposals without any payment. "If the labels solicit us to write up a concept," asserts Grodin, "we should be paid."[39] These producers also are irritated by the practice of soliciting multiple bids for a video and leading each production company to believe it was given the job. Producers want the record companies to notify them if their scripts are rejected so they do not spend valuable time and resources pursuing projects given to others.

Once a record label commissions a production company to make a video, the parties sign a contract obligating the firm to produce the video for a certain predetermined budget within a specified period of time. According to Ken Walz, the contracts are slanted in favor of the record labels' interests: "Contracts with the record companies are terrible. They say 'We'll give you your budget, and we want a video, no matter what. You have no rights; you're a hired hand.' It's totally skewed to the record companies."[40] Producers are often required to pay for any expenses exceeding the allocated budget. Contracts generally do not provide for royalties for the producer or director if the video clip is sold as a retail product, a source of irritation to Ken Walz, who produced Cyndi Lauper's acclaimed video, "Girls Just Want to Have Fun."[41] Walz, who claimed to make only $1,500 in profits from the production, bitterly recalled, "I know that I've made Lauper and Portrait Records an awful lot of money. . . . I don't even have a platinum record on my wall. They're selling both videos I did for Lauper on a compilation. Money is pouring into Cyndi's pockets and to CBS Records. . . . I'm partially responsible for that, and I've received virtually no compensation."[42] In general, the record labels claim video directors and producers are not entitled to any revenues derived from the music clip unless they help finance the production.

Producers and directors, except for those with superstar status, generally have limited bargaining leverage with the record labels during contract negotiations, compelling the video clip makers to consent to contracts that are heavily weighted in favor of the record companies. The highly competitive state of the video music market prevents most production companies from demanding too much from record labels, who can easily find other firms willing to produce a video on their stringent terms. Larry Solters, vice president of artist development for MCA Records, confidently says, "As soon as you hang up the phone with that [dissatisfied] video producer, there's another one on the phone who's done five less videos and is eager to take the shot. If he can deliver the same concept for cheaper, I'd be delinquent in my duty as a businessman not to accept it."[43]

The Production Budget

The producers' primary complaint is that record label budgets for video clip productions are too low, making it difficult to produce high-quality productions suitable for television. Chrisann Verges, who produced several videos with budgets of $40,000, explains, "I got out of them because the budgets remained the same. . . . It's very hard to do a non-union shoot. . . . There's also more emphasis on quality in video, and for professional quality you need professional crews."[44] Lenny Grodin claims that the stingy budgets force producers to "cut corners" in unethical or illegal ways in order to make the video for the allocated amount.[45] The limited budgets also make it hard for producers to earn profits from video clips comparable to the profit margin in related areas of production. Grodin says that "whether you're making videos, dresses or milk, you should be making 35% markup. We're lucky if we make 15 percent."[46]

In 1984, after producing a series of videos with marginal or no profits, Picture Music instituted a policy of refusing video production jobs that did not incorporate a 30 percent profit margin in the proposed budget. Producers like Walz say that limited and stagnant budgets encouraged them to move away from music video into commercials.[47] The record labels show little sympathy for producers' grievances. Larry Solters' uncompromising stand is typical of the labels, saying, "it's the free enterprise system. If [video producers] can't do the job and provide the quality of work that's expected [within the budget], they shouldn't take the job. If they can't operate within those restraints, maybe they should do commercials."[48]

Music clip budgets steadily increased throughout the 1980s, leveling off in the early 1990s. According to various trade magazine reports, the average budget for videos rose from $15,000 in 1981, to $40,000–$50,000 in 1984, and $50,000–$60,000 in 1988, remaining at $60,000–$80,000 in the 1990s. The average cost of video clips for producers varies according to their degree of stature in the industry. Large, established production companies command the highest budgets, in the $100,000 range, whereas smaller companies generally receive budgets of $60,000 or less. Estimates for first-time producers' budgets vary widely from $1,000 to $50,000. Budgets for video clips also vary according to the degree of commercial success of the recording artists featured in the production. Major stars like Madonna and Michael Jackson are usually featured in videos costing over $100,000. These artists often pay for their own videos to retain ownership rights to the production, entitling the musician to royalties derived from clip sales in the home-video market. David Fincher, a director at Propaganda, claimed in 1988 that "there are fewer stars willing to pay $100,000 for a great video."[49] However, in early 1995 there was a renewed burst of enthusiasm by superstar acts for wildly expensive videos. Michael Jackson's video for "Scream" from his new double album *HIStory: Past Present and Future—Book One* reportedly cost $7 million, perhaps the most expensive music clip ever made. Madonna's "Bedtime Story" was a $2 million production with elaborate special effects, and The Rolling

Stones' video for "Love Is Strong," featuring huge band members towering over a city, required $1 million. These artists pay huge sums to produce video spectacles that will hopefully bolster their superstar status—and in Jackson's case distract attention away from unsavory allegations about his personal life. Producers Jon Small and Alex Omeltchenko estimate that video budgets for medium-level recording acts range from $50,000 to $75,000, whereas videos for new artists cost up to $50,000.[50] Music clips for acts that are unsigned or affiliated with small independent labels often have minimal budgets under $10,000.

In the early 1990s, the major record labels adopted more fiscally conservative policies for music video, leading to substantially lower budgets for productions. Prominent producers of music video say that the quantity of music video clips remained constant, but the average budgets for these productions shrank. Len Epand, president of Flashframe Films and the East Coast chair of MVPA, said at the end of 1991 that "certain videos that may have been budgeted at $75,000 one or two years ago are often edging to $60,000."[51] Sixty thousand dollars is also the average budget for Lenny Grodin's GPA Films, which specializes in clips for dance and rap artists. Epand says the labels commission more music clips at substantially lower budgets. "Now we're hearing of $30,000–$35,000 videos when those didn't exist two years ago—you didn't do anything for under $40,000," he reports.[52] A major production company, Limelight, established a division for producing videos in the $20,000 to $50,000 range because of the growing label demand for low-budget videos, although this was later dismantled.[53] Music clip budgets dropped dramatically in Canada as well to an average of $30,000–$40,000 by early 1992, a steep decline from the mid-1980s when many artists had $100,000 videos.[54] Diminishing record label support for music video made it more difficult for production companies to survive, graphically illustrated by the failure of three major firms in 1991, AWGO, MGMM, and Calhoun Productions, and the retrenchment of established firms like Limelight and Vivid Productions.[55]

Production companies attribute the declining budgets to numerous factors. The labels shifted their emphasis from financing videos for adult contemporary artists to rap and R&B acts that historically received lower budgets than videos for comparable white performers. More expensive videos in the $100,000 range commissioned by the labels sometimes do not get played on MTV, much to the dismay of the record label executives who consider the money spent for those pricey productions wasted. If costly videos do not get played on prominent channels like MTV, record labels reason they might as well just fund more modest clips. Promotion executives also may decide to dispense with a video entirely, in favor of alternative means of exposure. "If you're going to spend $80,000 or $90,000 on a clip and not get exposure on a national show, maybe you should put the money toward the road," explained Emily Wittman, national director of video promotion for A&M Records.[56] The proliferation of aspiring first-time directors and small production companies in the late 1980s willing to make a video for next to nothing also depressed budgets, forcing more established production companies to make lower bids for music clip projects. Finally, record labels continue to limit expenses for videos because of the concern that this production is primarily a promotional form that does not recoup its own costs or make a profit.

Record Label Constraints on Video Clip Content

Whereas budgetary considerations impose constraints on producers and directors, record label executives also limit the creative latitude of video clip makers. When a record company commissions a video clip, the label often provides the producer with strong direction about the content and visual style of the proposed music video. Producers frequently are expected to make videos that visualize scripts or storyboards developed by the label video departments. The labels also express preferences for either "performance" videos, which portray groups performing the songs in a straightforward manner in front of the camera, inside a studio, or at a concert, or "concept" videos, which illustrate stories or abstract themes often with a surreal appearance. In 1988, record companies preferred conventional performance videos rather than more ambitious and imaginative concept-oriented clips, believing that performance videos more effectively establish the image of an act.[57] David Fincher, a director at Propaganda, remarked that labels often want a very specific mixture of these types of videos, saying "a label will come to you and say things like they want a 70/30 split between performance and concept with portrait-type breakaways and an overall glossy look."[58] However, although labels encourage performance videos, Pat Aufderheide notes that record companies prefer visuals of bands lip-synching to prerecorded music rather than tapes of artists singing "live" at concerts.[59] Record companies want video clips to feature the same studio-recorded music on albums in order to promote album sales.

Some video producers and directors allege that the record labels discourage creative and innovative productions, favoring conventional videos more likely to be aired by major video music program services like MTV. Brian Grant, a video director who made clips for Donna Summer, complains, "Innovation originally took place in video because there was no funding from the labels, no guidelines. Now, it's a business."[60] Mat Manurin, another video clip director, agrees that record companies have a conservative influence on videos, claiming "they're really afraid of trying something different, though there are exceptions."[61] Video clip producers worry that the establishment of industry rules and guidelines governing the production of clips will undermine the initially idiosyncratic, eccentric nature of video music, leading this media form to become more rigid and standardized. These video clip makers charge that the creativity of music videos suffers because record labels consider music videos solely as commercials rather than artistic endeavors in their own right. John Beug, vice president of video at Warner Brothers, seems to accept this diminished conception of music clips, saying "you have to maintain a perspective about what [the video maker] is doing. You're making a three-minute marketing tool. It's like designing an album cover. We're not making 'Gone With The Wind.'"[62] Yet director Josh Taft responds that music video has its own artistic integrity. "We're making a creative piece of visual marketing that has a life of its own, and should be treated as that," says Taft. "It's not just a cog in a wheel."[63] Moreover, directors and producers suggest that increasingly intrusive record label involvement in production matters is undermining the personal creativity of those involved in making the music clip.

Labels encourage producers and directors to pander to MTV's tastes by making videos that have the same visual style and content as videos that received heavy play on MTV in the past. Frequent plagiarism of popular videos on MTV created a series of hackneyed visual clichés that regularly recur in video clips, such as rising smoke, smashing glass, and scantily clad women. Increasing production of banal video clips dominated by overused images led Jeff Ayeroff, Warner Brothers' creative marketing vice president, to characterize most of the video clips being produced in the mid-1980s as "crap."[64] Ayeroff acknowledges that the record industry tendency to produce clips that pander to major music programs is the source of these abysmal productions. "I think that what we're producing is the lowest common denominator product," Ayeroff explains, "because the medium we're producing for demands that standard."[65] The problem of hackneyed videos became so pronounced that MTV spokespersons repeatedly asked record companies to stop producing videos that fit MTV's format and concentrate on making creative videos. In December 1989, MTV Networks chairman Tom Freston skewered the record labels for their substandard videos in his remarks at the eleventh annual *Billboard* Music Video Conference and appealed to the labels to "kill the cliches" in their productions.[66] Yet some video clip makers argue that MTV's increasingly conservative programming policies generally eschew unusual, avantgarde videos and contribute to the very tendency toward banal videos that MTV representatives claim they want to stop.

Producers and directors of music videos see a direct relationship between the budget and the degree of creative freedom they are afforded in the making of the clip, with record label interference growing exponentially, the larger the budget. Director Phil Mailard says that "on larger budgets, you get more politics."[67] "In the range of $20,000 to $50,000 you're given a lot of leeway," explains video director Adam Bernstein.[68] "But once you get between $70,000 to $100,000, you have to contend with a lot more input," having to deal with the various record company executives that have their own ideas about how a particular video should look. For higher-budget music clips, record labels want to be sure that their investment in the video will lead to publicity and exposure for the featured act.

Emerging Patterns in the Record Companies' Use of Video Clip Producers and Directors

Oligopoly of Large Production Firms

In 1982, when many independent producers and directors were making music videos during the initial burst of enthusiasm for this new media form, director

Richard Namm gloomily argued at a conference panel that video clip production would be "going through a shake down period. . . . In the next few years you'll see 10 to 15 companies on both coasts getting the lion's share of the work."[69] Namm's pessimistic prediction largely materialized; video clip production is increasingly dominated by an oligopoly of large, established production firms that specialize in music videos. The record labels rely on a small group of production companies to furnish video clips for their artists. According to a survey of video clip operations at twenty-six record companies, the production firms Propaganda, "O" Pictures, MGMM, F.Y.I., and The Company were commissioned for 22 percent of these record labels' video clip productions in progress during a six-week period ending October 1, 1988.[70]

Although many independent producers became involved in the field of music video in the early 1980s, these smaller production firms were hurt by declining video clip production at the major record labels after the initial novelty of music video subsided. Although the larger firms were able to adjust to shifting levels of production, more modest production companies were unable to prosper solely by making video clips. Producer Paul Flattery observes that "the big production companies can make money," but "those in the lower brackets can't survive on clips alone."[71]

The record labels also frustrated the development of independent producers by giving most of their business to the larger established companies. Stuart Samuals, a producer for the production company Zbig Vision, comments that this record label practice increased the dominance of larger firms and contributed to a more concentrated market. "What's happened is not so much clip burnout but fallout," says Samuals. "A lot of smaller production companies can't maintain themselves, and the bigger ones band together and get all the work because of the labels' need to trust established entities."[72] Record labels tend to rely on larger companies with established reputations for making technically proficient music clips in a short period of time within the allotted budget. Conversely, producers without an extensive background in music videos are seen as risks because there is no assurance that unknown producers will deliver music clips on schedule. The record companies' use of established firms parallels the U.S. commercial television networks' reliance on a core group of production studios to supply the bulk of their programming.

Increased Use of New Producers and Directors

Although record companies increased their use of established production firms, labels also pursued the seemingly contradictory policy of aggressively seeking out new and unknown directors and producers for some of their video clips. In December 1988, *Billboard* reported that the video departments at major labels were hiring new directors more actively than in the past several years.[73] For instance, Elektra Records selected Matt Mahurin, a young illustrator for several magazines who previously had made only one video clip, to direct the video for Tracy Chapman's "Fast Car." The labels use new talent because new directors and producers make clips with much lower budgets than more established video clip makers. MCA's Larry Solters argues that novice video producers and directors with minimal administrative expenses can make high-quality videos with a modest budget, saying, "I just had a brilliant video produced for $20,000 by two young unknown guys who were looking for a break. There are always going to be smaller companies who have no secretaries or business managers or telephones who can do it for less."[74] Darcy Myers, Warner Brothers manager of video production, agrees with this assessment, revealing that for one video project, "we had $10,000 for Throwing Muses and six or seven directors who wanted to do it."[75] The labels' use of unknown creative talent to make video clips also depresses the average budget for clips. Record labels encourage new directors and producers to underbid more established production companies for video jobs, forcing these firms to eventually lower their asking price for videos in order to remain competitive. By pitting novice video makers against other producers, budgets are restrained and the labels' overall video production expenses are limited.

Besides budgetary considerations, the record labels claim that novice directors are more likely to make original, innovative clips and avoid hackneyed video clichés. Motown's Traci Jordon says that her label commissioned several new directors for videos because "we're assured they won't be copying any of their earlier works, nor trying to climb out of conceptual ruts."[76] Peter Baron, head of video for Geffen Records, comments that his label is developing new directorial talent because "there's a feeling that we rely too heavily on established directors and that in many cases, their work begins to look much the same from video to video."[77]

Some record companies search for new potential directors at respected film schools at places like the University of Southern California and New York University as well as at student film festivals. Record company executives scout for prospective directors at these venues in the same way label A&R representatives attempt to find new musical talent at local bars featuring live bands. However, Len Epand, formerly Polygram's senior vice president of video, contends that most labels do not have the resources to seek out new talent at film schools. Rather, the record companies rely on the established video clip production companies to develop new directors. Epand says that firms like Propaganda Films "serve as something of a breeding ground for new talent. . . . They'll turn us on to people by saying, 'Hey, this guy's a director of photography and he's going to be a great director.'"[78] However, David "Preacher" Ewing, a video clip producer, argues that this tendency for new directors to emerge from production companies turned the video clip form into "a cameraman's medium in which visual style is used as a substitute for substance."[79]

Although record companies claim to regularly commission novice directors and producers, they exercise greater caution when using unknown talent. Novice directors are used for less urgent projects with ample time for production whereas more established firms are employed for clips with tight deadlines. Kris P., West

Coast director of videos for Columbia Records, recalls that for The Bangles' video "In Your Room," she assigned video director Tamra Davis, who "was known primarily for more avant-garde works with lower budgets, but [whom] I suspected would add the kind of edge the group needed." She concedes that she allowed Davis to direct this video only because there was sufficient production time, explaining, "If this wasn't a situation where we could have three weeks of meetings between the product manager, the artists, their manager and the director, I probably would have had to go with something safer using a more established name."[80]

However, some believe record companies' use of novice directors and producers is greatly exaggerated. Scott Kalvert, a director who made clips for Jazzy Jeff and the Fresh Prince, claims that he initially had great difficulty getting work from the labels despite his considerable experience directing such clips as Kool Moe Doe's "Wild Wild West."[81] Others claim that labels rely almost exclusively on established production firms specializing in music videos, while largely ignoring new independent video makers. Lionel Martin, principal director for Concept Productions based in New York, observes, "Labels have production companies that they constantly use, that are favorites, and it's difficult to break into that."[82]

Exclusion of Black Producers and Directors

In the late 1980s, major labels were charged with largely excluding blacks from the production of their video clips. Some African-Americans in the industry claim that record companies commission very few black producers and directors to make video clips. Jeff Newman, then senior producer of music video programming for BET, said, "There is a strong core group [of African-Americans] that is not being used by labels as much as it should be, for clips by both white and black artists."[83] Nelson George, a columnist for *Billboard,* claims that record company executives intentionally discriminate against black video clip makers, saying labels "won't consider black companies or won't tell artists and their managers of their availability."[84] Also, African-Americans are drastically underrepresented at white-owned production companies that make music videos. A *Billboard* survey in December 1990 revealed that less than 5 percent of the crews of these production companies are black.[85]

Blacks in the creative arts insist that even though African-American musicians are receiving more attention in video clips, the people who make their videos are usually white. Moreover, some blacks are especially outraged that video clips for successful black recording artists are mostly made by white producers and directors. George complains that the major labels "funnel black videos to the same small crew of [white] video producers."[86] Many in the black community expect African-American performers to include blacks in the production of their videos. Director Spike Lee argues, "I really place the blame on black artists. If they don't demand a black director, they should at least have a black publicist, black still photographer, a black choreographer, a black hair stylist and makeup artist."[87] Director Paris Barclay, head of Black & White Television, echoes this complaint, saying, "it's frustrating for me and some of the other black directors that black artists don't support us more."[88] However, he does see some increased sensitivity by black artists to this issue. "I feel [it's] changing. Michael Jackson let John Single-ton do 'Remember the Time,' and if he goes to another black director to do an-other cut for this album, it could really open things up."

When major labels do commission blacks to make a clip, directors and pro-ducers are often assigned videos for music in the black musical genres of R&B and rap, which generally have lower budgets than clips for white artists.[89] Lionel Mar-tin, a black director, laments, "We can work on clips for white acts, but we're not given the chance. Labels tend to put directors on rap videos, and they're mostly the lowest budget. That's how they start you out, and once you get good and make a name for yourself, labels figure that's all you do."[90] Martin's average budget for a video clip is $20,000–$30,000, substantially less than the industry average of $60,000. Millicent Shelton, director for Fat Productions and Idol Makers Films, experiences similar treatment despite her successful videos for Salt-N-Pepa and other artists. "This is a very racist industry," Shelton fumes.[91] "It's very difficult getting jobs as a black director. Black directors do black artists, they do R&B and rap. They tend not to do rap and R&B artists with video budgets over $100,000. As soon as the artist starts to cross over and the budgets start to exceed $100,000, the black director that brought that artist up is no longer considered for the video." Sherry Simpson of Black & White Television also sees this industry prac-tice as a type of "racism which says, 'You're black, so you have to direct black acts.' But white directors can direct anything. We're just trying to get people to see that talent across-the-board should be colorblind."[92]

The shoddy treatment of African-American producers and directors is repre-sentative of a broader pattern of discrimination in the record business. Although many black recording artists are commercially successful, African-Americans are underrepresented in positions of authority at major record companies. Sylvia Rhone, chairman and CEO of Atco/EastWest records, one of the industry's few high-level black executives, says that when she got her first job at a label as a sec-retary, "I had no reference point. There were no black people in senior positions."[93] In 1992, only four of the largest thirty-five record companies were managed by black executives, and two of these labels, Motown and RAL/Def Jam, primarily feature music by black artists.[94] Blacks are often confined to the nonbusiness side of labels, which stalls their career advancement. "Historically, most African-Amer-icans have been relegated to promotion positions in the industry," says Tony An-derson, general manager of R&B music at Polygram.[95] "But, until recently, upper management has not really accepted the idea that people from promotion could run record companies." African-Americans are also often limited to heading only black music divisions within labels, a restriction that results from the "perception that the strength of African-Americans in the record industry is limited to black music," explains David Harleston, president of RAL/Def Jam records.[96] This mir-rors the complaint of black directors and producers being confined to making clips for only black artists. The NAACP criticized the major record labels for their poor performance in hiring African-Americans in a 1987 report "The Discordant Sound of Music" and proposed a "Fair Share" policy to the labels to increase their employment of minorities.[97] The labels declined to abide by the NAACP proposal, claiming their own affirmative action programs were correcting past problems, prompting the NAACP to threaten a boycott of CBS, then owner of CBS Records.

Although production companies concede that relatively few video clips are made by blacks, they attribute this to a limited pool of black video directors and producers rather than discriminatory practices within the industry. Anne Marie Mackay, head of the music video division of Propaganda Films, comments that "there's a dearth of [black directors] in the music video industry," wishing "more would come forward."[98] Vivid Productions' Linda Valenzuela-Quakenbush expresses a similar view, saying "we've been aggressively looking for black directors. We're courting people. I've been looking at reels for five years and I really can't think of more than one black person that sent me a reel."[99] Amanda Pirie of Nitrate Films claims that their production crews are less than 5 percent black because they are not aware of black crew members. Yet the NAACP responds that there is an ample supply of competent black video makers who are not given sufficient production opportunities by the large production companies or record labels.

At the labels, Merritt Kleber, director of music video for Capitol Records, rejects accusations that record company executives are racist and intentionally use white producers and directors to make videos for black musicians. Attempting to shift blame to the recording artist, Kleber says "the selections of a director and a production company result from a process in which black artists and management are directly involved."[100] According to Kleber, production companies are chosen on the basis of a firm's artistic merit and its reputation for delivering videos on time and within allotted budgets. He argues, "race is not a consideration, nor should it be."[101] Michelle Webb of Atlantic Records says she actively encourages racially mixed production crews for her label's music clips. "When you have a black artist and everyone on the crew is white, it is extremely embarrassing," she admits.[102] Webb also claims that Atlantic Records hires black-owned production companies for about 10 percent of the label's productions.

Some production companies owned by minorities emerged to provide opportunities for black directors and crew members that are less available at other firms. In 1989, television and film producers Carl Craig and Richard Cummings Jr. founded Underdog Films, a video production company based in Los Angeles, to develop black talent. "I realized that there really was a lack of black directors involved with producing clips on black artists," says Cummings, "and talked with Carl about the idea of creating a whole company that would be able to focus on the pool of black talent and deliver qualified work."[103] Underdog Films offers a complete range of services for music video production with the available resources of four hundred people. Craig and Cummings want to provide African-

American recording artists with a company able to produce videos that reflect their identity and music as black people. According to Cummings, Underdog's goal is to have production crews composed of 60 percent minorities. Black & White Television, another minority-owned production firm, also tries to provide a forum for black directors. Paris Barclay, a director and Black & White's president, proudly reports that "of the 60-odd jobs we've done, 100% have been directed by blacks."[104] Yet although these minority-owned firms do create a space for black directors, such firms remain scarce. "When we started our company [in 1988]," says Barclay, "it was to increase minority participation, but we feel like we're [one of the few black-owned] production companies around having success."[105]

Despite the growth of firms like Black & White and Underdog, African-Americans and other minorities remained underrepresented in music video production, prompting the NAACP to address this problem in 1990. The Beverly Hills branch of the NAACP created a task force to lobby major record labels and production companies to increase their hiring of black directors and production crew members. Don Jackson of the NAACP task force explained, "There are two key areas that we're asking them to help us with. To increase the number of contracts that are given to African-American firms and the number of American-American technicians working with white firms on videos for African-American artists."[106] More specifically, the NAACP recommended that 40 percent of all music clips produced for black artists be made by black production companies, and that videos shot by white-owned production companies have crews at least 40 percent black.[107] To encourage this hiring, the NAACP distributed a directory of 280 African-American video production professionals to major production companies and a list of fifteen black-owned production companies to major record labels. Record label and production company responses to the NAACP proposals were unenthusiastic. Some continued to question whether a sufficient pool of qualified black talent existed to satisfy such policies, and others balked at numerical requirements for employment. "It's difficult to deal with a quota," cautioned Lenny Grodin of GPA Films, even though his production crews are usually about 40 percent black already.[108]

The NAACP also had two meetings with the Music Video Producers Association (MVPA) to stress the importance of hiring African-Americans in their productions. The first meeting in December 1990 was rocky, as NAACP representatives felt slighted by the MVPA in a short meeting lasting only twenty-five minutes. The NAACP believed that the production companies were not taking their concerns seriously. Michael Hamyln, MVPA president, claims that the problems stemmed from the British background of the MVPA members at the meeting who were not familiar with the NAACP or its objectives. "Three-fourths of the people in that room didn't understand. They're not American," explains Hamyln, who is himself British.[109] The parties were able to move beyond this initial misstep to cooperate on two successful job fairs, one on each coast, which introduced hundreds of available minority production crew members to major production companies.[110] Despite these constructive efforts, minorities are still underemployed behind the scenes in music video.

∿   ∿   ∿

Music video production is a business firmly controlled by the major record companies that finance the majority of music clips. These companies seem to follow three guidelines in selecting production companies and directors to be hired to make music clips. Label executives rely heavily on larger production companies like Propaganda and Picture Music that have established a reputation for reliability, will occasionally hire novice directors for some videos for minimal budgets, and finally, tend to hire African-Americans only for videos featuring black acts with lower budgets. Video producers and directors largely make music clips on terms dictated by the major labels. The record companies determine the budgets for videos and frequently make demands about the content of the music clip, curtailing the creative freedom of the director and producer.

The business arrangements are certainly not ideal for most video makers: Contracts are weighted toward record label interests, budgets are often skimpy with a minimal profit margin, and producers and directors receive no royalties from sales or broadcast licensing of the video. Further, the labels often act in an unscrupulous manner, stealing concepts and storyboards from these parties without compensation and dishonestly leading several firms to believe they have each been awarded a production contract. The trade association MVPA and individual production companies try to improve these conditions and increase budgets, but have little influence because of the intensely competitive nature of the industry. Smaller production companies and novice directors fresh from film school are always ready to underbid and undercut larger production companies, pressuring all video makers to take production jobs on terms offered by the labels, however imperfect. The undesirable working conditions and limited financial rewards encourage producers and directors to branch out into other types of productions like commercials or film, making music video more of a transitional occupation for many in the field. In general, the business for music video developed in a manner to serve the needs of record companies that want to promote their artists through video clips as cheaply as possible. Producers and directors are able to survive in this field only when they abide by the labels' stingy and self-interested policies.

9

MTV as Gatekeeper and Censor

MTV has become a powerful force in popular music today, shaping trends in music and providing invaluable exposure for recording artists through play of their video clips. MTV's presentation of these videos may cultivate an audience for an artist and often increases sales of an act's music. By contrast, music clips not presented on major program services like MTV have limited value as a form of promotion and the careers of artists featured in these unseen videos may be stalled due to lack of media exposure. The importance of MTV as a site of national exhibition for popular music and music clips raises the issue of MTV's role as a gatekeeper and its degree of influence over these forms of culture. How does MTV decide what music videos will be played and which submissions will be rejected? What criteria are used to determine the suitability of the music clips? MTV's control over the content of music video clips is also a pertinent issue. Is the channel able to require changes in the content of the videos to meet its standards? Can it persuade record labels and musicians to change the lyrics of songs performed in the videos as well? These questions are addressed in this chapter, which assesses to what extent MTV can impose its standards on the content of popular music and music clips, thus acting as a powerful censor over these two related media products.

The decisionmaking process within MTV for determining which videos are presented is examined, surveying the role of various departments within the program service. MTV's standards for videos, both stated and unstated, are reviewed. This survey examines the types of content considered objectionable and examples of specific videos initially rejected by MTV for unsuitable content. The relationship between MTV and various parties involved in the production of the music clip is explored, observing how these parties confront MTV's standards in the making of videos and react to its frequent requests to alter videos and lyrics after the completed clip is submitted to the channel. External pressures MTV encounters that influence its standards policies are assessed, such as complaints about program content from special interest groups and cable companies. Finally, the different pressures influencing the content of music video shows on broadcast and cable television, which account for the somewhat more relaxed standards on cable services like MTV, are compared.

MTV's Acquisition Committee

MTV has an elaborate screening process for deciding which videos will be added to its playlist. The channel must sift through a great quantity of music videos, receiving thirty-five to forty video clip submissions per week by November 1989.[1] These clips are first reviewed by MTV's Acquisition Committee, which meets once a week to decide if the videos will receive airplay. The rejection rate is high: About 80 percent of the videos received never make it on the channel.[2] This committee, originally composed of three members, expanded by 1990 to about ten people who serve on a revolving basis. Decisions about the fate of video clips are based on certain guidelines used for evaluating submissions such as whether the clips are consistent with the program service's format. MTV strongly embraces a "narrowcast" format playing only specific kinds of music designed to attract its desired young audience. Videos featuring music considered to fall outside the boundaries of the channel's rock format, such as country and easy listening music, are excluded. The production standards of clips are scrutinized for technical problems that make them unsuitable for airplay.

Other criteria for evaluating video clips are unacknowledged, such as the preference for clips by artists signed to major labels. Acts affiliated with major record companies are much more likely to be played on MTV than artists associated with smaller, independent labels. These independents often complain about being excluded from the channel. "Every week, long in advance of charts and sales, they're playing acts on major labels," says one president of an independent label. "They're willing to give it to the majors but not to the independents."[3] By contrast, MTV allows major record companies to select some of their own videos that will receive guaranteed play on the channel, a provision of contracts between MTV and the labels (described in Chapter 4) that amounts to an institutionalized form of payola.

MTV's Standards: Stated and Unstated

Once accepted by the Acquisition Committee, the clip is then evaluated by MTV's Program Standards and Public Responsibility Department, which determines whether the clip has any objectionable content. These guidelines are intended to prevent the presentation of videos that depict illegal drug use or excessive alcohol consumption, or "explicit, graphic or excessive depictions of sexual practices."[4] The videos cannot have scenes of gratuitous violence such as knifings or physical restraint. Music clips with "derogatory characterizations of ethnic or religious groups" also are not allowed on the channel, according to MTV's David

Horowitz.[5] Another MTV representative adds that visual shots of "naked women running around or throwing babies out of trucks" would not be permitted.[6]

MTV enforces these standards to deflect pressure from various groups complaining about sex and violence in videos and to demonstrate that management is competently handling the matter through its own screening process. Tom Freston, president of MTV Networks, explained, "We're caught between the rock and the hard place. We hear from advertisers, we hear from cable operators, we hear from individual consumers, and we can't get off violating those standards and have a business."[7]

MTV also does not allow videos to display brand-name products. "The idea behind not having product endorsements is to differentiate the videos from the commercials," explains MTV's Tina Exarhos.[8] The channel's ban is ironic since music videos are often derided for being nothing more than a commercial for an artist's compact discs and cassettes. The prohibition on brand names led record companies and producers to aggressively screen out logos in the making of music clips. "I have stood on the sets with black electrical tape and worked as logo police in order to save myself the headache and expense of having to edit [logos] out at a later date," revealed Jeff Newman, director of video production at Mercury Records.[9]

This policy was invoked to justify rejecting Neil Young's video, *This Note's for You,* which was a caustic, satirical commentary on the rampant commercialization of popular music. The song and video ridiculed and condemned the practice of popular performers endorsing products in music video–like television commercials. The music clip included parodies of famous pop stars in commercials, such as Michael Jackson hawking Pepsi and Whitney Houston selling Diet Coke. The song reinforced the mocking tone of the visuals with the lyrics, "Ain't singin' for Pepsi/Ain't singin' for Coke/I don't sing for nobody/Makes me look like a joke." Some critics suggested that the underlying reason for MTV's rejection of the video was to avoid embarrassing prominent advertisers on the channel that present these types of commercials featuring pop stars. "They've showed they have no backbone," claimes Laurel Sylvanus, Warner Brothers' national manager of video promotion.[10] "They're afraid their advertisers are going to be upset by it." Julien Temple, the video's director, agrees that "MTV is worried about biting the hand that feeds them," and Neil Young called MTV "spineless" in a letter sent to the network.[11] MTV ultimately provided some limited play of the video—only on its news program—after the channel was subjected to a blizzard of media criticism for its action. Yet the incident suggests that an unstated criterion for rejecting videos is if the content of the video embarrasses or criticizes the channel's advertisers.

Another unstated reason for rejecting a video is if the video is considered to be embarrassing or unflattering to MTV itself. One video was rejected because the word "Censored" was stamped over a particular scene as part of a statement against artistic censorship.[12] MTV refused to accept the video with this segment because channel executives feared viewers might assume that MTV was responsible for this action, drawing attention to its own role as a censor. This inference might undermine MTV's carefully constructed self-image as an irreverent rebel by revealing that MTV censors culture just like other establishment institutions. So, to maintain its hip facade, the channel avoids high profile attention to its own extensive censoring activities.

The "Committee"

MTV's Standards Department was established in April 1984 as a one-person operation and later expanded to five MTV staff members who review videos, some of whom also serve on the Acquisition Committee.[13] Neil Strauss reported in 1994 that this "committee" was still primarily one person, Michele Vonfeld, who has been responsible for MTV's standards enforcement for nine years. The record companies are not supposed to know the identity of Vonfeld and do not contact her directly. She consults with various people at the company when unsure whether a particular video violates the channels' standards. The committee reviews song lyrics as well as the video clip for potential problems, requiring record companies to submit lyrics along with each video. The decisions of the standards department are not unanimous within MTVN since the programming department often disagrees with it, leading to tension between these two areas.

Three possible actions are taken after evaluating a submission: The channel may accept the clip for airplay, reject it completely for standards violations, or require specific editing of the video before it can be added to the playlist. If MTV decides that some content in the video is unacceptable, the clip is sent to a member of MTV's talent relations department who explains to the record label why it cannot be aired and what editing is necessary to satisfy MTV. MTV does not edit music clips itself, but recommends that the record company make certain changes in the clip.

MTV's Freston concedes that this screening process is difficult and subjective: "Where it gets tricky is drawing the line. It's never a black-and-white issue. There's a lot of gray stuff. Is that too much or too little of Cher's ass? Somebody has to decide."[14] MTV spokesperson Carole Robinson characterizes this process as flexible, saying "our guidelines are fluid and open to interpretation so that each video can be looked at on a case-by-case basis."[15] She also claims that in borderline cases the channel usually presents the video: "When we have a difficult decision to make, we lean on the side of the artist and then see what the response of the viewer is. It's a balance between being a responsible programmer and respecting the artist's creative vision."[16] MTV is more likely to require videos from new artists to be edited than videos by more established acts with greater clout. "What's okay for Aerosmith is not okay for a lesser-known band," says Caprice Carmona, an independent video promoter who works with the small label Sub Pop. "And what's not okay for Green Day today will be okay for them in a year."[17]

Until 1989, Robinson said that the percentage of music videos rejected for unsuitable content remained relatively stable, "in the single digits, less than 10%."[18] Yet record label executives began charging that MTV's standards became more restrictive, prompting more requests for editing. Warner's Laurel Sylvanus explained, "We were asked to edit a scene in 'Personal Jesus' by Depeche Mode with the artist panting in the shadow between shots of dressed women. I think a year ago that video would have gone through, no problem."[19]

Some record companies attribute MTV's more stringent standards to the channel's policy of requiring lyrics to be submitted with the videos, which was instituted in 1989. "It's definitely made a difference now that they can read along," argues Michelle Peacock of Capitol Records.[20] "We've had several things sent back for lyrical interpretation and some of them probably would have gotten through before we had to turn in lyrics." Other record label personnel claim that MTV was reacting to a shift in public opinion toward music videos. Sam Kaiser, a senior vice president of promotion at Enigma and former vice president of programming for MTV, explains, "the standards and practices guidelines and mechanics are still much the same. However, when I was there we had a pretty liberal line and I think it's less liberal now because of the very conservative attitude around the nation. 'Girls Girls Girls' [by Motley Crue] probably wouldn't see the light of day now."[21]

In the past few years the channel has been returning a much greater proportion of music clips to record companies for editing. In 1993, MTV was sending back one out of every four videos it received, and became even more selective in 1994, rejecting one out of every three.[22] MTV president Judy McGrath admits, "We're taking a harder look at them," saying the network has become especially vigilant in not allowing music clips with scenes of violence. "The clips we play don't glorify gunplay or the stuff you see on reality television every day."[23] This prohibition on violence was considered appropriate since the network launched an antiviolence campaign in its programming in 1994. Some music video makers claim that MTV now requires editing in almost all the clips they make. "Nine and a half times out of ten, I have to scramble or edit out portions of videos I submit," complains one video production executive at a major label.[24] Marty Callner, a director for Aerosmith videos, charges that MTV objects to certain scenes "in just about every video I do. . . . It pisses me off."[25] Record company executives claim that some videos go back and forth between MTV and the record companies for editing up to six times.

Record labels charge that MTV's standards policies are too arbitrary and fail to provide clear guidelines to follow when making videos. Capitol's Peacock admits, "I just wish at times they'd be more consistent in what they allow and what they won't."[26] They also complain that the program service takes too long to screen clips, diminishing the promotional value of videos and undermining their attempts to develop new hit songs. MTV concedes that the increasing quantity of music clip submissions overwhelmed its standards department, resulting in lengthy delays in the reviewing process.

MTV has infrequently adopted an alternative to simply rejecting clips that violate its standards guidelines. The channel will sometimes play certain videos with excessive sexual content during later periods of the day when fewer young people are watching. In 1989, MTV played a provocative video of Cher dressed in a skimpy leather outfit dancing on a Navy battleship, but only after 9 P.M. The channel made a similar decision in June 1992 to play a video of *Baby Got Back* by Sir-Mix-A-Lot after 9 P.M., after receiving "many, many complaints from all of our constituencies over the entire period of time it had been on the air," according to MTV's Robinson.[27] The video included song lyrics of Sir-Mix-A-Lot rapping "I like big butts" and close-up shots of dancers' buttocks and fruits shaped like body parts. These decisions seem somewhat inconsistent since another music clip with similar subject matter, *Big Old Butt* by L. L. Cool J, was regularly played on the channel throughout the program day in 1989.

MTV's standards also apply to its programming other than music clips, which has been increasing rapidly in the past several years. *Beavis and Butt-head* is a popular and infamous animated show on the channel, which features two moronic teenagers wandering through suburbia acting vulgar and commenting on videos they watch on television. In 1993, MTV imposed restrictions on the show after a tragedy occurred in Moraine, Ohio, where a five-year-old boy set fire to the house killing his two-year-old sister. The boy's mother charged that the child began playing with matches and lighters after watching *Beavis and Butt-head,* imitating the actions of the characters who would frequently talk about setting fires. Although MTV denied responsibility, the channel belatedly imposed more restrictive standards on the show, removing all references to fire and also moving the program from 7 P.M. to 10:30 P.M. when fewer children would be watching.[28]

A Survey of Music Clips Rejected by MTV

Table 9.1 identifies various clips originally rejected by MTV for standards violations. The table is not an exhaustive or complete catalog of rejected clips, but rather depicts certain instances of MTV's refusal to play videos. The videos are grouped according to the general grounds for rejection, and the specific visual images or words for each video judged by MTV to be objectionable also are cited. This table illustrates that although MTV rejects videos for inappropriate sexual content, this standard violation is interpreted in numerous ways. The channel rejected a video for explicit nudity in a David Bowie clip called *China Girl* as well as for suggestive visuals where no graphic sex act or nudity was depicted, such as Bon Jovi's *Living in Sin* video portraying a band member placing a finger in the mouth of a woman who is fully clothed. MTV also rejected videos for sexually ex-

TABLE 9.1   Video Clips Rejected by MTV

General Category	Video Clip Title	Artist	Objectionable Content
Excessive sexual content	*China Girl*	David Bowie	nude beach scene
	Living in Sin	Bon Jovi	finger, object put in woman's mouth
	Justify My Love	Madonna	group sex, bisexuality, exposed breast
	Nine Months Later	Fuzztones	explicit song lyrics, reference to "rubbers"
Excessive violence	*Neighbors*	Rolling Stones	graphic portrayal of dismembered body
	Six, Six, Six	DeGarmo & Key	graphic portrayal of exploding body
Setting dangerous example	*Touch Me Tonight*	Shooting Star	visual shots of a drumstick busting light bulbs
	Nothing Can Stop Us Now	Serious-Lee-Fine	visual shots of basketball on fire
Racist content	*Do You Really Want to Hurt Me?*	Culture Club	visual shots of black-faced minstrels
Product mention	*This Note's for You*	Neil Young	specific depiction of brand-name products
	Kid Candy	Seaweed	depiction of brand-name product: soda with visible logo

plicit song lyrics where there are no objectionable visual images, such as the Fuzztones' *Nine Months Later,* which included the line "If you don't want to live this life of shame, be sure to wear your rubbers when you're out in the rain."[29] In response to MTV's request, the Fuzztones' record label, Beggar's Banquet Records, agreed to substitute the word *rubbers* with *raincoat* in the video in order to receive airplay.

Table 9.1 shows that MTV rejected videos for excessive violence when a clip graphically depicted bodily mutilation, such as The Rolling Stones' *Neighbors* video with visual scenes of a dismembered body in a suitcase.[30] The channel also refused to air videos because of concerns that a dangerous activity depicted in the clip could be copied by viewers. For example, Serious-Lee-Fine's rejected video depicted a basketball player dribbling a ball on fire and shooting it in a basket.[31] Although MTV also rejected videos for material alleged to be racist, such as a Culture Club video with scenes of black-faced minstrels, the channel aired clips considered by certain critics to include homophobic content, most notably Dire Strait's *Money for Nothing* video, which repeatedly mentions the word *faggot* in the song's lyrics.[32] MTV's prohibition of product mentions led the channel to reject the music video *Kid Candy* by Seaweed because of a shot of a person holding a soda with an identifiable logo.[33] MTV also initially banned Neil Young's video, *This Note's for You,* supposedly for its mention of product names, although D. J. Jazzy Jeff & the Fresh Prince's *Parents Just Don't Understand* was allowed on the channel's playlist despite its prominent display of brand-name products.[34] As mentioned previously, MTV may be more likely to reject a video with product mentions if the visual images or song lyrics ridicule or condemn advertiser practices like using pop stars to sell products.

Record Company and Artist Reaction to MTV

In almost all of the instances reported in Table 9.1, MTV said it would accept the videos if the clips were reedited to remove the offensive visual images or words. Neil Young's video was a notable exception to this policy as MTV executives initially refused to air the clip under any circumstances, even though Young and his record company offered to edit the clip to remove any content considered unacceptable by MTV.[35] In most cases, the record company and artist agree to edit the video to satisfy MTV because of the commercial importance of airplay of the clip on this premiere video music service. Record companies are willing to alter the video to satisfy MTV because in many instances the music clip was made primarily for showing on the channel. These labels rely heavily on MTV to provide national exposure for their artists and consider play of an act's video an invaluable form of promotion that can build an audience for an artist and increase album sales. Because of MTV's influence, the channel is able to impose its standards on most music videos financed by the major record labels.

Music clips are altered in various ways to satisfy MTV. The performers may record new lyrics for part of the song that MTV considers offensive, as the Fuzztones did for their music clip *Nine Months Later.* The trade magazine *Billboard* argued in an unsigned editorial that in some instances record labels strongly pressure their artists to revise the lyrics of their songs in order for MTV to accept the accompanying video clip.[36] An objectionable scene or image may be replaced with more palatable content. For example, DeGarmo & Key's video *Six, Six, Six* was rejected originally because the scenes of the Antichrist bursting into flames after an attack were deemed "too violent" according to an MTV spokesperson.[37] DeGarmo & Key agreed to reedit their video, and in the revised clip accepted by MTV, the burning Antichrist was replaced with a shot of a crystal ball depicting scenes of war and an atomic explosion. A computer scrambling device can be used to blur a certain portion of the screen that depicts an unsuitable image. Director Marty Callner used this technique to blur the image of a lewd hand gesture made by a woman in the Aerosmith music clip for "Crying." The scrambling technique is used frequently to cover up brand-name logos in videos.

As a result of MTV's vigorous enforcement of its standards, the record labels will infrequently commission multiple versions of music clips for a song: an unedited or "nasty" version to play on more permissive shows and sanitized, edited versions for more conservative programs. For instance, the act BWP made two versions for the video *We Want Money:* The edited version played on *Yo! MTV Raps* and the unedited clip was presented on The Playboy Channel's *Hot Rocks.* The record company may also sell the "nasty" version as a home video retail product using the marketing ploy that it contains provocative scenes not shown on television.

However, some artists refuse to edit their videos in any manner to placate MTV, such as Mick Jagger of The Rolling Stones, who says he never allows his music clips to be altered.[38] INXS would not remove sexually oriented scenes in the clip *Taste It.*[39] Public Enemy declined to take out an African riot scene from *Hazy Shade of Criminal.* The most publicized case of an artist's defiance of MTV's standards was Madonna, who refused to edit *Justify My Love,* a production filmed in black and white depicting erotic fantasies in a Paris hotel. The music clip had some brief scenes of nudity and an array of sexual practices, including male and female bisexuality, cross-dressing, sadomasochism, and group sex. MTV planned to debut the video in November 1990 with great fanfare as part of a weekend "Madonnathon," with programming devoted entirely to the artist's music videos, filmed concerts, and interviews. After failing to reach an agreement with Madonna, MTV released a terse statement announcing its decision, saying "We respect her work as an artist and think she makes great videos. This one is not for us."[40] The decision prompted a flurry of press attention that culminated in an edition of ABC's *Nightline* being devoted to the topic. *Nightline* presented the unedited video and an interview with the provocative artist.[41]

Madonna called attention to the more general double standard in media censorship of sex and violence. "Why is it that people are willing to go to a movie and watch someone get blown to bits for no reason and nobody wants to see two girls kissing or two men snuggling?" she asked.[42] MTV's action also illustrated differing standards for sexually explicit scenes in videos for male and female recording artists: Whereas MTV refused Madonna's video, the channel regularly presents videos by male heavy metal bands that portray women with sparse clothing and in sexually suggestive positions. As an MTV executive notes, "without lingerie, we'd be in trouble."[43] Gay media activists point out still another double standard represented by the banned video, charging that MTV is more likely to censor portrayals of homosexual sexuality than heterosexual acts. "MTV's rejection of Madonna's latest video, apparently because of its gay and lesbian imagery, is hypocritical and smacks of censorship," claims Stephen Beck, executive director of the New York chapter of the Gay and Lesbian Alliance Against Defamation (GLAAD).[44]

Some critics noted that MTV's video ban and resulting media attention had desirable economic benefits for Madonna, suggesting that the whole episode may have been planned. In order to capitalize on the substantial press attention to

MTV's action, Madonna's record label swiftly released the unedited clip as the first ever video single, which was quickly purchased by consumers anxious to view the "forbidden" video. Warner Reprise Video shipped almost 500,000 copies to stores in its first month of sales.[45] Also, this story was publicized soon after the release of her greatest hits album *Immaculate Collection,* including the new song "Justify My Love." Paul Grein, a *Billboard* columnist, suggested, "I don't think it's coincidental that all this hubbub is happening when the album is in its second week on the charts."[46]

Music Clip Rotation Categories

After a music clip is accepted by the Acquisition Committee and approved by the Program Standards and Public Responsibility Department, the clip becomes an "add-on" to be included in MTV's playlist. The committee assigns the "add-on" video to a particular rotation category, which roughly determines the clip's frequency of airplay on the channel. Play can range from once a week to six times a day.[47] MTV originally adopted a simple rotation system derived from album-oriented rock stations with categories titled light, medium, and heavy, indicating progressively more frequent play of a video. In 1984, MTV increased the number of rotation categories to seven because of the large size and complexity of the channel's playlist, including such categories as "new," a "testing ground for new videos," which received light play and, at the other extreme, "power," the slot for "sneak preview videos" that are "only on MTV videos" and might be played four to five times a day.[48] In December 1986, MTV streamlined this rotation system, dropping two categories and adding the "Hip Clip of the Week," a featured video played every three hours during a one-week period. Music Video Services, a company that monitored MTV's programming for record companies and advertisers, questioned the credibility of these categories, reporting that clips in a particular category often did not receive the frequency of play supposedly guaranteed by that category.

The Acquisition Committee's decisions about clip placement are increasingly dependent upon the commercial success of an artist. When MTV adopted a more hit-oriented format, current songs by popular artists acquired heavier airplay and now dominate most of MTV's airtime. Michael Goldberg reported that although MTV played over three hundred different video clips each week, only about thirty of these received more than one play a day, most featuring established recording stars.[49] MTV provides especially extensive play of "exclusive" videos by popular artists seen only on MTV for a certain period of time. Tom Freston concedes that even a clearly substandard video clip released by a well-known artist will receive airplay. Although MTV accepts videos by new artists on its playlist in order to give the channel the appearance of being on the "cutting edge," these clips are generally assigned to light rotation categories and played in late night hours when the audience is limited. MTV executives also determine a clip's rotation category by evaluating the video using such subjective criteria as the video's "quality," how well the clip fits the channel's format, and the executive's "gut feeling" about the clip.[50]

Decisions concerning the frequency of play for a new video also are dependent upon MTV's research findings. MTV's Tom Hunter explains that "millions of dollars are spent to find out what our viewers want to see."[51] MTV's research department of twenty employees regularly conducts telephone interviews with people identified as MTV viewers within the targeted demographic age group of twelve to thirty-four with sample sizes ranging from fifteen hundred to three thousand. These surveys ask respondents several questions about certain artists and videos. If a person has not heard a particular song, the interviewer plays a clip from the song and asks the respondent to rank his or her evaluation of the song on a scale from 1 to 10.[52]

MTV's research department also surveys retail music stores, gathering information on tape, compact disc, and video sales by artists featured on the channel. While still president of MTV, Bob Pittman said that he consulted other sources as well to determine the frequency of airplay for videos such as *Billboard*'s Hot 100 chart of top singles and RockAmerica's survey of popular videos in U.S. nightclubs.[53] These various sources of information are consulted not only to determine the initial rotation category for a video but also are used as a guide to evaluate whether a clip's frequency of airplay should be changed over a period of time due to shifting viewer response.

External Social Forces Influencing MTV's Standards

Local Communities and Cable Companies

MTV and other program services developed and enforced standards policies in response to pressure from various groups complaining about the sex and violence in music videos. Religious organizations and other conservative groups in small communities occasionally launch campaigns to persuade local cable companies and government officials to ban MTV from their cable service, with varying degrees of success. In 1983, a group of citizens in Emporia, Virginia, tried to get MTV dropped from their local cable system.[54] Although MTV was not completely banned, city officials requested Pembroke Cablevision to move the program service to a restricted access channel, requiring subscribers who wished to view MTV to pay an extra $10 per month. In 1984, two "born again" Christian women, who condemned music video as "decadent, morally degrading and evil," circulated a petition in the Boston suburb of Weymouth to have MTV removed from the local cable company.[55] Local officials responded to the petition in July by requiring the cable company to provide subscribers with an optional device that would block MTV, and ultimately the program service was completely banned from the cable system.

In Texarkana, Texas, the city's board of directors attempted to require their cable operator to drop MTV after the channel presented Cher's *If I Could Turn Back Time* video showing her in a revealing outfit.[56] Although the city attorney ruled that the board did not have the authority to take such an action, the local cable company, Dimension Cable Service, emulating Weymouth's solution, voluntarily offered its 22,000 subscribers the option of requesting a single-channel trap that would block MTV from the viewer's home. Greg Capranica, Dimension's general manager, said that only forty subscribers had requested the blocking device as of November 1989. MTV dismissed the significance of these events, saying that the community actions did not influence its program content. "This situation in Texas was definitely an isolated incident," said MTV's Carole Robinson. "We are getting no more cable pressure than normal and it's not affecting any of our decisions. There's nothing out of the ordinary there."[57] However, Sam Kaiser, a former MTV executive, countered that such attempts to ban MTV did indeed have an impact: "You have to understand the pressure MTV is under. If cable operators are pressured by the townships they're in, they'll put the pressure on MTV. If they really get in a battle, they'll consider jerking the system."[58]

More recently, MTV sought to stop two large multiple system operators (MSOs) that wanted to end their affiliation with the service. First, Tele-Community Antenna (TCA), a cable company with fifty-three systems serving 420,000 subscribers in six states including Texas, Arkansas, and Mississippi, shocked MTV by dropping the channel from its cable systems on June 28, 1991.[59] TCA executives claimed that they received many complaints from their subscribers about the sex and violence portrayed on MTV. "We operate in mostly rural [areas] and our customers told us they'd prefer not to have MTV," said TCA president, Fred Nichols.[60] One TCA executive called MTV "borderline pornographic" and said parents, teachers, and local government agencies pressured the company to drop the channel. Apart from the racy content, TCA canceled MTV in part because of a dispute in contract negotiations over the channel's distribution. TCA wanted to convert MTV from a basic service available to all subscribers into a pay cable channel available only to those who pay an additional monthly fee. MTV strongly opposed such a change, believing its audience and advertising revenue would sharply drop if it were offered as a pay service.

After TCA's decision, several local communities with TCA systems launched a campaign to compel the company to restore MTV, with numerous petitions and rallies in area colleges and high schools. A protest in College Station, Texas, site of Texas A&M University, encouraged more than seven hundred people to call TCA to complain and more than one thousand signed a petition to urge the company to bring back MTV.[61] A radio station in Amarillo, Texas, produced and aired a rap song that condemned TCA's "censoring" the channel.[62] MTV itself took an active role in fanning these protests. Although TCA claims that the unflattering publicity did not influence it, the company decided to restore MTV on most of its systems two weeks after dropping the channel.

This contest of wills between MTV and a major cable company was replayed with several similarities in November 1991 when Sammons Communications announced it would replace MTV with the Video Jukebox Network (VJN). Sammons, one of the twenty largest MSOs with fifty-five cable systems in nineteen states, replaced MTV with the Jukebox on four of its systems in January 1992 and considered where else these channels could be switched.[63] The primary conflict between MTV and Sammons that led to this action was once again the issue of distribution, as Sammons wanted to convert MTV from a basic to pay service. "We would like to carry services like MTV on an a la carte basis where we would sell it just to those audiences that want to see that kind of service," said Sherry Wilson, Sammons's vice president of marketing.[64] Sammons noted that some families would prefer not to have more sexually provocative channels like MTV and converting it into a pay service would give subscribers the choice of whether they wanted MTV. MTV again refused to become a pay "tier" channel since its audience and advertising revenue might drop.

Once again a public campaign was launched to compel Sammons to keep MTV on its systems. Subscribers organized the group Viewers Voice for MTV, which circulated a petition garnering more than fifteen hundred signatures and encouraged people to cancel premium services like HBO until Sammons relented.[65] MTV took an active role in these campaigns, sending vee-jays like Downtown Julie Brown into communities with Sammons cable systems to draw public attention to the issue. MTV aired several ads on local television and radio stations featuring well-known stars like Phil Collins and Paula Abdul telling viewers to call the cable company to demand that MTV be carried on the system. Sammons, like TCA, relented under the public pressure and agreed to restore MTV in March 1992.[66] The similarity of these organized protests against TCA and Sammons suggests that MTV has a prearranged plan for fostering public campaigns to encourage an MSO to keep MTV when a cable company announces its intention to drop the channel. So far these campaigns have been successful.

Parents Music Research Center

Video music television shows also were subjected to pressure from the Parents Music Research Center (PMRC), an organization created on May 5, 1985, by the wives of several prominent U.S. senators and White House cabinet members, including Mesdames Gore, Baker, Packwood, and Thurmond. The PMRC was formed because of charter members' growing concern about what they perceived as the gratuitous sex and violence in pop and rock music. "Tipper" Gore, wife of then Senator Al Gore, explained that her interest in the lyrics of rock music was aroused when she heard her eleven-year-old daughter listening to "Darling Nikki," a song from Prince's *Purple Rain* soundtrack, which described a woman's masturbation. The original primary goal of the PMRC was to persuade the record companies to establish a voluntary ratings system for albums based on the sex and violence depicted in the content of song lyrics and to place warning labels on records and tapes identifying the album's rating. Prominent rock artists including Frank Zappa and Jello Biafra charged that the PMRC was advocating censorship and attempting to impose its members' own conservative morality on popular music. Despite the protests, the major record companies eventually consented to the organization's demands and agreed to place warning labels on recorded music judged to contain suggestive lyrics. Albums that include explicit references to violence, sex, or drugs now have stickers that read "Explicit Lyrics— Parental Advisory."

Although the record companies were the major focus of PMRC's activities, the organization also sought to persuade video music program services such as MTV to adopt its proposals to develop a ratings scheme and label videos with objectional material. "Once again, we just want labelling," said Susan Baker, the vice president of PMRC and wife of then Treasury Secretary James Baker.[67] "Records that are going to have a warning on them should also have that [warning] noted before videos are played on MTV." On August 6, 1985, Baker discussed PMRC's recommendations for music video shows in more specific detail in an interview with Don Lyonds. She argued that offensive videos "should have a visible rating mark that should stay on the screen throughout the video. And it'd be a good idea to have a daily period, say from 2 to 6, when only benign music videos would be played."[68] The PMRC wanted MTV to have an "R" rating visible on an offensive music clip to inform parents, to help guide their children's viewing.

The issue of video music was discussed at a hearing on record labeling conducted by the Senate Committee on Commerce, Science, and Transportation held September 19, 1985, at the urging of PMRC's influential members. The hearing included a presentation by Senator Paula Hawkins of Florida who showed portions of some racy videos to the audience. After the clips were displayed, Hawkins said, "I think a picture is worth a thousand words. This issue is too hot not to cool down."[69] Jennifer Norwood, PMRC's executive director, said in April 1987 that the organization was still attempting to persuade MTV to label explicit videos. However, neither MTV nor any other major program services instituted any sort of labeling policy or had any plans to do so in the future.[70]

MTV said it was never overly concerned about the PMRC because there was no way that the organization could directly affect the program service since programming on cable television is subject to much less government regulation than broadcast television. Even so, MTV executives tried to address the PMRC's concerns, explaining to them that the channel had very stringent standards prohibiting the sexually explicit and obscene images and words in music clips that concerned the organization. MTV invited the PMRC to a presentation that highlighted its policy requiring edited versions of videos that omit objectionable scenes. The channel's representatives outlined their policies to the PMRC "to assure they were aware of the differences between us and other generic music video shows."[71] MTV's Michele Vonfeld explained that "often, although it may appear that we are running the same video as another show, we are actually showing an edited version."[72]

Pressure Groups and Campaigns Against Violence on MTV

Another frequent critic of MTV and music videos is the National Coalition on Television Violence (NCTV), an organization that *Rolling Stone* describes as "a small but strident group" that has monitored the presentation of violence on television programs since August 1980.[73] In October 1983, NCTV expanded its monitoring activities to include music video program services including MTV because of the organization's concern about the excessive acts of violence depicted in this programming. "The intensive sadistic and sexual violence of a large number of rock music videos is overwhelming," fumed Dr. Thomas Radecki, NCTV's chairman who is a psychiatrist at the University of Illinois School of Medicine.[74] "It's shocking to see this subculture of hate and violence becoming a fast-growing element of rock music entertainment for the young."

NCTV conducted content analyses of music television shows, which reported an average of 18 instances of violence each hour on MTV in 1983 and 17.9 instances of violence an hour on MTV and WTBS's music video shows the following year.[75] Further, the 1984 study of MTV and WTBS's programming reported that 22 percent of all music clips contained violence between men and women, and 13 percent of the violent videos included "sadistic violence where the attacker actually took pleasure out of committing the violence."[76] NCTV's critics question the credibility and objectivity of the organization's research studies, claiming that NCTV attempts to legitimize its partisan views with the aura of pseudoscientific data. The coalition lobbied unsuccessfully for legislation that would require music video services to devote a certain quantity of their program schedule to "nonviolent, nondegrading material," provide counteradvertising to diminish the alleged effects of violent videos, and present warning labels on music clips with violence.[77] A more recent NCTV study reported fewer depictions of violence and sexually degrading acts on MTV in 1991 than during the 1980s, but cautioned that rap videos had the most demeaning images of women. Another media-monitoring organization, the Center for Media and Public Affairs based in Washington, D.C., reported a modest decrease in violence portrayed on MTV in the mid-1990s. The center's content analysis of music videos presented on MTV found ninety scenes of violence during an eighteen-hour period in April 1994, a drop from 121 violent episodes during a similar time span in 1992.[78] The center's research director, Dan Amundson, attributed the decrease to MTV's heightened sensitivity to the problem of violence in society.

Despite this favorable assessment, MTV continues to be attacked by groups and individuals for presenting scenes of explicit violence in its music clips. In December 1994, James E. Davis, a former New York City police officer, began holding a series of press conferences and conducting a letter-writing campaign to encourage MTV to restrict its play of videos with excessive violence to the hours of 9 P.M. to 6 A.M. when supposedly fewer young people watch the channel.[79] This one-man crusade against MTV received ample mainstream press attention because Davis had been successful in a previous campaign to persuade the toy industry to stop making and selling realistic toy guns. Davis claims that the videos shown on MTV not only encourage young people to become more violent but misrepresent inner city African-Americans as gun-toting thugs.

At a more general level, government leaders are actively considering proposals to regulate violence on television, some of which could affect cable program services like MTV. In October 1993 U.S. Attorney General Janet Reno caused a stir by suggesting that "regulation of [entertainment] violence is constitutionally permissible," citing a 1987 Supreme Court decision that permits restrictions on indecent speech.[80] During that same month, the U.S. Senate Committee on Commerce, Science, and Transportation held hearings to consider proposals to regulate violence on television such as requiring warning labels on especially violent programs and prohibiting violence in programs during certain hours when children are most likely to be watching. All of these attempts to curtail violence on television are firmly denounced by media industries as an unacceptable abridgement of their First Amendment rights to freedom of speech and also as an unnecessary measure because they claim self-regulation led to a decrease in violent content without any government intervention.

Political Attacks on Popular Music

MTV and other music video programs are also subject to indirect pressure from more general political campaigns against objectionable content in popular music. These campaigns against explicit lyrics help create a more conservative climate where program services are more cautious about the content of their own music programming. In the early 1990s, there was a rash of actions by state governments and law enforcement agencies intended to curtail public access to music deemed obscene or merely objectionable. In Florida, an album by the rap group 2 Live Crew, *As Nasty as They Wanna Be,* was banned from music stores in 1990 after a federal judge ruled that it was obscene. A record store owner in Ft. Lauderdale, Florida, was later arrested and convicted for selling the album in his store to an undercover police officer.[81] 2 Live Crew itself was charged with violating obscenity laws after public performances of songs from the album in a Hollywood, Florida, club, but was found not guilty in the subsequent trial.[82]

In March 1992, Washington Governor Booth Gardner enacted a law prohibiting sales of albums considered obscene to minors, making music store owners and employees liable for criminal prosecution for such acts.[83] Several other states also included recorded and live music under their obscenity laws. At least a dozen states also proposed bills to require warning stickers on albums with explicit lyrics, but most of these attempts were withdrawn or defeated after the record industry agreed to voluntarily place stickers on albums. All of these actions help create an intolerant atmosphere where program services like MTV became more sensitive to content that might be considered objectionable, leading to more restrictive standards for music videos. Although MTV did not publicly comment on the influence of these political actions, the channel clearly has adopted more rigorous standards since these events transpired. As mentioned previously, whereas MTV rejected about 10 percent of submitted music clips for standards violations in 1989, this jumped to about 33 percent in 1994.

MTV's general response to various groups complaining about objectionable music clips is to claim that their own in-house standards department carefully reviews videos and prevents airplay of music clips with excessive displays of sex or violence. The channel also argues that these attempts to influence the content of their programming would abridge their First Amendment rights. David Horowitz, past president of MTV Networks, rejects NCTV's recommendations for counterprogramming to balance the violent videos as a violation of the channel's free speech rights. "Some of their proposals for legislative solutions would . . . interfere with freedom of speech," argues Horowitz. "That would be censorship, which is not permitted by the Constitution."[84] Yet these arguments based on the program service's free speech rights do not address the private in-house censorship by the company, which also abridges freedom of expression by limiting viewer access to certain images, lyrics, and ideas in the program content.

Content Regulation of Music Television Programs

Cable Television

The vulnerability of music television shows to pressure from various special interest groups and government officials varies according to the medium on which the program is presented. Music shows on cable like MTV are somewhat able to resist various attempts by groups to modify the content of clips because of the cable industry's relatively unregulated status. The high degree of First Amendment protection afforded cable program services allowed MTV to largely ignore various proposals by groups such as the PMRC and NCTV without any adverse consequences. However, local community groups are able to exert indirect pressure on MTV and other cable music shows by complaining to local cable companies about objectionable programming. As revealed by ex–MTV executive Sam Kaiser, cable operators will pressure MTV to alter its programming when the local franchise becomes the target of a campaign by an organized group protesting certain material on the service considered to be offensive.

Also, although there is little content regulation of cable programming, the Cable Communications Policy Act of 1984 does prohibit the presentation of obscene material on cable television. Under the provisions of the act, cable program services and local cable operators could be punished in certain instances for the presentation of video clips or other programming judged to be obscene. Section 639 of the act established penalties for presenting obscene program content on cable systems, which include being "fined not more than $10,000 or imprisoned not more than 2 years, or both."[85] In 1994, in a case not involving the FCC, a

county court in Texas convicted a host and producer of a show considered pornographic that was presented on an Austin cable television channel for violating obscenity laws.[86] However, in general it is relatively difficult to determine that program material is obscene under Supreme Court guidelines established in *Miller v.
California* (1973). Under this standard, a program can only be considered obscene
when an average person applying contemporary local community standards,
finds the work, taken as a whole, appeals to "prurient interests" and lacks "serious
literary, artistic, political or scientific value."[87] The vast majority of video clips distributed by the major record labels would be very unlikely to be considered obscene under these provisions. As of June 1994, soft-core pornography cable channels like Spice 1 and Adam & Eve had not violated obscenity laws and were
considered acceptable on cable systems as pay-per-view channels.[88]

Music program services on cable in the United States have much greater freedom than cable music shows in other countries, including Canada and the United
Kingdom, which have more heavily regulated cable systems with greater provisions for government regulation of program content. For example, the United
Kingdom's Cable Authority established a national code for acceptable content for
music videos presented on cable television in October 1989.[89] The Cable Authority stated that the code was intended to protect young viewers from videos with
sexually explicit scenes and an emphasis on violence as well as videos that favor-
ably portray alcohol or drug use.

Broadcast Television

Music shows on local broadcast stations in the United States are more vulnerable
to pressure from various groups protesting the depiction of sex and violence in
video clips because program content in broadcasting is more heavily regulated by
the FCC than cable television. Broadcasters must exercise care in the presentation
of videos to ensure that their programming does not violate FCC policies and
Communication Act prohibitions concerning both indecent speech and obscenity. Further, viewers offended by a particular video can file a complaint with the
commission, which may prompt an investigation into the matter if the clip was
judged to be indecent or obscene.

Since 1987, the FCC has defined indecency as "language or material that . . . depicts or describes, in terms patently offensive as measured by contemporary community standards for the broadcast medium, sexual or excretory activities or or-
gans."[90] Programs may be judged to violate the FCC's indecency standard because
they include an isolated word or image judged to be "indecent" regardless of the
overall artistic or social merit of the program. The commission's interpretation of
indecent speech is much broader than the standard for obscenity, making it much
easier to demonstrate that a program contains indecent rather than obscene content. Under these respective provisions, some recent music clips with nude scenes
or sexually suggestive song lyrics might be ruled to be indecent, but not obscene.

In June 1985, Edward Fritts, president of the National Association of Broadcasters, sent a letter to 807 radio and television station group owners expressing

his concern about the sexually explicit and violent nature of current pop songs and their accompanying videos. Fritts's letter, mailed soon after public announcements by the newly formed PMRC in May, emphasizes the broadcasters' obligation to adhere to FCC policies and Communication Act provisions: "The lyrics of some recent rock records and the tone of their related music videos are fast becoming a matter of public debate. . . . It is, of course, up to each broadcast licensee to make its decision as to the manner in which it carries out its programming responsibilities under the Communication Act."[91]

Broadcasters are more reluctant to air videos including content that might be considered offensive because of the FCC's increasingly aggressive enforcement of its policies regarding indecent speech over the past few years.[92] As of 1994 the FCC was imposing fines on about ten broadcast stations a year for indecent speech, mostly radio stations.[93] The now defunct Hit Video USA, which operated a daily program service available to broadcasters, received frequent complaints from television stations about clips, prompting the service to drop certain videos considered to be objectionable, including Cher's *If I Could Turn Back Time* video.[94] The Fox television network apologized to viewers after presenting Michael Jackson's controversial video for the song "Black or White." Fox received many complaints for airing this video, which included scenes of Jackson smashing a car with a crowbar and grabbing his crotch.[95] Jackson ultimately replaced the video with an edited version without the contentious scenes, explaining, "I've always tried to be a good role model and therefore have made these changes to avoid any possibility of adversely affecting any individual's behavior."[96]

In 1992, the FCC tried to refine its policy on indecency as directed by Congress to prohibit indecent program content between 6 A.M. and midnight, creating a "safe harbor" when such material could be aired in the remaining early morning hours. Yet, in November 1993, the U.S. Court of Appeals struck down the statute requiring the FCC to create a "safe harbor" period.[97] The court ruled that the ban on indecent programming from 6 A.M. to midnight was too broad and violated the First Amendment rights of broadcasters' freedom of speech.[98] Until the issue is resolved, the FCC plans to continue enforcement of its indecency rules, expanding the safe harbor from midnight to 8 A.M. Thus, while this policy is in place, more suggestive sexually explicit music videos could be played during these hours.

∾   ∾   ∾

MTV clearly has far-reaching influence over the content of videos clips featuring rock and popular music. Smaller, independent record companies cannot usually get their videos on MTV, often deriding it as a "majors only" channel. The major record companies willingly edit videos on a regular basis to conform to MTV's standards even as they complain about the arbitrary nature of these guidelines. The companies are also able to coerce artists to make changes in their song lyrics to suit MTV. Some artists do resist MTV's demands for alterations in their videos, although these tend to be more well-established acts like The Rolling

Stones and Madonna, who are less dependent on MTV for exposure, unlike new, aspiring artists who usually submit to MTV's demands. In many cases, the recording artist may not even have a say in the editing process if the record company owns the music video, as is frequently the case for new acts. The producer and director are obliged to edit a video to satisfy MTV and the record company since these parties work under contract to the company. In fact the video is originally made with an eye to satisfying MTV's guidelines since the record companies commission and finance videos for rock and pop music primarily for play on MTV. Music videos not played on MTV have less promotional value for artists because they are not as widely viewed, although the video can still be presented on programs with more permissive standards like The Box or sold as a retail home-video product.

Many of these guidelines limiting the portrayal of acts of sex and violence are designed to diffuse pressure from local community groups and cable companies, which often object to certain visual images and words in these clips. Other unstated guidelines seem more intended to exclude content that might embarrass or criticize advertisers or MTV itself. The extended review of MTV's rejection of the *Justify My Love* video illustrates certain double standards in these guidelines concerning the portrayal of sexuality.

Music shows on cable program services like MTV have comparatively more latitude over program content than shows on broadcast television due to less stringent regulation of content in this medium. However, MTV encounters pressure from local community groups and cable companies that sometimes try to get MTV banned from cable for objectionable content or at least converted into a restricted access premium channel. At a more general level, MTV's programming may be influenced indirectly by political campaigns against perceived excesses in popular music, prompted by groups such as the PMRC, state governments, and law enforcement agencies. These growing pressures may be responsible for MTV's increasing conservatism, demonstrated by the growing proportion of videos being rejected by the channel for standards violations between 1990 and 1995.

10

MTV, Music Video, and Creative Expression

The Power of Record Labels and MTV in the Video Music Business

This survey clearly demonstrates that the major record companies and program services dominate the video music business. As they developed this new media form, the record labels maintained control over all aspects of the making of video clips for their artists because they financed most of this production. Record companies also act as gatekeepers, determining which artists are provided with videos and which songs by these artists get accompanying videos.

The labels greatly influence the content of music videos. Record company executives severely limit the creative freedom of producers and directors by providing strong direction about the content of music videos, although certain established directors infrequently have more creative latitude. Label executives often develop a storyboard, script, or concept for video producers and directors to follow when making the clip. A continual conflict exists between the makers of videos, who want to create an artistic work, and label executives, who perceive videos solely as advertisements to sell discs and tapes. Directors often lose these struggles because record companies are the ultimate authority as the financial underwriter and owner of the clips. This heavy-handed direction by record labels suggests that cultural producers have limited creative autonomy in this market.

As for exposure media, the major program services, primarily MTV, exercise control over video music through their gatekeeping role. Although many videos are made by record companies, only a certain percentage of these clips are presented on music television shows. The programming decisions of major media outlets can directly affect recording artists featured in music clips by providing or withholding opportunities for exposure. For example, MTV's narrowcast policy of playing only certain musical genres hurt the careers of some recording artists excluded from MTV's playlist, notably black musicians whose videos were banned during the channel's early years.

Program services like MTV also exercise control by requiring submitted music videos to comply with their standards policies. Programming executives who enforce these standards regularly compromise the artistic independence of recording artists and clip directors by requiring changes in video images or song lyrics. Because of the importance of video airplay, artists, video directors, video producers, and record labels usually consent to this form of censorship, granting MTV substantial control over clip content. Record companies reportedly often pressure their artists to change the lyrics of songs to get videos accepted on MTV. Finally, MTV's influence is so pronounced that record companies regularly encourage producers and directors to pander to MTV by imitating the style and visual effects of popular videos played on the channel in the past, hoping that MTV will play these clips. This pressure often leads to a bland conformity in videos that are loaded with hackneyed visual clichés.

Interdependent Relationship Between MTV and Record Labels

The labels and MTV Networks have had a cooperative relationship where both parties' economic interests are served by promoting popular label acts: The clips featuring these acts get people to watch MTV and VH-1, increasing their audience, and the labels get valuable exposure for their artists, hopefully increasing album sales. The relationship between majors and program services like MTV can also be described as an interdependent one where neither party maintains complete dominance. Although record companies depend on program services, notably MTV, to play clips to promote their recording acts, these television shows depend on the labels for their primary source of programming. The corporate policies of one party can influence the other, but neither can directly control the other's actions. The playlists of major program services, primarily MTV, which emphasize certain musical genres, greatly influence the production policies of record companies but do not rigidly prescribe such policies. Moreover, program services' threats to refuse to play videos rarely influence record label policies. For example, bans by BET and some local television shows on videos by certain labels to protest certain objectionable actions such as the institution of license fees or exclusivity contracts with MTV did not compel the major labels to rescind these policies.

Similarly, the major record labels were unable to coerce leading program services like MTV to adopt certain policies sought by the labels that were not in the perceived best interests of the service. In one extraordinary instance, a record company allegedly did force MTV to take an action when CBS threatened to withdraw all of the label's videos unless the channel played Michael Jackson's clips. However, this action was unusual because of CBS's dominant share of the pop music market in the early 1980s. The labels are unable to persuade MTV to stop increasing its proportion of nonmusic video programming and are infrequently annoyed by MTV's reluctance to play certain videos by new acts despite the provisions of the exclusivity pacts that require play of some clips designated by the labels. MTV's periodic displays of independence encouraged several major labels to develop plans to launch their own music channel, providing them with the complete control over an exhibition outlet that they lack with MTV Networks' services.

Established Trends in Ownership and Control of the Music Video Business

Music video's development as a business clearly embodies the current trends affecting all culture industries reviewed in Chapter 1. The exhibition media for music video has a high degree of horizontal integration primarily due to the program services operated by MTV Networks. This company holds a dominant position in the market for music video programming by every possible measure, including total number of subscribers, audience ratings, advertising revenue, and press attention. MTVN regularly engaged in anticompetitive practices to enhance its dominance in this market. MTV's sister channel VH-1 was launched to undermine potential competitors with a similar format like Turner's CMC and Hit Video USA. MTV executives repeatedly tried to coerce recording artists to pledge an exclusive allegiance to the channel through such means as blacklisting artists who appeared on other video shows and banning videos by artists that premiered on a competitor's program service. Most significantly, MTV's exclusivity contracts with the major record labels were an attempt to strengthen its dominance and undermine potential competitors by gaining exclusive rights to popular videos.

Beyond MTVN's aggressive actions, other factors also intensified the concentration of exposure media, including the institution of license fees and decreased public interest in music video in the mid-1980s, both of which contributed to the demise of many video clip shows, leaving the field clear for more established programs like MTV. Despite the dominance of MTVN, there remain numerous television shows that continue to present a fairly wide range of music videos, including The Nashville Network (TNN), Black Entertainment Television (BET), and many regional and local video shows. However, none of these media outlets possess the influence and power MTVN's services have with the major record labels, recording artists, and the general public. This horizontal integration streamlines and limits the diversity of music presented on cable systems so that viewers only see videos of more conventional artists signed to major labels that are featured on MTV services, while the alternative and avant-garde artists ignored by MTV Networks go unheard and unseen.

Horizontal integration is also pronounced in the area of video clip production and distribution. The majority of music video clips are commissioned by the six major labels that dominate the record industry. Moreover, these record companies rely upon a small group of established production companies to make their clips, which collectively constitutes an emerging oligopoly in the field of video music production.

The institutionalized use of music video also reinforces concentration within the record industry by intensifying the dominance of the six major labels at the expense of smaller independent record companies. Most videos and music programs on MTV and VH-1 feature artists signed to major labels, perpetually promoting these acts. In contrast, the necessity of music video keeps independents at a disadvantage in the business. Although videos are an indispensable promotional tool for establishing new artists, independents generally lack the financial resources to underwrite costly video production and distribution on a regular basis. Further, when independent labels are able to produce clips, they have difficulty getting their music clips on major program services such as MTV.

Vertical integration is most pronounced between the major record companies and MTV Networks. MTV and the labels became integrated through contractual agreements designed to provide these companies with greater control over the distribution of music clips for their own mutual benefit. The record companies get guaranteed exposure for video clips featuring new artists, which helps establish these acts, and MTV has guaranteed exclusive rights to the most popular videos by top stars to keep viewers interested and increase the channel's ratings.

MTV's contracts were criticized by other music television shows, which claimed MTV was trying to monopolize the market for video music programming and eliminate competition. The pacts were also characterized as institutionalized payola because the contracts gave record companies guaranteed airplay for new artists that label executives wanted to promote. Although a series of legal actions challenged the legality of these contracts, including antitrust lawsuits by MTV's competitors, investigations by the FCC and FTC, and an inquiry by the Justice Department, none of these affected provisions of the pacts. Some record labels have discontinued these contracts in favor of plans to launch their own music video channel.

This vertical integration between MTV and the record labels intensified horizontal integration in two related media markets. In the record industry, this collusion provided major record companies with a valuable advantage over smaller independent record companies by granting these major labels guaranteed access to MTV to promote new artists, whereas artists signed to independents were usually excluded from MTV. In the market for music video programming, the cooperation between MTV and the labels gave MTV a crucial advantage over other music shows, enhancing its dominance in programming. The pacts contributed to the failure of many music program services, including CMC, Discovery, and Hit Video USA, leaving the market for music video firmly controlled by MTVN, owner of the only two full-time music program services on most U.S. cable systems. In general, MTV's collusion with the major labels provides these few companies with unprecedented control to shape the future direction of American pop music through their coordinated strategies to develop and promote certain artists and genres of music rather than others.

However, the vertical integration between MTV and the record labels is not complete. As discussed previously, the record companies do not have total control over major exhibition media, and conversely, program services cannot completely dictate the labels' production policies. Moreover, although MTV and the labels are able to cooperate to a certain extent for their mutual benefit, the divergent objectives of these companies (the labels want to promote their artists and MTV seeks high audience ratings) prevent more comprehensive corporate collusion. Direct ownership of music video program services like Viva in Germany and Channel V in Asia by major record companies provides these labels with the complete vertical integration among production, distribution, and exhibition that they apparently seek.

MTV Networks also pursued vertical integration between its cable program services and cable systems, both through contractual agreements and common ownership to ensure guaranteed exhibition of its programming and undercut competitors. MTV has long-term agreements with large multiple system operators (MSOs) that discourage the systems from carrying other companies' program services with formats duplicating those of MTV channels. Further, MTV's parent company, Viacom, owned a prominent MSO, Viacom Cable, which featured program services owned by Viacom subsidiaries like MTV Networks and Showtime Networks while often excluding competitors' services with similar program formats. The Box noted that its music channel was not welcome on Viacom systems. Viacom abandoned this form of vertical integration by selling its cable systems in 1995 and is likely to rely more heavily on contractual agreements with major MSOs to get guaranteed access for its programming.

MTV also is influenced by the tendency toward diversification of corporations in media markets. The program service has always been owned by a media conglomerate that practiced the policy of "synergy" by involving MTV in coordinated strategies with other related media divisions. In his 1984 letter to stockholders, Steven Ross acknowledged that MTV was part of a strategy including several media subsidiaries to promote Warner Brothers recording artists like Prince, when the program service was owned partially by Warner Communications.[1] However, Viacom, the successor corporate parent of MTV, even more aggressively developed synergy strategies through joint ventures between MTVN and other Viacom subsidiaries. The company coproduced programs for MTV through Viacom Productions and syndicated MTV programs through its division, Viacom Enterprises. MTV also launched a new production company, MTV Productions, that will distribute its programs through a Viacom subsidiary. Viacom's prodding to develop ancillary markets prompted MTV Networks to sell an increasing array of retail products with the MTV logo, including clothing and a series of *Club MTV Party to Go* discs and cassettes featuring music played on the channel. The company made more than $100 million from sales of products spun off from the MTV show *Beavis and Butt-head,* including video games and paperbacks like the best-selling *Ensucklopedia.* Future ventures being considered are an MTV exercise workout video, sex manual, and theatrical films. Viacom's recent acquisition of the media conglomerate Paramount also opens up seemingly endless possibilities for cross-media promotions and joint ventures between subsidiaries. For instance, MTV and VH-1 can promote new Paramount theatrical releases on their programming. In early 1995, another MTV Networks service, Nick at Night, heavily promoted the upcoming Paramount film, *The Brady Bunch Movie,* by playing old episodes of the original *Brady Bunch* sitcom series, later variety series, cartoon series, *The Brady Kids,* and made-for-television movies like *A Brady Christmas.* Ironically, the "diversification" of MTV Networks and its parent, Viacom, may ultimately lead to a lack of "diversity" of ideas and creative, innovative media content since the same narrow band of concepts and artists may be marketed in all of the conglomerate's increasingly interwoven subsidiaries.

As discussed earlier, communication conglomerates tend to distribute media products in other countries after the U.S. market is saturated. MTVN adopted this strategy in the late 1980s and early 1990s by developing foreign versions of its program service, including MTV Europe, MTV Australia, *MTV Internacional,* MTV Latino, and MTV Asia. Further, MTVN has taken full advantage of the demise of the Soviet Union by expanding its program services into Eastern Europe and Russia. MTV's reach is increasingly pervasive: In February 1995, MTV's music program services reached 251 million homes in fifty-eight countries.[2] MTV executives argue that the channel's worldwide program services appeal to an international youth culture based upon pop music. A primary objective of MTV's international shows is to develop a demographic target audience of young people throughout the world that can be delivered to transnational advertisers seeking to reach this specialized global audience.

MTV's services may also foster and cultivate a globalization of popular culture where young people around the world listen to the same music, watch the same films, and wear the same styles of clothing. Both MTV's programming and conventional advertising attempt to nurture audience desire for these increasingly homogenized products. The globalization of culture encouraged by MTV also poses a threat to the indigenous cultures of societies where MTV is available since the music, videos, and programming featured on most MTV services are largely American and, to a lesser extent, British. MTV provides comparatively little program time to local or regional acts and will usually only play these artists when they mimic American rock and pop styles. This lopsided emphasis between local and foreign music may encourage audience interest in U.S. and U.K. acts at the expense of indigenous musicians, further consolidating the cultural power and influence of Western transnational record companies while undermining local independent record labels. The relentless commercialization of MTV's services also promotes a value system based on consumerism that socializes young people to define their self-identity through the purchase of stylish consumer products featured on the channel, all of which grinds away at the traditional values of other societies that resist this commoditized conception of self.

Firms in the music video business developed policies designed to maximize their profit from the production and distribution of music clips. This objective led record companies to rationalize their investment in video clip production by limiting production expenses and exploiting their videos in as many venues as possible. The major labels developed a product recycling strategy similar to other cultural producers, designed to generate revenue from music videos from several different sources. Music clips are presented on program services as promotional devices, which ideally produce an indirect source of revenue by stimulating retail sales of the recorded music featured in videos. The record company simultaneously charges program services a license fee for the right to exhibit its videos. License fees are also paid by firms that package and distribute music videos for play in bars and dance clubs. And finally, the label sells its videos as a retail consumer good in the home-video market.

Conversely, whereas the labels try to increase revenues derived from music video, they also continually struggle with creative personnel to limit their production costs. The labels tried to shift the financial responsibility for videos to the recording artists by deducting the costs of production from the artists' royalties derived from sales of recorded music related to the video. Moreover, record companies strictly limit production budgets for music videos, prompting producers to complain that their profits from clips are minimal or nonexistent. The standard label contract reinforces this financial austerity by stipulating a predetermined budget and requiring the producer or director to pay for any unauthorized amount over the allotted budget. The labels also depress budgets by infrequently using novice talent willing to produce and direct videos for a reduced amount, forcing more established firms to cut their requested budgets in order to remain competitive.

Relationship Between Economic Structure and Ideology Within the Video Music Business

Although this study has not undertaken an extensive content analysis of video music presented on major program services, other critics noted that politically oriented videos are relatively absent from popular music television shows. This survey of the music video industry does include evidence supporting both instrumental and structural explanations for the general exclusion of videos that criticize social inequities and condemn injustices.

MTV's initial refusal to air Neil Young's *This Note's for You* video lends credence to the instrumentalist contention that MTV executives intentionally suppressed a video that overtly criticized certain aspects of the economic structure that sustains the program service. Despite MTV's claim that the video violated its standards policies, several parties, including Young and his record label, argued that MTV was afraid of offending the advertisers mentioned in the clip. Moreover, MTV appeared unwilling to present a production that mildly parodied certain commercial practices that provide the channel with its primary source of revenue. More generally, Tom Shales, television critic of the *Washington Post,* argues that politically oriented videos are not welcome on MTV because the program service constructed an insular world where music is the only relevant social force: "Rock stars adopt poses of surly rebelliousness, but what they portray themselves as rebelling against are things like table manners or having to go to school, never against the corporate or political powers that be."[3] MTV's tendency to ignore videos from independent labels contributes to the channel's avoidance of overtly political videos because such clips are more likely to come from independents that are more willing than majors to support artists whose music confronts controversial issues and challenges established authority. For instance, Bryan Turner of the independent Priority Records claimed that MTV refused to play a video for the rap group Low Profile indicting the Reagan and Bush Administrations for contributing to the U.S. drug crisis.

However, the more regular omission of overtly political videos may be due to structural forces. Recording artists' desire for commercial success may encourage them to avoid contentious, divisive topics in songs as well as their accompanying videos. Further, major program services seeking substantial ratings and advertising revenue may avoid playing videos with a partisan political message in order to avoid alienating any segment of a potential audience or offending sponsors. Such decisions regarding whether a politically oriented video will be produced or aired may be made solely on the basis of commercial considerations, rather than the ideological values held by an individual artist, record company executive, or program service executive. Yet the ideological conformity of the clips remains the same whatever the cause.

Video music clips rarely tend to confront specific political or social issues, but rather usually dwell on the more intimate themes of sex and romance. This perennial preoccupation with personal relationships in video music naturally reflects the larger focus on these matters in American pop music since the clips are drawn from current hit songs. At the major record labels, the relative lack of social dissent in music video also can likely be attributed to the operation of structural market forces rather than the result of a conscious corporate policy to suppress dissenting ideas. When allocating funds for videos, record label executives may believe that there is no market for clips with overt political themes and assume that such clips would have difficulty gaining television airplay. However, this rationale ignores consideration of the degree to which record buyers are conditioned through various media to conceptualize popular music as a purely apolitical medium.

Yet some artists take advantage of the inherent contradiction of cultural commodities described by Garnham.[4] These artists infrequently use music video as a forum for expressing dissent by producing music clips within the commodity production process that disparage central tenets of capitalist ideology. Established artists can use their substantial industry clout and financial resources to make a video for a politically oriented song in an attempt to generate public interest in an issue or cause embraced by the musician. For example, in 1987, Jackson Browne funded a video for "Lives in the Balance," the title song from his overtly political album, which harshly criticized the Reagan Administration's support of the Nicaraguan contras and more broadly condemned U.S. policy in Central America.[5] Browne also persuaded his record label, Elektra/Asylum, to release the song to college radio and commercial rock stations. The video, which used explicit scenes from documentaries on Central America, was shown on MTV. Browne aggressively promoted this video to sensitize young viewers to the consequences of American intervention in Nicaragua. "I want people to see the real faces of the Nicaraguans, the Nicaraguans who are mourning their dead," declared Browne. "I think Americans should see those faces."[6] Browne's video is a central example of this attempt by a socially conscious artist to exploit the latent contradictions of this cultural form.

Although successful artists like Browne have the opportunity to use this visual medium to publicize certain issues, artists seeking to maintain their commercial success often avoid addressing partisan political issues in their music or videos in order to reach the broadest possible audience and avoid alienating potential music buyers. Browne conceded that the relatively poor sales of this album compared to his other releases was likely due to the overtly political nature of the music. Further, less established or unknown artists generally lack the funds to make a broadcast quality video and may be unable to secure the cooperation of record labels and major program services necessary to effectively use the medium in this manner. Thus the structural operation of the market helps suppress an open dialogue on controversial issues through the medium of video music.

Pat Aufderheide says that when artists do attempt to convey a politically oriented theme in their videos, the conventional form of music video, which visualizes abstract fantasies, often undercuts their message.[7] Donna Summer wanted her video for the song "She Works Hard for the Money" to illustrate the plight of working women through a portrayal of the hard life of a waitress. Summer's performance in the video was modeled after a waitress she once met. David Bowie similarly sought to use his video for the song "Let's Dance" to address the issue of rights for Australian aborigines. Yet although working women appeared in Summer's video and aborigines were present in Bowie's production, neither music clip presented an intelligible position on a particular political issue. Aufderheide says that "in both cases, any message was lost in the disjunctive images and dreamy fantasy."[8]

Artists who deal with social issues in video clips are often criticized for capitalizing on these issues for their own financial gain. For example, the issues of homelessness and poverty are addressed in the songs and accompanying videos for Michael Jackson's "Man in the Mirror" and Phil Collins's "Another Day in Paradise." Because video clips are primarily promotional devices designed to sell recorded music, the images of homelessness included in these videos were used to promote sales of the respective albums by Jackson and Collins. These videos imply that the viewer can express concern about the social issue of homelessness by purchasing the associated album. Yet, although the plight of homeless people was exploited to increase sales of these albums, both songs were purely commercial efforts that raised money exclusively for Jackson, Collins, and their respective record labels. No revenue from sales of these albums was given to organizations providing support services for the homeless. Music critic Jon Pareles considers this type of video and song, profiting from the misery of others, especially repugnant because the song usually mentions a social issue in a vague, amorphous manner without advocating a specific course of action to remedy the problem. Pareles derisively refers to these as "pseudopolitical songs": "The songs point no fingers, reveal no underlying causes, assign no blame, suggest no action. They don't perform the essential political act: taking sides. That might alienate someone."[9]

Although video clips with politically oriented themes are rarely produced and seldom receive television airplay, some prominent videos designed to solicit charitable contributions received broad record industry support and extensive airplay on major program services. The first major attempt to employ music video to raise funds for a particular social cause was for the charity song, "Do They Know It's Christmas?/Feed the World," made by a collection of popular British recording artists under the name, "Band Aid." In 1984, Bob Geldof, leader of the Irish punk rock group, the Boomtown Rats, encouraged around forty U.K. performers to participate in the making of a song that would bring attention to the problem of famine in Ethiopia and solicit donations for food and other relief efforts. A video was made to accompany the song, "Do They Know It's Christmas?" which received extensive airplay on MTV as well as other major program services.

This group effort by British artists inspired a similar effort in 1985 by popular recording artists in the United States who, under the name "USA for Africa," recorded the song "We Are the World," which was also designed to raise funds for relief efforts in Africa. The song, written by Michael Jackson, Lionel Richie, and Quincy Jones, was recorded by an array of pop and rock stars after the American Music Awards on January 28, 1985. The organizers of USA for Africa also produced a video for "We Are the World," featuring the artists singing in a recording studio. The video was heavily played on MTV. These charity efforts for African relief culminated in an elaborate live telethon by Live Aid featuring performances by sixty American and U.K. musicians in Philadelphia and London. The Live Aid telethon was viewed by an estimated 1.5 billion people in 160 countries. In the United States, live coverage of the event was presented all day on MTV, 107 independent television stations presented the first eleven hours of performances, and ABC presented the final three hours in a prime-time show.

These charity-oriented videos and television events raised substantial funds for various social causes, with Band Aid generating $10 million alone from sales of the "Do They Know It's Christmas?" single. That money was donated to relief efforts in Ethiopia. However, these videos and accompanying songs were criticized for promoting a naive and simplistic understanding of the social problems that are confronted in their music. For example, both the USA for Africa and Band Aid songs and videos attempt to deal with the issue of hunger in Africa without identifying or criticizing the relevant social, political, or economic factors that may contribute to this desperate situation. Who's to blame? No one really knows from watching and listening to these videos. "Hunger" as a social phenomenon is discussed out of context from the widespread poverty and social inequities that exist in Africa as well as the United States and United Kingdom. No consideration is given to how Western colonial policies contributed to the widespread "hunger" in the first place. The refusal of these efforts to take a more overtly political stand on this issue led the *Village Voice* to deride USA for Africa's song as "no more than lowest-common denominator AOR dignified with a religious tinge and put in the service of toothless one-world do-goodism."[10] In general then, music videos that receive broad distribution and exposure on U.S. media systems only seem able to grapple with social problems like poverty in the most apolitical, inoffensive manner possible.

∾ ∾ ∾

Music video is usually considered to be one of the less consequential, significant sectors of the U.S. mass media. Media critics and academic scholars are more likely to focus their attention on areas like the press, which inform the public, or network television shows, which entertain mass audiences. Music video, by contrast, is perceived as a hybrid media form that provides a minor diversion for some young people who watch cable channels like MTV. The music clips are often derided as little more than commercials for record companies, and MTV is dismissed as an overheated promotional medium hawking everything in sight, most of all itself. Yet this survey of the music video business does raise crucial issues about such weighty topics as individual creativity, democracy, freedom of speech, and political expression. The form of music video provides the possibility to contribute to all of these lofty ideals. Producers and directors can conceivably use this new hybrid media form to express creative, innovative ideas and to artistically represent the experiences and struggles of various groups in society. Video makers can contribute to a discussion on pressing, controversial social issues through the lyrics and visual images in the music clip. Yet for the most part it hasn't worked out that way. The possibilities for artistry and innovation are unrealized, the new avenues for creativity unexplored. Instead, music clips presented on major program services like MTV and VH-1 are constructed as a way to promote and sell the products of media conglomerates: compact discs, cassettes, films, clothing, soft drinks, whatever. The major expression of creativity goes on not in front of the camera where hackneyed video clichés are repeated ad nauseam, but behind the camera in the corporate suites where executives in media conglomerates try to develop increasingly clever ways to use videos in cross-promotion strategies to sell more things to young people. The use of music video by major record companies and program services has not enhanced creative diversity in the U.S. mass media but has diminished it. Music clips are used as the linchpin in synergistic strategies to promote the same tired, recycled ideas in various media sectors, such as promoting the movie, soundtrack, television series, and product tie-ins all based on the same "creative" concept.

Yet, the possibilities still remain. Some MTV viewers are already rebelling at the unremitting barrage of merchandising and advertising for related media products, asking for something more. Viewers on the MTV Online computer bulletin board are increasingly castigating the channel, making such comments as "MTV used to speak to a generation . . . now they throw ads masquerading as programming at us twenty-four hours a day. . . . MTV died a long time ago," and "We're not as dumb as you think, oh corporate giant."[11] The disenchantment with the program service is reflected in its stagnant audience ratings, which stayed at roughly 0.5 in the mid-1990s, so that MTV is usually being watched in only one-half of one percent of its subscriber households.

Moreover, some cultural producers at the margins are exploring some of these prospects for more imaginative music video. As technological advances lower the cost of video production equipment, making it affordable to more people, independent record companies, recording artists, and freelance producers and directors are making their own low-cost, unconventional videos. These clips often break the clichés and formulas of typical videos on "Empty-Vee" as some call it, by using the form of music video in unexpected, provocative ways to express new creative ideas. They provide bracing challenges to the policies of political and business elites. These videos may be aired on certain local television music shows or some cable access channels, yet usually they go no farther than that. Because of the entrenched concentration and conglomeration of media firms, most videos presented on major program services like MTV remain safe, conventional, banal. The national distribution of music videos is largely controlled by MTV Networks, which acts as a gatekeeper limiting public access to clips. Further, most funding for videos comes from the major record labels, which insist on making videos that do not express ideas or creativity but instead primarily seek to sell their wares in related media markets. The challenge for society is to provide opportunities for production, distribution, and exhibition of clips outside of this market-driven conglomerate colossus, which may unlock the potential of music video and enhance rather than diminish a robust cultural democracy.

Notes

CHAPTER 1

1. Jon Pareles, "After Music Videos, All the World Has Become a Screen," *New York Times,* 10 December 1989, sec. 4, p. E6.

2. "How MTV Has Rocked Television Commercials," *New York Times,* 9 October 1989, D6.

3. Jane D. Brown and Kenneth Campbell, "Race and Gender in Music Videos: The Same Beat but a Different Drummer," *Journal of Communication* 36 (Winter 1986):98.

4. Ibid., 104.

5. Steven A. Seidman, "An Investigation of Sex-Role Stereotyping in Music Videos," *Journal of Broadcasting and Electronic Media* 36 (Spring 1992):209–215.

6. Nancy Signorielli, Douglas McLeod, and Elaine Healy, "Gender Stereotypes in MTV Commercials: The Beat Goes On," *Journal of Broadcasting and Electronic Media* 38 (Winter 1994):91–101.

7. Barry L. Sherman and Joseph R. Dominick, "Violence and Sex in Music Videos: TV and Rock 'n' Roll," *Journal of Communication* 36 (Winter 1986):79–93.

8. Richard C. Vincent, Dennis K. Davis, and Lilly Ann Boruszkowski, "Sexism on MTV: The Portrayal of Women in Rock Videos," *Journalism Quarterly* 64 (Winter 1987):750–754.

9. Sherman and Dominick, "Violence and Sex in Music Videos," 88.

10. Ibid.

11. Ibid., 86.

12. Brown and Campbell, "Race and Gender in Music Videos," 103.

13. Ibid.

14. Rebecca Rubin, Alan M. Rubin, Elizabeth M. Perse, Cameron Armstrong, Michael McHugh, and Noreen Faix, "Media Use and Meaning: A Music Video Exploration," *Journalism Quarterly* 63 (Summer 1986):353–359.

15. Dean Abt, "Music Television: Impact of the Visual Dimension," in *Popular Music and Communication: Social and Cultural Perspectives,* ed. James Lull (Beverly Hills, Calif.: Sage, 1987).

16. Se-Wen Sun and James Lull, "The Adolescent Audience for Music Videos and Why They Watch," *Journal of Communication* 36 (Winter 1986):116–117.

17. Ibid., 124.

18. E. Ann Kaplan, *Rocking Around the Clock* (New York: Methuen, 1987), 13.

19. Richard Gehr, "The MTV Aesthetic," *Film Comment* 19 (July/August 1983):39–40.

20. Pat Aufderheide, "The Look of the Sound," in *Watching Television,* ed. Todd Gitlin (New York: Pantheon Books, 1987), 111.

21. Kaplan, *Rocking Around the Clock,* 14, 15.

22. Margaret Morse, "Postsynchronizing Rock Music and Television," *Journal of Communication Inquiry* 10 (Winter 1986):16–17.

23. Virginia H. Fry and Donald L. Fry, "MTV: The 24 Hour Commercial," *Journal of Communication Inquiry* 10 (Winter 1986):29.

24. Ibid., 30–31.

25. Kaplan, *Rocking Around the Clock,* 12.

26. Aufderheide, "The Look of the Sound," 117.

27. Morse, "Postsynchronizing Rock Music and Television," 17.

28. John Fiske, "MTV: Post-Structural Post-Modern," *Journal of Communication Inquiry* 10 (Winter 1986):76.

29. Morse, "Postsynchronizing Rock Music and Television," 24.

30. Aufderheide, "The Look of the Sound," 117–118.

31. Pareles, "After Music Videos, All the World Has Become a Screen," sec. 4, p. E6.

32. "How MTV Has Rocked Television Commercials," D6.

33. Ibid.

34. Kaplan, *Rocking Around the Clock,* 5.

35. Jean Baudrillard, "The Implosion of Meaning in the Media and the Implosion of the Social in the Masses," in *The Myths of Information: Technology and Postindustrial Culture,* ed. K. Woodward (Madison, Wisc.: Coda Press, 1980), 142.

36. Kaplan, *Rocking Around the Clock,* 5.

37. Baudrillard, "The Implosion of Meaning," 137–148.

38. E. Ann Kaplan, "History, the Historical Spectator and Gender Address in Music Television," *Journal of Communication Inquiry* 10 (Winter 1986):6.

39. Kaplan, "Music Television," 12.

40. Hanno Hardt, "MTV: Towards Visual Domination, A Polemic," *Journal of Communication Inquiry* 10 (Winter 1986):65; and David J. Tetzlaff, "MTV and the Politics of Postmodern Pop," *Journal of Communication Inquiry* 10 (Winter 1986):87.

41. Tetzlaff, "MTV and the Politics of Postmodern Pop," 87.

42. Peter Golding and Graham Murdock, "Theories of Communication and Theories of Society," *Communication Research* 5 (July 1978):349.

43. Sherman and Dominick, "Violence and Sex in Music Videos," 79–93.

44. Fry and Fry, "MTV: The 24 Hour Commercial," 29–33.

45. Tetzlaff, "MTV and the Politics of Postmodern Pop," 88.

46. Golding and Murdock, "Theories of Communication," 350.

47. Kaplan, *Rocking Around the Clock.*

48. Golding and Murdock, "Theories of Communication," 349.

49. Robert W. McChesney, "Critical Communication Research at the Crossroads," in *Defining Media Studies,* eds. Mark R. Levy and Michael Gurevitch (New York: Oxford University Press, 1994), 340–346; and Vincent Mosco, "Introduction," in *The Critical Communications Review, Volume 1: Labor, the Working Class, and the Media,* eds. Vincent Mosco and Janet Wasko (Norwood, N.J.: Ablex, 1983), ix–xxviii.

50. Dallas Smythe, "On the Political Economy of Communications," *Journalism Quarterly* 37 (Autumn 1960):564.

51. Herbert Schiller, *Culture Inc.: The Corporate Takeover of Public Expression* (New York: Oxford University Press, 1989).

52. Ibid.; Michael Parenti, *Inventing Reality: The Politics of News Media,* 2nd ed. (New York: St. Martin's Press, 1993); Douglas Kellner, *Television and the Crisis of Democracy* (Boulder, Colo.: Westview Press, 1990); and Edward S. Herman and Noam Chomsky, *Manufacturing Consent: The Political Economy of the Mass Media* (New York: Pantheon Books, 1988).

53. Eileen R. Meehan, Vincent Mosco, and Janet Wasko, "Rethinking Political Economy: Change and Continuity," in *Defining Media Studies*, eds. Mark R. Levy and Michael Gurevitch (New York: Oxford University Press, 1994), 347–358.

54. Graham Murdock and Peter Golding, "Capitalism, Communication and Class Relations," in *Mass Communication and Society*, ed. James Curran, Michael Gurevitch, and Janet Woollacott (Beverly Hills, Calif.: Sage, 1979), 12–43.

55. Nicholas Garnham, "Toward a Theory of Cultural Materialism," *Journal of Communication* 33 (Summer 1983):321.

56. Larry Grossberg, "Strategies of Marxist Cultural Interpretation," *Critical Studies in Mass Communication* 1 (December 1984):398; and Stuart Hall, "The Rediscovery of 'Ideology': Return of the Repressed in Media Studies," in *Culture, Society and the Media*, ed. Michael Gurevitch, Tony Bennett, James Curran, and Janet Woollacott (New York: Methuen, 1982), 56–90.

57. Murdock and Golding, "Capitalism, Communication and Class Relations," 16.

58. Nicholas Garnham, "Contribution to a Political Economy of Mass Communication," in *Mass Communication Review Yearbook*, vol. 1 (Beverly Hills, Calif.: 1981), 123–146.

59. Schiller, *Culture Inc.*, Chapter 7.

60. Douglas Gomery, "Media Economics: Terms of Analysis," *Critical Studies in Mass Communication* 6 (March 1989):44.

61. Graham Murdock, "Large Corporations and the Control of Communication Industries," in *Culture, Society and the Media*, ed. Michael Gurevitch, Tony Bennett, James Curran, and Janet Woollacott (London: Methuen, 1982), 124.

62. Ibid., 122.

63. Karl Marx and Frederick Engels, *Selected Works* (London: Lawrence & Wishart, 1968), 40.

64. Garnham, "Contribution to a Political Economy of Mass Communication," 144.

65. Ibid.

66. Benjamin M. Compaine, "Preface to the Second Edition. An Editorial," in *Who Owns the Media?* 2d ed., ed. Benjamin M. Compaine (White Plains, N.Y.: Knowledge Industry Publishers, 1982), xii.

67. Laurence Kenneth Shore, "The Crossroads of Business and Music: A Study of the Music Industry in the United States and Internationally" (Ph.D. diss., Stanford University, 1983), 31–32.

68. Ibid., 32.

69. Richard Bunce, *Television in the Corporate Interest* (New York: Praeger Publishers, 1976), chap. 6.

70. Martin A. Lee and Norman Solomon, *Unreliable Sources* (New York: Carol Publishing, 1992).

71. Murdock, "Large Corporations and the Control of Communication Industries," 144.

72. Smythe, "On the Political Economy of Communications," 568–569.

73. Murdock, "Large Corporations and the Control of Communication Industries," 144.

74. Ibid.

75. Shore, "The Crossroads of Business and Music."

76. Garnham, "Contribution to a Political Economy of Mass Communication," 136.

77. For instance, see Parenti, *Inventing Reality;* and Lee and Solomon, *Unreliable Sources.*

78. Graham Murdock and Peter Golding, "For a Political Economy of Mass Communications," in *The Socialist Register 1973*, ed. Ralph Miliband and John Saville (London: The Merlin Press, 1974), 213.

79. Benjamin M. Compaine, "Introduction," in *Who Owns the Media?* 2d ed., ed. Benjamin M. Compaine (White Plains, N.Y.: Knowledge Industry Publishers, 1982), 15.

80. Gomery, "Media Economics: Terms of Analysis," 55.

81. Ben Bagdikian, *The Media Monopoly*, 4th ed. (Boston: Beacon Press, 1992), 21.

82. Ibid., 21–25.

83. Ibid., 4.

84. Garnham, "Toward a Theory of Cultural Materialism," 323–324.

85. Gomery, "Media Economics: Terms of Analysis," 48.

86. Compaine, "Introduction," 15.

87. Federal Communications Commission, Kenneth Gordon, et al., *Staff Report on FCC Policy on Cable Ownership* (Washington, D.C.: FCC Office of Plans and Policy, September 1981), p. 54, note 10. Preliminary draft.

88. Gomery, "Media Economics: Terms of Analysis," 49.

89. Murdock, "Large Corporations and the Control of Communication Industries," 119–120.

90. Murdock and Golding, "For a Political Economy of Mass Communications," 219.

91. Murdock and Golding, "Capitalism, Communication and Class Relations," 25–26.

92. Murdock, "Large Corporations and the Control of Communication Industries," 120.

93. Bagdikian, *The Media Monopoly*.

94. Thomas H. Guback, "Hollywood's International Market," in *The American Film Industry*, rev. ed., ed. Tino Balio (Madison: The University of Wisconsin Press, 1985), 463–465.

95. Ibid.

96. Shore, "The Crossroads of Business and Music," chapter 6.

97. Bagdikian, *The Media Monopoly*.

98. Schiller, *Culture Inc.;* Herbert Schiller, "Not Yet the Postimperialist Era," in *Communication and Culture in War and Peace*, ed. Colleen Roach (London: Sage, 1993), pp. 97–116; and Colleen Roach, "The Movement for a New World Information and Communication Order: A Second Wave?" *Media, Culture and Society* 12 (1990), 283–307.

99. Garnham, "Toward a Theory of Cultural Materialism," 322–323.

100. Garnham, "Contribution to a Political Economy of Mass Communication," 137.

101. Gomery, "Media Economics: Terms of Analysis," 54.

CHAPTER 2

1. The historical review in this section is taken primarily from the following sources: Tim Brooks and Earle Marsh, *The Complete Directory to Prime Time Network TV Shows*, 3d ed. (New York: Ballantine Books, 1985); R. Serge Denisoff, *Tarnished Gold* (New Brunswick, N.J.: Transaction Publishers, 1986); R. Serge Denisoff, *Inside MTV* (New Brunswick, N.J.: Transaction Publishers, 1989); Alex McNeil, *Total Television* (New York: Penguin, 1984); Sydney W. Head and Christopher H. Sterling, *Broadcasting in America*, 4th ed. (Dallas: Houghton Mifflin, 1987); and Laurence Kenneth Shore, "The Crossroads of Business and Music: A Study of the Music Industry in the United States and Internationally" (Ph.D. diss., Stanford University, 1983).

2. Denisoff, *Inside MTV,* 13.

3. Marjorie Williams, "MTV's Short Takes Define a New Style," *Washington Post,* 13 December 1989, A20.

4. Jon Pareles, "Pop Record Business Shows Signs of Recovery," *New York Times,* 28 November 1983, C13.

5. Ibid.

6. Ibid.

7. Robert Christgau, "Rock 'n' Roller Coaster," *Village Voice,* 7 February 1985, 37.

8. Warner Communications, Form 10-K for the fiscal year ending 31 December 1984, I–11.

9. Steven Levy, "Ad Nauseam: How MTV Sells Out Rock and Roll," *Rolling Stone,* 8 December 1983, 33.

10. Denisoff, *Inside MTV,* 44.

11. Williams, "MTV's Short Takes Define a New Style," A20.

12. MTV Networks, Form 10-K to the U.S. Securities and Exchange Commission (SEC) for the fiscal year ending 31 December 1984, 3.

13. Melinda Newman, "Freston: Let's Shun Cliched Clips," *Billboard,* 2 December 1989, 3.

14. Quote from *Wall Street Journal* reported in Christgau, "Rock 'n' Roller Coaster," 38.

15. Ibid.

16. Ibid.

17. Jim McCullaugh, "MTV Cable Spurs Disk Sales of Artists Aired," *Billboard,* 10 October 1981, 1, 68.

18. Ibid.

19. Rob Patterson, "Clips Sell—but How Much?" *Billboard,* 29 October 1983, 48.

20. Denisoff, *Inside MTV,* 84.

21. J. Max Robins, "Into the Groove," *Channels of Communication,* May 1989, 26.

22. Denisoff, *Inside MTV,* 83.

23. "MTV: 1981–1986," *Billboard,* 2 August 1986, MTV14. Advertising supplement. Given that the source of this information is MTVN Data, the figures might be inflated.

24. Leo Sacks, "Madison Ave. Warming to MTV," *Billboard,* 2 July 1983, 64.

25. Andrew C. Brown, "Products of the Year," *Fortune,* 28 December 1981, 66.

26. Sacks, "Madison Ave. Warming to MTV," 1.

27. Denisoff, *Inside MTV,* 125.

28. Cary Darling, "Labels See Video as Force to Be Reckoned with," *Billboard,* 14 November 1981, 64.

29. Cary Darling, "R&B Denied?" *Billboard,* 28 November 1981, 4, 62.

30. Ibid.

31. Christopher Connelly, "Rick James Blasts Vanity 6, Charges MTV with Racism," *Rolling Stone,* 14 April 1983, 47.

32. Transcript of *Nightline,* May 13, 1983.

33. Denisoff, *Inside MTV,* 110.

34. A transcript of this interview is presented in Levy, "Ad Nauseam," 37.

35. Ibid.

36. Ibid.

37. Richard Gold, "Labels Limit Videos on Black Artists," *Variety,* 15 December 1982, 78.

38. The details of this confrontation between CBS and MTV are recounted in Denisoff, *Inside MTV,* 102–104; and Levy, "Ad Nauseam."

39. Christgau, "Rock 'n' Roller Coaster," 40.

40. Ibid.

41. Ibid.; and Levy, "Ad Nauseam."

42. Denisoff, *Inside MTV,* 104.

43. Warner Communications, Form 10-K to the SEC for the fiscal year ending 31 December 1984, 1–13.

44. Ibid.; and William K. Knoedelseder Jr., "MTV's Stock Sales Snag on a State Law," *Los Angeles Times,* 4 September 1984, pt. 4, pp. 1, 2. MTV stock was not allowed to be sold in California because the state's regulatory agency, the Department of Corporations, found the unequal voting provisions of the MTV stock illegal under state law.

45. "Hit Parade," *Time,* 5 November 1984, 55; and Denisoff, *Inside MTV,* 123.

46. MTV Networks, Form 10-K to the SEC for the fiscal year ending 31 December 1984, 18.

47. Pareles, "Pop Record Business Shows Signs of Recovery," C13; and Warner Communications, 1984 Annual Report, 12.

48. Leo Sacks, "MTV's Impact at Retail and Radio," *Billboard,* 16 April 1983, 63.

49. Leo Sacks, "MTV Seen Aiding AOR Stations," *Billboard,* 28 May 1983, 66.

50. Contributing factors mentioned in this paragraph are discussed in Pareles, "Pop Record Business Shows Signs of Recovery," C13.

51. Denisoff, *Tarnished Gold,* 356.

52. Mark Potts, "MTV Hoping Its Stock Will Be 'Thriller' for Investors," *Washington Post,* 8 July 1984, G1.

53. "MTV: 1981–1986," MTV5.

54. Ibid.

55. Ellen Farley, "Videos Rock the Music Business," *Los Angeles Times,* 21 August 1983, pt. 1, 33.

56. "Joe Jackson Puts Down Video, Contending It Has Hurt Music," *Variety,* 13 June 1984, 71.

57. "Music Video," *Fortune,* 17 September 1984, 167.

58. Figures taken from ibid.; and Ken Terry, "Diskeries Ponder Music Video Business," *Variety,* 14 March 1984, 69.

59. Terry, "Diskeries Ponder Music Video Business," 69.

60. Ibid.

61. Ibid., 69, 76.

62. "Music Video," 169.

63. "Homevid Execs Wary of Musical Genre," *Variety,* 14 March 1984, 75.

64. "Music Video," 169.

65. Tony Seideman, "Video Outlets in CBS Boycott," *Billboard,* 8 June 1985, 1, 80.

66. Information presented in this paragraph regarding the WEA Record Group license fee plan is taken from Phil DiMauro, "WCI Labels to Charge for Clips," *Variety,* 21 August 1985, 121, 126.

67. Ibid.

68. Phil DiMauro, "Majors Consider Vidclip Charges in Wake of CBS, WEA Moves," *Variety,* 28 August 1985, 89.

69. Seideman, "Video Outlets in CBS Boycott," 1, 80.

70. Richard Gold, "Label Charges for Music Videos May Lead to Big Shakeout in Outlets That Broadcast Them," *Variety,* 14 March 1984, 69, 87.

CHAPTER 3

1. Serge Denisoff, *Inside MTV* (New Brunswick, N.J.: Transaction Publishers, 1989), 167.

2. "Turner Sets Launch Date for Music Video Service," *Broadcasting,* 3 September 1984, 37.

3. Paul Green, "New Turner Music Channel: Accent on Hits," *Billboard,* 20 October 1984, 72.

4. Figures reported in "Turner Sets Launch Date for Music Video Service," 36. The same estimated range of stock prices is reported in Maurice Christopher, "Turner Considers Competition for MTV," *Advertising Age,* 13 August 1984, 69. However, Alex Ben Block contends the expected price was the higher $18 per share and estimated loss was $15.4 million. Alex Ben Block, "Music for the Eyes," *Forbes,* 3 December 1984, 166.

5. Block, "Music for the Eyes," 166.

6. "Ted Turner Turns off the Music," *The Economist,* 8 December 1984, 77.

7. Turner's increasing dependence on banks is demonstrated vividly by statistics on long-term debt from the Selected Financial Data from Turner Broadcasting System's 1984 Annual Report:

Year	Long-term Debt
1980	$ 9,825,000
1981	7,165,000
1982	42,802,000
1983	122,404,000
1984	175,015,000

8. Susan Spillman, "Turner/MTV Face a 'Cutthroat' War," *Advertising Age,* 3 September 1984, 68.

9. Christopher, "Turner Considers Competition for MTV," 69. Christopher's account of Turner's meeting with Warner Amex's Drew Lewis is based on an unnamed "financial source." Denisoff, *Inside MTV* (p. 180), reports that Turner was compelled by lending institutions to meet with Warner to discuss the possibility of a merger.

10. Figures taken from Block, "Music for the Eyes," 162. The same figures are reported in Tony Seideman, "Rough Start for Turner's Music Channel," *Billboard.* 17 November 1984, 1, except that the amount for 1984 is $1.5 million instead of $1 million as reported by Block.

11. Tony Seideman, "Rough Start for Turner's Music Channel," 78. Seideman reports that TBS filed this prospectus as part of an attempt to raise $130 million to repay loans to banks that had insisted on incorporating the restrictive covenants into the loans.

12. "Hit Parade," *Time,* 5 November 1984, 55; and Denisoff, *Inside MTV,* 123.

13. Thomas E. Ricks, "Turner Broadcasting Is Ready to Close Music Channel, Sell Some Assets to MTV," *Wall Street Journal,* 29 November 1984, 6.

14. Denisoff, *Inside MTV,* 186.

15. Steven Dupler, "Settlement in Vidclip Exclusivity Suit," *Billboard,* 3 May 1988, 1.

16. "U.S. Senators Ask FTC to Probe MTV's Exclusive Video Contracts," *Variety,* 1 April 1987, 75–77.

17. Melinda Newman, "Hit Video USA Casts an Eye Toward Int'l Market," *Billboard,* 13 January 1990, 49.

214   *Notes*

18. Daniel Benedict, "Picking a Fight with the Champ," *Venture,* June/July 1989, 21, 22.

19. Melinda Newman, "Plug Pulled on Hit Video USA," *Billboard,* 20 October 1990, 10, 85.

20. Melinda Newman, "The Eye," *Billboard,* 13 April 1991, 42.

21. Fredric Dannen, "MTV'S Great Leap Backward," *Channels of Communication,* July/August 1987, 47.

22. Ibid.

23. Ibid.

24. Tony Seideman, "MTV Aging Via Second Net," *Billboard,* 1 September 1984, 58.

25. Steven Dupler, "MTV's VH-1 Opens on Optimistic Note," *Billboard,* 12 January 1985, 1.

26. "MTV's New Service Offers an Integrated Musical Mix," *Billboard,* 19 January 1985, 51.

27. Cathleen McGuigan, "Soft Rock and Hard Talk," *Newsweek,* 15 July 1985, 51.

28. Jeremy Gerard, "An MTV for Grown-Ups Is Seeking Its Audience," *New York Times,* 7 August 1989, C14.

29. Dannen, "MTV's Great Leap Backward," 47.

30. Susan Spillman, "MTV's New Music Network May Prove Tougher Ad Sell," *Advertising Age,* 27 August 1984, 10.

31. J. Max Robins, "Into the Groove," *Channels of Communication,* May 1989, 29. Advertising revenue for 1988 and 1989 is estimated.

32. Tony Seideman, "VH-1 Sending Sales Signals," *Billboard,* 16 February 1985, 1.

33. Steven Dupler, "Virgin Breaks Fordham Via VH-1, Press," *Billboard,* 26 November 1988, 30; and Steven Dupler, "Label Execs: VH-1 Is Coming of Age," *Billboard,* 7 March 1987, 51–52.

34. Figures are taken from Robins, "Into the Groove," 29; and Gerard, "An MTV for Grown-Ups Is Seeking Its Audience," C14.

35. Melinda Newman, "VH-1 Unveils 'Greatest-Hits' Campaign," *Billboard,* 8 September 1990, 53.

36. Clive Davis, "AMAs Reflect MTV-Influenced Homogenization. It's Time to Speak Up for Musical Diversity," *Billboard,* 16 February 1991, 12.

37. Melinda Newman, "Labels Weighing Video Costs vs. Gains," *Billboard,* 10 November 1990, 1, 75.

38. Andrew Grossman, "Freeze Frame: A Radical Departure," *Marketing & Media Decisions,* August 1989, 30.

39. Deborah Russell, "MTV Experiments to Hold Viewers," *Billboard,* 3 July 1993, 1, 84.

40. Form 10-K for Viacom for the fiscal year ending 31 December, 1991, I-19.

41. Peter Newcomb, "Music Video Wars," *Forbes,* 4 March 1991, 68, 70.

42. Melinda Newman and Phyllis Stark, "Jukebox Network Building Strong Rep as Maker of Hits," *Billboard,* 30 March 1991, 5, 125.

43. Peter Ainslie, "On the Jukebox Network, You Make the Call," *Rolling Stone,* 2 May 1991, 48, 63; and ibid.

44. Melinda Newman, "The Eye," *Billboard,* 15 June 1991, 54.

45. Newman and Stark, "Jukebox Network Building Strong Rep," 5, 125.

46. Rich Zahradnik, "Jukebox Network Expanding into U.K.," *Billboard,* 22 February 1992, 45.

47. Don Jeffrey, "VJN Cites Slow Growth, High Costs in Loss," *Billboard,* 30 November 1991, 32, 34.

48. Kirsten Beck, "BET Faces Music, Comes Up with Talk," *Channels of Communication,* June 1989, 58–60.

49. Janine McAdams, "BET in the '90s—Giving Viewers Even More of a Choice in the Decade of Diversity," *Billboard,* 22 September 1990, BET-2. Advertising supplement.

50. McAdams, "BET in the '90s," BET-2.

51. Jim Bessman, "Black Cable Network Makes Heavy Commitment to Clips," *Billboard,* 30 March 1985, 30.

52. Ibid.

53. McAdams, "BET in the '90s," BET-2.

54. Jeff Levenson, "BET to Bow Jazz Network," *Billboard,* 2 October 1993, 8, 55.

55. Beck, "BET Faces Music, Comes Up with Talk," 59.

56. Ibid.

57. Jube Shiver Jr., "Building a Network," *Los Angeles Times,* 27 August 1989, sec. 4, p. 1, 4.

58. Beck, "BET Faces Music, Comes Up with Talk," 58–60.

59. Jube Shiver Jr., "Ready to Do Lunch with Hollywood," *Los Angeles Times,* 19 August 1991, F1, F12.

60. Melinda Newman, "MTV Puts R&B in Spotlight with Weekly Video Show," *Billboard,* 26 October 1991, 5, 79.

61. Melinda Newman and Janine McAdams, "BET Pressures Labels to Curb MTV Exclusives," *Billboard,* 27 July 1991, 1, 42, 43.

62. Chris McGowan, "Music Video on TV: From Youth to Middle Age in Seven Years?" *Billboard,* 12 November 1988, V1.

63. Edward Morris, "Country Vids Expanding Horizons, Aristo Says," *Billboard,* 16 November 1991, 37.

64. Rob Tannenbaum, "Country's New Gold Rush," *Rolling Stone,* 16 April 1992, 16–17.

65. Morris, "Country Vids Expanding Horizons, Aristo Says," 37.

66. "CMT Europe's Reach Extends Across Continent," *Billboard,* 28 August 1993, 87.

67. Edward Morris, "Country Acts Find Non-Radio Routes to Fame," *Billboard,* 17 February 1990, 1, 43.

68. "5th Birthday Salute to Night Tracks," *Billboard,* 4 June 1988, N12. Advertising supplement.

69. Ibid., N1.

70. Melinda Newman, "'Night Tracks' on Alternative Path," *Billboard,* 20 July 1991, 41; and Melinda Newman, "It's the End of the Road for 'Night Tracks' on TBS," *Billboard,* 4 April 1992, 30.

71. "Local Stations are Offering 24-Hour Music Video," *New York Times,* 4 September 1984, C19.

72. Ibid.

73. Ibid.

74. "The Beat Goes on TV: Music Videos, Sign-on to Sign-off," *Broadcasting,* 25 June 1984, 53.

CHAPTER 4

1. Fredric Dannen, "MTV's Great Leap Backward," *Channels of Communication,* July/August 1987, 47.

2. Tony Seideman, "Exclusivity Key to MTV Deals, Says Pittman," *Billboard,* 14 April 1984, 3.

3. Ibid., 61.

4. The terms of the proposed agreement with Capitol are reported in Peter Hall, "MTV Wants It All," *Village Voice,* 21 February 1984, 48.

5. R. Serge Denisoff, *Inside MTV* (New Brunswick, N.J.: Transaction Publishers, 1989), 151.

6. Tony Seideman, "Four Labels Ink Vidclip Deals with MTV," *Billboard,* 23 June 1984, 1; and Ken Terry, "MTV Claims It Has Video Deals with Four Labels; Exclusivity May Be Double-Edged Sword," *Variety,* 20 June 1984, 60.

7. Fred Goodman, "Krasnow Says Electra Will Sign with MTV," *Billboard,* 25 August 1984, 1.

8. John Sippel, "Inside Track," *Billboard,* 25 May 1985, 86.

9. Adam White, "A Day in the Life of MTV: 164 Clips," *Billboard,* 17 November 1984, 31.

10. Seideman. "Four Labels," 1.

11. Ken Terry, "Pittman Sez MTV Exclusivity Will Be Re-evaluated Before Label Pacts Expire Next Year," *Variety,* 28 May 1986, 77.

12. Ibid.

13. MTV Networks, Form 10-K to the U.S. Securities and Exchange Commission (SEC) for the fiscal year ending 31 December 1984, 4.

14. Viacom International, Form 10-K to the SEC for the fiscal year ending 31 December 1985, 18.

15. The vague discussion of exclusivity pacts omitting the specific quantity of agreements began in the Form 10-K to the SEC for Viacom International for the fiscal year ending 31 December 1987, which stated: "MTV has concluded a *number* of agreements with record companies" (p. 21; italics added).

16. Viacom, Form 10-K to the SEC for the fiscal year ending 31 December 1991, I-3, I-5.

17. Seideman, "Four Labels," 1.

18. Ken Terry, "MTV's Exclusivity Deals Scored by New Music Seminar Panel," *Variety,* 15 August 1984, 78; and "Four Labels," 1.

19. Terry, "MTV's Exclusivity Deals Scored," 78.

20. Seideman, "Four Labels," 1.

21. Terry, "MTV's Exclusivity Deals Scored," 78; and Mark Potts, "Pacts of MTV, Record Firms Probed," *Washington Post,* 10 October 1984, C1.

22. Susan Spillman, "Contracts Prompt MTV Suit," *Advertising Age,* 24 September 1984, 105.

23. Terry, "MTV's Exclusivity Deals Scored," 78.

24. Denisoff, *Inside MTV,* 154.

25. Seideman, "Four Labels," 1, 67.

26. Faye Zuckerman, "Rock Artists Gather to Sing MTV's Praises," *Billboard,* 15 December 1984, 34.

27. Terry, "Pittman Sez MTV Exclusivity," 78.

28. Melinda Newman, "Fox Quick to Jump on Jackson Premieres," *Billboard,* 16 November 1991, 62.

29. Terry, "Pittman Sez MTV Exclusivity," 78.

30. Ibid.

31. Seideman, "Four Labels," 1.

32. Leo Sacks, Tony Seideman, and Bill Holland, "Other Clip Outlets Blast MTV Pacts," *Billboard,* 23 June 1984, 67.

33. Terry, "Pittman Sez MTV Exclusivity," 78.

34. Warner Communications, 1984 Annual Report, 2.

35. Tony Seideman, "MTV Plan Shakes Label Exec Suites," *Billboard,* 31 March 1984, 60.

36. Ibid.

37. Hall, "MTV Wants It All," 48.

38. Frank J. Kahn, ed., *Documents of American Broadcasting,* 4th ed. (Englewood Cliffs, N.J.: Prentice Hall, 1984), 481–482.

39. Fredric Dannen, *Hit Men: Power Brokers and Fast Money Inside the Music Business* (New York: Times Books, 1990). A review of Dannen's book is presented in Christopher Byron, "Bad Music," *New York,* 6 August 1990, 10–11.

40. Terry, "MTV's Exclusivity Deals Scored," 78.

41. Erik Hedegaard, "Discovery Network Sues MTV," *Rolling Stone,* 8 November 1984, 61.

42. Viacom, Form 10-K to the SEC for the fiscal year ending 31 December 1991, I-5.

43. Ken Terry, "Diskeries Ponder Music Video Business," *Variety,* 14 March 1984, 69, 76.

44. Seideman, "MTV Plan Shakes Label Exec Suites," 1.

45. Spillman, "Contracts Prompt MTV Suit," 105.

46. Tony Seideman, "MTV Pacts Stir Reaction," *Billboard,* 21 July 1984, 1.

47. Nelson George and Steven Dupler, "BET Boycotts Profile Product," *Billboard,* 23 August 1986, 3, 92.

48. Ibid.

49. Terry, "MTV's Exclusivity Deals Scored," 78.

50. Tom Girard, "Discovery Sues MTV, Charging It Has Violated Antitrust Laws; Polygram Inks Exclusivity Pact," *Variety,* 26 September 1984, 105; and Faye Zuckerman and Kip Kirby, "Lawsuit Challenges MTV Deals," *Billboard,* 29 September 1984, 1, 68.

51. Hedegaard, "Discovery Network Sues MTV," 61.

52. Girard, "Discovery Sues MTV," 110.

53. Potts, "Pacts of MTV, Record Firms Probed," C4.

54. Ibid., C1.

55. Girard, "Discovery Sues MTV," 110.

56. Peter Newcomb, ". . . and only here. . . ," *Forbes,* 3 December 1984, 202–204.

57. Steven Dupler, "Settlement in Vidclip Exclusivity Suit," *Billboard,* 3 May 1988, 1.

58. Ibid.

59. Ibid., 71.

60. Jimmy Guterman, "Rival Sues MTV," *Rolling Stone,* 5 December 1985, 16; and Denisoff, *Inside MTV,* 221–222.

61. Dupler, "Settlement," 71.

62. Guterman, "Rival Sues MTV," 16.

63. Review of allegations contained in the Wodlinger suit relies heavily upon information presented in Dupler, "Settlement," 1, 71; and Guterman, "Rival Sues MTV," 16.

64. Dupler, "Settlement," 71.

65. Guterman, "Rival Sues MTV," 16.

66. Viacom International, Form 10-K to the SEC for the fiscal year ending 31 December 1987, 21.

67. Melinda Newman, "Hit Video USA Casts an Eye Toward Int'l Market," *Billboard*, 13 January 1990, 49.

68. Daniel Benedict, "Picking a Fight with the Champ," *Venture*, June/July 1989, 21–22.

69. "U.S. Senators Ask FTC to Probe MTV's Exclusive Video Contracts," *Variety*, 1 April 1987, 75, 77.

70. Viacom International, Form 10-K to the SEC for the fiscal year ending 31 December 1987, 21.

71. Dannen, "MTV's Great Leap Backward," 47.

72. Potts, "Pacts of MTV, Record Firms Probed," C1.

73. Susan Spillman, "Feds Probe MTV's Video License Deals," *Advertising Age*, 21 September 1984, 63.

74. Ibid., 1.

75. Terry, "Pittman Sez MTV Exclusivity," 77–78.

76. "Exclusives Extended," *Billboard*, 11 October 1986, 90.

77. Terry, "Pittman Sez MTV Exclusivity," 77.

78. "Exclusives Extended," 90.

79. Melinda Newman and Janine McAdams, "BET Pressures Labels to Curb MTV Exclusives," *Billboard*, 27 July 1991, 1, 42, 43.

80. Les Garland, "MTV Exclusivity Deals Deprive Fans of Music," *Billboard*, 22 August 1992, 4.

81. Newman and McAdams, "BET Pressures Labels," 1, 42, 43.

82. Ibid.; and Jube Shiver Jr., "Ready to Do Lunch with Hollywood," *Los Angeles Times*, 19 August 1991, F1, F12.

83. Shiver Jr., "Ready to Do Lunch with Hollywood," F1.

84. Newman and McAdams, "BET Pressures Labels," 43.

85. Melinda Newman, "Growing Pains Aplenty," *Billboard*, 21 December 1991, 47.

86. Melinda Newman, "The Eye," *Billboard*, 2 February 1991, 50.

87. Newman, "Growing Pains Aplenty," 47.

88. Newman and McAdams, "BET Pressures Labels," 43.

89. Deborah Russell, "CMV Cashes in on Video Play," *Billboard*, 11 February 1995, 48.

90. Johnnie L. Roberts, "Are They Jackin' the Box?" *Newsweek*, 23 January 1995, 42, 43.

91. Kevin Zimmerman, "Independent Labels Want Their MTV," *Variety*, 23 May 1990, 85.

92. Don Jeffrey and Dominic Pride, "Majors Plan to Challenge MTV with Music Video Venture," *Billboard*, 29 January 1994, 5.

93. Mark Landler, "Will MTV Have to Share the Stage?" *Business Week*, 21 February 1994, 38.

94. Ellie Weinert, "Four Majors Said to Back Viva," *Billboard*, 21 August 1993, 40.

95. Landler, "Will MTV Have to Share the Stage?" 38; Don Jeffrey, "BMG, Cable Co. TCI May Join New Music Venture," *Billboard*, 2 July 1994, 3, 109; "Music Channel Is Shelved," *New York Times*, 7 June 1994, D19; "Bertelsmann to Join MTV Competition," *Wall Street Journal*, 29 June 1994, B8; and Jeffrey A. Trachtenberg and Mark Robichaux, "TCI and Bertelsmann Unit Drop Plans for Music, Home-Shopping Channel," *Wall Street Journal*, 6 June 1994, B5.

96. Jeffrey and Pride, "Majors Plan to Challenge MTV," 5.

97. Landler, "Will MTV Have to Share the Stage?" 38.

98. Deborah Russell, "MTV Reorganization Stresses More Music," *Billboard*, 1 October 1994, 12, 85.

99. Landler, "Will MTV Have to Share the Stage?" 38.

100. J. Max Robins, "New Music Net on Rocky Road," *Variety*, 25–31 July 1994, 24; Gregory A. Patterson and Christina Duff, "Five Music Companies Face Inquiry into Plans to Begin Video Channel in '95," *Wall Street Journal*, 25 July 1994, B4; Edmund L. Andrews, "Plan to Create MTV Rival Is Under Antitrust Scrutiny," *New York Times*, 23 July 1994, 35, 43; Bill Holland and Deborah Russell, "Will Justice Dept. Prove Tough for Majors?" *Billboard*, 1 August 1994, 4, 83.

101. Brett Atwood, "Majors Eye New Options for Vid Channel," *Billboard*, 22 July 1995, 5.

102. Steven Dupler, "Seminar Probes Video Exclusivity," *Billboard*, 18 August 1984, 54.

103. Denisoff, *Inside MTV*, 149.

104. Information about MTV's treatment of the videos by The Rolling Stones and Billy Joel is taken from ibid., 149–150.

105. Brian Donlon, "A 2-Front Challenge for MTV," *USA Today*, 18 June 1986, 3D.

106. Paul Green, "New Turner Music Channel: Accent on Hits," *Billboard*, 20 October 1984, 1, 72.

107. Ibid., 72.

108. Dannen, "MTV's Great Leap Backward," 47.

109. Ibid.

110. Denisoff, *Inside MTV*, 181.

111. Steven Dupler, "Hit Video Cuts Programming to 7 Early-Morning Hours," *Billboard*, 8 February 1988, 80.

112. Ibid.

113. John Dempsey, "VH1 Programmers Make Plan to Face the Music," *Variety*, 17–23 July 1995, 21, 22.

114. Information about MTV's petition is taken from Tony Seideman, "MTV Asks FCC to Block Competing Vidclip Outlet," *Billboard*, 13 July 1985, 78; and Paula Span, "Music Meets TV and KAPOW!" *Washington Post*, 1 August 1985, B3.

115. Ibid.

116. Verne Gay, "Viacom Sues Time Fearing Showtime's Fate," *Variety*, 10 May 1989, 3.

117. Warner Communications, 1984 Annual Report.

118. Viacom, Form 10-K to the SEC for the fiscal year ending 31 December 1991, I-9.

119. Ibid.

120. Peter Newcomb, "Music Video Wars," *Forbes*, 4 March 1991, 68, 70.

121. Jackie Calmes, "Tax Break Bill Could Affect Viacom Sale," *Wall Street Journal*, 8 February 1995, A3, A6.

122. "Music Channel Is Shelved," *New York Times*, 7 June 1994, D19.

123. "Viacom Sues Time for $2.4 Billion," *Broadcasting*, 15 May 1989, 28, 30; and Gay, "Viacom Sues Time," 1, 3.

124. Benedict, "Picking a Fight with the Champ," 21–22.

125. Mark Landler and Geoffrey Smith, "The MTV Tycoon," *Business Week*, 21 September 1992, 56–62.

CHAPTER 5

1. Steven Dupler, "Will Pan-Euro MTV Pan Out? Net Bows in 14 Countries," *Billboard*, 15 August 1987, 81; and Peter Newcomb, "Music Video Wars," *Forbes*, 4 March 1991, 68, 70.

2. "Tom Freston: The Pied Piper of Television," *Broadcasting & Cable,* 19 September 1994, 36–40.

3. Jonathan B. Levine and Mark Landler, "Cable Has a New Frontier: The Old World," *Business Week,* 28 June 1993, 74.

4. William K. Knoedelseder Jr., "MTV Goes Global," *Los Angeles Times,* 18 December 1988, pt. 4, p. 1.

5. Ibid.

6. Don Jeffrey, "MTV Networks' Revenues Up for 1st Quarter," *Billboard,* 15 May 1993, 90.

7. "Wired for Losses?" *Economist,* 8 August 1987, 59, 62; and Steve Clarke, "Cold Warrior Now Head Honcho for Hot Channel," *Variety,* 16 November 1992, 35–36.

8. "Maxwell Sells MTV Stakes," *Los Angeles Times,* 21 August 1991, D2; "Viacom Plans to Buy MTV Europe Stake Owned by Maxwell," *Wall Street Journal,* 21 August 1991, B7; and "Viacom Gets MTV Europe," *New York Times,* 31 August 1991, 41.

9. Jeremy Coopman and David Laing, "MTV Has Europe's Ear," *Variety,* 26 August 1991, 5, 103; and Steve Clarke, "Rock Conquers Continent," *Variety,* 16 November 1992, 35–36.

10. Bill Roedy, "MTV Europe Does Play Local Acts," *Billboard,* 28 March 1992, 8.

11. "MTV Europe Open to Broader Range," *Variety,* 3 February 1988, 145.

12. "How MTV Plays Around the World," *New York Times,* 7 July 1991, sec. 2, p. H22.

13. Deborah Russell, "MTV Europe Tackles Racism with Unity Forum," *Billboard,* 27 March 1993, 38.

14. Dominic Pride, "MTV Europe on the Move," *Billboard,* 31 July 1993, 8, 58.

15. Roedy, "MTV Europe Does Play Local Acts," 8.

16. Nick Robertshaw, "Pacts Clears MTV for Europe," *Billboard,* 25 April 1987, 5.

17. Dominic Pride, "MTV Europe Sues Majors in Battle over Video Rights," *Billboard,* 21 August 1993, 6, 16.

18. Pride, "MTV Europe on the Move," 8, 58.

19. Dominic Pride and Melinda Newman, "MTV Deal Marks Strategy Shift for Sony," *Billboard,* 12 November 1994, 5, 117.

20. Knoedelseder, "MTV Goes Global," pt. 4, p. 4.

21. Pride, "MTV Europe on the Move," 8, 58.

22. Ibid.

23. Steve Clarke, "Music Network's Goal: Get into Every Home," *Variety,* 16 November 1992, 36.

24. Coopman and Laing, "MTV Has Europe's Ear," 5, 103.

25. Clarke, "Rock Conquers Continent," 35–36.

26. Kari Helopaltio, "Static Surrounds MTV Europe's Scandinavian B'casting Deals," *Billboard,* 18 January 1992, 35.

27. Jeff Green, "MTV Yanked off Air by Norwegian Cable Cos," *Billboard,* 18 April 1992, 37.

28. Clarke, "Rock Conquers Continent," 35–36; and Pride, "MTV Europe on the Move," 8, 58.

29. Coopman and Laing, "MTV Has Europe's Ear," 5, 103.

30. Ibid.

31. Clarke, "Cold Warrior Now Head Honcho," 35–36.

32. Ibid, 35.

33. "Rolling Through the Years," *Variety,* 16 November 1992, 36; and David Lieberman, "Is Viacom Ready to Channel the World?" *Business Week,* 18 October 1989, 72.

34. Don Groves, "MTV-E Spins More than Vids: Eyeing Profitability by 1992," *Variety,* 17 January 1990, 45.

35. Kevin Zimmerman, "Labels Looking East for Room to Grow," *Variety,* 14 January 1991, 121.

36. Stephen Engelberg, "Occident Prone in Poland," *New York Times,* 7 July 1991, sec. 2, p. H22.

37. Ibid.

38. Chris Fuller, "East-West Vidclips Debated," *Billboard,* 6 January 1990, 62.

39. Ken Wells, "Lithuanians Find They're Missing One Perk of Red Army Occupation," *Wall Street Journal,* 11 November 1991, B1.

40. Elizabeth A. Brown, "MTV's 'Cultural Colonialism,'" *Christian Science Monitor,* 6 August 1991, 11.

41. Wells, "Lithuanians Find They're Missing," B1.

42. Judith Graham, "MTV, CNN Move into Bloc," *Advertising Age,* 4 December 1989, 4.

43. Alessandra Scanziani, "Perestroika Perks: McDonald's and MTV," *New York Times,* 7 July 1991, sec. 2, p. H22; and "MTV Goes to Russia," *Wall Street Journal,* 12 October 1990, B4.

44. Scanziani, "Perestroika Perks," sec. 2, p. H22; and Bill Carter, "MTV to Provide Programming for Soviets," *New York Times,* 12 October 1990, D4.

45. Scanziani, "Perestroika Perks," sec. 2, p. H22.

46. Carter, "MTV to Provide Programming for Soviets," D4.

47. Clarke, "Cold Warrior Now Head Honcho," 35–36.

48. "MTV International," 31 August 1991, *Billboard,* 28, Advertising supplement; and Paul Taylor, "Video Connoisseurs in Koolyanobbing," *New York Times,* 7 July 1991, sec. 2, p. H22.

49. Tony Mitchell, "Treaty Now! Indigenous Music and Music Television in Australia," *Media, Culture and Society,* vol. 15, 1993, 299–308.

50. Taylor, "Video Connoisseurs in Koolyanobbing," sec. 2, p. H22.

51. Mitchell, "Treaty Now!" 299–308.

52. Steve McClure, "Plug Pulled on 'MTV Japan' Program," *Billboard,* 29 June 1991, 5; and Knoedelseder Jr., "MTV Goes Global," pt. 4, p. 1.

53. Steve McClure, "Japan Getting 'Music Channel,'" *Billboard,* 2 May 1992, 52; and David Sanger, "Sayonara, MTV," *New York Times,* 7 July 1991, sec. 2, p. H22.

54. Sanger, "Sayonara, MTV," sec. 2, p. H22.

55. McClure, "Japan Getting 'Music Channel,'" 52.

56. Steve McClure, "MTV's Japanese Licensee Sets Sights on Winning More Viewers," *Billboard,* 29 October 1994, 52, 54.

57. Viacom International, 10-K Report to the Securities and Exchange Commission (SEC) for the year ending 31 December 1991; "Asian Venture Joined by MTV," *New York Times,* 9 May 1991, D8; "Asia to Get Its Own MTV," *Wall Street Journal,* 9 May 1991, A10; and Rhonda Palmer, "Asia to Get Its MTV, Courtesy HK's Star-TV," *Variety,* 20 May 1991, 31. Hutchvision is a joint venture of Hutchison Whampoa, Hong Kong's third largest company, and a private company controlled by Li Ka Shing.

58. Melinda Newman, "Asia to Get Its MTV via Hong Kong's Hutchvision," *Billboard,* 18 May 1991, 8.

59. Hans Ebert, "MTV Asia Debuts in Hong Kong," *Billboard,* 28 September 1991, 14, 67.

60. Hans Ebert, "MTV Asia Hits the Road to Herald Launch," *Billboard,* 10 August 1991, 62, 64.

61. Mike Levin, "Satellites Bring MTV Asia Home," *Billboard,* 3 April 1993, 40, 44.

62. Jerry D'Souza and Mike Levin, "Indian Artists Benefiting from MTV Asia Exposure," *Billboard,* 4 December 1993, 42, 46.

63. Levin, "Satellites Bring MTV Asia Home," 40, 44.

64. Ibid. The *New York Times* estimated that China had about 500,000 satellite dishes as of November 22, 1993. Patrick E. Tyler, "CNN and MTV Hanging by a 'Heavenly Thread,'" *New York Times,* 22 November 1993, A4.

65. Tyler, "CNN and MTV Hanging," A4.

66. Ebert, "MTV Asia Debuts in Hong Kong," 14.

67. Ibid., 76.

68. Frederik Balfour, "Rock Around the Clock," *Far Eastern Economic Review,* 25 February 1993, 54–55.

69. Ibid.

70. Levin, "Satellites Bring MTV Asia Home," 40, 44.

71. Ibid.

72. Mike Levin, "MTV Asia Debuts Mandarin Video Chart," *Billboard,* 13 November 1993, 48.

73. Mike Levin, "MTV Asia in Limbo over Cantopop Vids," *Billboard,* 6 November 1993, 56.

74. Levin, "Satellites Bring MTV Asia Home," 40, 44.

75. D'Souza and Levin, "Indian Artists Benefiting," 42–46.

76. Balfour, "Rock Around the Clock," 54–55.

77. Mike Levin, "Satellites Bring MTV Asia Home," 40, 44.

78. Tyler, "CNN and MTV Hanging," A4.

79. Steve Coll, "MTV Age Dawning in India," *Washington Post,* 5 March 1992, A31; and Levin, "Satellites Bring MTV Asia Home," 40, 44.

80. Balfour, "Rock Around the Clock," 54–55.

81. Ibid.

82. Levin, "Satellites Bring MTV Asia Home," 40, 44.

83. Balfour, "Rock Around the Clock," 54–55.

84. Paul Farhi, "Murdoch Deal to Buy Satellite TV," *San Francisco Chronicle,* 28 July 1993, E1.

85. Levin, "MTV Asia in Limbo over Cantopop Vids," 56.

86. "MTV Drops Asia Partner," *New York Times,* 3 May 1994, D22.

87. Sally D. Goll, "MTV Asia Taps Peter Jamieson to Be President," *Wall Street Journal,* 8 February 1995, B10; Mike Levin, "MTV Reveals New Asia Chief, Plans for Two Services," *Billboard,* 18 February 1995, 6; and Rhonda Palmer, "MTV Sets Its Sights on Asia's Biggest Star," *Variety,* 5–11 September 1994, 52.

88. Palmer, "MTV Sets Its Sights on Asia's Biggest Star," 52.

89. Ibid.

90. Mike Levin, "Majors Take 50% Stake in STAR TV's V Music Channel," *Billboard,* 14 January 1995, 6, 77.

91. Carlos Agudelo, "Latin Music Television Comes of Age," *Billboard,* 15 October 1988, 60.

92. Daisann McLane, "No Julio Allowed," *New York Times,* 7 July 1991, sec. 2, p. H22.

93. John Lannert, "New Shows Serve Burgeoning Hispanic Youth Market," *Billboard*, 14 September 1991, 79; and "MTV International," 28.

94. Adrienne Bard, "In Mexico, a Video Veto," *New York Times*, 7 July 1991, sec. 2, p. H22.

95. Elizabeth Hellman Brooke, "Yo! They're Dancin' in the Streets," *New York Times*, 7 July 1991, sec. 2, p. H22.

96. Ibid.

97. "Say It in Spanish: 'Yo Deseo Mi MTV,'" *Variety*, 29 March 1993, 56.

98. John Lannert, "21 Countries Plugged in for MTV Latino Debut," *Billboard*, 2 October 1993, 8, 55.

99. Ibid.

100. "Say It in Spanish: 'Yo Deseo Mi MTV,'" 56.

101. Lannert, "21 Countries Plugged in," 8, 55.

102. Ibid.

103. "Pop Charts," *San Francisco Sunday Examiner and Chronicle*, 25 December 1994, Datebook section, p. 42. Presented chart of top music videos from MTV Latino taken from *Billboard*, 24 December 1994.

104. John Lannert, "Labels Assess Impact of MTV Latino," *Billboard*, 2 July 1994, 6, 94.

105. Lannert, "21 Countries Plugged in," 8, 55.

106. Bard, "In Mexico, a Video Veto," sec. 2, p. H22.

107. Ibid.

108. "Say It in Spanish: 'Yo Deseo Mi MTV,'" 56.

109. Dupler, "Will Pan-Euro MTV Pan Out?" 81.

110. Knoedelseder Jr., "MTV Goes Global," pt. 4, p. 1.

111. Ibid.

112. Alan Bunce, "MTV: Tomorrow the World?" *Christian Science Monitor*, 16 February 1989, 10.

113. Elizabeth A. Brown, "Music Television Turns 10," *Christian Science Monitor*, 6 August 1991, 10.

114. Julie Skur Hill, "Coke Teaches the World to Vote for Music Videos," *Advertising Age*, 27 October 1986, 3.

115. Ibid.

116. Alan Goldsand, "Coca-Cola Ambushes Pepsi with Global Cable TV Buy," *Mediaweek*, 27 January 1992, 3.

117. Robert Hilburn and Chuck Philips, "Rock's New World Order," *Los Angeles Times*, 29 November 1992, 7, 58, 59.

118. Ibid., 58.

119. Adam Dawtrey, "Global Audio Sales $24 Bil," *Variety*, 7 October 1991, 208.

120. Ibid.

121. "Recorded Music Sales Rose Almost 4% in '91; Unit Sales Fell 7.5%," *Wall Street Journal*, 20 March 1992, B10.

122. Hilburn and Philips, "Rock's New World Order," 7, 58, 59.

123. Dawtrey, "Global Audio Sales $24 Bil," 208.

124. Hilburn and Philips, "Rock's New World Order," 7, 58, 59.

125. Dawtrey, "Global Audio Sales $24 Bil," 208.

126. Hilburn and Philips, "Rock's New World Order," 7, 58, 59.

127. Ibid.

128. Ibid.

129. Adam White, "A Day in the Life of MTV: 164 Clips," *Billboard*, 17 November 1984, 31, 33.

130. Chris McGowan, "Music Video on TV: From Youth to Middle Age in Seven Years?" *Billboard*, 12 November 1988, V1.

131. Pride, "MTV Europe on the Move," 8, 58.

132. D'Souza and Levin, "Indian Artists Benefiting," 42–46.

133. Coll, "MTV Age Dawning in India," A31.

134. Ibid.

135. Ibid.

136. Levin, "Satellites Bring MTV Asia Home," 40, 44.

137. Brown, "MTV's 'Cultural Colonialism,'" 11.

138. Bunce, "MTV: Tomorrow the World?" 10.

139. Ibid.

140. Jim Bessman, "MuchMusic is Much Different," *Billboard*, 9 March 1991, 63.

141. Ibid.; and Kirk LaPointe, "MuchMusic Network Enjoying MuchSuccess," *Billboard*, 2 September 1989, 67.

142. Bessman, "MuchMusic is Much Different," 63.

143. LaPointe, "MuchMusic Network Enjoying MuchSuccess," 67.

144. Nick Krewen and Larry LeBlanc, "Budgets Challenge Canada's Directors," *Billboard*, 21 March 1992, 52.

145. Ibid.

146. Edward Morris, "CMA Asks Canada to Keep U.S. Country Show on TV," *Billboard*, 12 November 1994, 30; Edward Morris, "Citing NAFTA, CMT Takes Action to Stay in Canada," *Billboard*, 7 January 1995, 24; and Edward Morris, "Exiled from Canada, CMT Begins Boycott," *Billboard*, 21 January 1995, 31; Edward Morris, "New Vid Network on Air in Canada; Replaces CMT," *Billboard*, 21 January 1995, 34.

147. Edward Morris, "CMT Boycott Fuels More Accusations," *Billboard*, 28 January 1995, 35.

148. "Tom Freston: The Pied Piper of Television," 36–40.

149. Deanna Robinson, Elizabeth B. Buck, Marlene Cuthbert, and the International Communication and Youth Consortium, *Music at the Margins: Popular Music and Global Cultural Diversity* (Beverly Hills, Calif.: Sage Publications, 1991), 193–195.

150. Ibid.

151. Pride, "MTV Europe on the Move," 8, 58.

152. Robinson et al., *Music at the Margins*, 194.

153. "Venture Is Set to Rival MTV," *New York Times*, 1 February 1994, D7.

154. Ellie Weinert, "Four Majors Said to Back Viva," *Billboard*, 21 August 1993, 40.

155. Miranda Watson, "German Music Biz Welcomes Viva," *Billboard*, 26 March 1994, 62, 70.

156. Mark Dezzani, "Euro Channels Link Programming and Resources, Challenging MTV Europe," *Billboard*, 29 October 1994, 52–54.

157. Don Jeffrey and Dominic Pride, "Majors Plan to Challenge MTV with Music Video Venture," *Billboard*, 29 January 1994, 5.

158. "Venture is Set to Rival MTV," D7.

159. Mike Rubin, "MTV Consumer Guide," *Village Voice*, 7 June 1994, 46; "Music Channel Is Shelved," *New York Times*, 7 June 1994, D19; and "Bertelsmann to Join MTV Competition," *Wall Street Journal*, 29 June 1994, B8.

160. Mark Dezzani, "Videomusic Takes Investment Bids," *Billboard*, 21 January 1995, 44.

161. Chris Fuller, "BMG Charges Abuse of Power by MTV Europe," *Billboard*, 3 September 1994, 6, 123.

CHAPTER 6

1. Fredric Dannen, "MTV's Great Leap Backward," *Channels of Communication*, July/August 1987, 45–47.

2. Warner Communications, 1985 Annual Report, 2; Carolyn Friday, "Viacom's Rise to Stardom," *Newsweek*, 25 November 1985, 71; and Kenneth M. Miller, "Video Giant Wants Its MTV," *Rolling Stone*, 10 October 1985, 12. Friday reported that Viacom spent $694 million for the entire purchase, whereas Miller stated that the value of the transaction was $690 million.

3. Viacom International, Form 10-K to the U.S. Securities and Exchange Commission (SEC) for the fiscal year ending 31 December 1988, 7.

4. Viacom International, Form 10-K to the SEC for the fiscal year ending 31 December 1985, 13.

5. Ibid.

6. Viacom International, Form 10-K to the SEC for the fiscal year ending 31 December 1988, 3.

7. Ibid.

8. Kathryn Harris, "Viacom Seeks a Role in the Land of Media Giants," *Los Angeles Times*, 19 November 1989, D1; and Virginia Munger Kahn, "Analysts Say Viacom Management Deal Will Fly," *Cablevision*, 13 October 1986, 20, 22.

9. David Lieberman, "Is Viacom Ready to Channel the World?" *Business Week*, 18 October 1989, 72.

10. Don Jeffrey, "MTV Networks Boosts Viacom," *Billboard*, 4 November 1989, 82; and Viacom International, Form 10-K to the SEC for the fiscal year ending 31 December 1988, 7.

11. Harris, "Viacom Seeks a Role," D1, D5.

12. Ibid., D1.

13. Ibid., D1, D4; and Lieberman, "Is Viacom Ready to Channel the World?" 73, 74.

14. "Firm Revises Credit Pact, Extends Revolving Portion," *Wall Street Journal*, 27 January 1992, A9.

15. Jeffrey, "MTV Networks Boosts Viacom," 82; and Viacom, Form 10-K to the SEC for the fiscal year ending 31 December 1991, II-4.

16. Lisa Gubernick, "Sumner Redstone Scores Again," *Forbes*, 31 October 1988, 44, 48.

17. Geraldine Fabrikant, "Viacom Is Winner Over QVC in Fight to Get Paramount," *New York Times*, 16 February 1994, 1, D5; and Geraldine Fabrikant, "Viacom Now Owns Paramount," *New York Times*, 12 March 1994, 37.

18. Fabrikant, "Viacom Is Winner Over QVC," 1, D5.

19. Ibid.

20. Ibid.

226   *Notes*

21. Michael Meyer and Nancy Hass, "Simon Says, 'Out!'" *Newsweek,* 27 June 1994, 42–44.

22. Ibid.

23. Mark Robichaux, "It's a Book! A T-Shirt! A Toy! No, Just MTV Trying to Be Disney," *Wall Street Journal,* 8 February 1995, pp. A1, A9.

24. Peter J. Boyer, "After Rebellious Youth, MTV Tries the System," *New York Times,* 9 May 1988, D8.

25. Steven Dupler, "New MTV Prez: No Big Changes Planned at Channel," *Billboard,* 27 May 1989, 55.

26. Viacom International, 1985 Annual Report, 15.

27. Martin Peers, "Blockbuster Set to Face the Music," *Variety,* 22–28 May 1995, 110.

28. Ibid.

29. Larry Jaffee, "MTV to Stand for Merchandise TV?" *Billboard,* 28 January 1995, 43, 44; and Robichaux, "It's a Book! A T-Shirt! A Toy! No, Just MTV Trying to Be Disney," A1, A9.

30. John Motavalli, "MTV Sees Low Cost Programming Ingenuity as Key to Sustaining High Profitability," *Cablevision,* 15 September 1986, 26.

31. Dannen, "MTV's Great Leap Backward," 47.

32. Although the 1.0 rating of MTV viewers was based on official A. C. Nielsen ratings, MTV sources provided the estimate of households watching the program service with this rating. Statistics furnished by MTV in this study should be kept in proper perspective. MTV is likely to present self-serving information about its corporate activities. In this instance, the company may have inflated figures about audience ratings.

33. Robert Pittman, in "Letters" column, *Rolling Stone,* 23 May 1985, 2.

34. Steven Dupler, "Nielsen Publishes Disputed MTV 4th-Quarter Ratings," *Billboard,* 26 April 1986, 84.

35. Ibid.; and James Traub, "Gotterdammerung for Video Music?" *Channels of Communication,* July/August 1986, 9.

36. J. Max Robins, "Into the Groove," *Channels of Communication,* May 1989, 29.

37. R. Serge Denisoff, *Inside MTV* (New Brunswick, N.J.: Transaction Publishers, 1989), 63.

38. Ibid., 207.

39. Steven Dupler, "Now, Dance Hits are OK on MTV," *Billboard,* 24 October 1987, 108.

40. Michael Goldberg, "MTV's Sharper Picture," *Rolling Stone,* 8 February 1990, 62; and Steven Dupler, "'Hit-Driven' MTV Irks Majors, Net Replies: We Still Help New Artists," *Billboard,* 2 April 1988, 1, 66.

41. Michael Goldberg, "MTV's Sharper Picture," 62.

42. Steven Dupler, "Record Industry Mixed on MTV Plan to Daypart Videos," *Billboard,* 17 September 1988, 1, 82.

43. Goldberg, "MTV's Sharper Picture," 64.

44. Boyer, "After Rebellious Youth," D8.

45. Denisoff, *Inside MTV,* 63.

46. Melinda Newman, "MTV Dips Slightly in Nielsen," *Billboard,* 20 January 1990, 62. Although MTV's ratings have averaged 0.6, the program service's ratings dropped to 0.5 for the fourth quarter of 1989. The 0.1 ratings decrease represented a drop of approximately 50,000 households.

47. Steven Dupler, "Vidclip Output Faces Trim," *Billboard*, 19 April 1986, 1; and Ken Terry, "Diskeries Change Clip Output Stance, Cutback Reported at Some Labels," *Variety*, 14 May 1986, 85, 88.

48. Dannen, "MTV's Great Leap Backward," 47.

49. Dupler, "Vidclip Output Faces Trim," 91.

50. Marjorie Williams, "MTV's Short Takes Define a New Style," *Washington Post*, 13 December 1989, A21.

51. Carrie Borzillo, "MTV, Modern Rock Keys to Success for Capitol Bands," *Billboard*, 28 August 1993, 10, 87.

52. Goldberg, "MTV's Sharper Picture," 62.

53. Mark Robichaux, "MTV Is Playing a New Riff: Responsibility," *Wall Street Journal*, 9 February 1993, B1, B8.

54. Ibid.

55. J. Max Robins, "MTV Hitches Ride on Bubba's Bandwagon," *Variety*, 18 January, 1993, 1, 97.

56. Don Jeffrey, "MTV Networks' Revenues Up for 1st Quarter," *Billboard*, 15 May 1993, 90.

57. Don Jeffrey, "Rumor of MTV Making Public Offer Persists," *Billboard*, 14 March 1992, 11, 98.

58. John McManus, "P&G Nears $50M MTV Cable Buy," *Advertising Age*, 21 May 1990, 3, 57.

59. Mark Landler, "I Want My MTV—Stock," *Business Week*, 18 May 1992, 55.

60. Matthew Schifrin, "I Can't Even Remember the Old Star's Name," *Forbes*, 16 March 1992, 44–45.

61. Mike Rubin, "MTV Consumer Guide," *Village Voice*, 7 June 1994, 46.

62. "MTV Fights Fire with No Fire," *Broadcasting and Cable*, 18 October 1993, 22–23.

63. Jay Martel, "The Perils of Pauly . . . ," *Rolling Stone*, 9–23 July 1992, 54–57.

64. J. Max Robins, "Blue-Chip Ad Buyers Want Their MTV (News)," *Variety*, 29 June 1992, 1, 86.

65. J. Max Robins, "Reality TV: Politics Rates," *Variety*, 26 October 1992, 21–22.

66. Robins, "MTV Hitches Ride," 1, 97.

67. Christopher Georges, "Mock the Vote," *Washington Monthly*, May 1993, 30–35.

68. Ibid.

69. John Lippman, "MTV Will Split into 3 Cable Channels," *Los Angeles Times*, 31 July 1991, D1.

70. Ibid.

71. "MTV Announces Its Move to Multiplexing," *Broadcasting*, 5 August 1991, 39, 40; and "Freston May Go Multiplex with MTV, Nick, VH-1," *Broadcasting*, 29 July 1991, 28.

72. Matt Rothman, "Viacom Interacts with Future," *Variety*, 29 June 1992, 29.

73. Melinda Newman, "'Nick Jr. Rocks!' to Roll in Summer," *Billboard*, 23 March 1991, 56, 57.

74. Sharon D. Moshavi, "MTV Said to Consider Infomercial Channel," *Broadcasting*, 27 January 1992, 31.

75. Dan Shaw, "Home Shopping's New Beat," *New York Times*, 28 August 1994, sec. 1, p. 39, 42.

CHAPTER 7

1. Jim Bessman, "Credit Atlantic Success to Videos," *Billboard,* 4 February 1989, 50.

2. Chris McGowan, "Record Companies: Realistic Marketing, Budding Catalogs Help Music Video Come Alive at Retail," *Billboard,* 12 November 1988, V4.

3. Cary Darling, "Labels See Video as Force to Be Reckoned with," *Billboard,* 14 November 1981, 64.

4. Ibid.

5. Melinda Newman, "Video: A Key Ingredient for R&B Success," *Billboard,* 27 June 1992, R-8.

6. Steven Dupler, "Targeting the Video," *Billboard,* 28 September 1985, NT3.

7. Jim Bessman, "'One' Plus MTV Equals Wider Metallica," *Billboard,* 18 March 1989, 57.

8. Ethlie Ann Vare, "Beyond Video: Media Flips for Clips," *Billboard,* 28 September 1985, NT3.

9. Michael Goldberg, "MTV's Sharper Picture," *Rolling Stone,* 8 February 1990, 62.

10. Ibid.

11. Ibid.

12. Ibid.

13. Parke Puterbaugh, "Concert-611 Blues! Long, Cold Summer," *Rolling Stone,* 15 September 1983, 45.

14. Patrick Goldstein, "In Rock to Be or Not to Be May Depend on MTV," *Los Angeles Times,* 2 August 1983, pt. 6, p. 6.

15. Pat Aufderheide, "The Look of the Sound," in *Watching Television,* ed. Todd Gitlin (New York: Pantheon Books, 1987), 131.

16. Jeff Berke, "The Problem with Record Contracts," *Billboard,* 4 June 1988, 9.

17. Kevin Zimmerman, "Ruckus over Record Royalties," *Variety,* 28 October 1991, 58, 59.

18. Stephen Holden, "Madonna Makes a $60 Million Deal," *New York Times,* 20 April 1992, C11, C16; and Stephen Holden, "Big Stars, Big Bucks and the Big Gamble," *New York Times,* 24 March 1991, sec. 2, pp. H25–H26.

19. Zimmerman, "Ruckus over Record Royalties," 58, 59.

20. Laurence Kenneth Shore, "The Crossroads of Business and Music: A Study of the Music Industry in the United States and Internationally" (Ph.D. diss., Stanford University, 1983), 168.

21. Zimmerman, "Ruckus over Record Royalties," 58, 59.

22. Shore, "The Crossroads of Business and Music," 168.

23. Lauri Foti, "New Act Pacts Take Vidclip $ from Royalties," *Billboard,* 2 July 1983, 1.

24. Moira McCormick, "Wild West," *Billboard,* 23 November 1985, VM16.

25. Dennis Kneale, "Weirder Is Better in the Red-Hot Land of the Rock Videos," *Wall Street Journal,* 17 October 1983, 1.

26. Michael Goldberg, "MTV's Sharper Picture," 62.

27. Jon Pareles, "As MTV Turns 10, Pop Goes the World," *New York Times,* 7 July 1991, sec. 2, pp. 1, 19.

28. Stephen Holden, "Strike the Pose: When Music Is Skin Deep," *New York Times,* 5 August 1990, H1.

29. R. Serge Denisoff, *Inside MTV* (New Brunswick, N.J.: Transaction Publishers, 1989), 263.

30. Aufderheide, "The Look of the Sound," 124.

31. Goldberg, "MTV's Sharper Picture," 118.

32. Ibid., 118.

33. Kevin Zimmerman, "That Synching Feeling: Vanilli Not Alone?" *Variety*, 26 November 1990, 66, 68; Thom Duffy and Larry Flick, "Milli Vanilli Didn't Start the Fire," *Billboard*, 8 December 1990, 4, 89; and Brent Staples, "Unseen but Not Unsung," *New York Times*, 19 December 1990, A24.

34. Kim Neely, "Backup Singer Sues Abdul over Vocals," *Rolling Stone*, 30 May 1991, 25; and Greg Reibman, "New Kids Sue Over Allegations of Vocal Fakery," *Billboard*, 22 February 1992, 12, 87.

35. Wendy Blatt, "Spirit of Independents Burns on," *Billboard*, 21 March 1992, I-3, I-24, I-25.

36. Don Jeffrey, "Indie-Major Romances and Marriages," *Billboard*, 21 March 1992, I-6, I-32.

37. David Wykoff, "Independent Labels & Distributors," *Billboard*, 11 March 1989, I-1, I-20.

38. Kevin Zimmerman, "Indie-Label Ranks Thinned as Polygram Acquires A&M," *Variety*, 18–24 October 1989, 85.

39. Kevin Zimmerman, "Premature Burial for Indies?" *Variety*, 4 November 1991, 71, 73.

40. David Browne, "The Independents See Vultures Circling Overhead," *New York Times*, 27 October 1991, sec. 2, pp. 26, 35.

41. Phyllis Stark, "Indie-Distrib Single Beats the Odds," *Billboard*, 16 February 1991, 9, 72.

42. Robert Hilburn and Chuck Philips, "Rock's New World Order," *Los Angeles Times*, 29 November 1992, Calendar section, 7, 58, 59.

43. Sallie Hofmeister, "Rifts Shake and Rattle Warner Music," *New York Times*, 1 November 1994, D1, D22.

44. "Corporate Monoliths Threaten Entrepreneurs," *Billboard*, 13 May 1989, 9, 75.

45. Chris McGowan, "The New Strength of Independent Distribution," *Billboard*, 11 March 1989, I-3, I-22.

46. Havelock Nelson, "Ice-T Stages New Aural Invasion," *Billboard*, 17 April 1993, 19; and Chris Morris, Bill Holland, Charlene Orr, Paul Verna, and Ed Christman, "Quayle, Congressmen, L.A. Pols Joining 'Cop Killer' Posse," *Billboard*, 4 July 1992, 1, 83.

47. Ibid.

48. Ibid.

49. Stark, "Indie-Distrib Single Beats the Odds," 9, 72.

50. Browne, "The Independents See Vultures," sec. 2, p. 26, 35.

51. Kip Kirby, "Indie Label 'Risk Takers' Discuss the Search for Alternative Clip Outlets," *Billboard*, 15 December 1984, 35.

52. Ibid.

53. Steven Dupler and Jim Bessman, "Vidclip Panels: Useful, Not Earthshaking," *Billboard*, 30 June 1988, 5, 72.

54. Bruce Buckley and Melinda Newman, "Indie Labels Seeing Increased Success with Vids," *Billboard*, 20 June 1992, 44.

55. Ibid.

56. Ibid.

57. Adam White, "A Day in the Life of MTV: 164 Clips," *Billboard*, 17 November 1984, 31, 33.

58. Kevin Zimmerman, "Independent Labels Want Their MTV," *Variety*, 23 May 1990, 85.

59. Buckley and Newman, "Indie Labels Seeing Increased Success with Vids," 44.

60. Zimmerman, "Independent Labels Want Their MTV," 85.

61. Ibid.

62. Ibid.

63. Kirby, "Indie Label 'Risk Takers' Discuss the Search," 35.

64. Buckley and Newman, "Indie Labels Seeing Increased Success with Vids," 44.

65. Ibid.

CHAPTER 8

1. Janine McAdams, "Millicent Shelton Blazes a Trail as Video Director," *Billboard*, 6 June 1992, 37.

2. Moira McCormick, "Producers Hold Creative Keys in Struggle to Make Music Video a Happy Medium," *Billboard*, 23 November 1985, VM20.

3. Ken Terry, "Diskeries Change Clip Output Stance," *Variety*, 14 May 1986, 88.

4. Ken Terry, "Videoclip Producers Ready to Organize," *Variety*, 13 June 1984, 76.

5. Ibid.

6. Melinda Newman, "GPA Films Expanding to Reel in West Coast Biz," *Billboard*, 9 February 1991, 63.

7. Jim Farber, "Clip Corporation," *Rolling Stone*, 23 August 1990, 137.

8. Melinda Newman, "Propaganda Spreading in Video, Film Arenas," *Billboard*, 9 May 1992, 38–39.

9. Peter Kerr, "Music Video's Uncertain Payoff," *Billboard*, 29 July 1984, F4.

10. Melinda Newman, "Lucasfilm Empire Expands to Incorporate Music Video," *Billboard*, 13 July 1991, 47.

11. Melinda Newman, "Pam Tarr's Production Co. Does More than Squeak By," *Billboard*, 2 November 1991, 70.

12. Ibid.

13. Steven Dupler and Jim Bessman, "Vidclip Panels: Useful, Not Earthshaking," *Billboard*, 30 June 1988, 72.

14. Melinda Newman, "Do Budget Demands Stifle Creativity?" *Billboard*, 3 August 1991, 60.

15. Richard Harrington, "Fame Without a Name," *Washington Post*, 3 August 1984, B4.

16. Terry, "Videoclip Producers Ready to Organize," 76.

17. McAdams, "Millicent Shelton Blazes a Trail," 37.

18. Ibid.

19. Steven Dupler, "Wanted: New Blood for Music Vids," *Billboard*, 17 December 1988, 1.

20. McCormick, "Producers Hold Creative Keys," VM20.

21. Peter Occiogrosso, "Video Dreams: MTV Goes to the Movies," *Village Voice*, 31 July 1984, 36, 37, 87.

22. Ibid.

23. Ibid.

24. Terry, "Videoclip Producers Ready to Organize," 76.

25. Ibid.

26. Steven Dupler, "Rolling the Credits," *Billboard*, 21 December 1985, 30.

27. Ken Terry, "Music Video Producers Assn. Issues a Clip Production Guide," *Variety*, 1 January 1986, 127, 130.

28. Melinda Newman, "Vidclip Makers See Red in Label Deals," *Billboard,* 20 April 1991, 1, 53.

29. Deborah Russell, "Vid Producers Face Economic Woes," *Billboard,* 7 December 1991, 39.

30. Ibid.

31. Ibid.

32. Ibid.

33. Moira McCormick, "Wild West," *Billboard,* 23 November 1985, VM4.

34. Dupler, "Rolling the Credits," 30.

35. McCormick, "Wild West," VM16.

36. Ibid.

37. Deborah Russell, "Who Owns Ideas in Music Vid Biz?" *Billboard,* 23 April 1994, 40, 41.

38. John Sippel, "Producers, Directors Ask Greater Role," *Billboard,* 15 December 1984, 33.

39. McCormick, "Wild West," VM16.

40. Ibid.

41. Ibid.

42. Faye Zuckerman, "Clip Makers Focus on Royalties," *Billboard,* 2 March 1985, 37.

43. Terry, "Videoclip Producers Ready to Organize," 76.

44. Terry, "Diskeries Change Clip Output Stance," 88.

45. Terry, "Videoclip Producers Ready to Organize," 71.

46. McCormick, "Wild West," VM16.

47. Terry, "Diskeries Change Clip Output Stance," 88.

48. Terry, "Videoclip Producers Ready to Organize," 76.

49. Mark Weinstein, "Videoclips: Still-Evolving Form Struggles to Transcend Limitations; Filmmaking Winning Emphasis over Effects," *Billboard,* 12 November 1988, V8.

50. Terry, "Diskeries Change Clip Output Stance," 88.

51. Newman, "Vidclip Makers See Red," 1, 53.

52. Ibid.

53. Newman, "Vidclip Makers See Red," 1, 53; and Melinda Newman, "Limelight's Video Division Moves Back to Main Office," *Billboard,* 26 October 1991, 54.

54. Nick Krewen and Larry LeBlanc, "Budgets Challenge Canada's Directors," *Billboard,* 21 March 1992, 52.

55. Newman, "Vidclip Makers See Red," 1, 53.

56. Melinda Newman, "Labels Weighing Video Costs vs. Gains," *Billboard,* 10 November 1990, 1, 75.

57. Jim Farber, "Director's View: Creativity and Innovation Harder to Come By in '88; MTV, Labels, Music Itself to Blame," *Billboard,* 12 November 1988, V3.

58. Weinstein, "Videoclips: Still-Evolving Form Struggles to Transcend Limitations," V8.

59. Pat Aufderheide, "The Look of the Sound," in *Watching Television,* ed. Todd Gitlin (New York: Pantheon Books, 1987), 122.

60. Kip Kirby, "Video Music Conference," *Billboard,* 21 December 1985, 25.

61. Farber, "Director's View: Creativity and Innovation Harder to Come By in '88," V3.

62. Russell, "Who Owns Ideas in Music Vid Biz?" 40, 41.

63. Ibid.

64. Sam Sutherland, "Label Execs Air Common Woes," *Billboard,* 15 December 1984, 32; and Tony Seideman, "Video Music Meet Looks at Prosperity, Pitfalls," *Billboard,* 1 December 1984, 1, 78.

65. Sutherland, "Label Execs Air Common Woes," 32.

66. Melinda Newman, "Freston: Let's Shun Cliched Clips," *Billboard*, 2 December 1989, 3.

67. Newman, "Do Budget Demands Stifle Creativity?" 60.

68. Jim Farber, "Budget Genius," *Rolling Stone*, 10 August 1989, 99, 100.

69. Nelson George, "Four Offer Divergent Views on Role of the Artist," *Billboard*, 18 December 1982, 46.

70. Weinstein, "Videoclips: Still-Evolving Form Struggles to Transcend Limitations," V8.

71. McCormick, "Producers Hold Creative Keys," VM6, VM20.

72. Jim Bessman, "Videoclips: For Producers and Directors There's Still Room Enough to Grow, Especially in Creative Directions," *Billboard*, 21 November 1987, V3.

73. Dupler, "Wanted: New Blood for Music Vids," 1, 63.

74. Kerr, "Music Video's Uncertain Payoff," F4.

75. Newman, "Do Budget Demands Stifle Creativity?" 60.

76. Ibid.

77. Ibid.

78. Ibid.

79. Weinstein, "Videoclips: Still-Evolving Form Struggles to Transcend Limitations," V8.

80. Ibid.

81. Ibid., V3, V8.

82. Janine C. McAdams, "Black Directors: Talent Pool Waiting to Be Tapped," *Billboard*, 8 April 1989, 55.

83. Ibid.

84. Merritt B. Kleber, "Label Clip Execs Not Racist," *Billboard*, 16 July 1988, 9.

85. Melinda Newman and Janine McAdams, "NAACP: Let's Give Minorities More Music-Vid Work," *Billboard*, 15 December 1990, 1, 83.

86. Kleber, "Label Clip Execs Not Racist," 9.

87. McAdams, "Black Directors: Talent Pool Waiting to be Tapped," 53.

88. Melinda Newman, "Video: a Key Ingredient for R&B Success," *Billboard*, 27 June 1992, R-8.

89. Janine McAdams, "Focus on African-American Music," *Billboard*, 29 June 1991, 48, 49.

90. McAdams, "Black Directors: Talent Pool Waiting to Be Tapped," 53, 55.

91. Newman, "Video: A Key Ingredient for R&B Success," R-8.

92. Jim Bessman, "Black & White Comes Thru 1st Year with Flying Colors," *Billboard*, 19 May 1990, 50.

93. Kevin Zimmerman, "Is the Music Biz Color Blind?" *Variety*, 30 March 1992, 82.

94. Ibid.

95. Ibid.

96. Ibid.

97. Janine McAdams and Bruce Haring, "NAACP Is on the Brink of CBS Boycott," *Billboard*, 24 February 1990, 5, 95.

98. McAdams, "Black Directors: Talent Pool Waiting to Be Tapped," 53, 55.

99. Newman and McAdams, "NAACP: Let's Give Minorities More Music-Vid Work," 1, 83.

100. Kleber, "Label Clip Execs Not Racist," 9.

101. Ibid.

102. Newman and McAdams, "NAACP: Let's Give Minorities More Music-Vid Work," 1, 83.

103. David Nathan, "Underdog Champions the Role of Black Vid Directors," *Billboard*, 30 September 1989, 67.

104. Newman and McAdams, "NAACP: Let's Give Minorities More Music-Vid Work," 1, 83.

105. Ibid.

106. Ibid.

107. Melinda Newman, "Growing Pains Aplenty," *Billboard*, 21 December 1991, 47.

108. Newman, "GPA Films Expanding to Reel in West Coast Biz," 63.

109. Newman and McAdams, "NAACP: Let's Give Minorities More Music-Vid Work," 1, 83.

110. Newman, "Video: A Key Ingredient for R&B Success," R-8.

CHAPTER 9

1. Melinda Newman, "MTV Taking a Harder Look at Vids?" *Billboard*, 18 November 1989, 1.

2. Richard Harrington, "Madonna at the Hype of Her Career," *Washington Post*, 4 December 1990, D1, D3.

3. Kevin Zimmerman, "Does Music Biz Want Its MTV?" *Variety*, 5 August 1991, 105, 106.

4. Michael Goldberg, "MTV's Sharper Picture," *Rolling Stone*, 8 February 1990, 64.

5. Andrew Roblin, "Study on Violence Endorsed," *Billboard*, 12 January 1985, 32.

6. R. Serge Denisoff, *Inside MTV* (New Brunswick, N.J.: Transaction Publishers, 1989), 367.

7. Goldberg, "MTV's Sharper Picture," 64.

8. Neil Strauss, "Free Your Mind, Blur Your Video," *Village Voice*, 24 May 1994, 64.

9. Ibid.

10. Amy Dawes, "'This Note's For You': Neil Young Criticizes MTV's Ban of Parody," *Variety*, 6 July 1988, 58.

11. Ibid.

12. Strauss, "Free Your Mind, Blur Your Video," 64.

13. Robert Love, "'Washington Wives' Set Their Sights on Video," *Rolling Stone*, 10 October 1985, 18; and Newman, "MTV Taking a Harder Look at Vids?" 92.

14. Goldberg, "MTV's Sharper Picture," 64.

15. Strauss, "Free Your Mind, Blur Your Video," 64.

16. Newman, "MTV Taking a Harder Look at Vids?" 92.

17. Strauss, "Free Your Mind, Blur Your Video," 64.

18. Newman, "MTV Taking a Harder Look at Vids?" 92.

19. Ibid.

20. Ibid.

21. Ibid.

22. Strauss, "Free Your Mind, Blur Your Video," 64.

23. Deborah Russell, "New MTV Campaign Tackles Violence," *Billboard*, 22 January 1994, 1, 95.

24. Strauss, "Free Your Mind, Blur Your Video," 64.

25. Ibid.

26. Newman, "MTV Taking a Harder Look at Vids?" 95.

27. Jack Anderson and Dale Van Atta, "Cher's Dirty Dance Embarrasses Navy," *Washington Post,* 5 January 1990, E5; and Craig Rosen and Melinda Newman, "Mix-A-Lot Clip Gets Pushed Back to After 9 on MTV," *Billboard,* 27 June 1992, 4, 70.

28. "MTV Fights Fire with No Fire," *Broadcasting and Cable,* 18 October 1993, 22–23; "MTV Moves 'Beavis and Butt-head,'" *Broadcasting and Cable,* 25 October 1993, 29; and "Smokey and the Butt-Head," *The Education Digest,* January 1994, 76.

29. Goldberg, "MTV's Sharper Picture," 64.

30. Denisoff, *Inside MTV,* 75.

31. Newman, "MTV Taking a Harder Look at Vids?" 92.

32. Although MTV did play the Dire Straits video, Tony Seideman reports that this clip "had caused some problems" for other program services "due to both its imagery and the use of the word 'faggot.'" Tony Seideman, "Rockamerica Panel Takes Close Look at TV," *Billboard,* 17 August 1985, 31.

33. Strauss, "Free Your Mind, Blur Your Video," 64.

34. Jean Rosenbluth, "Singles Click as Mad Ave. Jingles," *Billboard,* 27 August 1988, 77.

35. Jon Pareles, "Young vs. MTV: A Case of Modest Revenge," *New York Times,* 14 August 1988, 26.

36. "Free Speech Outweighs Minority Concerns," *Billboard,* 25 November 1989, 11.

37. Andrew Roblin, "Antichrist Cooled Down for MTV Debut," *Billboard,* 4 May 1985, 37.

38. Denisoff, *Inside MTV,* 75.

39. Strauss, "Free Your Mind, Blur Your Video," 64.

40. Stephen Holden, "Madonna Video Goes Too Far for MTV," *New York Times,* 28 November 1990, C13.

41. *Nightline* spokeswoman Laura Wessner disclosed that the network's attorneys said it would be acceptable to show the video "because of its news value, because the focus of our show is censorship in the arts and because of the lateness of the hour." Harrington, "Madonna at the Hype of Her Career," D1, D3.

42. Holden, "Madonna Video Goes Too Far for MTV," C13.

43. Robert Goldberg, "Madonna's Dirty Dancing," *Wall Street Journal,* 10 December 1990, A9.

44. "Etcetera," *The Advocate,* 1 January 1991, 72.

45. Greg Evans, "Madonna Video May 'Justify' Controversy as Selling Point," *Variety,* 31 December 1990, 57.

46. Paul Grein quoted in Harrington, "Madonna at the Hype of Her Career," D1, D3.

47. Goldberg, "MTV's Sharper Picture," 64.

48. Denisoff, *Inside MTV,* 219–220.

49. Goldberg, "MTV's Sharper Picture," 118.

50. Jim Bessman, "Radio May Not Be Watching, but It Is Listening," *Billboard,* 15 April 1989, M6.

51. Goldberg, "MTV's Sharper Picture," 118.

52. Steven Levy, "Ad Nauseam: How MTV Sells Out Rock and Roll," *Rolling Stone,* 8 December 1983, 34.

53. Denisoff, *Inside MTV,* 76.

54. R. Serge Denisoff, *Tarnished Gold* (New Brunswick, N.J.: Transaction Publishers, 1986), 367.

55. Love, "'Washington Wives,'" 18; and Seideman, "Rockamerica Panel Takes Close Look at TV," 31.

56. Newman, "MTV Taking a Harder Look at Vids?" 92.

57. Ibid.

58. Ibid.

59. "Texas Cable TV Operator Drops Its Offering of MTV," *Wall Street Journal,* 1 July 1991, B2.

60. Melinda Newman, "TCA Cable Dropping MTV, Citing Viewer Complaints," *Billboard,* 6 July 1991, 76.

61. Melinda Newman, "Several TCA Cable Systems to Get MTV Picture Again," *Billboard,* 27 July 1991, 42, 44.

62. "Rock 'n' Roll Is There to Stay," *Broadcasting,* 22 July 1991, 24; and Newman, "Several TCA Cable Systems to Get MTV Picture Again," 42, 44.

63. Melinda Newman, "4 Towns Lose Their MTV, Get VJN Instead," *Billboard,* 25 January 1992, 6, 86.

64. Ibid.; and John Dempsey, "Basic Nets Fear for Tiers," *Variety,* 17 February 1992, 33, 38.

65. Jerry Gray, "Taking 'I Want My MTV' Seriously in Vineland," *New York Times,* 24 January 1992, B5.

66. "MTV Restored in Several Areas," *New York Times,* 21 March 1992, 28.

67. Love, "'Washington Wives,'" 18.

68. Denisoff, *Inside MTV,* 309.

69. Ibid., 303–304.

70. Henry Schipper, "Rock Censorship Debate Rages; Parents Org Has Corp Support; MTV Asked to Label 'X' Videos," *Variety,* 2 April 1987, 2, 92.

71. Steven Dupler, "Lyrics: Video Outlets Seen Confident," *Billboard,* 21 September 1985, 3, 72.

72. Ibid.

73. Love, "'Washington Wives,'" 18.

74. Roblin, "Study on Violence Endorsed," 32.

75. Denisoff, *Inside MTV,* 285.

76. Faye Zuckerman, "Coalition Blasts Violence in Clips," *Billboard,* 22 December 1984, 35.

77. Love, "'Washington Wives,'" 18; Zuckerman, "Coalition Blasts Violence in Clips," 35; and Elizabeth Brown, "Music Television Turns 10," *Christian Science Monitor,* 6 August 1991, 10.

78. Jay Mathews, "'Toy Gun' Cop Targets MTV Videos," *San Francisco Chronicle,* 26 December 1994, E1–E3.

79. Ibid.

80. Katia Hetter, "Can She Censor the Mayhem?" *U.S. News & World Report,* 9 May 1994, 44.

81. "Jury Finds Vendor Guilty of Selling 'Obscene' LP," *Jet,* 22 October 1990, 32.

82. "2 Live Crew Freed by Jury in Obscenity Trial; Black Historian Defends Group," *Jet,* 5 November 1990, 14–15.

83. Timothy Egan, "Washington Governor Signs Measure on Obscene Music," *New York Times,* 21 March 1992, 6.

84. Roblin, "Study on Violence Endorsed," 32.

85. Cable Communications Policy Act of 1984, Section 639, Public Law 98-549, 98th Congress.

86. Audrey Duff, "Shock TV," *Texas Monthly,* November 1993, 106–112; and Andrea Gerlin, "Legal Beat: Cable TV Show on Safe Sex Leads to Obscenity Convictions in Texas," *Wall Street Journal,* 20 April 1994, B12.

87. *Miller v. California,* 413 U.S. 15 (1973).

88. John Dempsey, "Cablers Comforted by Softcore Services," *Variety,* 13 June 1994, 33, 43.

89. Nigel Hunter, "U.K. Sets Vidclip Content Standards," *Billboard,* 5 August 1989, 56.

90. Denise Wharton, "Big Brother's Watching: FCC Explores 24-hr 'Indecency' Ban," *Variety,* 11 July 1990, 60.

91. Bill Holland, "NAB President Speaks out on 'Porn Rock,'" *Billboard,* 1 June 1985, 6.

92. "Indecent Broadcasts Lead to F.C.C. Fines on 4 Radio Stations," *New York Times,* 27 October 1989, B6.

93. Bill Holland, "Bureaucracy, Legalities Slow FCC's Regulation of Indecency," *Billboard,* 25 June 1994, 1, 105.

94. Melinda Newman, "Hit Video USA Casts an Eye Toward Int'l Market," *Billboard,* 13 January 1990, 49.

95. Cara Applebaum, "Jackson Video Heads Back for Cosmetic Surgery," *Adweek's Marketing Week,* 18 November 1991, 5; and Meg Cox, "Jackson Video Is Marketing Success: Some Criticism, but Millions See Tape," *Wall Street Journal,* 18 November 1991, B5.

96. Applebaum, "Jackson Video Heads Back for Cosmetic Surgery," 5.

97. "Indecency 'Safe Harbor' Invalid, Court Rules," *News Media and the Law* 18 (Winter 1994):42–43; and Sean Scully, "Court Throws out Indecency Ban," *Broadcasting and Cable,* 29 November 1993, 10.

98. Mary Lu Carnevale, "Appeals Court to Reconsider TV Indecency," *Wall Street Journal,* 22 February 1994, B6.

CHAPTER 10

1. Warner Communications, 1984 Annual Report, 2.

2. Mark Robichaux, "It's a Book! A T-Shirt! A Toy! No, Just MTV Trying to Be Disney," *Wall Street Journal,* 8 February 1995, p. A1, A9.

3. Tom Shales, "The Pop Network That's Dim & Ditzy to Decor," *Washington Post,* 1 August 1985, B1, B9.

4. Nicholas Garnham, "Contribution to a Political Economy of Mass Communication," in *Mass Communication Review Yearbook,* vol. 1 (Beverly Hills, Calif.: 1981), 123–146.

5. Anthony DeCurtis, "Video Verite," *Rolling Stone,* 27 January 1987, 12.

6. Ibid.

7. Pat Aufderheide, "The Look of the Sound," in *Watching Television,* ed. Todd Gitlin (New York: Pantheon Books, 1987), 130.

8. Ibid.

9. Jon Pareles, "A Political Song That Casts Its Vote for the Money," *New York Times,* 6 March 1988, sec. 2, p. 32.

10. Serge Denisoff, *Inside MTV* (New Brunswick, N.J.: Transaction Publishers, 1989), 271.

11. Robichaux, "It's a Book! A T-Shirt! A Toy!" A1, A9.

References

Abt, Dean. "Music Television: Impact of the Visual Dimension." In *Popular Music and Communication: Social and Cultural Perspectives,* ed. James Lull. Beverly Hills, Calif.: Sage, 1987.

Agudelo, Carlos. "MTV, ATI Aiming Music Shows at Hispanic Market." *Billboard,* 5 March 1988, 1, 81.

———. "Latin Music Television Comes of Age." *Billboard,* 15 October 1988, 60.

Ainslie, Peter. "On the Jukebox Network, You Make the Call." *Rolling Stone,* 2 May 1991, 48, 63.

Allan, Blaine. "Musical Cinema, Music Video, Music Television." *Film Quarterly,* Spring 1990, 2–14.

"All-Comedy HBO Channel." *New York Times,* 6 October 1989, D17.

Anderson, Jack, and Dale Van Atta. "Cher's Dirty Dance Embarrasses Navy." *Washington Post,* 5 January 1990, E5.

Andrews, Edmund L. "Judge Backs Cable TV on Music Fees." *New York Times,* 19 August 1991, D1–D2.

———. "Plan to Create MTV Rival Is Under Antitrust Scrutiny." *New York Times,* 23 July 1994, 35, 43.

Appelbaum, Cara. "Beyond the Blonde Bombshell." *Adweek's Marketing Week,* 3 June 1991, 18–20.

———. "Jackson Video Heads Back for Cosmetic Surgery." *Adweek,* 18 November 1991, 5.

Appleford, Steve. "MTV Expands Political Platform." *Billboard,* 5 September 1992, 41.

"A Professor's Class Video Runs into an MTV Protest." *New York Times,* 18 May 1991, 46.

"Asian Venture Joined by MTV." *New York Times,* 9 May 1991, D8.

"Asia to Get Its Own MTV." *Wall Street Journal,* 9 May 1991, A10.

Astor, David. "Unplugged Tabitha Soren Tries Column." *Editor & Publisher,* 20 November 1993, 42–44.

Atwood, Brett. "Majors Eye New Option for Vid Channel." *Billboard,* 22 July 1995, 5.

Aufderheide, Pat. "The Look of the Sound." In *Watching Television,* ed. Todd Gitlin. New York: Pantheon Books, 1987, 111–135.

"A*Vision, VH-1 Venture into Vid Deal." *Billboard,* 13 July 1991, 47–48.

Ayers, Anne. "TV's In-Vogue Video Vamp." *TV Guide,* 19 May 1990, 20–22.

Azerrad, Michael. "Now They Spell It 'Wood$tock.'" *Rolling Stone,* 6 April 1989, 17.

———. "Independents Daze." *Rolling Stone,* 18 April 1991, 54.

Bagdikian, Ben. *The Media Monopoly,* 4th ed. Boston: Beacon Press, 1992.

Balfour, Frederik. "Rock Around the Clock." *Far Eastern Economic Review,* 25 February 1993, 54–55.

Banks, Jack. "Current Developments in the Political Economy of Video Music Exposure Media." *Studies in Communication and Culture* 1 (Spring 1987):155–184.

———. "An Introduction to the Critical Theory of Jurgen Habermas." *Studies in Communication and Culture* 1 (Fall 1989):89–131.

Baran, Paul A., and Paul M. Sweezy. *Monopoly Capital.* New York: Modern Reader Paperbacks, 1966.

Barbieri, Richard. "Music Videos: Programs or Record Promos?" *Channels of Communication,* July/August 1985, 10.

Bard, Adrienne. "In Mexico, a Video Veto." *New York Times,* 7 July 1991, sec. 2 H22.

Baudrillard, Jean. "The Implosion of Meaning in the Media and the Implosion of the Social in the Masses." In *The Myths of Information: Technology and Postindustrial Culture,* ed. K. Woodward. Madison, Wisc.: Coda Press, 1980, 137–148.

"The Beat Goes on TV: Music Videos, Sign-on to Sign-off." *Broadcasting,* 25 June 1984, 50–53.

Beck, Kirsten. "BET Faces Music, Comes Up with Talk." *Channels of Communication,* June 1989, 58–60.

Benedict, Daniel. "Picking a Fight with the Champ." *Venture,* June/July 1989, 21–22.

Berke, Jeff. "The Problem with Record Contracts." *Billboard,* 4 June 1988, 9.

Berle, A. Jr., and G. C. Means. *The Modern Corporation and Private Property.* New York: Harcourt, Brace, and World, 1932.

Bernstein, Roberta. "When Money Matters." *Channels of Communication,* 25 June 1990, 30–32.

"Bertelsmann to Join MTV Competition." *Wall Street Journal,* 29 June 1994, B8.

Bessman, Jim. "Local Focus Pays off for 'Video 22.'" *Billboard,* 12 January 1985, 31–32.

———. "UHF Linkup for Long Island's WBLI." *Billboard,* 23 February 1985, 32.

———. "Black Cable Network Makes Heavy Commitment to Clips." *Billboard,* 30 March 1985, 30, 31.

———. "Boston's Channel 66 Makes Heavy Investment in Clips." *Billboard,* 20 April 1985, 29.

———. "Showtime Continuing Varied Musical Menu." *Billboard,* 4 May 1985, 36, 37.

———. "New Ways of Establishing Sponsorship Explored." *Billboard,* 17 August 1985, 31.

———. "CBS Records Tells Pools: Don't Give Our Clips Away." *Billboard,* 1 February 1986, 32.

———. "Vidclip Makers Ask: 'Where's the Recession?'" *Billboard,* 9 August 1986, 54, 64.

———. "Label Execs: MTV's Hip Clip Boosts Sales." *Billboard,* 17 January 1987, 46.

———. "Music Ties Corporate Promo, Clips." *Billboard,* 20 June 1987, 54, 54–55.

———. "'Night Flight' Soars on Diverse Fare." *Billboard,* 11 July 1987, 45.

———. "Duran Erects Vid Wall for Concerts." *Billboard,* 6 August 1987, 60.

———. "California Clip Channel Is a Survivor." *Billboard,* 5 September 1987, 57.

———. "Videoclips: For Producers and Directors There's Still Room Enough to Grow, Especially in Creative Directions." *Billboard,* 21 November 1987, V3, V6.

———. "Fla. Jazz Show Mixes Clips, Live Performances." *Billboard,* 28 November 1987, 53.

———. "Cutting Crew Gives Polaroid Pitch." *Billboard,* 28 May 1988, 51, 53.

———. "Reprise's Siberry Peddles Clip at Shows." *Billboard,* 28 May 1988, 51.

———. "Capitol Gives Clips Clout with Computer Tracking." *Billboard,* 20 August 1988, 46.

———. "Credit Atlantic Success to Videos." *Billboard,* 4 February 1989, 50, 70.

———. "'One' Plus MTV Equals Wider Metallica." *Billboard,* 18 March 1989, 57.

———. "County Vids Grow in Style, Number." *Billboard,* 25 March 1989, 52, 53.

———. "The Changing Look of Longform: Producers, Directors Cast Consumers in Leading Role for Future Video Sales." *Billboard,* 15 April 1989, M2, M10.

————. "Radio May Not Be Watching, but It Is Listening. . . " *Billboard,* 15 April 1989, M6, M8.

————. "Chrysalis Beefs up Video Dept." *Billboard,* 24 June 1989, 66.

————. "Black & White Comes Thru 1st Year with Flying Colors." *Billboard,* 19 May 1990, 50.

————. "MuchMusic Is Much Different." *Billboard,* 9 March 1991, 63.

————. "CRS Panel Stresses Country Vidclips' Vital Role." *Billboard,* 30 March 1991, 62.

————. "WANTED: The Risk-taker's Fresh, Creative Video Vision." *Billboard,* 11 May 1991, MV1, MV4.

————. "Flashframe Making a Splash in Music-Vid Pool." *Billboard,* 8 June 1991, 60–61.

Bierbaum, Tom. "Attorneys Mull Impact of Ruling That 'Synch Licenses' Don't Clear Program's Music for Vid Per Se." *Variety,* 4 May 1988, 547.

Blatt, Wendy. "Spirit of Independents Burns On." *Billboard,* 21 March 1992, I-3, I-24–26, I-33–34.

Block, Alex B. "Music for the Eyes." *Forbes,* 3 December 1984, 162, 166.

————. "Now, What?" *Forbes,* 30 June 1986, 131–132.

Borger, Gloria. "Setting Words to Music Over Values." *U.S. News & World Report,* 29 June 1992, 9.

Borzillo, Carrie. "MTV, Modern Rock Keys to Success for Capitol Bands." *Billboard,* 28 August 1993, 10. 87.

Boyer, Peter J. "After Rebellious Youth, MTV Tries the System." *New York Times,* 9 May 1988, D8.

Brandt, Pam. "MTV/Music Television: The Beat Goes On . . . for Better, for Worse." *Ms.,* November 1983, 42, 44–45.

Breen, Julian H. "Replace Confrontation with Compromise. Radio, Music Biz Aren't Married." *Billboard,* 13 April 1991, 11.

Brooke, Elizabeth Hellman. "Yo! They're Dancin' in the Streets." *New York Times,* 7 July 1991, H22.

Brooks, Tim, and Earle Marsh. *The Complete Directory to Prime Time Network TV Shows.* 3d ed. New York: Ballantine Books, 1985.

Brown, Andrew C. "Products of the Year." *Fortune,* 28 December 1981, 66.

Brown, Elizabeth A. "MTV's 'Cultural Colonialism.'" *Christian Science Monitor,* 6 August 1991, 11.

————. "Music Television Turns 10." *Christian Science Monitor,* 6 August 1991, 10.

Brown, Jane D., and Kenneth Campbell. "Race and Gender in Music Videos: The Same Beat but a Different Drummer." *Journal of Communication* 36 (Winter 1986):94–106.

Browne, David. "The Independents See Vultures Circling Overhead." *New York Times,* 27 October 1991, sec. 2, pp. 26, 35.

Brubach, Holly. "Rock-and-Roll Vaudeville." *Atlantic,* July 1984, 99, 100, 102.

Brunelli, Richard, and Alan Goldsand. "Coca-Cola Ambushes Pepsi with Global Cable TV Buy." *Mediaweek,* 27 January 1992, 3.

Buckley, Bruce, and Melinda Newman. "Indie Labels Seeing Increased Success with Vids." *Billboard,* 20 June 1992, 44.

Bunce, Alan. "MTV: Tomorrow the World?" *Christian Science Monitor,* 16 February 1989, 10.

Bunce, Richard. *Television in the Corporate Interest.* New York: Praeger Publishers, 1976.

Bunzel, Reed E. "RIAA Analysis Shows Change in Buying Patterns." *Broadcasting,* 1 July 1991, 36.

Burris, Val. Lecture in Political Sociology Class, Winter 1987. University of Oregon, Eugene.

Byron, Christopher. "Bad Music." *New York,* 6 August 1990, 10–11.

Calmes, Jackie. "Tax Break Bill Could Affect Viacom Sale." *Wall Street Journal,* 8 February 1995, A3, A6.

Campbell, Richard and Rosanne Freed. "'We Know It When We See It': Postmodernism and Television." *Television Quarterly,* 1993, 75–87.

"Canadian Channel Bans Rap Group." *New York Times,* 7 February 1990, C14.

"The Candidates and Fun Power." *New York Times,* 24 September 1988, 34.

Capuzzi, Cecilia. "Selling the Children." *Channels of Communication,* June 1987, 60–61.

Carey, Chase. "When Money Matters." *Channels of Communication,* 25 June 1990, 30–35.

Carlson, Timothy. "Rock's Leading Ladies. How They Conquered the Music World." *TV Guide,* 1 September 1990, 2–6.

Carnevale, Mary Lu. "Appeals Court to Reconsider TV Indecency." *Wall Street Journal,* 22 February 1994, B6.

Carson, Tom. "Don't Try This at Home." *Rolling Stone,* 23 November 1993, 99–104.

Carter, Bill. "An MTV Comedy Channel Will Compete with HBO's." *New York Times,* 19 May 1989, D5.

———. "HBO and MTV Begin a Serious Battle over Comedy." *New York Times,* 22 May 1989, D8.

———. "MTV Rolling out Comedy Channel." *New York Times,* 29 March 1990, D22.

———. "MTV to Provide Programming for Soviets." *New York Times,* 12 October 1990, D4.

———. "MTV's 10th Birthday Show to Be Broadcast on ABC." *New York Times,* 12 June 1991, C17.

Chapple, Steve, and Reebee Garofalo. *Rock 'n' Roll Is Here to Pay: The History and Politics of the Music Industry.* Chicago: Nelson-Hall, 1977.

"Cher's Dirty Dance Embarrasses Navy." *Washington Post,* 5 January 1990, E5.

"Chris Kreski Is into His Seventies." *New Yorker,* 14 February 1994, 37–38.

Christgau, Robert. "Rock 'n' Roller Coaster." *Village Voice,* 7 February 1985, 37, 38, 40–45.

Christman, Ed. "NARM Retailers See Sales Strength in Music Video." *Billboard,* 4 November 1989, 9, 91.

Christopher, Maurice. "Turner Considers Competition for MTV." *Advertising Age,* 13 August 1984, 69.

Citron, Alan. "Fretting It. Despite Recent High Sales Note, Record Firms See Tough Times." *Los Angeles Times,* 12 December 1991, D1, D3.

Clarke, Steve. "Cold Warrior Now Head Honcho for Hot Channel." *Variety.* 16 November 1992, 35–36.

———. "Rock Conquers Continent." *Variety,* 16 November 1992, 35–36.

———. "Music Network's Goal: Get into Every Home." *Variety,* 16 November 1992, 36.

Clark-Meads, Jeff, and Adam White. "Paul Conroy to Head Virgin's U.K. Labels." *Billboard,* 4 January, 8, 69.

"Clinton Wants His MTV for Political Forum." *Variety,* 15 June 1992, 29.

"CMT Among 4 Most-Watched Cable Networks." *Billboard,* 16 November 1991, 37.

"CMT Europe's Reach Extends Across Continent." *Billboard,* 28 August 1993, 87.

Cocks, Jay. "A Nasty Jolt for the Top Pops." *Time,* 1 July 1991, 78–79.

Coe, Steve. "'Diversification, Not Uniformity' Key to Successful International TV." *Broadcasting,* 4 March 1991, 68.

———. "Sports, Soaps and Video Specials." *Broadcasting,* 28 October 1991, 58.

———. "FOX, MTV Team on AIDS Concert." *Broadcasting,* 16 March 1992, 20.

———. "MTV's Lofty Take on 'The Real World.'" *Broadcasting,* 6 July 1992, 42.

———. "Nick's Big Deal Is the Cat's Meow." *Broadcasting,* 13 July 1992, 22–24.

Coleman, Beth. "The Politics of Dancing." *Village Voice,* 28 July 1992, 38–39.

Colford, Steven W. "D.C. Wives Aim at MTV; Ads Next?" *Advertising Age,* 19 August 1985, 1, 72.

Coll, Steve. "MTV Age Dawning in India." *Washington Post,* 5 March 1992, A31, A38.

Comer, Brooke S. "Cut to the Beat. Music Video Editors Take Technology and Tradition Seriously." *Theater Craft,* December 1985, 81–88.

Compaine, Benjamin M. "Preface to the Second Edition. An Editorial," "Introduction," "Newspapers," "Who Owns the Media Companies?" and "Conclusion: How Few Is Too Few?" In *Who Owns the Media?* 2nd ed., ed. Benjamin M. Compaine. White Plains, N.Y.: Knowledge Industry Publishers, 1982.

Connelly, Christopher. "Rick James Blasts Vanity 6, Charges MTV with Racism." *Rolling Stone,* 14 April 1983, 47.

Coopman, Jeremy, and Dave Laing. "MTV Has Europe's Ear." *Variety,* 26 August 1991, 5, 103.

"The Copycats That Are Chasing Music Television." *Business Week,* 3 September 1984, 57, 58.

"Corporate Monoliths Threaten Entrepreneurs." *Billboard,* 13 May 1989, 9, 75.

Cox, Meg. "Jackson Video Is Marketing Success: Some Criticism, but Millions See Tape." *Wall Street Journal,* 18 November 1991, B5.

Dagnoli, Jadann. "Rockin' Rascals." *Advertising Age.* 2 October 1989, 56.

Dalesandro, Anthony D. "Indie Labels Prosper with Indie Distributors." *Billboard,* 27 February 1988, 9.

Dannen, Fredric. "MTV's Great Leap Backward." *Channels of Communication,* July/August 1987, 45–47.

———. *Hit Men: Power Brokers and Fast Money Inside the Music Business.* New York: Times Books, 1990.

Darling, Cary. "Labels See Video as Force to Be Reckoned with." *Billboard,* 14 November 1981, 58, 64, 69.

———. "R&B Denied?" *Billboard,* 28 November 1981, 62.

———. "Label Execs Kick Video Around." *Billboard,* 19 December 1981, 53, 57.

Davis, Clive. "AMAs Reflect MTV-Influenced Homogenization. It's Time to Speak Up for Musical Diversity." *Billboard,* 16 February 1991, 12.

Davis, Erik. "I Am My MTV." *Village Voice,* 25 August 1992, 46–47.

Dawes, Amy. "'This Note's For You': Neil Young Criticizes MTV's Ban of Parody." *Variety,* 6 July 1988, 58.

Dawtrey, Adam. "Global Audio Sales $24 Bil." *Variety,* 7 October 1991, 208.

"The Day the Music Returned." *Broadcasting,* 23 March 1992, 97.

DeCurtis, Anthony. "Stars Reject Videos." *Rolling Stone,* 5 June 1986, 11.

———. "Pittman Leaving MTV." *Rolling Stone,* 25 September 1986, 17.

———. "Video Verite." *Rolling Stone,* 27 January 1987, 12.

———. "80s." *Rolling Stone,* 15 November 1990, 59–65, 170.

Dempsey, John. "'Solid Gold' Strip Scares Competition." *Variety,* 14 March 1984, 75–76.

———. "Basic Nets Fear for Tiers." *Variety,* 17 February 1992, 33, 38.

———. "Cablers Comforted by Softcore Services." *Variety,* 13 June 1994, 33, 43.

———. "VH1 Programmers Make Plan to Face the Music." *Variety,* 17–23 July 1995, 21, 22.

Denisoff, R. Serge. *Tarnished Gold.* New Brunswick, N.J.: Transaction Publishers, 1986.

———. *Inside MTV.* New Brunswick, N.J.: Transaction Publishers, 1989.

"Department Store Fashions Clip to Boost Sales." *Billboard,* 15 December 1984, 40.

Deutschman, Alan. "Trump the Video: Too Hot for MTV?" *Fortune,* 14 January 1991, 13.

Dezzani, Mark. "Euro Channels Link Programming and Resources, Challenging MTV Europe." *Billboard,* 29 October 1994, 52–54.

———. "Videomusic Takes Investment Bids." *Billboard,* 21 January 1995, 44.

DiMartino, Dave. "Rock the Vote Rolls into New Phase." *Billboard,* 26 January 1991, 14, 102.

DiMauro, Phil. "Label Execs Happy About Advent of Adult Contempo MTV Spinoff." *Variety,* 29 August 1984, 89, 92.

———. "WCI Labels to Charge for Clips." *Variety,* 21 August 1985, 121, 126.

———. "Majors Consider Vidclip Charges in Wake of CBS, WEA Moves." *Variety,* 28 August 1985, 89.

———. "MTV Launches Ad Campaign with Network TV Time Buys." *Variety,* 30 October 1985, 91.

———. "WEA Postpones Deadline for Start of TV Vidclip Payments." *Variety,* 13 November 1985, 119–120.

"Dodge Rocks with MTV." *Advertising Age,* 9 December 1991, 34.

Donaton, Scott, and Alison Fahey. "Cross-Media Allies Falter." *Advertising Age,* 30 March 1992, 3, 59.

Donlon, Brian. "A 2-Front Challenge to MTV." *USA Today,* 18 June 1986, 3D.

D'Souza, Jerry, and Mike Levin. "Indian Artists Benefiting from MTV Asia Exposure." *Billboard,* 4 December 1993, 42, 46.

Duff, Audrey. "Shock TV." *Texas Monthly,* November 1993, 106–112.

Duffy, Glen. "It's a Miserable Life." *Esquire,* February 1990, 122–126.

Duffy, Susan. "Will a Little Less Rock Get MTV Rolling Faster?" *Business Week,* 30 April 1990, 62, 66.

Duffy, Thom, and Larry Flick. "Milli Vanilli Didn't Start the Fire." *Billboard,* 8 December 1990, 4, 89.

Dupler, Steven. "Seminar Probes Video Exclusivity." *Billboard,* 18 August 1984, 3, 54.

———. "Sony, WEA, CBS, Polygram Team in MTV Push for CD." *Billboard,* 1 September 1984, 3.

———. "Turner Channel Advertisers 'Watchful.'" *Billboard,* 1 December 1984, 3.

———. "Clip Directors 'Dream' Out Loud About Getting Hollywood to Call." *Billboard,* 15 December 1984, 37.

———. "MTV's VH-1 Opens on Optimistic Note." *Billboard,* 12 January 1985, 1, 61.

———. "Lyrics: Video Outlets Seen Confident." *Billboard,* 21 September 1985, 3, 72.

———. "Targeting the Video." *Billboard,* 28 September 1985, NT3, NT8.

———. "The Shattering Bubble of Special Effects." *Billboard,* 23 November 1985, VM10.

———. "Dubin Speaks His Mind on Industry Woes." *Billboard,* 21 December 1985, 23.

———. "Programming for Depth of Field." *Billboard,* 21 December 1985, 28.

———. "Rolling the Credits." *Billboard,* 21 December 1985, 30.

———. "Vidclip Charges Create Program Casualties." *Billboard,* 22 February 1986, 3, 76.

————. "CBS May Pass on MTV 'Countdown.'" *Billboard,* 6 March 1986, 1, 92.

————. "Impact of VH-1 Debated: Does Channel Sell Records?" *Billboard,* 12 April 1986, 1, 84.

————. "Vidclip Output Faces Trim." *Billboard,* 19 April 1986, 1, 91.

————. "Nielsen Publishes Disputed MTV 4th-Quarter Ratings." *Billboard,* 26 April 1986, 84.

————. "Settlement in Vidclip Exclusivity Suit." *Billboard,* 3 May 1986, 1, 71.

————. "CBS Ups Production of Home Tapes." *Billboard,* 17 May 1986, 60.

————. "MTV Chief Speaks Out." *Billboard,* 17 May 1986, 60.

————. "See Pittman's Departure from MTV in Mid-'87." *Billboard,* 23 August 1986, 92.

————. "New Superstar Videoclips Defy the Budget Cutters." *Billboard,* 13 September 1986, 1, 93.

————. "MTV: Changes at the Channel." *Billboard,* 11 October 1986, 1, 90.

————. "Music Vid Meet: Cautious Optimism. Industry Reduces Sell-Through Hopes." *Billboard,* 6 December 1986, 3, 77.

————. "Label Execs: VH-1 Is Coming of Age." *Billboard,* 7 March 1987, 51–52.

————. "On Behalf of Hit Video USA Senators Request MTV Probe." *Billboard,* 4 April 1987, 1, 85.

————. "Blake Segues from Photos to Clips." *Billboard,* 20 June 1987, 54.

————. "MTV Bash Signals Invasion of Europe." *Billboard,* 15 August 1987, 81.

————. "Will Pan-Euro MTV Pan Out? Net Bows in 14 Countries." *Billboard,* 15 August 1987, 1, 81.

————. "Now, Dance Hits are OK on MTV." *Billboard,* 24 October 1987, 1, 108.

————. "The Eye." *Billboard,* 6 February 1988, 53.

————. "Hit Video Cuts Programming to 7 Early-Morning Hours." *Billboard,* 6 February 1988, 1, 80.

————. "Vidclip Shows Follow Radio on Dance/Crossover Format." *Billboard,* 27 February 1988, 1, 89.

————. "'Hit-Driven' MTV Irks Majors, Net Replies: We Still Help New Artists." *Billboard,* 2 April 1988, 1, 66.

————. "MTV Ratings Nos. Overlook College Dorms, Bars Viewers." *Billboard,* 2 April 1988, 66.

————. "Konowitch Takes Program Helm at MTV." *Billboard,* 13 August 1988, 8, 88.

————. "Record Industry Mixed on MTV Plan to Daypart Videos." *Billboard,* 17 September 1988, 1, 82.

————. "MTV to Step Up Minority Hiring." *Billboard,* 24 September 1988, 5, 100.

————. "Bush Leads in MTV Poll." *Billboard,* 1 October 1988, 58.

————. "Virgin Breaks Fordham Via VH-1, Press." *Billboard,* 26 November 1988, 30.

————. "Wanted: New Blood for Music Vids." *Billboard,* 17 December 1988, 1, 69.

————. "New MTV Prez: No Big Changes Planned at Channel." *Billboard,* 27 May 1989, 55.

————. "CEMA, BMG, MCA to Take Longform Video Plunge." *Billboard,* 3 June 1989, 1, 76.

————. "Metalheads Rock to Rap as Crossover Idiom Grows." *Billboard,* 15 July 1989, 1, 66, 78.

Dupler, Steven, and Jim Bessman. "Vidclip Panels: Useful, Not Earthshaking." *Billboard,* 30 June 1988, 5, 72.

Ebert, Hans. "MTV Asia Hits the Road to Herald Launch." *Billboard,* 10 August 1991, 62, 64.

———. "MTV Asia Debuts in Hong Kong." *Billboard,* 28 September 1991, 14, 67.

Egan, Timothy. "Washington Governor Signs Measure on Obscene Material." *New York Times,* 21 March 1992, 6.

Engelberg, Stephen. "Occident Prone in Poland." *New York Times,* 7 July 1991, sec. 2 H22.

"Etcetera." *The Advocate,* 1 January 1991, 72.

Evans, Greg. "Madonna Video May 'Justify' Controversy as Selling Point." *Variety,* 31 December 1990, 57.

"Exclusives Extended." *Billboard,* 11 October 1986, 90.

Fabrikant, Geraldine. "Viacom to Sell a 50% Stake in Showtime TV Service." *New York Times,* 18 October 1989, D22.

———. "When Leverage Works." *New York Times,* 24 December 1989, F1, F8.

———. "Cable Company in Texas Planning to Drop MTV." *New York Times,* 29 June 1991, L46.

———. "Viacom Is Winner over QVC in Fight to Get Paramount." *New York Times,* 16 February 1994, 1, D5.

———. "Viacom Now Owns Paramount," *New York Times,* 12 March 1994, 37.

Fahey, Alison. "Cable Plots International Growth." *Advertising Age,* 14 October 1991, 6.

Fahey, Alison, and Scott Donaton. "Mags Jam with MTV." *Advertising Age,* 21 October 1991, 16.

Farber, Jim. "Director's View: Creativity and Innovation Harder to Come By in '88; MTV, Labels, Music Itself to Blame." *Billboard,* 12 November 1988, V3, V8.

———. "Budget Genius." *Rolling Stone,* 10 August 1989, 99–100.

———. "Beyond the Big Hair." *Rolling Stone,* 14–28 December 1989, 235–236.

———. "Clip Corporation." *Rolling Stone,* 23 August 1990, 137.

Farhi, Paul. "Murdoch Deal to Buy Satellite TV." *San Francisco Chronicle,* 28 July 1993, E1.

Farley, Ellen. "Videos Rock the Music Business." *Los Angeles Times,* 21 August 1983, pt. 1, pp. 1, 33–34.

Farley, Ellen, Mark N. Vamos, and Christine Dugas. "How Many Teenagers Still Want Their MTV?" *Business Week,* 4 August 1986, 73.

Federal Communications Commission, Kenneth Gordon, et al. *Staff Report on FCC Policy on Cable Ownership.* Washington, D.C.: FCC Office of Plans and Policy, September 1981. Preliminary draft.

"5th Birthday Salute to Night Tracks." Advertising supplement. *Billboard,* 4 June 1988, N1–N20.

"Firm Revises Credit Pact, Extends Revolving Portion." *Wall Street Journal,* 27 January 1992, A9.

Fisher, Christy. "Military's Ads Shoot for the 'Hip.'" *Advertising Age,* 30 August 1993, 12.

Fiske, John. "MTV: Post-Structural Post-Modern." *Journal of Communication Inquiry* 10 (Winter 1986):74–79.

Fleming, Charles. "Barry Diller Scores at the Buzzer." *Newsweek,* 6 December 1993, 41.

Flick, Larry, and Melinda Newman. "Clubs Getting the Music-Vid Picture Again." *Billboard,* 25 May 1991, 1, 71.

"'Flight' Merits 2-Year Renewal on USA Cable." *Billboard,* 19 December 1981. 60.

Flint, Joe. "Viacom's 'Real Time' Tackles Access." *Broadcasting & Cable,* 16 August 1993, 19.

———. "MTV Fights Fire with No Fire." *Broadcasting & Cable,* 18 October 1993, 22–23.

———. "MTV Moves 'Beavis and Butt-head.'" *Broadcasting & Cable,* 25 October 1993, 29.

Fong-Torres, Ben. "The Decline and Fall Season of Rock on TV." *Rolling Stone,* 9 October 1975, 14.

Forrest, Rick. "Compact Hardware Revolution Paces Technological Changes." *Billboard,* 14 November 1981, 60, 76.

———. "Video New Wave: Music Greets Image Manipulation." *Billboard,* 19 December 1981, 56.

Foti, Lauri. "MTV Cable Channel Exposing New Acts." *Billboard,* 15 August 1981, 3, 58.

———. "Stereo Sound Prominent in Music TV Offerings." *Billboard,* 1 May 1982, 16.

———. "New Act Pacts Take Vidclip $ From Royalties." *Billboard,* 2 July 1983, 1, 58.

———. "Vidclip $$ Issue Heats Up." *Billboard,* 30 July 1983, 1, 54.

———. "MTV, Labels Talk Payments." *Billboard,* 11 February 1984, 1, 74.

Frank, Allan D. "And the Beat Goes On." *Forbes,* 18 May 1987, 40–44.

Frankenheimer, John T. "Smallness Allows Greater Focus, Speed. New Labels Have Several Advantages." *Billboard,* 2 February 1991, 15.

Freeman, Kim. "MTV Links with Pretenders." *Billboard,* 28 January 1984, 40.

———. "Radio Caught up in New Controversy over Lyrics." *Billboard,* 8 June 1985, 1, 78.

Freeman, Mike. "New Media Sales Firm Bullish on Barter." *Broadcasting,* 24 February 1992, 22.

"Free Speech Outweighs Minority Concerns." Unsigned editorial. *Billboard,* 25 November 1989, 11.

"Freston May Go Multiplex with MTV, Nick, VH-1." *Broadcasting,* 29 July 1991, 28.

Friday, Carolyn. "Viacom's Rise to Stardom." *Newsweek,* 25 November 1985, 71.

Fry, Virginia H., and Donald L. Fry. "MTV: The 24 Hour Commercial." *Journal of Communication Inquiry* 10 (Winter 1986):29–33.

Fuller, Chris. "East-West Vidclips Debated." *Billboard,* 6 January 1990, 62.

———. "BMG Charges Abuse of Power by MTV Europe." *Billboard,* 3 September 1994, 6, 123.

Gallese, Liz R. "'I Get Exhilerated by It.'" *Forbes,* 22 October 1990, 54, 56, 60.

Ganot, Harvey K. "Fifth Estater." *Broadcasting & Cable,* 21 June 1993, 71.

Garcia, Guy. "Look, Ma—No Amps!" *Time,* 1 July 1991, 79.

Garfield, Bob. "Burger King Tunes in to Teens on 'BK TeeVee.'" *Advertising Age,* 19 October 1992, 54.

Garland, Les. "MTV Exclusivity Deals Deprive Fans of Music." *Billboard,* 22 August 1992, 4.

Garnham, Nicholas. "Contribution to a Political Economy of Mass Communication." In *Mass Communication Review Yearbook,* vol. 1. Beverly Hills, Calif.: 1981, 123–146.

———. "Toward a Theory of Cultural Materialism." *Journal of Communication* 33 (Summer 1983):314–329.

Gaudioso, Angela. "Clip Offers an Anti-Drug Message." *Billboard,* 4 May 1985, 36, 37.

Gay, Verne. "Viacom Sues Time Fearing Showtime's Fate." *Variety,* 10 May 1989, 1, 3.

Gehr, Richard. "The MTV Aesthetic." *Film Comment* 19 (July/August 1983):37–40.

George, Nelson. "Four Offer Divergent Views on Role of the Artist." *Billboard,* 18 December 1982, 46.

———. "Slick Rick Says MTV Is Sick." *Billboard,* 19 February 1983, 32.

———. "At Last, Black Acts Making MTV Inroads." *Billboard,* 8 April 1989, 20.

George, Nelson, and Steven Dupler. "BET Boycotts Profile Product." *Billboard,* 23 August 1986, 3, 92.

Georges, Christopher. "Mock the Vote." *Washington Monthly,* May 1993, 30–35.

Gerard, Jeremy. "An MTV for Grown-Ups Is Seeking Its Audience." *New York Times,* 7 August 1989, C14.

Gerlin, Andrea. "Legal Beat: Cable TV Show on Safe Sex Leads to Obscenity Convictions in Texas," *Wall Street Journal,* 20 April 1994, B12.

Gett, Steve. "Pop Soundtracks Caught in Updraft of Video Revolution's Impact on TV & Movies." *Billboard,* 21 June 1986, S3, S10–S11.

Giges, Nancy. "Global Spending Patterns Emerge." *Advertising Age,* 11 November 1991, 64.

"Giraldi's Prod. Co. Deals with Artists, Not Record Labels." *Variety,* 13 June 1984, 76.

Girard, Tom. "HBO-Cinemax Studies Indicate Their Videos Boost Album Sales." *Variety,* 14 December 1983, 2, 109.

———. "Discovery Sues MTV, Charging It Has Violated Antitrust Laws; Polygram Inks Exclusivity Pact." *Variety,* 26 September 1984, 105, 110.

Glasberg, Davita Silfen, and Michael Schwartz. "Ownership and Control of Corporations." In *Annual Review of Sociology* 9 (1983): 311–332.

Gold, Richard. "Labels Limit Videos on Black Artists." *Variety,* 15 December 1982, 73, 78.

———. "Black Video Production Is Increasing." *Variety,* 14 March 1984, 127–128.

———. "Label Charges for Music Videos May Lead to Big Shakeout in Outlets That Broadcast Them." *Variety,* 14 March 1984, 69, 87.

———. "Cash Clout & Chutzpah Keys to Redstone's Takeover of Viacom; $3.4-Bil Deal Seen as Solid Buy." *Variety,* 11 March 1987, 3, 116.

———. "Globalization of Music Markets Seen on Certain but Bumpy Road." *Variety,* 3 February 1988, 145–146.

Goldberg, Michael. "Payola: The Record-Label Connection." *Rolling Stone,* 21 April 1988, 15, 114.

———. "MTV's Sharper Picture." *Rolling Stone,* 8 February 1990, 61–64, 118.

———. "More Bad News for Ticket Buyers." *Rolling Stone,* 8 August 1991, 28.

———. "Music Business Hits the Skids." *Rolling Stone,* 5 September 1991, 15–16.

———. "Atco Folds; More Cuts Expected." *Rolling Stone,* 14 November 1991, 15, 27.

Goldberg, Robert. "Madonna's Dirty Dancing." *Wall Street Journal,* 10 December 1990, A9.

"Golden West Syndicates WABC-TV Video Show." *Variety,* 18 January 1984, 91.

Golding, Peter, and Graham Murdock. "Theories of Communication and Theories of Society." *Communication Research* 5 (July 1978):339–356.

Goldman, Kevin. "NBC Gets Short End of McDonald's Tie-In." *Wall Street Journal,* 12 October 1990, B4.

Goldsand, Alan. "Television." *Mediaweek,* 4 November 1991, 23.

———. "MTV Quizzes World Teen Buys, Sex." *Mediaweek,* 11 November 1991, 29.

———. "Coca-Cola Ambushes Pepsi with Global Cable TV Buy." *Mediaweek,* 27 January 1992, 3.

Goldstein, Patrick. "In Rock to Be or Not to Be May Depend on MTV." *Los Angeles Times,* 2 August 1983, pt. 6, pp. 1, 6.

Goll, Sally D. "MTV Asia Taps Peter Jamieson to Be President." *Wall Street Journal,* 8 February 1995, B10.

Gomery, Doulgas. "Media Economics: Terms of Analysis." *Critical Studies in Mass Communication* 6 (March 1989):43–60.

Goodman, Fred. "Krasnow Says Electra Will Sign with MTV." *Billboard,* 25 August 1984, 1, 70.

————. "MTV Nixes Neil Young's Acerbic 'This Note's for You' Video." *Rolling Stone,* 11 August 1988, 25.

Graham, Judith. "MTV, CNN Move into Bloc." *Advertising Age,* 4 December 1989, 4.

Gray, Jerry. "Taking 'I Want My MTV' Seriously in Vineland." *New York Times,* 24 January 1992, B5.

Green, Jeff. "MTV Yanked off Air by Norwegian Cable Cos." *Billboard,* 18 April 1992, 37.

Green, Paul. "Once Promotion Tool, Video Filming Now Consumer Art." *Billboard,* 19 December 1981, 54, 57.

————. "New Turner Music Channel: Accent on Hits." *Billboard,* 20 October 1984, 1, 72.

Grim, Matthew. "Why Hire Madonna When You Can Custom Order a Pop Endorser?" *Adweek,* 15 January 1990, 17.

Grossberg, Larry. "Strategies of Marxist Cultural Interpretation." *Critical Studies in Mass Communication* 1 (December 1984):392–421.

Grossman, Andrew. "Freeze Frame: A Radical Departure." *Marketing & Media Decisions,* August 1989, 30.

Groves, Don. "MTV-E Spins More than Vids: Eyeing Profitability By 1992." *Variety,* 17 January 1990, 45, 47.

Guback, Thomas H. "Theatrical Film." In *Who Owns the Media?* 2d ed., ed. Benjamin M. Compaine, 199–298. White Plains, N.Y.: Knowledge Industry Publishers, 1982.

————. "Hollywood's International Market." In *The American Film Industry.* Rev. ed., ed. Tino Balio. Madison: The University of Wisconsin Press, 1985, 463–486.

Gubernick, Lisa. "Sumner Redstone Scores Again." *Forbes,* 31 October 1988, 44, 48.

"Gulf + Western + Viacom?" *Broadcasting,* 15 May 1989, 59, 60.

Gunther, Max. "The Beat." *TV Guide,* 22 July 1978, 2–4, 6, 8.

————. "The Beat Doesn't Go On." *TV Guide,* 29 July 1978, 18–19, 21.

Guterman, Jimmy. "Rival Sues MTV." *Rolling Stone,* 5 December 1985, 16.

————. "MTV Has a New Rival." *Rolling Stone,* 30 January 1986, 10.

Hall, Peter. "MTV Wants It All." *Village Voice,* 21 February 1984, 48.

————. "The Sweet Sound of Success." *Financial World,* 4 September 1985, 72–74.

Hall, Stuart. "The Rediscovery of 'Ideology': Return of the Repressed in Media Studies." In *Culture, Society and the Media,* ed. Michael Gurevitch, Tony Bennett, James Curran and Janet Woollacott. New York: Methuen, 1982, 56–90.

Hardt, Hanno. "MTV: Towards Visual Domination, a Polemic." *Journal of Communication Inquiry* 10 (Winter 1986):64–65.

Haring, Bruce. "1989 to Test Mettle of PPV Music Events." *Billboard,* 18 February 1989, 1, 93.

————. "Music Business Stumbles in '91, RIAA Reports." *Variety,* 30 September 1991, 79.

Harrington, Richard. "Fame Without a Name." *Washington Post,* 3 August 1984, B1, B4.

————. "Madonna at the Hype of Her Career." *Washington Post,* 4 December 1990, D1, D3.

————. "Rock Around the Clock." *Washington Post,* 28 July 1991, G1, G4.

Harris, Kathryn. "Sumner Redstone Prevails by Force of Will." *Los Angeles Times,* 19 November 1989, D5.

————. "Viacom Seeks a Role in the Land of Media Giants." *Los Angeles Times,* 19 November 1989, D1, D4, D5.

Head, Sydney W., and Christopher H. Sterling. *Broadcasting in America.* 4th ed. Dallas: Houghton Mifflin, 1987.

Hedegaard, Erik. "Discovery Network Sues MTV." *Rolling Stone,* 8 November 1984, 61.

Held, David. *Introduction to Critical Theory.* Berkeley: University of California Press, 1980.

Helopaltio, Kari. "Static Surrounds MTV Europe's Scandinavian B'casting Deals." *Billboard,* 18 January 1992, 35.

Hennessey, Mike. "Three Firms Join in European Music Channel." *Billboard,* 28 April 1984, 28, 33.

———. "More European Clip $$ Deals in Place." *Billboard,* 22 March 1986, 47.

Herman, Edward S., and Noam Chomsky. *Manufacturing Consent: The Political Economy of the Mass Media.* New York: Pantheon Books, 1988.

Hetter, Katia. "Can She Censor the Mayhem?" *U.S. News & World Report,* 9 May 1994, 44.

Hilburn, Robert, and Chuck Philips. "Rock's New World Order." *Los Angeles Times,* 29 November 1992, Calendar section, 7, 58, 59.

Hill, Julie Skur. "Coke Teaches the World to Vote for Music Videos." *Advertising Age,* 27 October 1986, 3.

Hirschorn, Michael. "Why MTV Matters." *Esquire,* October 1990, 90.

"A Hit Is a Hit Is a Hit." Unsigned editorial. *Billboard,* 24 December 1983, 12.

"Hit Parade." *Time,* 5 November 1984, 55.

Hofmeister, Sallie. "Rifts Shake and Rattle Warner Music." *New York Times,* 1 November 1994, D1, D22.

Hoineff, Nelson. "Music Video Growing in Brazil; Local Production Is Starting Up." *Variety,* 3 October 1984, 103–104.

Holden, Stephen. "Signs of Intelligent Life in Music Television." *New York Times,* 30 October 1988, sec. 2, p. 26

———. "The Pop Life." *New York Times,* 3 January 1990, C18.

———. "Strike the Pose: When Music Is Skin Deep." *New York Times,* 5 August 1990, H1, H21.

———. "Madonna Video Goes Too Far for MTV." *New York Times,* 28 November 1990, C13.

———. "Big Stars, Big Bucks and the Big Gamble." *New York Times,* 24 March 1991, sec. 2, H25–H26.

———. "Madonna Makes a $60 Million Deal." *New York Times,* 20 April 1992, C11, C16.

Holland, Bill. "U.S. Continues Look at MTV." *Billboard,* 20 October 1984, 1, 72.

———. "NAB President Speaks Out on 'Porn Rock.'" *Billboard,* 1 June 1985, 6, 77.

———. "Music Business Urges Congress to Adapt Performance Right." *Billboard,* 3 April 1993, 6, 99.

———. "Bureaucracy, Legalities Slow FCC's Regulation of Indecency." *Billboard,* 25 June 1994, 1, 105.

Holland, Bill, and Deborah Russell, "Will Justice Dept. Prove Tough for Majors?" *Billboard,* 1 August 1994, 4, 83.

"Homevid Execs Wary of Musical Genre." *Variety,* 14 March 1984, 75.

Horn, Miriam. "Torching Television Violence (Heh Heh)." *U.S. News & World Report,* 27 December 1993, 91.

"Houston's TV5 Has 'Community Touch.'" *Billboard,* 5 October 1985, 33.

"How MTV Has Rocked Television Commercials." *New York Times,* 9 October 1989, D6.

"How MTV Plays Around the World." *New York Times.* 7 July 1991, sec. 2 H22.

Huff, Richard. "MTV Is Planning to Divide and Conquer." *Variety,* 5 August 1991, 37.

————. "MTV & FOX Seek Talent, Develop Shows." *Variety,* 11 May 1992, 60.

Hunt, Dennis, and Daniel Cerone. "MTV's Big Surprise. Network Scores a TV Wallop with Pee-Wee." *Los Angeles Times,* 7 September 1991, F1, F9.

Hunter, Nigel. "U.K. Sets Vidclip Content Standards." *Billboard,* 5 August 1989, 56.

"Indecency 'Safe Harbor' Invalid, Court Rules." *News Media and the Law* 18 (Winter 1994): 42–43.

"Indecent Broadcasts Lead to F.C.C. Fines on 4 Radio Stations." *New York Times,* 27 October 1989, B6.

Ivany, John Shelton. "Lowering the Boom on Heavy Metal." *Billboard,* July 6, 1985, 10.

Jaffee, Larry. "An Operator to Run VH-1." *Cablevision,* 8 May 1989, 16.

————. "MTV to Stand for Merchandise TV?" *Billboard,* 28 January 1995, 43, 44.

Jeffrey, Don. "MTV Networks Boosts Viacom." *Billboard,* 4 November 1989, 9, 82.

————. "Mixed Results for Viacom." *Billboard,* 9 March 1991, 92.

————. "MTV Networks Sees Profits Rise by 48%." *Billboard,* 18 May 1991, 98.

————. "Study: Slower Growth in Spending on Music." *Billboard,* 13 July 1991, 8, 89.

————. "MTV Nets Plugs into Profit." *Billboard,* 17 August 1991, 70.

————. "Viacom Posts Loss Despite MTV Nets Gain." *Billboard,* 16 November 1991, 93.

————. "VJN Cites Slow Growth, High Costs in Loss." *Billboard,* 30 November 1991, 32, 34.

————. "Rumor of MTV Making Public Offer Persists." *Billboard,* 14 March 1992, 11, 98.

————. "Indie-Major Romances and Marriages." *Billboard,* 21 March 1992, I-6, I-32.

————. "MTV Networks Reports Rise in 1st-Qtr. Revenues, Profits." *Billboard,* 23 May 1992, 38.

————. "Joint Project from Jive, New Line Poses 'Menace' to Society." *Billboard,* 24 April 1993, 47.

————. "MTV Networks' Revenues Up for 1st Quarter." *Billboard,* 15 May 1993, 90.

————. "MTV Says 2nd Quarter Revenues Up." *Billboard,* 14 August 1993, 67.

————. "BMG, Cable Co. TCI May Join New Music Venture." *Billboard,* 2 July 1994, 3, 109.

Jeffrey, Don, and Dominic Pride. "Majors Plan to Challenge MTV with Music Video Venture." *Billboard,* 29 January 1994, 5.

Jensen, Jeff. "MTV 'Unplugged.'" *Advertising Age,* 5 July 1993, S–21.

"Joe Jackson Puts down Video, Contending It Has Hurt Music." *Variety,* 13 June 1984, 1.

Joseph, Regina, and Alan Goldsand. "Newsweek and MTV Axis Caps a Multimedia Flurry." *Mediaweek,* 14 October 1991, 3.

"Jury Finds Vendor Guilty of Selling 'Obscene' LP." *Jet,* 22 October 1990, 32.

Kahn, Frank, J., ed. *Documents of American Broadcasting.* 4th ed. Englewood Cliffs, N.J.: Prentice Hall, 1984.

Kahn, Virginia Munger. "Analysts Say Viacom Management Deal Will Fly." *Cablevision,* 13 October 1986, 20, 22.

Kaplan, David, and Debra Rosenberg. "They Want Their MTV Back." *Newsweek,* 20 May 1991, 68.

Kaplan, E. Ann. "History, the Historical Spectator, and Gender Address in Music Television." *Journal of Communication Inquiry* 10 (Winter 1986):3–14.

————. *Rocking Around the Clock.* New York: Methuen, 1987.

Katz, Rich. "Pay-per-view Music Videos: Will Viewers Ante Up to Play Them?" *Channels of Communication,* January 1989, 16.

Kellner, Douglas. *Television, and the Crisis of Democracy.* Boulder, Colo.: Westview Press, 1990.

Kerr, Peter. "Music Video's Uncertain Payoff." *Billboard,* 29 July 1984, F4.

Kindred, Jack. "MTV-Style Cable Channel Planned for West Germany." *Variety,* 12 October 1983, 87.

Kirby, Kip. "New 24-Hour Vidclip Net Due in December." *Billboard,* 4 August 1984, 1, 62.

———. "It's Turner's Turn for Cable Rocker." *Billboard,* 18 August 1984, 1, 60.

———. "Indie Label 'Risk Takers' Discuss the Search for Alternative Clip Outlets." *Billboard,* 15 December 1984, 35.

———. "Hollywood Finally Flashes That Proud Soundtrack Smile." *Billboard,* 23 November 1985, VM6, VM11, VM13, VM15.

———. "Video Music Conference." *Billboard,* 21 December 1985, 25.

Kleber, Merritt B. "Label Clip Execs Not Racist." *Billboard,* 16 July 1988, 9, 68.

Kleinfield, N. R. "Barefoot in the Loft: A Real New York Study." *New York Times,* 22 March 1992, sec. 2, pp. 33, 42.

Kneale, Dennis. "Weirder Is Better in the Red-Hot Land of the Rock Videos." *Wall Street Journal,* 17 October 1983, 1, 19.

———. "MTV's Game Show Tries to Be Dumb, and Fully Succeeds." *Wall Street Journal,* 11 August 1989, A1, A8.

Knoedelseder, William K. Jr. "MTV's Stock Sales Snag on a State Law." *Los Angeles Times,* 4 September 1984, pt. 4, pp. 1, 2.

———. "MTV Goes Global." *Los Angeles Times,* 18 December 1988, pt. 4, pp. 1, 4.

"Konowitch Reassigned at MTV." *Variety,* 24 February 1992, 263.

Kozak, Roman. "Warner Amex MTV: Debuting New Music." *Billboard,* 22 August 1981, 12.

———. "Top Video Producers Put the Spotlight on Creativity." *Billboard,* 18 December 1982, 46.

Krewen, Nick, and Larry LeBlanc. "Budgets Challenge Canada's Directors." *Billboard,* 21 March 1992, 52–53.

"Kuhn Named Head of Video Production Arm at RCA Records." *Variety,* 18 January 1984, 91, 93.

Landler, Mark. "I Want My MTV—Stock." *Business Week,* 18 May 1992, 55.

———. "Will MTV Have to Share the Stage?" *Business Week,* 21 February 1994, 38.

Landler, Mark, and Geoffrey Smith. "The MTV Tycoon." *Business Week,* 21 September 1992, 56–62.

Landro, Laura. "Warner Unit's MTV Plans Public Offering, Signs Video Accords." *Wall Street Journal,* 15 June 1984, 10.

Langenberg, Amy. "Hey, Look Me Over." *Adweek,* 2 April 1990, 38.

Lannert, John. "New Shows Serve Burgeoning Hispanic Youth Market." *Billboard,* 14 September 1991, 79.

———. "21 Countries Plugged for MTV Latino Debut." *Billboard,* 2 October 1993, 8, 55.

———. "Labels Assess Impact of MTV Latino." *Billboard,* 2 July 1994, 6, 94.

LaPointe, Kirk. "Canada 'MTV' Plans Presented." *Billboard,* 11 February 1984, 3.

———. "CHUM to Offer Canadian 'MTV.'" *Billboard,* 14 April 1984, 3, 61.

———. "New Music Channel Hits Snag." *Billboard,* 23 June 1984, 65.

———. "MTV Deals Haunt Much Music." *Billboard,* 8 September 1984, 58.

———. "MuchMusic Network Enjoying MuchSuccess." *Billboard,* 2 September 1989, 67.

Lawren, Bill. "Calling Dr. MTV." *Omni,* February 1994, 32.

Lee, Martin A., and Norman Solomon. *Unreliable Sources.* New York: Carol Publishing, 1992.

Leland, John, and Marc Peyser. "Searching for Nirvana II." *Newsweek,* 30 March 1992, 62–63.

Lenin, V. I. *Imperialism, the Highest State of Capitalism.* New York: International, 1917.

Leo, John. "The Seven Video Sins." *U.S. News & World Report,* 23 August 1993, 19.

Lev, Michael. "MTV Contests: The Odder the Better." *New York Times,* 12 June 1989, D12.

Levenson, Jeff. "BET to Bow Jazz Network." *Billboard,* 2 October 1993, 8, 55.

Levin, Mike. "Satellites Bring MTV Asia Home." *Billboard,* 3 April 1993, 40, 44.

———. "MTV Asia in Limbo Over Cantopop Vids." *Billboard,* 6 November 1993, 56.

———. "MTV Asia Debuts Mandarin Video Chart." *Billboard,* 13 November 1993, 48.

———. "Majors Take 50% Stake in STAR TV's V Music Channel." *Billboard,* 14 January 1995, 6, 77.

———. "MTV Reveals New Asia Chief, Plans for Two Services." *Billboard,* 18 February 1995, 6.

Levine, Jonathan B., and Mark Landler. "Cable Has a New Frontier: The Old World." *Business Week,* 28 June 1993, 74.

LeVlanc, Larry. "Diverse Programming Adds up for Quebec's MusiquePlus." *Billboard,* 18 April 1992, 36, 40.

Levy, Steven. "Ad Nauseam: How MTV Sells out Rock and Roll." *Rolling Stone,* 8 December 1983, 30–34, 37, 74–78.

Lieberman, David. "Now Playing: The Sound of Money." *Business Week,* 15 August 1988, 86–90.

———. "Is Viacom Ready to Channel the World?" *Business Week,* 18 October 1989, 72–74.

———. "Take My Comedy Programming, Please." *Business Week,* 18 October 1989, 73.

"Lights! Camera! Playback!" *Canadian Composer,* December 1989, 20, 22, 40.

Lipman, Joanne. "MTV Style Abandoned by Many Shops." *Wall Street Journal,* 12 February 1991, B6.

Lippert, Barbara. "Pepsi's Prayer Answered by Madonna's Pop Imagery." *Adweek,* 6 March 1989, 79.

Lippman, John. "MTV Will Split into 3 Cable Channels." *Los Angeles Times,* 31 July 1991, D1, D3.

Livingston, Guy. "Boston Music-Video Outlet Going Heavy on Local Shows in Evening." *Variety,* 21 May 1986, 90.

"Local Stations Are Offering 24-Hour Music Video." *New York Times,* 4 September 1984, C19.

Love, Robert. "'Washington Wives' Set Their Sights on Video." *Rolling Stone,* 10 October 1985, 18.

Mabry, Donald J. "The Rise and Fall of Ace Records: A Case Study in the Independent Record Business." *Business History Review,* Autumn 1990, 411–450.

"Madonna's 'Like a Prayer' Clip Causes a Controversy." *Rolling Stone,* 20 April 1989, 22.

Magiera, Marcy. "MTV Has Shoe Biz Tie." *Advertising Age,* 4 September 1989, 8.

———. "Cutting New Tracks. Record Labels Promote Albums with Paid Media." *Advertising Age,* 28 October 1991, 54.

Marion, Jane. "The Night Belongs to Janet." *TV Guide,* 1 September 1990, 4–5.

Martel, Jay. "The Perils of Pauly: Weazin' Buff Nugs and Chillin' with MTV's Pauly Shore, the Star of Encino Man." *Rolling Stone,* 9–23 July 1992, 54–57.

Marx, Karl, and Frederick Engels. *Selected Works.* London: Lawrence & Wishart, 1968.

Mathews, Jay. "'Toy Gun' Cop Targets MTV Videos." *San Francisco Chronicle,* 26 December 1994, E1–E3.

"Maxwell Sells MTV Stake." *Los Angeles Times,* 21 August 1991, D2.

"Maxwell to Sell Stake in MTV." *New York Times,* 21 August 1991, D17.

Mayfield, Geoff. "Music Video: The Picture Brightens." *Billboard,* 15 October 1988, 1, 80.

McAdams, Janine C. "Clips Are Key to Motown Renewal." *Billboard,* 21 January 1989, 62.

———. "Black Directors: Talent Pool Waiting to Be Tapped." *Billboard,* 8 April 1989, 53, 55.

———. "Local Black Outlets Cater to Hometown Tastes." *Billboard,* 1 July 1989, 34, 36.

———. "BET in the '90's—Giving Viewers Even More of a Choice in the Decade of Diversity." *Billboard,* 22 September 1990, BET-2, BET-8.

———. "'Mandela Is Coming' in Music Video." *Billboard,* 2 March 1991, 62.

———. "Focus on African-American Music." *Billboard,* 29 June 1991, 48–49.

———. "Millicent Shelton Blazes a Trail as Video Director." *Billboard,* 6 June 1992, 37.

———. "R&B Women Clear Historical Hurdle." *Billboard,* 3 April 1993, 1, 95.

———. "EastWest Touts Snow for All Seasons." *Billboard,* 24 April 1993, 12.

———. "'Real' Sound Keeps Levert Fresh." *Billboard,* 24 April 1993, 16–17.

———. "Not the Same Old Song. Majors Respond to R&B Surge with Specialists and Talent Sweeps." *Billboard,* 8 May 1993, M14–M16.

———. "Stronger Mktg. Impact Felt at This Year's Meet." *Billboard,* 8 May 1993, 20–21.

McAdams, Janine, and Bruce Haring. "NAACP Is on the Brink of CBS Boycott." *Billboard,* 24 February 1990, 5, 95.

McChesney, Robert W. "Critical Communication Research at the Crossroads." *Defining Media Studies,* eds. Mark R. Levy, and Michael Gurevitch. New York: Oxford University Press, 1994, 340–346.

McClure, Steve. "Plug Pulled on 'MTV Japan' Program." *Billboard,* 29 June 1991, 5.

———. "New Joint Venture Aims to Bring Japan Its MTV Again." *Billboard,* 4 January 1992, 32.

———. "Japan Getting 'Music Channel.'" *Billboard,* 2 May 1992, 52.

———. "MTV's Japanese Licensee Sets Sights on Winning More Viewers." *Billboard,* 29 October 1994, 52, 54.

McCormick, Moira. "Producers Hold Creative Keys in Struggle to Make Music Video a Happy Medium." *Billboard,* 23 November 1985, VM6, VM20.

———. "Wild West." *Billboard,* 23 November 1985, VM4, VM16.

———. "Local Black Outlets Cater to Hometown Tastes." *Billboard,* 1 July 1989, 34, 36.

———. "Sound Scan: Boon or Bane for Indies?" *Billboard,* 21 March 1992, I-4, I-28.

McCullaugh, Jim. "Nesmith's Pacific Arts Preps for Coming Videodisk Market." *Billboard,* 1 March 1980, 33.

———. "Cable Channel Seen Helping Record Sales." *Billboard,* 14 March 1981, 1, 80.

———. "MTV Cable Spurs Disk Sales of Artists Aired." *Billboard,* 10 October 1981, 1, 68.

———. "Ground-Breaking Still in Progress but . . . The Video Show Must Go On." *Billboard,* 23 November 1985, VM3.

———. "Paramount to 'Rattle' Sell-Through with U2 Vid." *Billboard,* 21 January 1989, 51.

———. "LIVE Aiding L.A. Vid Stores with Free Copies of Tapes." *Billboard,* 13 June 1992, 10.

McGowan, Chris. "Label Connection: Breakout Power Still the Single Most Persuasive Argument for Improving Video Ties." *Billboard,* 21 November 1987, V3, V6.

————. "Music Video." *Billboard,* 15 April 1988, M1, M8.

————. "The Night Tracks Story—from the Beginning." Advertising supplement. *Billboard,* 4 June 1988, N1–N17.

————. "Music Video on TV: From Youth to Middle Age in Seven Years?" *Billboard,* 12 November 1988, V1, V5.

————. "Record Companies: Realistic Marketing, Budding Catalogs Help Music Video Come Alive at Retail." *Billboard,* 12 November 1988, V4, V9.

————. "The Spreading Market: Music Industry Feels New Presence Building in Record Stores." *Billboard,* 12 November 1988, V1, V8.

————. "The New Strength of Independent Distribution." *Billboard,* 11 March 1989, I-3, I-22.

————. "Billboard Spotlight on Music Video." *Billboard,* 15 April 1989, M1, M8.

————. "Format Explosion: The Shape—and Size—of Music Video to Come." *Billboard,* 15 April 1989, M6, M8, M15–M16.

————. "Music Titles Lure Buyers to CDV." *Billboard,* 15 April 1989, 58, 61.

————. "The Shape of Music Video to Come: It's a Two-Format Universe in '91." *Billboard,* 11 May 1991, MV4.

McGuigan, Cathleen. "Rock Music Goes Hollywood." *Newsweek,* 11 March 1985, 78.

————. "Soft Rock and Hard Talk." *Newsweek,* 15 July 1985, 51.

McLane, Daisann. "No Julio Allowed." *New York Times,* 7 July 1991, sec. 2, H22.

McManus, John. "P&G Nears $50M MTV Cable Buy." *Advertising Age,* 21 May 1990, 3, 57.

McNeil, Alex. *Total Television.* New York: Penguin, 1984.

Meehan, Eileen R., Vincent Mosco, and Janet Wasko. "Rethinking Political Economy: Change and Continuity." *Defining Media Studies,* eds. Mark R. Levy and Michael Gurevitch. New York: Oxford University Press, 1994, 347–358.

Meyer, Michael. "OK Sumner, Take That!" *Newsweek,* 1 November 1993, 47.

Meyer, Michael, and Nancy Hass. "Simon Says, 'Out!'" *Newsweek,* 27 June 1994, 42–44.

"Michael Jackson Co-Directs Music Film, 'In the Closet.'" *Jet,* 27 April 1992, 56, 57.

Mifflin, Margot. "The Auteur Theory of Music Video Means No More Pretty Cliches." *Billboard,* 20 January 1991, sec. 2, pp. H28, H37.

Miliband, Ray. *Marxism and Politics.* London: Oxford University Press, 1977.

Millard, Bob. "Country Music Video Budgets Rise as More Outlets Open." *Variety,* 14 March 1984, 74.

Miller, Kenneth M. "Video Giant Wants Its MTV." *Rolling Stone,* 10 October 1985, 12.

Miller, Stuart. "MTV Wants Its Collegiate Crowd." *Variety,* 20 May 1991, 27.

Miller, Trudi. "How Indies Survive Star Departures." *Billboard,* 21 March 1992, I-6, I-22.

Miller v. California. 413 U.S. 15 (1973).

"Missing Kids Video Planned." *Advertising Age,* 12 August 1985, 47.

Mitchell, Elvis. "Video Valium: The VH-1 Experience." *Village Voice,* 4 June 1985, 39.

————. "Monkee Business." *Channels of Communication,* May 1986, 8, 12.

Mitchell, Tony. "Treaty Now! Indigenous Music and Music Television in Australia." *Media, Culture and Society,* vol. 15 1993, 299–308.

Monet, Jack. "French Ante Frances for Vidclips; Nurturing Hikes Homegrown Fare." *Variety,* 3 October 1984, 103.

Monsco, Pat. "U.S. Vid Programmers Ready to Accept Broadcast Payments; Europeans Already Used to It." *Variety,* 2 October 1985, 141, 148.

Moore, Frazier. "More Sound for Less." *Channels of Communication,* July/August 1989, 72.

Morgan, Timothy C. "Sloth, Avarice, and MTV." *Christianity Today,* 4 October 1993, 14–15.

Morgenson, Gretchen. "Look Who's Coming to Dinner." *Forbes,* 1 March 1993, 104–105.

Morris, Chris. "California Is Latest State to Ponder Lip-Syncing Bill." *Billboard,* 22 December 1990, 14.

———. "Music-Biz Coalition Plans Suit Over Wash. 'Erotic' Bill." *Billboard,* 20 June 1992, 7, 97.

Morris, Chris, Bill Holland, Charlene Orr, Paul Verna, and Ed Christman. "Quayle, Congressmen, L.A. Pols Join 'Cop Killer' Posse." *Billboard,* 4 July 1992, 1, 83.

Morris, Chris, Irv Lictman, and Melinda Newman. "Staff Cuts Deep at Chrysalis, EMI, SBK Labels." *Billboard,* 14 December 1991, 1, 79.

Morris, Edward. "Country Acts Find Non-Radio Routes to Fame." *Billboard,* 17 February 1990, 1, 43.

———. "Country Acts Going Prime-Time on NBC." *Billboard,* 26 October 1991, 5.

———. "Country Vids Expanding Horizons, Aristo Says." *Billboard,* 16 November 1991, 37.

———. "Music Videoclips Are Redefining Country." *Billboard,* 13 June 1992, 29.

———. "CMA Asks Canada to Keep U.S. Country Show on TV." *Billboard,* 12 November 1994, 30.

———. "Citing NAFTA, CMT Takes Action to Stay in Canada." *Billboard,* 7 January 1995, 24.

———. "Exiled from Canada, CMT Begins Boycott." *Billboard,* 21 January 1995, 31.

———. "New Vid Network on Air in Canada; Replaces CMT." *Billboard,* 21 January 1995, 34.

———. "CMT Boycott Fuels More Accusations." *Billboard,* 28 January 1995, 35.

Morse, Margaret. "Postsynchronizing Rock Music and Television." *Journal of Communication Inquiry* 10 (Winter 1986):15–28.

Mosco, Vincent. "Introduction." *The Critical Communications Review, Volume 1: Labor, the Working Class, and the Media,* eds. Vincent Mosco, and Janet Wasko. Norwood, N.J.: Ablex, 1983, ix–xxviii.

Moshavi, Sharon D. "MTV: Moving with the Music." *Broadcasting,* 2 July 1990, 39–40.

———. "ABC, Viacom Sign Deal to Air Same TV Sitcom." *Broadcasting,* 3 June 1991, 33–34.

———. "ABC Gets Cable Friendlier." *Broadcasting,* 17 June 1991, 45–46.

———. "MTV Announces Its Move to Multiplexing." *Broadcasting,* 5 August 1991, 39–40.

———. "MTV Sues Worldvision Over Hanna-Barbera." *Broadcasting,* 21 October 1991, 30.

———. "MTV Said to Consider Infomercial Channel." *Broadcasting,* 27 January 1992, 31.

———. "Kid Vid." *Forbes,* 7 June 1993, 124.

Motavalli, John. "MTV Sees Low Cost Programming Ingenuity as Key to Sustaining High Profitability." *Cablevision,* 15 September 1986, 26.

"MTV: 1981–1986." Advertising supplement. *Billboard,* 2 August 1986, MTV1–MTV14.

"MTV Announces Its Move to Multiplexing." *Broadcasting,* 5 August 1991, 39, 40.

"MTV Europe Open to Broader Range." *Variety,* 3 February 1988, 145.

"MTV Europe Stake Is Sold." *New York Times,* 13 February 1990, D20.

"MTV Fights Fire with No Fire." *Broadcasting and Cable,* 18 October 1993, 22–23.

"MTV Files Suit over Turner Deal." *Mediaweek,* 21 October 1991, 35.

"MTV Goes to Russia." *Wall Street Journal,* 12 October 1990, B4.
"MTV International." Advertising supplement. *Billboard,* 31 August 1991, 28.
"MTV Moves 'Beavis and Butt-head,'" *Broadcasting and Cable,* 25 October 1993, 29.
MTV Networks. Form 10-K to the U.S. Securities and Exchange Commission (SEC) for the fiscal year ending December 31, 1984.
"MTV Plans 3 Channels." *New York Times,* 31 July 1991, D6.
"MTV Profit $4.5 Million." *New York Times,* 6 February 1985, D18.
"MTV Restored in Several Areas." *New York Times,* 21 March 1992, 28.
"MTV Rumors Affect Viacom." *New York Times,* 24 March 1992, D4.
"MTV's Decade." Unsigned editorial. *Wall Street Journal,* 15 December 1989, A10.
"MTV Service Enters Music Stores." *Advertising Age,* 16 December 1991, 8.
"MTV's Impact at Retail and Radio." *Billboard,* 16 April 1983, 63.
"MTV's New Service Offers an Integrated Musical Mix." *Billboard,* 19 January 1985, 51, 54.
"MTV's Rejection of Madonna Video Smacks of Censorship." *The Advocate,* 19 January 1991, 72.
"MTV to Be in 4½–5 Mil Homes: Lack." *Billboard,* 10 October 1981, 68, 82.
"MTV Turns Ten." *Rolling Stone,* 12–26 December 1991, 71.
Mundy, Chris. "Trouble in Paradise. Violence Erupts After MTV Event in New Jersey." *Rolling Stone,* 6 August 1992, 16.
Mungo, Paul. "British Take Lead in Video Production." *Variety,* 14 March 1984, 71, 74.
Murdock, Graham. "Large Corporations and the Control of Communication Industries." In *Culture, Society and the Media,* ed. Michael Gurevitch, Tony Bennett, James Curran, and Janet Woollacott. London: Methuen, 1982, 118–150.
Murdock, Graham, and Peter Golding. "For a Political Economy of Mass Communications." In *The Socialist Register 1973,* ed. Ralph Miliband, and John Saville. London: Merlin Press, 1974, 205–234.
———. "Capitalism, Communication and Class Relations." In *Mass Communication and Society,* ed. James Curran, Michael Gurevitch, and Janet Woollacott. Beverly Hills: Sage, 1979, 12–43.
Murr, Andrew, and John Schwartz. "Solid Gold for Cold Cash." *Newsweek,* 26 March 1990, 34.
"Music-Biz Blues." *Rolling Stone,* 12–26 December 1991, 64.
"Music Channel Is Shelved." *New York Times,* 7 June 1994, D19.
"Music Video." *Fortune,* 17 September 1984, 167–170.
"Music Video a Syndie Trend: Group W, Viacom and Par Lead Red-Hot Firstrun Strip Parade." *Variety,* 4 April 1984, 47, 74.
"Music Videocassette Sales Aren't Ready to Rock." *Business Week,* 3 September 1984. 58.
"Music Video Directors' Symposium." *Variety,* 14 March 1984, 70, 78, 80, 82, 86, 88.
"Music Video '89: V.I.P. Sell-Through Forum." *Billboard,* 15 April 1988, M4, M12–M13, M16–M19.
"Music Video's Mellower Mood." *Time,* 3 September 1984, 65.
"Must Be Strong, Like Jean-Claude Van Damme." *Rolling Stone,* 29 April 1993, 44–48.
"Mystery Dance." *The Economist,* 22 February 1992, 67.
"NARM Retailers See Sales Strength in Music Video." *Billboard,* 4 November 1989, 9, 91.
Nathan, David. "Underdog Champions the Role of Black Vid Directors." *Billboard,* 30 September 1989, 67.

Neely, Kim. "Backup Singer Sues Abdul Over Vocals." *Rolling Stone,* 30 May 1991, 25.

———. "Nirvana Tops Album Chart." Rolling Stone, 20 February 1992, 15–16.

———. "Clinton: I Want the MTV Vote." *Rolling Stone,* 6 August 1992, 22.

Nelson, Havelock. "Naughty by Nature Takes Its Course." *Billboard,* 27 March 1993, 23.

———. "Ice-T Stages New Aural Invasion." *Billboard,* 17 April 1993, 19.

———. "Run-D.M.C. Back in the Running with Hit Single." *Billboard,* 8 May 1993, 12, 16.

Neuman, Al. "Alternative to MTV Produced in Atlanta." *Downbeat,* June 1990, 53.

Newcomb, Peter. ". . . and only here . . ." *Forbes,* 3 December 1984, 202–204.

———. "Music Video Wars." *Forbes,* 4 March 1991, 68, 70.

———. "Yo, Dude, You're Fired." *Forbes,* 20 January 1992, 18–19.

———. "The Sound of Money." *Forbes,* 11 May 1992, 102.

"New Era Starting with Video Jockeys." *Billboard,* 8 August 1981, 29.

Newman, Melinda. "Public TV Gives New Music a Spin." *Billboard,* 13 May 1989, 53.

———. "Janet's Longform Vid to Follow Album by 1 Month." *Billboard,* 7 October 1989, 6, 67.

———. "MTV Promotes Three in Programming, Creative." *Billboard,* 7 October 1989, 6.

———. "Country Network Rides into Town." *Billboard,* 21 October 1989, 45.

———. "Creativity, Not Cash, Called Crucial to Clips." *Billboard,* 11 November 1989, 63.

———. "MTV Taking a Harder Look at Vids?" *Billboard,* 18 November 1989, 1, 92, 95.

———. "Freston: Let's Shun Cliched Clips." *Billboard,* 2 December 1989, 3, 75.

———. "Hit Video USA Casts an Eye Toward Int'l Market." *Billboard,* 13 January 1990, 49.

———. "More Outlets Added as County Clips Multiply." *Billboard,* 20 January 1990, 62.

———. "MTV Dips Slightly in Nielsen." *Billboard,* 20 January 1990, 62.

———. "TBS Pulls Plug on Metal 'Power Hits' Program." *Billboard,* 3 February 1990, 58.

———. "BET to Reorganize Music Dept." *Billboard,* 24 March 1990, 43.

———. "Vid Channels Gear Up for Summer." *Billboard,* 2 June 1990, 68.

———. "'Light Music' Looks to Mainstream." *Billboard,* 14 July 1990, 32.

———. "VH-1 Unveils 'Greatest Hits' Campaign." *Billboard,* 8 September 1990, 53.

———. "Plug Pulled on Hit Video USA." *Billboard,* 20 October 1990, 10, 85.

———. "Labels Weighing Video Costs vs. Gains." *Billboard,* 10 November 1990, 1, 75.

———. "Banned Madonna Clip to Be Issued as Video Single." *Billboard,* 8 December 1990, 1, 92.

———. "NAACP, Music Vid Assn. Discuss Hiring Issue." *Billboard,* 22 December 1990, 12, 99.

———. "H'wood Records Offers Fresh Approach." *Billboard,* 2 February 1991, 50–51.

———. "The Eye." *Billboard,* 2 February 1991, 50.

———. "GPA Films Expanding to Reel in West Coast Biz." *Billboard,* 9 February 1991, 63.

———. "Vid Outlets Mark Black History Month." *Billboard,* 23 February 1991, 40.

———. "Video Track America to Bow Via New Cable TV System." *Billboard,* 23 February 1991, 40.

———. "The Eye." *Billboard,* 9 March 1991, 62.

———. "Producer/Director Jon Small's Vision of the Music-Video Biz." *Billboard,* 16 March 1991, 39–40.

———. "'Nick Jr. Rocks!' to Roll in Summer." *Billboard,* 23 March 1991, 56–57.

———. "Steve Vai Takes Turn Behind the Camera." *Billboard,* 23 March 1991, 56.

———. "New Directors Step into Limelight." *Billboard,* 6 April 1991, 59–60.

———. "The Eye." *Billboard,* 13 April 1991, 42.

————. "Vidclip Makers See Red in Label Deals." *Billboard*, 20 April 1991, 1, 53.

————. "Warner Bros.' Stevenson Revs Up Video Promotion." *Billboard*, 27 April 1991, 42A–43A.

————. "Desert Music Pix Keeps Options Open." *Billboard*, 11 May 1991, 45–46.

————. "IMPACT: What Was Once a Luxury Is Now a Necessity." *Billboard*, 11 May 1991, MV1, MV8.

————. "Asia to Get Its MTV Via Hong Kong's HutchVision." *Billboard*, 18 May 1991, 8, 98.

————. "Labels Extend Songs' Appeal with Alternative Vids." *Billboard*, 25 May 1991, 48–49.

————. "The Eye." *Billboard*, 15 June 1991, 54.

————. "Radio Vision Rolls out 'Global Jam.'" *Billboard*, 15 June 1991, 54–55.

————. "MTV Making a Splash with New Block Programming." *Billboard*, 22 June 1991, 32.

————. "TCA Cable Dropping MTV, Citing Viewer Complaints." *Billboard*, 6 July 1991, 76.

————. "Lucasfilm Empire Expands to Incorporate Music Video." *Billboard*, 13 July 1991, 47.

————. "'Night Tracks' on Alternative Path." *Billboard*, 20 July 1991, 41.

————. "Several TCA Cable Systems to Get MTV Picture Again." *Billboard*, 27 July 1991, 42, 44.

————. "Do Budget Demands Stifle Creativity?" *Billboard*, 3 August 1991, 60.

————. "Labels Ecstatic Over Idea of MTV 3 Times." *Billboard*, 10 August 1991, 1, 76.

————. "Promoting Vidclips Can Be Academic." *Billboard*, 24 August 1991, 46.

————. "The Reel Story on MTV's Founding Fathers & Mothers." *Billboard*, 31 August 1991, 47–48.

————. "BMG Vid International's Workman Ethic." *Billboard*, 28 September 1991, 53.

————. "There's an 'Other Side' to Callner's Sexy-Vid Image." *Billboard*, 28 September 1991, 51.

————. "Limelight's Video Division Moves Back to Main Office." *Billboard*, 26 October 1991, 54.

————. "MTV Puts R&B in Spotlight with Weekly Video Show." *Billboard*, 26 October 1991, 5, 79.

————. "Rock Chips Fall off Blocks on MTV." *Billboard*, 26 October 1991, 54, 56.

————. "Pam Tarr's Production Co. Does More than Squeak By." *Billboard*, 2 November 1991, 70.

————. "Fox Quick to Jump on Jackson Premieres." *Billboard*, 16 November 1991, 62–63.

————. "Epic Nixes Sale of 11-Minute Jackson Vid." *Billboard*, 30 November 1991, 12.

————. "Vidclip Exposure Soars to New Heights." *Billboard*, 14 December 1991, 38–39.

————. "Growing Pains Aplenty." *Billboard*, 21 December 1991, 47.

————. "The Time & Place for Midnight Films." *Billboard*, 4 January 1992, 27.

————. "4 Towns Lose Their MTV, Get VJN Instead." *Billboard*, 25 January 1992, 6, 86.

————. "MTV Offers New Means of Exposure." *Billboard*, 25 January 1992, 38.

————. "VH-1 Shows Its Stuff with Plans for Original Programs." *Billboard*, 25 January 1992, 38–39.

————. "Channels Cast Eye to Black History." *Billboard*, 15 February 1992, 39.

————. "More Fans Face the Music Via 'USA.'" *Billboard*, 22 February 1992, 43–44.

————. "Andy Morahan Shows Faith in Music Vid." *Billboard*, 7 March 1992, 35–36.

————. "Garth's 'Wind' Prevails Sans Videos." *Billboard*, 14 March 1992, 48–49.

————. "It's the End of the Road for 'Night Tracks' on TBS." *Billboard*, 4 April 1992, 30.

————. "Oil Factory Seeps into New Territories." *Billboard*, 2 May 1992, 50–51.

————. "Propaganda Spreading in Video, Film Arenas." *Billboard*, 9 May 1992, 38–39.

————. "BET Saluting Black Music Month." *Billboard*, 30 May 1992, 36.

————. "Rock the Vote in High Gear with TV, Retail, Tour Drives." *Billboard*, 13 June 1992, 14, 83.

————. "MTV Fires up Box-Office Grosses." *Billboard*, 20 June 1992, 1, 88.

————. "MTV Cans Sports Fests After N.J. Fracas." *Billboard*, 27 June 1992, 3, 79.

————. "MVPA's Electees; Prince's Un-'Sexy M.F.'; Eye's Vid Picks." *Billboard*, 27 June 1992, 34.

————. "Video: A Key Ingredient for R&B Success." *Billboard*, 27 June 1992, R-8.

————. "Carvey to Host Expanded MTV Awards." *Billboard*, 4 July 1992, 31.

————. "Mix-a-Lot Vid Goes to Retail." *Billboard*, 4 July 1992, 88.

————. "Siobhan Barron in Limelight; Ashley Exits CMC; Getting in Sync." *Billboard*, 4 July 1992, 31.

————. "Konowitch, Shore Leaving; MJ's 'Jam' Jells Via Human Touch." *Billboard*, 11 July 1992, 34.

————. "New Titles, Faces at Reorganized MTV." *Billboard*, 11 July 1992, 34.

————. "'Request' Runs with Hits; Endless Addition; Torch Passed to Bennett." *Billboard*, 18 July 1992, 37.

————. "'Unplugged' Sets Making Sparks at Retail." *Billboard*, 18 July 1992, 8, 75.

————. "Outlets Display Conventional Wisdom; 'Bohemia' Rhapsodies." *Billboard*, 25 July 1992, 33.

Newman, Melinda, and Larry LeBlanc. "Budgets Challenge Canada's Directors." *Billboard*, 21 March 1992, 52–53.

Newman, Melinda, and Janine McAdams. "NAACP: Let's Give Minorities More Music-Vid Work." *Billboard*, 15 December 1990, 1, 83.

————. "BET Pressures Labels to Curb MTV Exclusives." *Billboard*, 25 July 1991, 1, 42, 43.

Newman, Melinda, and Jim McCullaugh. "MTV Fires up Box-Office Grosses." *Billboard*, 20 June 1992, 1, 88.

Newman, Melinda, and Edward Morris. "Music Row Summit Probes Video-Radio Synergy." *Billboard*, 13 June 1992, 38, 40.

Newman, Melinda, and Phyllis Stark. "Jukebox Network Building Strong Rep as Maker of Hits." *Billboard*, 30 March 1991, 5, 125.

Nichols, Peter. "Will Iraq Rock and Singapore Swing?" *New York Times*, 7 July 1991, H22.

Nightline. Transcript of May 13, 1983, episode.

"No Longer Just Promo Fodder, Music Videos Open Prods.' Eyes to New Type of Playoff, Payoff." *Variety*, 14 March 1984, 71.

Nonglows, Paul. "Wall Street Plugs in to Viacom." *Variety*, 23 August 1993, 29.

Norris, Floyd. "Viacom Avoiding 'Leveraged' Label." *New York Times*, 30 April 1990, D6.

Nunziata, Susan. "Recording Studios Feel Budget Pinch." *Billboard*, 12 January 1991, 1, 69.

Occiogrosso, Peter. "Video Dreams: MTV Goes to the Movies." *Village Voice*, 31 July 1984, 36, 37, 87.

On Cable, 23 January 1985, 1, 31, 61.

"On the Flipside: Trouble in Music-Video Land." *Broadcasting,* 10 February 1986, 53, 56, 58.

Orr, Charlene, Tom Duffy, Susan Nunziata, and Chris Morris. "Texas Police Pursue 'Cop Killer.'" *Billboard,* 27 June 1992, 1, 79.

Paige, Earl. "Video Distributors Moving into Music." *Billboard,* 4 March 1989, 3, 57.

Palmer, Rhonda. "Asia to Get Its MTV, Courtesy HK's Star-TV." *Variety,* 20 May 1991, 31.

———. "MTV Sets Its Sights on Asia's Biggest Star." *Variety,* 5–11 September 1994, 52.

Pareles, Jon. "Pop Record Business Shows Signs of Recovery." *New York Times,* 28 November 1983, C13.

———. "MTV Makes Changes to Stop Ratings Slump." *New York Times,* 12 June 1986, C21.

———. "Rock Video Refocuses on the Music." *New York Times,* 23 August 1987, 20.

———. "A Political Song That Casts Its Vote for the Money." *New York Times,* 6 March 1988, sec. 2, p. 32.

———. "Young vs. MTV: A Case of Modest Revenge." *New York Times,* 14 August 1988, 26.

———. "After Music Videos, All the World Has Become a Screen." *New York Times,* 10 December 1989, sec. 4, p. 6.

———. "Louisiana Bill Would Require Warnings on Recordings." *New York Times,* 7 July 1990, 16.

———. "Tot-Rock: A Mini-Boom in Pop Music." *New York Times,* 30 September 1990, H1, H32.

———. "Sex, Lies and the Trouble with Videotapes." *New York Times,* 2 June 1991, H31, H40.

———. "As MTV Turns 10, Pop Goes the World." *New York Times,* 7 July 1991, sec. 2, pp. 1, 19.

———. "MTV Aims to Startle at Its Awards, and Does." *New York Times,* 7 September 1991, 48.

Parenti, Michael. *Inventing Reality: The Politics of News Media,* 2nd ed. New York: St. Martin's Press, 1993.

Park, Aloma H. "Regulation of Music Videos: Should the FCC 'Beat It?'" *Computer Law Journal,* Summer 1988, 287–310.

Patterson, Gregory A., and Christina Duff. "Five Music Companies Face Inquiry into Plans to Begin Video Channel in '95." *Wall Street Journal,* 25 July 1994, B4.

Patterson, Rob. "Clips Sell—but How Much?" *Billboard,* 29 October 1983, 48, 51.

"Paula Abdul Says Album Was Solely Her Effort." *San Francisco Chronicle,* 28 July 1993, E3.

Peers, Martin. "Blockbuster Set to Face the Music." *Variety,* 22–28 May 1995, 1, 16, 110.

Pendleton, Jennifer. "Chalk up Another Victory for Trend-Setting Rock 'n' Roll." *Advertising Age,* 9 November 1988, 160.

———. "Hollywood Buys the Concept." *Advertising Age,* 9 November 1988, 158, 160.

Peterson-Lewis, Sonya, and Shirley A. Chennault. "Black Artists' Music Videos: Three Success Strategies." *Journal of Communication* 36 (Winter 1986):107–114.

Pettigrew, Jim Jr. "Atlanta Meet 'Faces the Music.'" *Billboard,* 14 May 1983, 53, 56.

Pfeffer, J., and G. R. Salancik. *External Control of Organizations: A Resource Dependence Perspective.* New York: Harper & Row, 1978.

Philips, Chuck. "Mega Contracts Still Alive for Madonna, Stones." *Los Angeles Times,* 19 November 1991, F1, F9.

Pittman, Robert. In "Letters" column. *Rolling Stone,* 23 May 1985, 2.

"PMI's Clip Strategy: Multiple Use." *Billboard,* 3 November 1984, 42.

Polskin, Howard. "You Can Win a Pink House—or a Camel Ride in Egypt with Tom Petty." *TV Guide,* 5 December 1987, 13.

"Polygram, RCA/Columbia Promote Videos on MTV." *Variety,* 3 October 1984, 103.

Pond, Steve. "The Industry in the Eighties." *Rolling Stone,* 15 November 1990, 113–117.

———. "Raitt Keeps the Faith." *Rolling Stone,* 8 August 1991, 15–16.

"Pop Charts." *San Francisco Sunday Examiner and Chronicle.* 25 December 1994, Datebook section, 42.

Potts, Mark. "MTV Hoping Its Stock Will Be 'Thriller' for Investors." *Washington Post,* 8 July 1984, G1, G4, G5.

———. "2 More Music Channels Planned." *Washington Post,* 10 August 1984, E1, E2.

———. "Pacts of MTV, Record Firms Probed." *Washington Post,* 10 October 1984, C1, C4.

Powell, Rachel. "Making the Jump from MTV to the Retail Shelves." *New York Times,* 21 April 1991, sec. 3, p. F4.

Price, Deborah E. "Christian Music Vid Beginning to Spread Its Wings." *Billboard,* 18 May 1991, 58–59.

Pride, Dominic. "MTV Europe on the Move." *Billboard,* 31 July 1993, 8, 58.

———. "MTV Europe Sues Majors in Battle over Video Rights." *Billboard,* 21 August 1993, 6, 16.

Pride, Dominic, and Melinda Newman. "MTV Deal Marks Strategy Shift for Sony." *Billboard,* 12 November 1994, 5, 117.

"Prince Gives His Fans Double Delight with Two Versions of Video." *Jet,* 27 April 1992, 65.

Prince, Greg, and Marty Fredericks. "Music Makes TV Hits! Video Rockwaves Quake the Tube." *Billboard,* 23 November 1985, VM3, VM7, VM9.

Ptacek, Greg. "Majors Return to Nuts and Bolts of Pre-MTV Metal Marketing Days." *Billboard,* 27 April 1985, HM3, HM15.

Puterbaugh, Parke. "Concert-611 Blues! Long, Cold Summer." *Rolling Stone,* 15 September 1983, 45, 53.

"Radio May Not Be Watching, but It Is Listening . . ." *Billboard,* 15 April 1989, M6.

"Recorded Music Sales Rose Almost 4% in '91; Unit Sales Fell 7.5%." *Wall Street Journal,* 20 March 1992, B10.

"Record Labels Pay for Cinema Run of Vidclips." *Variety,* 22 February 1984, 1, 109.

Reibman, Greg. "New Kids Sue Over Allegations of Vocal Fakery." *Billboard,* 22 February 1992, 12, 87.

Ressner, Jeffrey. "To Sticker or Not to Sticker . . ." *Rolling Stone,* 7 February 1991, 17.

Reynolds, Simon. "Translating MTV into English." *New York Times,* 7 July 1991, H22.

Richmond, Ray. "'Spoken Word' Is Pure Poetry on MTV." *San Francisco Chronicle,* 28 July 1993, E1–E2.

Ricks, Thomas E. "Turner Broadcasting Is Ready to Close Music Channel, Sell Some Assets to MTV." *Wall Street Journal,* 29 November 1984, 6.

Rimassa, Milena Balandzich. "Act Longevity Comes First, Attorneys Agree." *Billboard,* 19 December 1981, 54.

Roach, Colleen. "The Movement for a New World Information and Communication Order: A Second Wave?" *Media, Culture and Society* 12 (1990):283–307.

Roberts, Johnnie L. "Are They Jackin' the Box?" *Newsweek,* 23 January 1995, 42, 43.

Robertshaw, Nick. "European Vidclips Aim at U.S." *Billboard,* 1 September 1984, 3.

————. "Pact Clears MTV for Europe." *Billboard,* 25 April 1987, 5, 86.

————. "Clip Income Remains Ill-defined." *Billboard,* 13 June 1987, 47, 48.

Robichaux, Mark. "MTV Is Playing a New Riff: Responsibility." *Wall Street Journal,* 9 February 1993, B1, B8.

————. "It's a Book! A T-Shirt! A Toy! No, Just MTV Trying to Be Disney." *Wall Street Journal,* 8 February 1995, A1, A9.

Robins, J. Max. "A Baby-Boom Makeover." *Channels of Communication,* May 1989, 26.

————. "Into the Groove." *Channels of Communication,* May 1989, 22–23, 25–26, 28–29.

————. "MTV News Hits Skid Row." *Channels of Communication,* 23 April 1990, 15.

————. "MTV Gives War a Chance." *Variety,* 25 February 1991, 1, 269.

————. "MTV Unbuttons Resources." *Variety,* 10 June 1991, 28.

————. "Blue-Chip Ad Buyers Want Their MTV (News)." *Variety,* 29 June 1992, 1, 86.

————. "Reality TV: Politics Rates." *Variety,* 26 October 1992, 21–22.

————. "MTV Hitches Ride on Bubba's Bandwagon." *Variety,* 18 January 1993, 1, 97.

————. "New Music Net on Rocky Road." *Variety,* 25–31 July 1994, 24.

Robinson, Deanna Campbell, Elizabeth B. Buck, Marlene Cuthbert, and the International Communication and Youth Consortium. *Music at the Margins: Popular Music and Global Cultural Diversity.* Beverly Hills, Calif.: Sage Publications, 1991.

Roblin, Andrew. "Cable Show Boycotting Two Labels' Vidclips." *Billboard,* 25 August 1984, 4.

————. "Study on Violence Endorsed." *Billboard,* 12 January 1985, 32.

————. "New Ploys from Clip Jukebox Firms." *Billboard,* 23 February 1985, 32, 34.

————. "Antichrist Cooled Down for MTV Debut." *Billboard,* 4 May 1985, 37.

"Rock 'n' Roll Is There to Stay." *Broadcasting,* 22 July 1991, 24.

Roedy, Bill. "MTV Europe Does Play Local Acts." *Billboard,* 28 March 1992, 8.

"Rolling Through the Years." *Variety,* 16 November 1992, 36.

Rosen, Craig. "Lennon Song Served Up Again as Anti-War Anthem." *Billboard,* 26 January 1991, 5, 107.

————. "MCA, Capitol, Sony Bolstering Music Vids by Way of Big Screen." *Billboard,* 21 December 1991, 97.

————. "Labels Slow Pace of New Signings." *Billboard,* 4 January 1992, 1, 69.

————. "MTV Vets: Once VJs, Now DJs." *Billboard,* 6 June 1992, 64.

————. "Depeche Mode's Modus Operandi. Band Meets Challenge of Mass Success." *Billboard,* 17 April 1993, 6, 84.

————. "Labels, MTV Keep Plugging Away." *Billboard,* 8 May 1993, 1, 68.

————. "Soundtrack Race Getting Hotter." *Billboard,* 31 July 1993, 9.

Rosen, Craig, and Melinda Newman. "Mix-A-Lot Clip Gets Pushed Back to After 9 on MTV." *Billboard,* 27 June 1992, 4, 70.

Rosenblum, Debbie. "The Multi-Channel Matrix." *Billboard,* 21 December 1985, 29.

————. "RPM to Frames per Second." *Billboard,* 21 December 1985, 29.

Rosenbluth, Jean. "Singles Click as Mad Ave. Jingles." *Billboard,* 27 August 1988, 1, 77.

Ross, Sean. "Beyond the Bashing: Notes on UC's New Conservativism." *Billboard,* 11 January 1992, 63, 65.

————. "Soft AC Reconsiders Its Sources." *Billboard,* 11 January 1992, 63.

Rothman, Matt. "Viacom Interacts with Future." *Variety,* 29 June 1992, 29.

Rubin, Mike. "Nazi as They Wanna Be." *Village Voice,* 22 June 1993, 48.

————. "MTV Consumer Guide." *Village Voice.* 7 June 1994, 46.

Rubin, Rebecca, Alan M. Rubin, Elizabeth M. Perse, Cameron Armstrong, Michael McHugh, and Noreen Faix. "Media Use and Meaning: A Music Video Exploration." *Journalism Quarterly* 63 (Summer 1986):353–359.

Russell, Deborah. "Closed Captioning of Clips Increases." *Billboard,* 2 December 1989, 48.

———. "Deaton Flanigen Is Kicking up Its Heels." *Billboard,* 26 January 1991, 61–62.

———. "Vid Producers Face Economic Woes." *Billboard,* 7 December 1991, 39.

———. "N'ville Studio Emphasizes Country Consciousness." *Billboard,* 8 February 1992, 32.

———. "Majors Now Using the Indie Pipeline." *Billboard,* 21 March 1992, I-4, I-30.

———. "No-Risk Retail: Useful Indie Tool?" *Billboard,* 21 March 1992, I-3, I-16

———. "'T2' in Action at MTV Awards." *Billboard,* 20 June 1992, 88.

———. "MTV Europe Tackles Racism with Unity Forum." *Billboard,* 27 March 1993, 38.

———. "Eyes & Ears on MTV Movie Awards." *Billboard,* 15 May 1993, 40.

———. "MTV, Viacom Form Production Branch." *Billboard,* 15 May 1993, 4, 90.

———. "Kennedy Offers 'Alternative.'" *Billboard,* 26 June 1993, 96.

———. "MTV in 2nd Decade: A True Network." *Billboard,* 26 June 1993, 1, 96.

———. "MTV Experiments to Hold Viewers." *Billboard,* 3 July 1993, 1, 84.

———. "It's Ready, Set, Action for BET." *Billboard,* 7 August 1993, 34.

———. "MTV Announces Video Award Noms." *Billboard,* 7 August 1993, 34–35.

———. "Beavis, Butt-head a Boon for Bands." *Billboard,* 4 September 1993, 1, 90.

———. "Pearl Jam, Kravitz Get a Boost from MTV Award Show." *Billboard,* 18 September 1993, 8, 99.

———. "MTV Ups Execs Levinson, McGrath to President Posts." *Billboard,* 6 November 1993, 16, 86.

———. "New MTV Campaign Tackles Violence." *Billboard,* 22 January 1994, 1, 95.

———. "Who Owns Ideas in Music Vid Biz?" *Billboard,* 23 April 1994, 40, 41.

———. "MTV Reorganization Stresses More Music." *Billboard,* 1 October 1994, 12, 85.

———. "CMV Cashes in on Video Play." *Billboard,* 11 February 1995, 48.

Sacks, Leo. "MTV's Impact at Retail and Radio." *Billboard,* 16 April 1983, 63, 80.

———. "MTV Seen Aiding AOR Stations." *Billboard,* 28 May 1983, 1, 66.

———. "MTV Tests Promo Power with Police." *Billboard,* 18 June 1983, 1, 72.

———. "Madison Ave. Warming to MTV." *Billboard,* 2 July 1983, 1, 64.

———. "Promo Clips: Who Should Pay?" *Billboard,* 16 July 1983, 35.

Sacks, Leo, Tony Seideman, and Bill Holland. "Other Clip Outlets Blast MTV Pacts." *Billboard,* 23 June 1984, 1, 67.

Sagal, Peter. "Thriller." *New Republic,* 30 March 1992, 12–13.

Sampson, Jim. "Vidclip Compensation in Germany." *Billboard,* 25 February 1984, 3.

Sanger, David E. "Sayonara, MTV." *New York Times,* 7 July 1991, H22.

"Say It in Spanish: 'Yo Deseo Mi MTV.'" *Variety,* 29 March 1993, 56.

Scanziani, Alessandra. "Perestroika Perks: McDonald's and MTV." *New York Times,* 7 July 1991, sec. 2 H22.

Schalin, Scott. "Video Impact: Their Fiery Brand of Raunch 'n' Rebellion Has Made Them MTV Favorites and Certified Celluloid Heroes." *Billboard,* 28 September 1991, M10.

Schifrin, Matthew. "I Can't Even Remember the Old Star's Name." *Forbes,* 16 March 1992, 44–45.

Schiller, Herbert. *Culture Inc.: The Corporate Takeover of Public Expression.* New York: Oxford University Press, 1989.

————. "Not Yet the Postimperialist Era." *Communication and Culture in War and Peace*, ed. Colleen Roach. London: Sage, 1993, 97–116.

Schipper, Henry. "Survey Claims MTV Has Passed Radio as Disk Sales Stimulus." *Variety*, 6 November 1985, 87.

————. "Rock Censorship Debate Rages; Parents Org Has Corp Support; MTV Asked to Label 'X' Videos." *Variety*, 2 April 1987, 2, 92.

Schneider, Steve. "Music Channel Seeks Mature Viewers." *New York Times*, 24 February 1985, sec. 2, p. 34.

Schoemer, Karen. "Teen-Agers Get Down to Issues." *New York Times*, 17 May 1992, H27.

Scovell, Nell. "A Cool Show That's Getting Hot." *Rolling Stone*, 8 September, 1988, 36.

Scully, Sean. "Court Throws Out Indecency Ban," *Broadcasting and Cable*, 29 November 1993, 10.

Segers, Frank. "Videotape Theater open for Business in Chicago Suburb." *Variety*, 26 September 1984, 1, 114.

Seideman, Tony. "Documentaries Sell Best in Music Video Market." *Variety*, 14 March 1984, 69, 87.

————. "MTV Plan Shakes Label Exec Suites." *Billboard*, 31 March 1984, 1, 60.

————. "Exclusivity Key to MTV Deals, Says Pittman." *Billboard*, 14 April 1984, 3, 61.

————. "CBS Records Will Demand Vidclip Payment." *Billboard*, 21 April 1984, 1, 61.

————. "Four Labels Ink Vidclip Deals with MTV." *Billboard*, 23 June 1984, 1, 67.

————. "Labels Split on Video Service." *Billboard*, 14 July 1984, 4, 68.

————. "RCA Enters Video Distribution." *Billboard*, 14 July 1984, 68.

————. "MTV Pacts Stir Reaction." *Billboard*, 21 July 1984, 1, 69.

————. "Video Clubs Called Lawbreakers." *Billboard*, 25 August 1984, 4, 78.

————. "MTV Aging via Second Net." *Billboard*, 1 September 1984, 1, 58.

————. "Labels Weigh Vidclip Economies." *Billboard*, 22 September 1984, 3, 71.

————. "Changes in MTV Playlist." *Billboard*, 3 November 1984, 42, 44.

————. "Rough Start for Turner's Music Channel." *Billboard*, 17 November 1984, 1, 78.

————. "Discovery Network Thinks Big." *Billboard*, 1 December 1984, 3.

————. "Video Music Meet Looks at Prosperity, Pitfalls." *Billboard*, 1 December 1984, 1, 78.

————. "MTV Readies Beefed-Up News Coverage." *Billboard*, 15 December 1984, 40, 48.

————. "Programming Executives' Panel Marked by Heated Exchanges of Opinion." *Billboard*, 15 December 1984, 36.

————. "MTV Revenues, Profits Up." *Billboard*, 16 February 1985, 4.

————. "VH-1 Sending Sales Signals." *Billboard*, 16 February 1985, 1, 84.

————. "VH-1 off to Fast Start." *Billboard*, 30 March 1985, 30.

————. "Video Outlets in CBS Boycott." *Billboard*, 8 June 1985, 1, 80.

————. "MTV Asks FCC to Block Competing Vidclip Outlet." *Billboard*, 13 July 1985, 78.

————. ". . . newsline . . ." *Billboard*, 17 August 1985, 32.

————. "Rockamerica Panel Take Close Look at TV." *Billboard*, 17 August 1985, 31–32.

————. "From Promises to Profits." *Billboard*, 21 December 1985, 27.

Seideman, Tony, and Kip Kirby. "Rights Payment Warning: 'Publishers Are Watching' Clip Broadcast Industry." *Billboard*, 15 December 1984, 35.

Seidman, Steven A. "An Investigation of Sex-Role Stereotyping in Music Videos." *Journal of Broadcasting and Electronic Media* 36 (Spring 1992):209–215.

"September." *Rolling Stone,* 10–24 December 1992, 80.

Shales, Tom. "The Pop Network That's Dim & Ditzy to Decor." *Washington Post,* 1 August 1985, B1, B9.

Shalett, Mike. "Studying MTV's Impact on Consumers." *Billboard,* 8 September 1984, 21.

"Shameless Self Promotion. A *Billboard* Advertising Supplement." *Billboard,* 31 August 1991, MTV4, MTV28.

Shapiro, Michael J. *Language and Political Understanding.* New Haven: Yale University Press, 1981.

Shaw, Dan. "Home Shopping's New Beat." *New York Times,* 28 August 1994, sec. 1, pp. 39, 42.

Shaw, Russell. "Research Firm Offering 24-Hour MTV Monitoring." *Billboard,* 17 November 1984, 31.

Shemel, Sidney, and M. William Krasolovsky. *This Business of Music.* Los Angeles: Billboard Publishing Co., 1979.

Shepherd, Stephanie. "Exposing the Role of MTV." *Billboard,* 30 June 1984, 8.

Sherman, Barry L., and Joseph R. Dominick. "Violence and Sex in Music Videos: TV and Rock 'n' Roll." *Journal of Communication* 36 (Winter 1986):79–93.

Sherrid, Pamela. "Emotional Shorthand." *Forbes,* 4 November 1985, 214–215.

Shiver, Jube Jr. "Building a Network." *Los Angeles Times,* 27 August 1989, sec. 4, pp. 1, 4.

———. "Red-Hot Record Sales Starting to Cool Off." *Los Angeles Times,* 21 February 1990, D2, D6.

———. "Record Companies Taking a Spin at the Video Business." *Los Angeles Times,* 25 June 1990, D1, D8.

———. "New Record Labels Defying Industry Trend." *Los Angeles Times,* 11 December 1990, D2, D5.

———. "Ready to Do Lunch with Hollywood." *Los Angeles Times,* 19 August 1991, F1, F12.

Shore, Laurence Kenneth. "The Crossroads of Business and Music: A Study of the Music Industry in the United States and Internationally." Ph.D. diss., Stanford University, 1983.

Signorielli, Nancy, Douglas McLeod, and Elaine Healy, "Gender Stereotypes in MTV Commercials: The Beat Goes On." *Journal of Broadcasting and Electronic Media* 38 (Winter 1994):91–101.

Sippel, John. "Producers, Directors Ask Greater Role." *Billboard,* 15 December 1984, 33.

———. "Inside Track." *Billboard,* 25 May 1985, 86.

Smith, Chris. "The Man Who Should Be Conan." *New York,* 10 January 1994, 36–39.

"Smokey and the Butt-Head." *The Education Digest,* January 1994, 76.

Smythe, Dallas. "On the Political Economy of Communications." *Journalism Quarterly* 37 (Autumn 1960):563–572.

Solomon, Jolie, Michael Meyer, Rich Thomas, and Charles Fleming. "The Dueling Dudes." *Newsweek,* 11 October 1993, 54–55.

"Some Vid Execs Wary of Musical Genre." *Variety,* 14 March 1984, 75.

Spahr, Wolfgang. "German TV Sours on Music Shows." *Billboard,* 12 November 1988, 45.

———. "The German Sound Goes Global. A New Generation Is Overcoming Old Barriers." *Billboard,* 3 April 1993, 53, 56, 59.

Span, Paula. "Music Meets TV and KAPOW!" *Washington Post,* 1 August 1985, B1–B3.

Spillman, Susan. "MTV's New Music Network May Prove Tougher Ad Sell." *Advertising Age,* 27 August 1984, 10.

———. "Turner/MTV Face a 'Cutthroat' War." *Advertising Age,* 3 September 1984, 2, 68.

———. "Feds Probe MTV's Video License Deals." *Advertising Age,* 21 September 1984, 1, 63.

———. "Contracts Prompt MTV Suit." *Advertising Age,* 24 September 1984, 105.

Staples, Brent. "Unseen but Not Unsung." *New York Times,* 19 December 1990, A24.

Stark, Phyllis. "Indie-Distrib Single Beats the Odds." *Billboard,* 16 February 1991, 9, 72.

———. "'Roses' Breaks Bon Jovi at AC." *Billboard,* 24 April 1993, 61.

Sterling, Christopher H. "Cable and Pay Television." In *Who Owns the Media?* 2d ed., ed. Benjamin M. Compaine, 373–450. White Plains, N. Y.: Knowledge Industry Publishers, 1982.

———. "Television and Radio Broadcasting." In *Who Owns the Media?* 2d ed., ed. Benjamin M. Compaine, 299–372. White Plains, New York: Knowledge Industry Publishers, 1982.

Stewart, Al. "Despite Hits, Video Dealers Not Sold on Music Titles." *Billboard,* 25 February 1989, 1, 77.

Strauss, Neil. "The Real World." *Village Voice,* 2 June 1992, 43–44.

———. "Free Your Mind, Blur Your Video." *Village Voice,* 24 May 1994, 64.

Sun, Se-Wen, and James Lull. "The Adolescent Audience for Music Videos and Why They Watch." *Journal of Communication* 36 (Winter 1986):115–125.

Sutherland, Sam. "Copyright Body Debates MTV." *Billboard,* 23 January 1983, 43.

———. "Agents, Managers Offer Their Views on Support." *Billboard,* 15 December 1984, 33.

———. "Label Execs Air Common Woes." *Billboard,* 15 December 1984, 32.

———. "Clips Connect with Afterlife Beyond Video." *Billboard,* 23 November 1985, VM12, VM21.

———. "Videos Termed Effective." *Billboard,* 10 May 1986, 1, 91.

Sweeting, Paul. "Shanachie Plans to Release 100 Titles in '92." *Billboard,* 11 January 1992, 48, 52.

Tannenbaum, Rob. "Country's New Gold Rush." *Rolling Stone,* 16 April 1992, 16–17.

Taylor, Gail D. "MTV Nets Rock with Promotions." *Advertising Age,* 11 September 1989, 111.

Taylor, Paul. "Video Connoisseurs in Koolyanobbing." *New York Times,* 7 July 1991, sec. 2, p. H22.

Tedesco, Richard. "HA! Signs Several Off-Net Sitcoms As Comedy War Widens." *Cablevision,* 18 December 1989, 12, 14.

"Ted Turner Turns off the Music." *The Economist,* 8 December 1984, 83.

"Telemundo-MTV Pact." *New York Times,* 10 June 1988, D16.

Terry, Ken. "Diskeries Ponder Music Video Business." *Variety,* 14 March 1984, 69, 76.

———. "Countdown Begins for Video Jukeboxes." *Variety,* 28 May 1984, 75, 78.

———. "Videoclip Producers Ready to Organize." *Variety,* 13 June 1984, 1, 76.

———. "MTV Claims It Has Video Deals with Four Labels; Exclusivity May Be Double-Edged Sword." *Variety,* 20 June 1984, 57, 60.

———. "MTV's Exclusivity Deals Scored By New Music Seminar Panel." *Variety,* 15 August 1984, 78.

———. "Music Video Producers Assn. Issues a Clip Production Guide." *Variety,* 1 January 1986, 127, 130.

———. "Diskeries Change Clip Output Stance, Cutback Reported at Some Labels." *Variety,* 14 May 1986, 85, 88.

————. "Pittman Sez MTV Exclusivity Will Be Re-evaluated Before Label Pacts Expire Next Year." *Variety,* 28 May 1986, 77, 78.

————. "ASCAP, BMI Face Cuts in TV Fees." *Billboard,* 4 March 1989, 3, 93.

————. "BMI OKs Pact with Showtime, MTV Networks." *Billboard,* 3 August 1991, 75.

————. "The Year in the Music Business." *Billboard,* 21 December 1991, YE-46.

————. "Major Labels Try Direct-Sales Route." *Billboard,* 18 January 1992, 1, 49, 52.

————. "Music Units Drop in World Markets." *Billboard,* 2 May 1992, 1, 29.

Terry, Ken, and Melinda Newman. "Music-Vid Biz Lacks Info on Home-Taping." *Billboard,* 6 July 1991, 5, 69.

Tetzlaff, David J. "MTV and the Politics of Postmodern Pop." *Journal of Communication Inquiry* 10 (Winter 1986):80–91.

"Texas Cable Company Bans MTV." *Los Angeles Times,* 29 June 1991, D2.

"Texas Cable TV Operator Drops Its Offering of MTV." *Wall Street Journal,* 1 July 1991, B2.

Texier, Catherine. "Have Women Surrendered in MTV's Battle of the Sexes?" *New York Times,* 22 April 1990, H29, H31.

"A Third Music Network Heard From." *Broadcasting,* 3 September 1984, 27.

"30 Years on, 'Bandstand' Still Targeting the Teens." *Billboard,* 31 October 1981, 3, 16.

"Tom Freston: The Pied Piper of Television." *Broadcasting & Cable,* 19 September 1994, 36–40.

"Tom Freston: The Sound Business of Music." *Broadcasting,* 4 September 1989, 79.

Trachtenberg, Jeffrey A., and Mark Robichaux. "TCI and Bertelsmann Unit Drop Plans for Music, Home-Shopping Channel." *Wall Street Journal,* 6 June 1994, B5.

"Tracking the Players in Race for Exposure." *Billboard,* 23 November 1985, VM4, VM22–VM23.

Traub, James. "Gotterdammerung for Video Music?" *Channels of Communication,* July/August 1986, 9.

Turner Broadcasting System. 1984 Annual Report.

"Turner Sets Launch Date for Music Video Service." *Broadcasting,* 4 September 1984, 36–37.

"Turner to Sell Music Channel to Competing MTV Networks." *Washington Post,* 29 November 1984, C3.

"2 Live Crew Freed by Jury in Obscenity Trial; Black Historian Defends Group." *Jet,* 5 November 1990, 15.

"238 Videos Rotated in CMT Orbit in '91." *Billboard,* 25 January 1992, 32.

Tyler, Patrick E. "CNN and MTV Hanging by a 'Heavenly Thread.'" *New York Times,* 22 November 1993, A4.

U.S. Congress. Cable Communications Policy Act of 1984, Section 639. Public Law 98-549, 98th Congress.

"U.S. Senators Ask FTC to Probe MTV's Exclusive Video Contracts." *Variety,* 1 April 1987, 75–77.

Vare, Ethlie Ann. "L.A. Alive with Sight of Music." *Billboard,* 28 January 1984, 40, 44.

————. "USA for Africa Producers Work Fast." *Billboard,* 30 March 1985, 30.

————. "MTV Retreat Threatens to Cast Metal Back into Dark Age—with Gold Lining." *Billboard,* 27 April 1985, HM4, HM17.

————. "Beyond Video: Media Flips for Clips." *Billboard,* 28 September 1985, NT3, NT10.

————. "Artists on Video." *Billboard,* 23 November 1985, VM14.

————. "Cutting Room Floor to Cutting Edge." *Billboard,* 21 December 1985, 27.
————. "Melody Filmgroup Gearing for 'New Approach.'" *Billboard,* 21 December 1985, 23.
————. "On Your Mark." *Billboard,* 21 December 1985, 26.
————. "AFI TV Workshop Sets New Clip Awards." *Billboard,* 17 May 1986, 60.
"Venture Is Set to Rival MTV." *New York Times,* 1 February 1994, D7.
Verna, Paul. "Battles In-Store for Music Vid Firms." *Billboard,* 10 November 1990, 49, 52–53.
————. "Indies Use Vid Promos to Reel in Sales." *Billboard,* 10 November 1990, 52.
————. "Fans Justify Madonna Video at Retail." *Billboard,* 22 December 1990, 11, 107.
————. "Video Outlets Embracing Longforms." *Billboard,* 23 February 1991, 42–43.
————. "MTV Laserdisc Service to Bow at Retail." *Billboard,* 21 December 1991, 16.
————. "Prince's 'Retirement' Perplexes Trade." *Billboard,* 8 May 1993, 10.
"Viacom Gets MTV Europe." *New York Times,* 31 August 1991, 41.
"Viacom Inc." *Hoover's Handbook,* 1991, 572.
"Viacom Inc. Reports First Quarter Profit, 5.7% Revenue Rise." *Wall Street Journal,* 29 April 1992, 138.
"Viacom Inc." *Wall Street Journal,* 8 March 1991, B10.
"Viacom International Inc." *Wall Street Journal,* 15 July 1991, B4.
Viacom International. 1984 Annual Report.
————. Form 10-K to the SEC for the fiscal year ending 31 December 1984.
————. 1985 Annual Report.
————. Form 10-K to the SEC for the fiscal year ending 31 December 1985.
————. Form 10-K to the SEC for the fiscal year ending 31 December 1987.
————. Form 10-K to the SEC for the fiscal year ending 31 December 1988.
————. Form 10-K to the SEC for the fiscal year ending 31 December 1991.
"Viacom LBO Bid Imperiled." *Broadcasting,* 9 February 1987, 49.
"Viacom Plans to Buy MTV Europe Stake Owned by Maxwell." *Wall Street Journal,* 21 August 1991, B7.
"Viacom's MTV Will Split into 3 Diverse Channels." *Wall Street Journal,* 31 July 1991, B6.
"Viacom Sues Time for $2.4 Billion." *Broadcasting,* 15 May 1989, 28, 30.
"Video Files." *Rolling Stone,* 12–26 December 1991, 33.
Vincent, Richard C., Dennis K. Davis, and Lilly Ann Boruszkowski. "Sexism on MTV: The Portrayal of Women in Rock Videos." *Journalism Quarterly* 64 (Winter 1987):750–754.
Voros, Drew. "Beavis and Butt-head Show." *Variety,* 15 March 1993, 67.
Wall, Kevin. "There Is a Market for Music Video." *Billboard,* 27 June 1987, 9.
"Wall St. Report Calls Music Video Major Area for Disk Biz Growth." *Variety.* 18 January 1984, 91, 93.
Walz, Ken. "Videoclip Production Has Grown Up." *Billboard,* 28 May 1988, 9.
Warner Communications. 1981 Annual Report.
————. Form 10-K to the SEC for the fiscal year ending 31 December 1981.
————. 1982 Annual Report.
————. 1983 Annual Report.
————. Form 10-K to the SEC for the fiscal year ending 31 December 1983.
————. 1984 Annual Report.
————. Form 10-K to the SEC for the fiscal year ending 31 December 1984.

————. 1985 Annual Report.

————. Form 10-K to the SEC for the fiscal year ending 31 December 1985.

Warner, Fran. "Too Old to Rock 'n' Roll? Nuts!" *Brandweek,* 9 November 1992, 20–22.

"Warner to Buy Out American Express; MTV to Go Private." *Broadcasting,* 12 August 1985, 29–30.

Watanabe, Teresa. "Pulling the Plug on Pirate Videos." *Los Angeles Times,* 8 January 1990, D3.

Waters, Harry. "Down to the Sea in Shtik." *Newsweek,* 19 March 1990, 55.

Watson, Miranda. "German Music Biz Welcomes Viva." *Billboard,* 26 March 1994, 62, 70.

Weaver, Jane. "Live, from MTV Sports: Headbanger Hoops." *Mediaweek,* 22 April 1991, 5.

Weinert, Ellie. "BMG Ariola to Promote Vid Mags, Folk Longforms." *Billboard,* 25 August 1990, 55.

————. "Something Old Rocks Germany." *Billboard,* 27 March 1993, 1, 85.

————. "Four Majors Said to Back Viva." *Billboard,* 21 August 1993, 40–41.

Weinger, Harry. "RockAmerica, RCA in Tour Experiment." *Billboard,* 12 January 1985, 31.

Weinstein, Mark. "Videoclips: Still-Evolving Form Struggles to Transcend Limitations; Filmmaking Winning Emphasis over Effects." *Billboard,* 12 November 1988, V3, V8.

Weiss, Elizabeth. "Breaking Through." *Working Woman,* March 1994, 12.

Wells, Ken. "Lithuanians Find They're Missing One Perk of Red Army Occupation." *Wall Street Journal,* 11 November 1991, B1.

Wharton, Denise. "Big Brother's Watching: FCC Explores 24-hr 'Indecency' Ban." *Variety,* 11 July 1990, 60.

White, Adam. "A Day in the Life of MTV: 164 Clips." *Billboard,* 17 November 1984, 31, 33.

————. "Acts Rarely Seen on Sister Channel Get Exposure." *Billboard.* 12 January 1985, 1, 61.

————. "Warner Int'l Aims to Conquer Europe." *Billboard,* 18 January 1992, 36–37.

White, Armond. "Running on Recall." *Film Comment,* August 1987, 72, 74–75.

Williams, Marjorie. "MTV's Short Takes Define a New Style." *Washington Post,* 13 December 1989, A1, A20, A21.

Winslow, Ken. "Music Videos: Hollywood Handmaiden in a Hit Movie Business." *Billboard,* 14 November 1981, 58, 74–76.

"Wired for Losses?" *Economist,* 8 August 1987, 59, 62.

Witt, Karen. "MTV Puts the Campaign on Fast Forward." *New York Times,* 8 February 1992, 8.

Wood, Gerry. "Problems and Potential of Programming Examined." *Billboard,* 18 December 1982, 43.

Wykoff, David. "Olive Jar Reshapes Clay Animation." *Billboard,* 6 June 1987, 52, 53.

————. "Independent Labels & Distributors." *Billboard,* 11 March 1989, I-1, I-20, I-26.

Yang, Jeff. "When MTV Met SNL . . ." *Village Voice,* 6 October 1992, 50–51.

Zahradnik, Rich. "Jukebox Network Expanding into U.K." *Billboard,* 22 February 1992, 45.

Zimmerman, Kevin. "MTV Striving for 'Not Normal' with Non-Music Video Shows." *Variety,* 28 September 1988, 70.

————. "Indie-Label Ranks Thinned as Polygram Acquires A&M." *Variety,* 18–24 October 1989, 85.

————. "Indies Live on Despite Sale of Geffen to MCA." *Variety,* 21 March 1990, 69–70.

————. "New Labels Peel off in All Directions." *Variety,* 11 April 1990, 91.

————. "Independent Labels Want Their MTV." *Variety,* 23 May 1990, 85.

————. "That Synching Feeling: Vanilli Not Alone?" *Variety,* 26 November 1990, 66, 68.

————. "Labels Looking East for Room to Grow." *Variety,* 14 January 1991, 121.

————. "Does Music Biz Want Its MTV?" *Variety,* 5 August 1991, 105–106.

————. "These Megadeals Won't Last." *Variety,* 30 September 1991, 79, 81.

————. "Record Biz in Global Spin." *Variety,* 14 October 1991, 254, 264.

————. "Rockers Miss the Bus." *Variety,* 21 October 1991, 1, 94.

————. "Ruckus over Record Royalties." *Variety,* 28 October 1991, 58–59.

————. "Premature Burial for Indies?" *Variety,* 4 November 1991, 71, 73.

————. "Pink Slips Have Biz Spinning." *Variety,* 18 November 1991, 41, 47.

————. "Is the Music Biz Color Blind?" *Variety,* 30 March 1992, 82, 89.

————. "Who Wants Their MTV Awards?" *Variety,* 14 September 1992, 70.

————. "Music Biz Targets Global Markets." *Variety,* 22 March 1993, 42.

Zucchino, David. "Big Brother Meets Twisted Sister." *Rolling Stone,* 7 November 1985, 9, 10, 15–17, 62, 64–66.

Zuckerman, Faye. "MTV Greets 'Mistress of the Dark.'" *Billboard,* 3 November 1984, 44.

————. "Rock Artists Gather to Sing MTV's Praises." *Billboard,* 15 December 1984, 34.

————. "Coalition Blasts Violence in Clips." *Billboard,* 22 December 1984, 35, 36.

————. "MTV Outlines Plans for About-to-Debut VH-1." *Billboard,* 22 December 1984, 86.

————. "Clip Makers Focus on Royalties." *Billboard,* 2 March 1985, 37–38.

Zuckerman, Faye, and Kip Kirby. "Lawsuit Challenges MTV Deals." *Billboard,* 29 September 1984, 1, 68.

About the Book and Author

In August 1981, Music Television—now popularly known as MTV—was launched. Within a matter of years it revitalized a struggling record industry; made the careers of leading pop stars like Madonna, Boy George, Cyndi Lauper, and Duran Duran; infiltrated traditional network television and the movie industry; revolutionized the advertising industry; and stimulated purchases in several markets, most notably fashion apparel. The reach of MTV has proven long and profitable. In this book, Jack Banks examines the historical development of music video as a commodity and analyzes the existing structures within which music video is produced, distributed, and exhibited on its premier music channel, MTV.

Who controls MTV? What part do record companies play in the financing and production of music video? How do the power brokers in the business influence the ideological content of music video? Given the tight sphere of influence within the music industry, what are the future trends for music video and for artistic freedom of expression? Banks tackles these questions in an intelligent, lively, and sophisticated investigation into one of the most influential media enterprises of our society.

Jack Banks is assistant professor of communication at the University of Hartford.

Index

A&M Records, 39, 43, 76, 132, 137, 148, 165
  acquired by Polygram, 148
  catalog of music videos for children, 132
  exclusivity contracts between MTV Networks and, 76
ABC, 25, 48, 204
Abdul, Paula, 99, 140, 146, 157, 187
Abt, Dean, 4
A.C. Nielsen, 37, 123
Adam & Eve, 192
Adam Ant, 123
Adams, Bryan, 110, 140
Adolescents, 4
Advertising Age, 54
Advertising and advertisers, 1
  MTV's global reach with, 105–106
  MTV's relations with, 37–38
  music videos as, 4, 6
  See also Commercials; Globalization
Aerosmith, 103, 178, 179, 182
African Americans, 26. *See also* Black Entertainment Television; Blacks
AIDS, 129
Air Supply, 36
Alabama, 53
Allen, Don, 111
Allen, Steve, 25
"All Night Long" video, 43
Althusser, Louis, 95
American Association of Advertising Agencies, 6
American Bandstand, 25, 26
American Express, 31, 32, 41, 86, 117. *See also* Warner Amex Cable Communications
American Film Institute, 156

American Music Awards, 204
American Television & Communications (ATC), 84
Amos 'n' Andy, 24
Amundson, Dan, 189
Anderson, Ray, 69
Anderson, Tony, 171
Anticompetitive practices
  and American film studios, 115
  and attempts by MTV to coerce artists, 83–84
  and attempts by MTV to control access to cable, 84–87
  and MTV's exclusivity agreements with record companies, 63–78
Antitrust lawsuits
  by MTV competitors, 198
Apache Indians, 100
Arista Records, 37, 39, 149
Armstrong, Louis, 23, 24
Artura, Robert, 79
Association of Music Video Broadcasters, 62
Astra satellites, 93, 94
Atlantic Records, 44, 64, 76, 137, 149
Atwood, Brett, 82
Aufderheide, Pat, 4, 6, 105, 145, 166, 203
Avalon, Frankie, 25
AWGO, 165
Ayeroff, Jeff, 39, 167

Bagdikian, Ben, 14, 16, 17, 150
Bailando, 102
Baker, Anita, 54
"Band Aid," 204, 205
Bangles, The, 170
Barclay, Paris, 170
Baron, Peter, 139

Barron, Steve, 160
Baudrillard, Jean, 6
Bauman, John "Bowser," 53
BBC, 99
Beatles, The, 24, 25, 26, 148
Beavis and Butt-head, 125
    copycat acts and, 128–129, 180
    dubbed in Spanish, 104
    video games, 121, 200
    videos, 122
Beavis and Butt-head Megamodel Jam, 133
Beck, Dan, 145
Beck, Stephen, 183
"Bedtime Story" (Madonna), 164
Behavioralist communication research, 4
Bellamy, Bill, 129
Benatar, Pat, 34, 38
Benetton, 96
Benjamin, David, 61, 70, 71, 83
Bennett, Joel, 74
Bennett, William, 150
Bergman, Jo, 39
Berke, Jeff, 143
Berkeley, Busby, 23
Berle, Milton, 25
Bernstein, Adam, 167
Bertelsmann A. G., 17, 106, 113, 133, 148
Bertelsmann Music Group, 80, 108
BET. *See* Black Entertainment Television
Beug, John, 166
B-52s, The, 26
Billboard magazine, 36, 51, 65, 82, 152,
        168, 170, 182
    black album chart in, 153
    country music singles chart in, 145
    "Hot One Hundred" chart in, 40, 42,
        126, 149, 185
    Music Video Conference, 167
    and "Video Programming" chart, 42
Biller, Gary, 60
"Billie Jean" (Jackson), 40
Billie Jean video, 40
Biondi, Frank, 87, 120, 121
Black & White Television, 170, 171, 173
Black Entertainment Television (BET),
        57–59, 66, 72, 141, 170, 197
    attacks MTV's deals with record labels,
        76–78

bans on videos by certain labels, 196
    competition from MTV, 131, 133
    focus on black artists by, 63, 139
    videos by black artists on, 53, 140
Blacks
    exclusion of artists by MTV, 39–41
    exclusion of producers and directors of
        video clips, 170–174
    on VH-1, 53
    and video funding policies, 139
Black Showcase, 57
Blige, Mary J., 79
Blind Melon, 127
Blockbuster Entertainment, 120
Blockbuster Video
    coordinated cross-promotion with
        MTV, 121, 122
BMG Music International, 102, 107, 114,
        148
Bobby Jones Gospel Show, 57
Bon Jovi, 103, 146, 180
Boom boxes, 42
Boomtown Rats, The, 204
Boruszkowski, Lilly Ann, 3
Bowie, David, 38, 92, 157
    China Girl, 180
    "Let's Dance," 203
    questions lack of black artists on MTV,
        39, 40
Box, The, 33, 55–56, 63, 86, 132, 194,
        199
    attacks MTV's deals with record labels,
        76–78
    launching of, 55
Boycotts by Black Entertainment Tele-
        vision, 77–78
Boy George, 1
Bozi, Denise, 38
Brady Bunch (sitcom), 200
Brady Bunch Movie, The, 200
Brady Christmas, A, 200
Brady Kids, The, 200
"British Invasion," 25
British Telecommunications, 91
Brooks, Garth, 56, 145
Brown, Bobby, 145
Brown, James, 153
Brown, Jamie, 72

Brown, Jane, 2, 4
Brown, Julie, 125, 129
Browne, Jackson, 203
Bryant, Karyn, 129
Buggles, The, 34, 36
Bunce, Richard, 11
Burger King, 129
Bus Boys, 40
Bush, George, 129, 153
Bush Administration, 16, 130, 202
Buzz, 103

Cable Authority (United Kingdom), 192
Cable Communications Policy Act of
    1984, 191, 192, 193
Cable Jazz Channel, 58
Cable Music Channel (CMC), 48, 53, 66,
    72, 73, 85, 197
  failure of, 49, 60, 198
  launching of, 63, 83
Cable News Network (CNN), 48, 86, 90,
    91, 99, 105
Cable systems
  in Europe, 93, 94
  in Mexico, 104
  interactive, 132
  MTV attempts to control access to,
    84–87
  and multiplexing, 130–131
Cable television
  content regulation of music television
    programs on, 191–193
  growth in early 1980s, 30
  See also Satellites and satellite commu-
    nication; Television
Cablevision (Mexico), 104
Caifanes, 103
Calhoun Productions, 165
Callner, Marty, 179, 182
Calloway, Cab, 23, 24
Campbell, Glen, 28
Campbell, Kenneth, 2, 4
Canada, music video production in,
    110–111, 114
Canadian Radio-Television and Telecom-
    munications Commission (CRTC),
    111
Candyman, 56

Capitalism, cultural forms structured
    within, 9
Capitol Records, 65, 127, 138, 148, 186
Captain and Tennille, The, 28
Captain Beefheart, 26
Carey, Mariah, 128
Carmona, Caprice, 154, 178
Carson, Johnny, 61
Cassette tapes, 42
CBS, 196
CBS/Fox Home Video, 44
CBS Music Video (CMV), 138
CBS records, 31, 40, 44, 64, 126, 163, 172.
    See also Sony Music
Censorship
  and content regulation of music televi-
    sion programs, 191–193
  and external social factors influencing
    MTV's standards, 185–190
  MTV as gatekeeper and, 175, 178–180
  and MTV's standards, 176–178
  and music clip rotation categories on
    MTV, 184–185
  of music clips, 153, 180–182
  on network television, 27
  and Parents Music Research Center,
    187–188
  and political attacks on popular music,
    190–191
  of rock lyrics, 150
  of violence on MTV, 189–190
Channels of Communication, 57–58
Channel V, 102, 113, 199
Chapman, Tracy, 168
Cher, 180, 186, 193
Chicago, 53
Childs, Darren, 110
Chomsky, Noam, 9
Christgau, Robert, 35, 36
Chrysalis Records, 64, 126, 148
Chudnoff, Jack, 37
CHUM, 110
Cinderella (rock group), 124, 145
Cinderella (film), 122
Cinemascope, 13
Cinemax, 53
Cineplex Odeon Corporation, 111
Clapton, Eric, 128

Clark, Dick, 25
Clayton Act, 74
Clinton, Bill, 2, 129, 130
Club MTV, 124
Club MTV Party to Go, 199
CMC. *See* Cable Music Channel
CMT. *See* Country Music Television
CNN. *See* Cable News Network
Cobain, Kurt, 130, 163
Coca-Cola, 101, 105, 106, 116, 157
Coca-Cola World Music Video Awards, The,
    105
Cohen, Marshall, 33
Coke Time, 25
Cole, Nat "King," 24
College Music Video, 78
Collins, Phil, 92, 99, 187, 204
Columbia Records, 31, 77, 148, 170
Comedy Central, 118
Commercials
    on MTV, 3, 4
    music videos differ from, 5
    See also Advertisers and advertising
Common ownership, 86
Communication conglomerates, 16
Compact discs
    conversion from vinyl records to, 151
Compaine, Benjamin, 11, 14, 15
Concept Productions, 170
"Concept" videos, 3, 166
Concert films, 138
Condit, Hilary, 90
Consumerism, MTV's promotion of, 5, 8,
    96, 104–105, 114, 116, 133, 200
Consumer sovereignty argument, 11, 12
Cooke, Sam, 25
Corbijn, Anton, 163
Corbin, C. Paul, 59
Corcoran, Barbara, 102, 103
Corporate activity
    action-oriented study approach of, 10,
    11
    structural analysis of, 11
Corporations, allocative and operational
    control within, 11. *See also* individual
    corporations
Cortese, Dan, 129

Cosby Show, The, 119, 159
Costello, Elvis, 26
Couch, Tommy, 148
Country and western programs, 59–60
Country Music Television (CMT), 56,
    59–60, 111
Country Music Television Europe, 60
Craig, Carl, 172
Crawford, Cindy, 129
Cross-media promotion strategies, 16, 121,
    131, 200
Crow, Sheryl, 55, 102
CSSR-TV, 96
Cultural imperialism, 17
"Cultural materialism," 9, 10
Culture Club, 123, 181
Cummings, Richard, Jr., 172, 173
Curry, Adam, 129

Daid, Dan, 139
Davidson, Juli, 54
Davis, Clive, 55
Davis, Dennis, 3
Davis, James E., 189, 190
Davis, Martha, 66
Davis, Marvin, 120
Davis, Zelma, 146
DeGama & Key, 182
Delicious Vinyl, 147
Dempsey, Don, 43
Denisoff, R. Serge, 41
De Palma, Brian, 158
Depeche Mode, 103, 179
Desai, Rajiv, 109
DeVoe, Bell Birv, 59
Dial MTV, 56
Diamond, Brian, 91
Diller, Barry, 119
Dimension Cable Service, 186
Dire Straits, 91, 182
"Discordant Sound of Music, The," 172
Discovery Music Network (DMN), 50–51,
    66, 71, 73, 75, 85, 198
Disney, 132
Diversification, 18
D. J. Jazzy Jeff & the Fresh Prince, 170, 182
DMN. *See* Discovery Music Network

Dobbis, Rick, 39
Documentaries, 138
Dolby, Thomas, 35
Dominick, Joseph, 3, 8
Dornemann, Michael, 108
"Do They Know It's Christmas?/Feed The
    World," 204, 205
Drug crisis, U.S., 153, 202
Duff, Bruce, 153, 154
Dukes of Hazzard, 11
Dupler, Steve, 54
Duran Duran, 1, 35, 36, 123, 143, 157
Duran Duran (Picture Music Interna-
    tional) video, 44

Earache U.S., 152
Earth, Wind & Fire, 39
Eastern Europe, MTV's presence in, 95–97
Easybeats, 98
Economic function, related to ideological
    content of commoditized culture, 12
Economist, The, 49
Elektra, 44, 76, 149, 168
Elephant Parts, 29
Ellington, Duke, 24
EMF, 56
EMI Music, 80, 82, 102, 106
End TV, 79
Epand, Len, 42, 165
Epic/Portrait/CBS Associated Labels, 43
Epic Records, 142, 148, 153
Equity Associates, 55
Eric, Dain, 71, 73
ESPN, 86, 90, 131
Europe
    collective licensing system used in, 92
    introduction of pop and rock music in,
        28
    See also MTV Europe; Viva
European Commission, 114, 115
European Community, 90, 107
Eurythmics, The, 35
Ewing, David "Preacher," 169
Exarhos, Tina, 177
Exclusivity pacts between record labels
    and MTV, 141. *See also* Record labels

Exposure media
    record label production dependent on,
        138–139
    role in record label's promotional strat-
        egy, 140–142

Fabian, 25
Falco, Peter, 86
Family Channel, The, 90
FCC. *See* Federal Communications Com-
    mission
Fear, 26
Federal Communications Commission
    (FCC), 75, 191, 192,193, 198
Federal Trade Commission (FTC), 75,
    198
Fifield, Jim, 106, 107
Film, music in from 1920s to 1960s, 23–24
Film Craft, 23
Film industry
    international marketing of American, 16
    vertical integration within, 15
Financial News Network (FNN), 50
Fincher, David, 164, 166
First Amendment, 190, 191, 193. *See also*
    Censorship
Fisher, Eddie, 25
Fiske, John, 5
Fitch Investor Services, 121
Fitzgerald, Larry, 142
Fixed bidding, 162
Flashdance, 1
Flashframe Films, 165
Flattery, Paul, 155, 168
Fleetwood Mac, 31, 144
Fleischer, Max, 23
Flock of Seagulls, A, 35
FNN. *See* Financial News Network
Fordham, Julia, 54
Fortune magazine, 38, 43
48 Hours, 1
Foundation to Assist Canadian Talent on
    Records, 111
Fox, Laurence, 65, 66
Fox Network, 66, 101, 105
Freedom of expression, 14, 15. *See also*
    Censorship

Freston, Tom, 35, 97, 167, 184
   quoted, 37, 82, 89, 90, 101, 110, 112,
     130, 131, 177, 178
Friday Night Videos, 61, 66, 70, 71, 83
Friesen, Gil, 43
Fritts, Edward, 192, 193
Fry, Donald, 5, 8
Fry, Virginia, 5, 8
FTC. *See* Federal Trade Commission
Fuentes, Daisy, 102
Fuzztones, 181, 182

Gabor, Zsa Zsa, 25, 27
Gannett News Service, 14
Ganot, Harvey, 106
Gap Band, 39
Gardner, Booth, 190
Garland, Les, 36, 56, 77, 83, 84
Garnham, Nicholas, 9, 10, 11, 13, 17, 202
Gasner, Rudi, 107
GASP! Productions, 67
Gay and Lesbian Alliance Against Defama-
   tion (GLAAD), 183
Gaye, Marvin, 39
Geffen, David, 149
Geffen/DGC video, 163
Geffen Records, 64, 76, 142
Gehr, Richard, 4
Geldof, Bob, 204
Gender stereotypes in MTV music videos,
   3. *See also* Women
General conglomerates, 16
General Electric, 12
General Motors, 58
George, Nelson, 170
Georges, Christopher, 130
Gerardo, 56, 77
Gerbner, George, 4
Giraldi, Bob, 158, 159
GLAAD. *See* Gay and Lesbian Alliance
   Against Defamation
Globalization, 134
  and alternatives to MTV, 110–113
  and major record labels' marketing
   campaigns, 106–109
  MTV Asia, 98–102
  MTV Australia and MTV Japan, 97–98

MTV Europe, 91–97, 116
MTV in Latin America, 102–104
MTV's corporate incentives to develop
   international markets, 89–91
MTV's global advertisers, 105–106
MTV's international youth culture,
   104–105
and one-way flow of music and culture,
   109–110, 113
of popular culture, 17, 200
Gold, Jeff, 127
Goldberg, Michael, 184
Goldblum, Jeff, 55
Golding, Peter, 8, 9, 10, 13, 14
Golin, Steve, 156
Gomery, Douglas, 10, 14, 15, 17
Gone Taiwan, 100
Goodman, Benny, 24
Goodman, Mark, 34, 39, 40
Goods, The, 133
Gore, Al, 129, 130, 187
Gostelradio, 96
Gottlieb, Tony, 111
Government, and music video as cultural
   form, 10
GPA Films, 156
Grant, Brian, 166
Grant, Eddy, 41
"Grazing," MTV strategy to stop viewer,
   128
Green, Mike, 71, 72
Greenpeace, 55
Grein, Paul, 184
Grodin, Lenny, 156, 159, 161, 162, 164,
   165, 173
Group W cable systems, 38
Grunge style, 5
Guback, Thomas, 16
Guy, 59

Hachette S. A., 17
Hall, Peter, 68
Hamlyn, Michael, 162, 173
Hammer, 66, 78, 145
Hance, Jeannie, 151, 152
Hard Day's Night, A, 24
Hardt, Hanno, 7

Harleston, David, 171
Hate crimes, 129
Hawkins, Paula, 188
HBO. *See* Home Box Office
Headbangers' Ball, 122, 124
Healy, Elaine, 3
Heavy D. & the Boyz, 59, 78
Help, 24
Henley, Don, 157
Herman, Edward, 9
Hermeneutic epistemology, 2
Hershleder, Jim, 158
Himmelman, Peter, 158
Hirschman, Celia, 140
HIStory: Past Present and Future—Book One (Jackson), 164
Hit Men: Power Brokers and Fast Money Inside the Music Business (Dannen), 69
Hit Video USA, 52, 83, 84, 85, 87, 193
    competitor of MTV, 66, 197
    failure of, 72, 198
    launching of, 51, 63
    owned by Wodlinger Broadcasting, 74, 75
Holden, Stephen, 145, 148
Hollywood film studios, 15
Hollywood Hotel, 24
Home Box Office (HBO), 30, 58, 87, 118, 131, 187
    creates Cinemax, 53
Homelessness, 129, 203, 204
Home shopping, 130–132, 142
Home videos, four types of music-related titles in, 138
Horizontal integration
    within media markets, 14, 198
    in music video business, 18
    in video clip production and distribution, 197
    See also Vertical integration
Horowitz, David, 85, 176–177, 191
House of Style, 129, 132
Houston, Whitney, 59, 148, 177
    "I Will Always Love You," 101
Hullabaloo, 25
Human League, The, 35

"Hungry Like the Wolf" (Duran Duran), 36
Hunter, Rachel, 55
Hunter, Tom, 96, 103, 104, 185, 109, 110
Hutchvision, 98, 99

Ice-T, 150
Ideological state apparatuses (ISAs), 95
Idol, Billy, 157
IFPI. *See* International Federation of the Phonographic Industry
Iglesias, Julio, 54, 102
Imus, Don, 53
In Concert, 26
Independent Label Coalition, 151
Indus Creed, 100
Instrumentalism, 12
International Communication and Youth Consortium (ICYC), 112
International Federation of the Phonographic Industry (IFPI), 107
INXS, 183
ISA. *See* Ideological state apparatuses
Isaacs, Steve, 129
Isgro, Joseph, 69
Island Records, 76, 148, 156, 158
ITT Corporation, 120
"I Want My MTV" (campaign), 38, 123

"Jackin' The Box," 79
Jackson, Don, 173
Jackson, Janet, 67, 72, 124, 127, 145, 148, 149
Jackson, J. J., 146
Jackson, Joe, 43, 145
Jackson, Michael, 99, 103, 177, 196
    "Black or White," 193
    commissions Giraldi for videos, 159
    concerts recreate video scenes, 142
    Dangerous, 66
    director for "Billie Jean", 160
    first black artist aired on MTV, 40, 41
    funds own video productions, 164, 165
    HIStory: Past Present and Future—Book One, 164
    limits MTV exclusivity on video showings, 67

"Man in the Mirror," 204
popularity of, 44
"Remember the Time," 171
Thriller, 42, 123
"We Are the World," 204
Jagger, Mick, 183. *See also* Rolling Stones,
    The
Jailhouse Rock, 24
Jamaica Broadcasting Corporation, 111
Jamaican Federation of Musicians, 112
James, Jay, 38
James, Rick, 39, 53
Jazz Singer, The, 23
Jazzy Jeff, 170
Jeffreys, Garland, 41
Jian, Cui, 99
Jodeci, 56
Joel, Billy, 83
John, Elton, 53, 91
Johnson, Robert L., 57, 58, 59
Jolson, Al, 23
Jones, Grace, 145
Jones, Quincy, 204
Jones, Tom, 55
Jordan, Traci, 169
Justify My Love (Madonna), 56, 183, 184,
    194
Justman, Paul, 160

Kaiser, Sam, 179, 186, 191
Kalvert, Scott, 170
Kaplan, Ann, 4, 6, 7
Kasem, Casey, 26, 39
Kellner, Douglas, 9
Kelly, R., 79
Kerslake, Kevin, 163
Khalid, 100
Kirshner, Don, 25, 26
Kiss, 145
Kleber, Merritt, 172
KMSF-TV, 61
Knotts, Don, 27
Konowitch, Abbey, 124, 140, 141, 142, 146
Kool Moe Doe, 170
KRLR-TV, 62
Kross, Kris, 77

Lack, John A., 32
L.A. Gear, 96
lang, k.d., 60, 110
Latin America, MTV in, 102–104
Lauper, Cyndi, 1, 145, 157
    "Girls Just Want to Have Fun" video,
        163
Laybourne, Geraldine, 132
Lee, Martin, 12
Lee, Spike, 170
Levin, Gerald, 150
Levinson, Mark, 157
Levinson, Sara, 99, 103, 104
Levi Strauss, 101
Lewis, Drew, 49
Lewis, Jerry, 25
Li, Richard, 99
License fees, MTV benefits from, 45
"Like a Virgin," (Madonna), 43
Limelight Films and Videos, 156, 165
"Limousine culture perks," 18
Lip-synching
    allegations of, 146, 147
    on commercial television, 25
    on video clips, 166
Live Aid, 105, 204
L. L. Cool J, 180
Loder, Kurt, 129
Lois Pitts Gershon (LPG agency), 37, 38
Loiterton, Nicky, 102
"Longest Time, The," (Joel), 83
Los Angeles Times, 50
Lovett, Lyle, 60
Loving You (film), 24
Low Profile, 202
Lucas, George, 157
Lucasfilm Commercial Productions, 157
Lucky Strikes, 24
Lull, James, 4
Lynch, David, 156
Lynch, Monica, 154
Lynch, Tom, 60
Lynch, William, 185

McCartney, Paul, 124
McGhan, John, 83
McGrath, Judy, 81, 130, 179

McGuigan, Cathleen, 53
MacKay, Anne Marie, 172
McLeod, Douglas, 3
MacNeil/Lehrer Report, 11
Madison Square Garden, 119, 120
Madonna, 1, 16, 17, 54, 102, 103, 124
  "Bedtime Story," 164
  on censorship, 183
  concerts recreate video scenes, 142
  contracts for, 148
  exclusivity time limits on videos of, 67
  funds own videos, 164
  Immaculate Collection, 184
  Justify My Love, 56, 183, 184, 194
  "Like a Virgin" video, 43
  multiyear contracts for, 149
  ownership rights to video clips by, 66
  provocative visual appearance of, 145
  reinvention of persona by, 139
  royalty rate for, 144
  Truth or Dare, 156
  "Vogue," 157
Magnasound India, 99
Mahurin, Matt, 168
Mailard, Phil, 158, 167
"Making of Michael Jackson's *Thriller,*
  The," 44
Maldita Vecindad, 103
Males, white, on MTV videos, 2
Malone, John, 56, 57, 120
Mammoth Records, 152
Manger, Steve, 144
Manhattan Cable, 38
Manilow, Barry, 53
Manurin, Mat, 166
Marsh, John, 156
Martin, Lionel, 170, 171
Marx, Karl, 9, 11
Mass media
  centralized control by corporations
    within, 151
  concentration of ownership in, 14, 17,
    18, 148, 149
  trends in ownership and control of,
    14–18
Masterpiece Theatre, 11
Masters, Lee, 108, 125

Matsushita, 148, 149
Mattel Toys, 58
Matting technique, 6
Maxwell, Robert, 91
Maxwell Communications Corporation,
  91
Mazer, Larry, 145
MCA Home Video, 138
MCA Music Entertainment, 108
MCA Records, 33, 45, 59, 149, 163
  Black Entertainment Television boycott
    of, 78
  buys Geffen, 148
  discontinues exclusivity agreement with
    MTV, 76
  and MCA Home Video, 138
  MTV exclusivity agreement with, 64, 70
MCM Service (France), 113
Media economics, 10
Media institutions, examined through po-
    litical economy, 9
Meehan, Eileen, 9
Melnyk, Alex, 157
Men at Work, 98
Mercury Records, 76, 148, 177
Merrill Lynch, 86
Metallica, 140
MGMM, 165, 168
Miami Vice, 1
Midnight Special, 26, 27
Miller v. California (1973), 192
Milli Vanilli, 128, 145, 146, 147
Mills Novelty Company, 23
Minoco, 23
Minorities
  in MTV music videos, 2, 3
  See also Black Entertainment Television;
    Blacks
Mister Rock 'n' Roll, 24
Mitchell, Steve, 41
Mitchell, Tony, 97, 98
Monkees, The, 25, 26, 29
Monkees, The, 25, 125
Monty Python's Flying Circus, 125
Moral philosophy, 9
MOR Music, 133
Morse, Margaret, 5, 6

Mosco, Vincent, 9
Motion pictures, music clips in, 1. *See also*
    Film industry
Motley Crue, 92, 179
Motown Records, 126, 149, 171
Motown Video, 39
Movie Channel, The, (TMC), 32, 70, 87
Movie musicals, 23
MSOs. *See* Multiple system operators
MTV (Music Television)
    alternatives to, 110–113
    audience research behind, 33
    exclusion of black artists by, 39–41
    external social forces influencing stan-
        dards on, 185–190
    global programming services of, 19
    launching of, 1
    music clip rotation categories on,
        184–185
    novel early years of, 29–41
    and power of record labels in video
        music business, 195–197
    premiere of, 34
    pressure groups and campaigns against
        violence on, 189–190
    promotional function of, 5, 8
    ratings decline of, 122–123
    record company artist's reaction to,
        182–184
    resurgence of, 127–130
    stimulates record sales, 36–37
    See also MTV Networks; VH-1 (Video
        Hits One); Video music clips
MTV Asia, 80, 89, 98–102, 109, 110, 134
MTV Australia, 97–98, 200
MTV Brazil, 103
MTV Coca Cola Report, 92
MTV Europe, 65, 91–97, 110, 113, 114,
        116, 134, 200
    growth of, 127
    lack of German artists played on, 80,
        112
    launching of, 89
    ownership of, 86
MTV Internacional, 102, 200
MTV Japan, 97–98
MTV Latino, 89, 103, 104, 109, 134, 200

MTV Mandarin, 80, 101
MTV Merchandise Catalog, 122
MTV Movie Awards, 120, 129
MTV Networks
    acquired by Viacom, 19, 41, 65, 117–118
    Acquisition Committee of, 176, 178,
        184
    anticompetitive practices by, 63
    antitrust action against, 73–76
    attempts to coerce artists by, 83–84
    attempts to control access to cable sys-
        tems, 84–87
    coordinated cross-media promotion
        strategies by, 121
    corporate acquisitions of, 117–122
    corporate activities through 1984, 41
    dominance in exhibiting music clips, 18
    exclusivity agreements with record com-
        panies, 63–67
    future programming for, 130–134
    as gatekeeper and censor, 175–176
    growth in advertising sales of, 127
    launches VH-1 (Video Hits One), 49, 53
    license fees, 44–45
    Program Standards and Public Respon-
        sibility Department, 176, 178, 184
    relations with cable companies and ad-
        vertisers, 37–38
    renews record labels contracts, 76
    severs ties with Star TV, 102
    stated and unstated standards of, 176–178
    strategies to revitalize channel, 123–127
    See also Globalization
MTV online computer bulletin, 206
MTV Productions, 128, 134
MTV Roadshow, 99
MTV sports, 129
MTV3, 133
MTV Top 20 Video Countdown, 121
MTV2, 133
MTV Unplugged, 122
MTV Video Music Awards, 129
MuchMusic, 89, 110, 111
Mulcahy, Russell, 160
Multinational corporate capitalism, 6
Multiple system operators (MSOs), 38, 49,
        53, 86, 87

MTV long-term agreements with, 199
seeking to end MTV affiliation, 186, 187
Viacom's ranking as, 118
Multiplexing, 130, 133
Multivision, 104
Murdoch, Rupert, 17, 91, 101, 105
Murdock, Graham, 8, 9, 10, 11, 12, 13, 14, 16
Music
    Asian ethnic, 100
    country and western, 59–60
    dance, 146
    heavy metal, 124, 127, 139
    hip-hop, 150
    new, 35, 140
    new wave, 148
    political attacks on popular, 190–191
    pop, on commercial television, 24–28
    punk, 148
    R & B, 131, 139, 171
    rap, 3, 127, 131, 139, 148, 150, 159, 171
    reggae, 100, 112
    salsa, 103
Musical Youth, 40
Music Channel (Japan), 98
Music-oriented films, 138
Music Video Producers Association (MVPA), 161–162, 165, 173
Music videos, 205–206
    for children, 132
    in commercial culture, 1
    as consumer culture, 4–6
    content analysis of sexual behavior in, 8
    cultural studies of, 4–7
    decline in the mid-1980s, 122–127
    early years of, 23–29
    economic structure and ideology within business of, 201–205
    functions at major record labels, 137, 138–139
    growth of other program services with, 47–62
    increased use of new producers and directors of, 168–170
    at independent and major record labels, 147–154

oligopoly of large production firms producing, 167–168
political economic study of, 18–19
as postmodern culture, 6–7
and Producer's Association, 161–162
production as transitional occupation with, 160–161
quantitative empirical studies of, 2–4
replace touring in promotional strategies, 142–143
trends in ownership and control of business of, 197–201
Music Video Services, 184
MusiquePlus, 110
"Must carry rules," 37, 85
MVPA. *See* Music Video Producers Association
Myers, Darcy, 169

Nabors, Jim, 25
Namm, Richard, 168
Nashville Network, The, 56, 59–60, 63, 111, 140, 197
National Amusements, 118
National Association for Advancement of Colored People (NAACP), 172, 173
National Association for Record Manufacturers, 42
National Association of Broadcasters, 62, 192
National Cable Television Association, 57
National Coalition on Television Violence (NCTV), 189, 191
National Nine Network (Australia), 97
Naughty by Nature, 56
NBC, 12, 25
NCTV. *See* National Coalition on Television Violence
Neer, Richard, 42
Neoclassical market economy theory, 11
Neo-Marxist economic analysis, 9, 11
Nesmith, Michael, 29, 32
"Network, The," 69
New Country Network (NCN), 111
Newhouse Broadcasting Corporation, 55
New Kids on the Block, 139, 145, 146

New Line Distribution, 70
Newman, Jeff, 72, 170, 177
New Music, 35
News Corporation, 17, 101, 105
New York Knicks, 119
New York Rangers, 119
New York University, 169
Nichols, Fred, 186
Nick at Night, 128, 200
Nickelodeon, 32, 65, 86, 89, 132, 133
Nick Jr. Rocks, 132, 133
Nielsen ratings, 123
Night Flight, 29
Nightline, 39, 183
Night Tracks, 52, 60, 72
Nike, 101
1934 Communications Act, Section 508,
    68, 70
1992 Presidential Campaign (U.S.), 2
Nirvana, 103, 130, 163
Noone, Peter, 55
Norwood, Jennifer, 188
Nuclear power industry, 12
Nugent, Ted, 129
N.W.A., 153

O'Connor, Sinead, 153
Omeltchenko, Alex, 156, 165
1–800–COUNTRY, 111
"One Night Stand" contest, 36
Orion Pictures, 70
Otto, Frank, 80

Pacific Arts Corporation, 32
Panorams, 23, 24
Paramount Communications, 121
    Viacom acquires, 70, 119, 200
Paramount decision (1948), 15, 70
Pareles, Jon, 6, 143, 204
Parenti, Michael, 9
Parents Music Research Center, 150,
    187–188, 191, 193, 194
Parton, Dolly, 28
Payne, Antony, 67
Payola
    illegal schemes, 141
    institutionalized, 198

and label agreements with other music
    programs, 78–79
    prohibited in radio, 68, 69
Peacock, Michelle, 179
Pembroke Cablevision, 185
Pendulum Productions, 156
Pentagon Papers, 12
Pepsi, 94
Pepsico, 38
"Performance" videos, 166
Personal identity and consumerism in
    music videos, 5, 133, 201
Philips, 17
Philips Electronics N.V., 148
Picture Music International (PMI), 44,
    138, 156, 157, 164, 174
Pioneer Electronic Corporation, 98
Piracy
    coordinated record label effort to stem,
        107
    MTV encounters in Latin America, 103
Pittman, Robert, 33, 34, 36, 49, 68, 185
    on artist's ownership of own videos, 67
    on black music, 40
    derides heavy metal, 124
    on exclusivity, 74, 76
    hiring of, 32
    on license fees for videos, 64
    on MTV ratings, 122
    and multiyear contracts with cable sys-
        tems, 84
    on VH-1, 52, 53
Playboy Channel, 183
PLG Records, 76
PMRC. *See* Parents Music Research Center
Poison, 92, 124
Political economic analysis of music video
    industry, 2, 18–19
Political economy, 12
    of communications, 8–10
    factors contributing to music program
        service, 29–31
    and study of corporate activity, 10
Polygram Investments, 70
Polygram Music Video, 137
Polygram Records, 33, 37, 42, 45, 80, 102,
    113, 147

and creation of Viva, 112
exclusivity agreement with MTV, 64
joint ownership with MTV of Asia ser-
vices, 82
Polygram Taiwan, 101
Pop Clips, 32
Popular culture
globalization of, 17
impact of MTV and music video on
American, 2
Portrait Records, 163
Positivist epistemology, 2
Postmodernism, 6, 7
Potts, Mark, 66
Poverty, 203
Praad, Mehesh, 109, 110
Praxis, 9
Premiere, 81
Presley, Elvis, 24, 25, 27, 29
Pressure groups, and music video as cul-
tural form, 10
Pretenders, The, 34
Prince, 41, 66, 67, 139, 199
Diamond and Pearls, 107
Purple Rain, 187
Priority Records, 153, 202
Proctor & Gamble, 58
Profit maximization, 17, 19
Profile Records, 72, 151
Propaganda Films, 156, 157, 164, 166, 168,
169, 172, 174
Psychoanalysis, 2
Public Enemy, 183
Pulse with Swatch, The, 92
Purple Rain (Prince) 1, 138
Pushing technique, 6

Quality Records, 147, 149
Qube, 33
Quinn, Martha, 129
Quinol, Katrin, 146
Q2, 133
QVC Networks, 119, 120, 133

Race and MTV music videos, 3. *See also*
Blacks
Radecki, Thomas, 189

Radio Fun, 96
Radiohead, 127
Radio Zet, 95, 96
Rage (Australia), 97, 98
RAL/Def Jam records, 171
Ramones, The, 35
Rap City, 57
Ratings, 37, 122–123
RCA Corporation, 17, 76, 149, 157
RCA Music, 149
RCA Records, 37, 45, 64, 80, 126
R. C. M., 23
Ready! Steady! Go!, 29
Reagan, Ronald, 153
Reagan Administration, 16, 202, 203
Real World, The, 128
Reardon, John, 121
Record companies
and artist reaction to MTV, 182–184
and artists, 143–147
Canadian, 111
control of music video production by, 18
influence of video music on artists' careers at, 145–147
MTV exclusivity agreements with,
63–67
participation in new music channel,
33
payola agreements with other music
programs, 78–79
role in video music production and distribution, 137
video music incorporated into, 137–138
Recorded music, early combinations with
visual media, 23–28
Recording industry, 1
advocacy of consumer sovereignty by,
11
corporate exercise of power within, 18
and expanded involvement in video
music, 41
racial discrimination within, 170–174
severe recession in, 31
See also Record companies; Record
labels
Recording Industry Association of America (RIAA), 31, 107, 123

Record labels
  artists' contracts with, 143–145
  challenge of music video for indepen-
    dent, 151–154
  and constraints on video clip content,
    166–167
  contracts with video clip producers and
    directors, 162–166
  contractual creation of vertical integra-
    tion between MTV and, 67–71
  create own music video channel, 79–82
  decrease in video music production,
    125–127
  global cooperation between MTV and,
    108–109
  global marketing campaigns by,
    106–109
  increased investment in music videos
    by, 42–46
  independent, 147
  legal payola agreements with other
    music programs, 78–79, 87
  MTV exclusivity agreements with, 64
  music videos at independent and major,
    147–154
  power and MTV in video music busi-
    ness, 195–197
  and record labels renew contracts, 76
  and television show reaction to MTV
    contracts, 71–72
Recoupment of label expenses, 143, 144
Reddy, Helen, 27
Redstone, Sumner, 75, 81
  acquires Viacom, 118–122
Regan, Russ, 147
Reid, Tim, 59
Renault, 96
Reno, Janet, 190
Repressive state apparatuses (RSAs), 95
Resnick, Ron, 153
Rhone, Sylvia, 171
RIAA. *See* Recording Industry Association
  of America
Richie, Lionel, 43, 124, 204
Righteous Brothers, The, 25
"Rio" (Nesmith), 29
Roach, Colleen, 17

Roadhouse, 160
Robbins, Cory, 151
Robinson, Carole, 178, 179, 186
Robinson, Mark, 160
Robinson, Smokey, 39
RockAmerica, 185
Rock Around the Clock, 24
Rock Concert, 26
Rock music in film narratives, 24
Roedy, Bill, 92, 93, 94, 95
Rolling Stone, 122
Rolling Stones, The, 27, 67, 83, 133, 183,
    193–194
  "Love Is Strong," 164–165
  Neighbors video, 181
  1994 Voodoo Lounge tour, 142
Ronstadt, Linda, 36
Roseanne, 129
Roseman, Jon, 160, 161, 163
Rosenblatt, Eddie, 142
Rosencrans, Robert, 57
Rosenfeld, Scott, 160
Ross, Diana, 53
Ross, Steven, 67, 199
Rossin, Herb, 44
Rossmiller, Stuart, 121
Rough Trade, 148
Royalties, 143, 144
Rrazhash, Andrei L., 96
RSA. *See* Repressive state apparatuses
Rubin, Mike, 128
Rubin, Rebecca, 4
"Rule of One," 48
Rumours, 31
Rundgren, Todd, 29, 34
Run-D.M.C., 72
Rush, 110
Rusk, Cory, 152
Russia, MTV's presence in, 95

"Safe harbor," 193
Salstone, John, 149
Salt-N-Pepa, 159, 171
Sammons Communications, 187
Samuals, Stuart, 168
Satellite News Channels, 48

Satellites and satellite communications, 30
  and globalization of popular culture, 90,
    93, 98, 99, 100, 101, 109
  and transponder compression, 131
Satellite Television Asian Region Service.
  See Star TV
Saturday Night Fever, 26, 31
Sayles, John, 158
Schiller, Herbert, 9, 10, 17
Scorsese, Martin, 158
Scott, Rick, 62
Scripps-Howard Cable Sacramento, 84
Seagram Company, 148
Seal, Kevin, 125
SEC. *See* Securities and Exchange Com-
  mission
"Second Russian Revolution," 96
Securities and Exchange Commission
  (SEC), 65, 75, 117
Seghal, Baba, 100
Segregation, racial, in "soundies," 24. *See*
  also Blacks; Minorities
Seidman, Steven, 2
Self-identity, consumption as, via MTV,
  105
Semiotics, 2
Serious-Lee-Fine, 181
Sex Pistols, The, 35
Seymour, Michael, 132
Shales, Tom, 201
Sha Na Na, 53
Shannon, Scott, 53
Shapiro and Steinberg, 144
Shelton, Millicent, 155, 159, 171
Sherman, Barry, 3, 8
Sherman Anti-Trust Act, 74
She Was Hot (The Rolling Stones), 83
Shindig, 25
Shore, Laurence, 13, 17, 11
Shore, Pauly, 129
Showtime Networks, 199
Showtime/The Movie Channel, 70, 87,
  117, 118, 131
Sierra Club, 55
Sight on Sound, 32, 33
Sighvantsson, John, 156
Signorielli, Nancy, 3

Silverman, Tommy, 79
Simmons, Gene, 142
Simon & Schuster, 119, 120
Simply Red, 107
Simpson, Sherry, 171
Singapore Cablevision, 101
Sire, 149
Sir-Mix-A-Lot, 180
Sky Broadcasting Corporation, 101
Sky Channel, 91, 105
Sloane, Robin, 140
Small, Jon, 165
Smid, Milan, 96
Smith, Bob, 36
Smithwick, Gary, 61
Smothers Brothers Comedy Hour, 27
Smythe, Dallas, 9, 13
Snyder, Richard, 120
Social totality, 9
Soda Stereo, 103
Solid Gold, 26
"Solid Gold Dancers," 26
Solomon, Norman, 12
Solters, Larry, 163, 164, 169
"Some People Just Don't Get It" (cam-
  paign), 123
Sonny and Cher, 28
Sony Corporation, 80, 102, 106, 148, 157
Sony Music, 44, 92, 94, 112
Sony Music Video, 138
Sony Walkman, 42
Soren, Tabitha, 129
Soul Train, 26
"Soundies," 23–24
Sound Recording Development Program,
  111
Sound Warehouse, 42
Soviet Union, former, MTV's presence in,
  95–97
Spice 1, 192
Springsteen, Bruce, 54, 67
Stanton, Amy, 126
Star TV, 80, 99, 102
  Channel V, 80
  Murdoch's purchase of, 101
  See also Channel V
Stefiej, Leszek, 96

Stereo signal transmission, 30
Stevenson, Steve, 76
Stewart, Jon, 129
Stewart, Rod, 83, 92
Sting, 55, 92, 103, 132, 146
Strauss, Neil, 178
Stray Cats, The, 36, 157
Sudden Impact, 154
Sullivan, Ed, 25, 27
Summer, Donna, 166, 203
Sun, Se-Wen, 4
Super Channel, 91, 96
Sykes, John, 40
Sylvanus, Laurel, 177, 179
Synergy strategies, 16, 19, 120, 121, 122, 199

Taft, Josh, 166, 167
Tao, Nonie, 100
Tarr, Pam, 157, 158, 162
Taylor, Glen, 51
TBS. *See* Turner Broadcasting Systems
TCA. *See* Tele-Community Antenna
TCI. *See* Telecommunications
TDK Corporation, 98
Technology
    and boom boxes, 42
    and boom in satellite communications, 90
    and music video as cultural form, 10
    and popularity of Sony Walkman, 42
    and television audio, 30
    and widespread penetration of VCRs, 44
Tele-Communications (TCI), 80, 113, 133
    and Black Entertainment Television, 57, 58
    and The Box, 56,
    MTV signs long-term contract with, 84
    sued by Viacom, 120
Tele-Community Antenna (TCA), 186
Telemundo network, 102
Televisa network, 104
Television
    content regulation of music television programs on, 191–193
    fragmentation of, 131
    pop music on commercial, 24–26

pop music on network, 26–28
video music shows on commercial broadcast, 61–62
worldwide distribution of American shows on, 17
See also Cable systems; Cable television
Teller, Al, 76, 108, 126
Temple, Julien, 160, 177
Terry, Ken, 65
Tetzlaff, David, 7, 8
Texas A&M University, 186
Textual analysis
    limitations of, 7–8
    of music video industry, 2
This Note's for You (Young), 177
Thompson Twins, The, 83
Thorn-EMI, 106, 112, 113, 157
    buys Virgin Records, 148
Thriller (Jackson), 42, 123
Time magazine, 41, 48, 119, 144, 149
Time, 16, 17, 30, 80, 87, 112, 113
    and HBO, 118
    law enforcement officer's boycott against, 150
    Viacom files antitrust suit against, 87
    See also TimeWarner
TNN. *See* Nashville Network, The
Tokyo Agency, 98
Tokyo Broadcasting System, 98
Tommy Boy Records, 153, 154
Top of the Pops, 29
Top 20 Countdown, 76
Touch and Go Records, 152
Transponder compression, 131. *See also* Satellites and satellite communication
Triple X Records, 153, 154
Tri-Star, 70
Truth or Dare (Madonna), 156
Tu Musica, 102
Turner, Bryan, 153, 202
Turner, Ted, and Cable Music Channel, 48, 49, 52, 53, 72, 73, 83, 197
Turner Broadcasting Systems, 48
TV Asahi, 98
TV5, 51, 74
20/20, 39

2 Live Crew, 190
Tyler, Karen, 50

Underdog Films, 172, 173
United Kingdom
  acts on MTV from, 35
  pop music on television in, 29
  public broadcasting system in, 28
United Satellite Corporation (USC), 72
United States, media ownership and class
    structure in, 9
United States Congress, 68
United States Court of Appeals, 193
United States Department of Justice, 69,
    115, 198
  Antitrust Division of, 75, 82
United States Senate Committee on Com-
    merce, Science, and Transportation,
    188, 190
Unity Weekend, 92
University of Illinois School of Medicine,
    189
University of Southern California, 169
Univision Spanish language network, 102
Unplugged, 128, 130, 147
"USA for Africa," 204, 205
USA Network, 29, 86, 90
USC. *See* United Satellite Corporation
Utopian Videos, 29
U2, 102

Valenzuela-Quakenbush, Linda, 172
Vanilla Ice, 56
Variety, 65, 144
Vee-jays. *See* VJs
Verges, Chrisann, 164
Vertical integration, 81, 82, 84, 85, 87, 88
  contractually between MTV and record
    labels, 67–71
  between major record companies and
    MTV Networks, 198
  at major record labels, 147
  between MTV, cable program services,
    and cable systems, 199
  in media companies, 63
  in media ownership, 15, 16
  for music video production, 138

within Viacom, 121
through Viacom's cable system hold-
    ings, 118
VH-1 (Video Hits One), 52–55, 65, 81, 82,
    108, 121, 124, 130, 140, 205
  channel expansion plans of, 131
  home shopping on, 133
  launched, 197
  ownership of, 86, 118
  promoted in franchise agreement, 85
  reach of, 127
  and record labels relationship to, 196
  tour promotions on, 142
  videos with higher budgets on, 152
  videos with major artists, 154
Viacom, 74, 76, 81, 86, 125, 128
  acquires Blockbuster, 120
  acquires MTV Networks, 19, 41, 65,
    117–118
  interactive video system plans of, 132
  and ownership of MTV Europe, 91
  owns Viacom Cable, 199
  partnership with Hutchvision, 98
  purchase of Paramount Communica-
    tions, 70, 119, 200
  Redstone's acquisition of, 118–122
Viacom Cable Television, 86
Viacom Enterprises, 121, 199
Viacom Networks Group, 118
Viacom Productions, 199
Video clip compilation, 138
VideoFACT. *See* Video Foundation to As-
    sist Canadian Talent
Video Foundation to Assist Canadian Tal-
    ent (VideoFACT), 110, 111
Video games, 42
Video Jukebox Network (VJN), 36, 55, 187
"Video Killed the Radio Star," 34, 36
Videomusic (Italy), 112, 113
Video Music Channel, 71, 72
Video music clips
  birth of, as promotional films, 28–29
  directors of, 155–158
  in early years of MTV, 35, 36
  and exclusion of black producers and
    directors, 170–174
  historical background of, 23–24

producers of, 155–158
promotion of, 139–143
record label constraints on content in, 166–167
record labels coordinate production of, 43–46
record labels distribution system for, 138
rejected by MTV, 180–182
rotation categories for, 184–185
Video Performance Limited, 92
Videos for tots, 130, 132
Video Soul, 57
Video Vibrations, 57
Vietnam War, 12
Viewers Voice for MTV, 187
Village Voice, 35, 128, 205
Vincent, Richard, 3
Violence
campaigns against MTV featuring of, 189–190
portrayals in music clips, 3, 4
Virgin Records, 76, 148
Visual media, early combinations with recorded music, 23–28
Viva (Germany), 80, 92, 102, 112, 113, 115, 199
Vivid Productions, 165, 172
VJs (vee-jays),
on MTV, 34, 35, 36
on MTV Asia, 100
on MTV Europe, 92
MTV rotation of, 129
on VH-1, 53, 54
"Vogue" (Madonna), 157
Vonfeld, Michele, 178, 188
Voting campaign (1992), 129–130
Vowell, Wayne, 84

Wall Street Journal, 35
Walt Disney Company, 122
Walt Disney Pictures, 70
Walz, Ken, 157, 161, 162, 163
Warlock Records, 159
Warner Amex, 38, 49, 67, 73, 74
Warner Amex cable, 31, 41, 86
Warner Amex Cable Communications, 31
ownership of MTV Networks by, 41

Warner Amex Satellite Entertainment Company (WASEC), 31, 33, 37, 38, 86
dissolved, 41
and treatment of black artists, 40
Warner Brothers, 44, 67, 126, 149, 166, 167
Warner Communications, 49, 67, 86, 117, 199
develops new music program service, 31–41
merges with Time, 118
Warner Music, 149
Warner Music Group, 82, 102
Warner Records, 147
Warner Reprise Video, 184
WASEC. *See* Warner Amex Satellite Entertainment Company
Wash, Martha, 146
Washington Post, 202
Wasko, Janet, 9
WEA Record Group, 44
"We Are the World," 204
Weather Girls, 146
Webb, Michelle, 172
Welch, Jim, 151
Western film genre, 23
Westheimer, Ruth, 55
Westinghouse, 48
White, Maurice, 39
Wilde, Nancy Leviska, 39
Willenson, Seth, 72
Wilson, Sherry, 187
Winter, Johnny, 153
Wittman, Emily, 165
WLXI-TV, 44, 61
WNEW-FM, 42
Wodlinger, Constance, 51, 52, 74, 75, 84, 87
Wodlinger, Mark, 51, 83
Wodlinger Broadcasting, 51, 74
Women
and demeaning images on MTV, 127
in MTV music videos, 2, 3
obstacles to directing video music by, 159
Wonder, Stevie, 39
Workman, Adrian, 107
World Alerts campaign (VH-1), 55

World Music Video Awards, 105
Wrangler, 94, 96
WTBS, 189
  Night Tracks, 60
WWHT, 85

Yellow Submarine, 24
Yetnikoff, Walter, 40
Yo! MTV Raps, 92, 103, 124, 139, 183

Young, Neil, 177
  This Note's for You, 182, 201, 202
Young M.C., 78
Young Ones, The, 125
Your Hit Parade, 24

Zappa, Frank, 188
Z-TV (Scandinavia), 113